reviews MT June '87 P. 332
M+L 68: 298-299. Aug '87
ML Notes 45: 756-7. June '89.

The Thames and Hudson Encyclopaedia of

20th-CENTURY MUSIC

The Thames and Hudson Encyclopaedia of

20th-CENTURY MUSIC

Paul Griffiths

THAMES AND HUDSON

for Ru Reiss
who kept asking

First published in Great Britain in 1986
by Thames and Hudson Ltd, London

© 1986 Paul Griffiths

First published in the USA in 1986
by Thames and Hudson Inc., New York

Library of Congress Catalog Card Number 85-51468

Printed and bound in Hungary

Contents

A reader's guide
to the use of this book

Music in the 20th c. is notoriously a vast and varied field, for at least two reasons that may conceivably be linked: the many new notions of what music is, and the huge number of active composers. More people have written music seriously since 1901 than in all the several previous centuries of composed music put together, probably by several-fold. And the increase has been not just numerical but also geographical. A concise encyclopaedia of 19th c. music would have occasion to mention very few composers who were not German, Austrian, Italian, French or Russian, whereas the present volume includes also substantial numbers from Great Britain, the Nordic lands, central Europe, Latin America and, most particularly, the United States. Similarly in the area of topics and terms, there are concepts that would have seemed alien indeed to Brahms.

The aim of this book is to provide a basic gazetteer to this confused but stimulating world. Most of the entries concern individual composers: over 500 are covered, at varying length. This is, of course, nothing like a complete roll-call of those who have produced interesting music in the century: the hope can only be that it includes the top 100 who would appear on any rational person's list. But if quality is an awkward criterion (*see* AESTHETICS: cross-references are always thus indicated by small capitals), chronology is surprisingly helpful, for 1901 turns out to be a very workable watershed. Verdi died that year; Brahms was recently in his grave; Wolf and Dvořák died within the next 3 years. On the other hand, Debussy, Mahler and Strauss still had enough to contribute to make them very much 20th c. figures, and Janáček, older than any of them, composed the whole of his important output in the new century. The oldest composer included is Saint-Saëns (born, incidentally, 125 years before the youngest here), but he is one of remarkably few essentially 19th c. composers with a significant 20th c. output: the only others of note are Fauré and Rimsky-Korsakov.

In these cases the **lists of works** appended to entries include only their 20th c. compositions. Otherwise the lists are selective in accordance with the size of the entry: most of the small entries have no list, while the longest are accompanied by **brief catalogues** of all important works, with dates of composition or, where there is an asterisk, details of the first performance. The abbreviations used for instruments and standard genres are self-explanatory; they follow the system of *The New Grove* with some slight modification. In particular it should be noted that there is a distinction between S, A, T, B (4 vocal soloists) and SATB (4-part chorus), that fl/vn indicates flute *or* violin, and that C signifies C major, while c stands for C minor. At the ends of lists, or at the ends of entries where there is no list, the composer's principal **publishers** and **record companies** are listed in square brackets thus: [publishers; record companies]. The longer entries include miniature **bibliographies**, limited to books published in English. A **general bibliography** follows at the end of the book, after a **chronology** of the century's major works. The transliteration of Russian names also follows the system used in *The New Grove*.

Apart from the entries on composers, there are also definitions of specifically 20th c. musical terms, notes on instruments, institutions and major works, and articles on a range of themes in 20th c. music. The selection of performers and other people has been guided not so much by intrinsic merit as by importance in connection with 20th c. composers. The **subject index** may provide a quick indication of the coverage in this and other areas: its intention is to suggest some possible pathways through the pages that follow.

As mentioned above, cross-references are indicated by SMALL CAPITALS. Obvious cross-references are not designated: generally speaking, they are given only when the extra information is particularly significant or relevant, or when the reader might not otherwise expect to find it.

Subject index

Entries are here grouped within the following categories:

COMPOSERS

Argentina
Australia
Austria
Belgium
Brazil
Canada
Cuba
Czechoslovakia
Denmark
Finland

France
Germany
Great Britain
Greece
Hungary
Israel
Italy
Japan
Korea
Mexico

Netherlands
Norway
Poland
Romania
Russia
Spain
Sweden
Switzerland
United States
Yugoslavia

OTHER ENTRIES

Performers
Other people
Places
Institutions

Instruments
Elements and definitions
Techniques and styles
Genres

Operas
Other theatre works
Concert works
Reception

COMPOSERS

Argentina
Ginastera, Alberto
Kagel, Mauricio

Australia
Antill, John
Butterley, Nigel
Conyngham, Barry
Grainger, Percy
Lumsdaine, David
Meale, Richard
Sculthorpe, Peter
Williamson, Malcolm

Austria
Apostel, Hans Erich
Berg, Alban
Bittner, Julius
Cerha, Friedrich
David, Johann Nepomuk
Deutsch, Max
Einem, Gottfried von
Gruber, H. K.

Hauer, Josef M.
Heiller, Anton
Jelinek, Hanns
Korngold, Erich
Krenek, Ernst
Lehár, Franz
Mahler, Gustav
Marx, Joseph
Schmidt, Franz
Schoenberg, Arnold
Schreker, Franz
Ullmann, Viktor
Webern, Anton
Wellesz, Egon
Zemlinsky, Alexander

Belgium
Absil, Jean
Boesmans, Philippe
Gilson, Paul
Goeyvaerts, Karel
Jongen, Joseph
Peeters, Flor

Pousseur, Henri

Brazil
Villa-Lobos, Heitor

Canada
Archer, Violet
Beckwith, John
Garant, Serge
Mather, Bruce
Schafer, Murray
Somers, Harry
Tremblay, Gilles

Cuba
Brouwer, Leo
Roldán, Amadeo

Czechoslovakia
Burian, Emil F.
Cikker, Jan
Eben, Petř
Foerster, Josef B.

Index

Index

cello
cencerros
cimbalom
clarinet
crotales
double bass
electric guitar
electrochord
electronic organ
electronium
flexatone
flugelhorn
flute
gongs
guitar
harmonium
harp
harpsichord
heckelphone
horn
intonarumori
mandolin
marimba
mechanical instruments
oboe
ondes martenot
organ
oscillator
percussion
piano
pianola
prepared piano
Renaissance instruments
ring modulator
saxophone
sequencer
sphaerophon
string piano
synthesizer
theremin
timpani
trautonium
trombone
trumpet
vibraphone
viola
violin
xylophone

Elements and definitions
acoustic
aggregate
ametric
amplitude

arhythmic
athematic
beat
block
blue note
canon
cell
chromatic
cluster
composition
decay
derived set
duration
dyad
envelope
form
formant
formula
frequency
group
harmony
Hauptstimme
hexachord
hierarchy
history
inversion
Klangfarbenmelodie
mode
motif
movement
music
Nebenstimme
noise
notation
organized sound
palindrome
parameter
pitch class
point
polymetre
polyphony
polyrhythm
pulse
quotation
resonance
retrograde
rhythm
secondary set
silence
simultaneity
sound
timbre
time
tetrachord

texture
trichord
voice

Techniques and styles
acrostic
action music
aleatory
amplitude modulation
antiphony
arrangement
atonality
avant garde
bitonality
blues
bruitism
chance operations
cipher
collage
colour
combinatoriality
computers
dada
dodecaphony
electronic music
epiç theatre
experimental music
Expressionism
Fibonacci series
Fluxus
formalism
frequency modulation
fugue
furniture music
Futurism
Gebrauchsmusik
golden section
graphic notation
happening
heterophony
Impressionism
improvisation
indeterminacy
intermodulation
intuitive music
jazz
Kulturbolschewismus
live electronic music
magic square
metric modulation
microtones
minimal music
mixed media
mobile form

Index

A

Abraham and Isaac 1. Britten's *Canticle II* for contralto, tenor and piano, text from Chester miracle play. *Ferrier, Pears, Britten, Nottingham, 21 Jan 1952. 2. Stravinsky's 'sacred ballad' for baritone and chamber orchestra, text from Genesis in Hebrew. *Ephraim Biran, Israel Festival Orchestra/Craft, Jerusalem, 23 Aug 1964.

Abrahamsen, Hans (1952-) Danish composer. Studied the horn at the Copenhagen Conservatory and composition with Gudmundsen-Holmgren and Nørgård. His works show a natural, simple coming-together of various materials, and include orchestral and chamber pieces (*Walden* for wind quintet, 1978; *Winternacht* for seven instruments, 1976-9; String Quartet no. 2, 1981). [Hansen]

Absil, Jean (1893-1974) Belgian composer. Studied as an organist, then with Gilson for composition. At first he followed his teacher's late Romantic style, but then concerts by the Pro Arte Quartet introduced him to the music of Berg, Milhaud, Hindemith, Schoenberg and others. In the mid-1930s he spent some time in Paris, which encouraged his development of a Milhaud-influenced polytonal style, deployed in clear forms; he was also inspired by his admiration for Bartók to work with folk music. His output was of Milhaudesque proportions, amounting to 162 works with opus numbers and covering every genre except opera and ballet.

accordion Instrument generally confined to light music but occasionally used by serious composers in the 20th c., whether for picturesque effect (on-stage tavern ensemble in Act 2 of *Wozzeck*) or not (Gerhard's Nonet, Symphony no.2 and Concert for Eight).

acoustic 1. The sound-diffusing qualities of an environment, so that a hall may be said to have 'a good acoustic for chamber music'. 2. In plural form, the science of sound diffusion in buildings, or rather the art, since acoustics is far from being an exact and firmly based area of study. Sometimes the term 'room acoustics' is preferred for this meaning, so that 'acoustics' can refer also to the physics of musical instruments and voices. 3. Used as adjective to distinguish natural from electrically amplified instruments: hence 'acoustic guitar'.

acrostic Text which can in some way be read vertically as well as horizontally. Webern likened the serial properties of his Concerto op.24 to the ancient word square SATOR AREPO TENET OPERA ROTAS, and other composers have been fascinated with such verbal models of close forming.

action music Term occasionally used for music in which the actions of the performers would seem to be at least as important as the sounds they make. Classic examples come from the music of Cage, particularly the piano music he wrote for Tudor in the 1950s.

Adams, John (1947-) American composer and conductor. Studied at Harvard under Kirchner, Kim and Sessions, and in 1972 began teaching at the San Francisco Conservatory. His works, using a sophisticated variety of MINIMAL MUSIC techniques, include *Shaker Loops* for seven strings (1979) and electronic pieces. [Philips, ECM]

Adler, Samuel (1928-) German–American composer. Arrived in the USA in 1939 and studied at Harvard with Piston, Thompson and Hindemith. After military service as conductor of the Seventh Army Symphony Orchestra he taught at North Texas State University and then from 1966 at the Eastman School, where he became chairman of the composition department in 1973. His works include operas, symphonies, synagogue music and much else.

Adorno, Theodor Wiesengrund (1903-69) German philosopher, active in Frankfurt apart from periods in Oxford (1934-8) and the USA (1938-49). In his youth he practised music criticism and studied composition with Berg, and music continued to be a principal subject of his enquiries. Writing in notoriously convoluted prose, he was one of the first to consider music in relation to SOCIETY: he felt composers should be resistant to commercial and political pressures, that their usefulness to society depended on an obedience to progressive tendencies within the musical tradition, which he saw as essentially Germanic; on those grounds he praised Schoenberg and his pupils. Books translated into English include *The Philosophy of New Music* (1973), *Introduction to the Sociology of Music* (1976) and *In Search of Wagner* (1981).

aesthetics One result of the diversification of music in the 20th c. has been to complicate issues in aesthetics. Diatonic traditions had provided some standards by which the symphonies of Raff, for instance, might be judged inferior to those of Brahms. Those traditions had encouraged too some confidence in views of the meaning and purpose of music to express emotion, to tell stories, to paint pictures, to generate moral uplift, to convey order (these were different purposes, of course, but they had their particular genres). 20th c. musicians have been less certain of what music is for, and therefore less sure in making value judgments. In addition to more or less disguised survivals of the old views, music has been seen as concerned with the relationship between man and TIME (Stravinsky), as an introduction to the chaos of life (Cage), as a means of changing the world (*see* POLITICS), as an expression of social structure (*see* SOCIETY) and as a system of signs.
□ L. B. Meyer, *Emotion and Meaning in Music* (1956)

African music Little European-style composition has been practised in Africa, except in Egypt (*see* ARAB MUSIC) and the Republic of South Africa (*see* RAINIER). Through recordings, however, black African music has excited the interest of Messiaen, Boulez, Stockhausen and others. A few composers, like Reich and Swayne, have studied it on the spot.

aggregate 1. Collection of notes in a composition, but not necessarily part of its organization, representing every pitch class just once; thus Webern's Concerto op.24, like many another 12-note composition by him and others, opens with a 12-note aggregate. 2. In Cage's terminology, collection of sounds heard at the same instant. The notion grew out of his work with the prepared piano, where often the pressing of a key produces not a single sound but an aggregate of 2 or 3 sounds separately distinguishable. He then worked with composed aggregates in his String Quartet and other pieces.

Agon Ballet by Stravinsky, choreographed by Balanchine: it is a sequence of 12 abstract dances for 12 dancers, with prelude and interludes, the whole scored for a highly variegated orchestra. ★New York City Ballet, NY, 1 Dec 1957 (concert performance Los Angeles, 17 June 1957).

Ägyptische Helena, Die (Helen in Egypt) Opera by Strauss and Hofmannsthal on Helen of Troy and Menelaus as both mythic and modern personages. ★Dresden, 6 Jun 1928; with revised 2nd act, Salzburg, 14 Aug 1933.

Alain, Jehan (1911-40) French composer and organist. Studied with Dukas and Dupré at the Paris Conservatoire, and like his contemporary Messiaen was influenced by Asian music as well as by Debussy: hence the modalities, the rhythmic irregularities and the ecstatic ostinatos of his works, which are mostly for the organ or the Catholic mass. The former group includes *2 danses à Agni Yavishta* (1934), *2 Fantaisies* (1934, 1936), an Intermezzo (1935), *Litanies* (1937) and *3 danses* (1937-9). He met his death as a soldier. [Leduc]

Albéniz, Isaac (1860-1909) Spanish composer and pianist. After sufficient musical training for him to be giving recitals, he stowed away to South America when he was 12, and thereafter was rarely in one place for long. He was in Weimar with Liszt, in Paris with Dukas and Debussy, and in London with a banker whose librettos he set in return for a guaranteed income. Musically, however, he remained in Spain. The great bulk of his creative output consists of piano works in which Spanish folk idioms are projected with a flamboyance that came from Liszt and in turn influenced the Hispanic music of Debussy and Ravel. The *Suite Iberia*, in 4 substantial volumes published between 1905 and 1908, is the crown of his work.

Albert, Eugène (or Eugen) **d'** (1864-1932) Composer and pianist of German–French–Italian origins born in Glasgow. Studied in London and was influenced by Liszt. He and his wife Teresa Carreño were among the great pianists of their day, but his output of piano music is small: his creative energies were directed to the theatre. His operas include both comedies and tragedies, of which *Tiefland* (★Prague, 1903) is the best known.

Albert Herring Opera by Britten and Eric Crozier transferring a comic Maupassant story about a village innocent to an English setting, and scored for chamber forces. ★Glyndebourne, 20 Jun 1947.

Aldeburgh Fishing port on the east coast of England which was Britten's home town from 1947 and the site of an annual festival from 1948, centred on his music. Since his death the festival has continued its specialization, though it has always had wider interests too, and has presented much new music other than its founder's.

aleatory (from Latin *alea* = dice.) Adjective used of music in which the composer deliberately makes room for chance occurrences or choices by performers. This definition would include such long-established phenomena as keyboard improvisation, the cadenza and the ossia, as well as musical games published in the 18th c., providing rules for dances to be strung together according to dice throws. However, the term is normally reserved for 20c. music, beginning with Ives, some of whose scores include exhortations to freedom, unusually important alternatives, and unrealizable notations that silently invite the performer to find a solution. Ives's example was important to Cowell, who used what he called 'elastic' notations, including the provision of fragments to be assembled by the players (String Quartet no.3 'Mosaic', 1934). Grainger also favoured 'elastic scoring'. But Ives's most extreme heir is Cage, who began using CHANCE OPERATIONS in the early 1950s, and whose music from later in that decade leaves a very great deal to chance (*see* GRAPHIC NOTATION and INDETERMINACY), following a Zen principle of non-intention.

Even so, the term 'aleatory' is more usually applied to European music, where the background was different. Stockhausen was impressed by the appearance of unpredictable elements in physical analyses of sounds, and composed his *Klavierstück XI* (1956) as an assortment of fragments spread over a large sheet of paper to be joined freely by the player. Boulez at the same time took note of Mallarmé's efforts to make chance artistically functional, and offered choices of route through his Third Piano Sonata (1956-7). Both these works exemplify MOBILE FORM, which retained its attraction for Boulez, though Stockhausen gradually went further, especially in works composed for his own electronic group: scores were replaced by simple sign systems (*Prozession*, 1967) or short texts (*Aus den sieben Tagen*, 1968). Stockhausen's return to exact notation in *Mantra* (1970) was seen at the time as a volte-face, but was merely the first striking indication of a general dwindling of interest in the aleatory.

Alfano, Franco (1876-1954) Italian composer. Studied in Naples and Leipzig, and scored an early success with the verismo opera *Risurrezione* (after Tolstoy, 1902-3, ★Turin, 1904). Later he was influenced by Debussy and Strauss, most importantly in *La leggenda di Sâkuntala* (1914-20, ★Bologna, 1921). It was the rich orchestration and exotic atmosphere of this opera, based on a Sanskrit play, that brought him the invitation to complete Puccini's *Turandot* in 1925, though in the event his ending was drastically cut by Toscanini and remained virtually unknown until the rediscovery of his manuscript in the 1980's. His other works include 2 symphonies, 3 string quartets, and violin and cello sonatas.

Alfvén, Hugo (1872-1960) Swedish composer and choral conductor. Studied at the Stockholm Conservatory and privately with Lindegren. The great Impressionist of Swedish music, he was influenced by Debussy, folksong and voyages on the Baltic, composing 5 symphonies and many other orchestral pieces, a large quantity of choral music and many songs.

all-interval set 12-note set in which each interval from minor 2nd to major 7th is represented.

Alphabet für Liège (Alphabet for Liège) Work by Stockhausen exhibiting in several rooms the physical and psychological effects of sound. One stand in the exhibition is taken by his ceremony of Indian songs *Am Himmel wandre ich. .,.* (★Liège, 23 Sep 1972).

American Composers Orchestra Ensemble established in the 1970s, with Dennis Russell Davies as conductor, for the performance of contemporary American scores in New York.

Amériques Work by Varèse for large orchestra, evoking not so much his new homeland as new worlds of the imagination. ★Philadelphia/ Stokowski, Philadelphia, 9 Apr 1926.

ametric Lacking a stable metre, usually because of elaborate cross-rhythms or an absence of pulsation.

AMM Enigmatic acronym chosen as name by a group of musicians engaged in free IMPROVISATION in London in the second half of the 1960s, and occasionally thereafter. The regular members were Cornelius Cardew, Lou Gare, ·Christopher Hobbs, Eddie Prévost and Keith Rowe, recorded on Mainstream MS 5002.

amplifier Electrical device for increasing a signal, used in all systems for reproducing sound.

amplitude A synonym for loudness, or more exactly the measure of the furthest disturbance in a wave or vibration.

amplitude modulation Change to the amplitude of a wave. By means of such changes information can be put into an electromagnetic wave (hence AM radio).

Amy, Gilbert (1936-) French composer and conductor. Studied with Messiaen at the Paris Conservatoire and was decisively influenced by Boulez, whom he succeeded as director of the Domaine Musical (1967-73). As an orchestral conductor, notably with the Orchestre National, he has specialized in contemporary music. His own compositions generally follow Boulezian models and include a Piano Sonata (1957-60), several large orchestral works (*Chant*, 1967-9; *Refrains*, 1972; *D'un espace déployé* with soprano singing Mallarmé, 1972-3) and works for smaller ensembles (*Cycle* for 6 percussionists, 1964-6; *Sonata pian' e forte* for voices and instruments, 1974) [UE, Heugel; Erato]

analysis The study of musical structure, attempting to discern how a composition was made or how it is heard (which is, of course, not necessarily the same thing at all). Analysis in the 20th c. has been most influenced by the work of SCHENKER, and in particular by his view of tonal compositions as operating on three levels: a background (the basic harmonic progression underlying a work or movement), a middleground (the elaboration of the latter which begins to give the work or movement its identity) and a foreground (the detail actually presented by the music). The main alternative to this position has seen music as proceeding through the continuous evolution of some thematic element, as Réti proposed, but the two are not essentially opposed: many later analysts have found it possible to use aspects of both.

For instance, Schenkerian methods alone seem to have nothing to say about atonal music, of which he himself disapproved. Allen Forte, however, has attempted the analysis of atonal works in terms of sets, or small groups of notes, that the composition redistributes and transposes, while he retains the concept of levels. Schenker's thinking has even touched composers of atonal music, especially composers of serial music in the USA, and Babbitt has very consciously and precisely sought to implant the model of Schenkerian levels into his works, so that in his case analysis precedes composition.

Other methods of analysis have applied ideas from information theory or semiology, though they have tended to produce new ways of describing rather than analysing music, and again have produced creative results that may outweigh their scientific benefit: information theory has been important to Stockhausen and Xenakis among others, semiology to Berio.

Anderson, Laurie (1947-) American composer and performer. Studied at Barnard College and Columbia (MFA in sculpture). Since the late 1970s she has appeared internationally as a 'performance artist' in her own solo pieces combining music, threatre and visual art.

Andriessen, Hendrik (1892-1981) Dutch composer, organist and teacher. Studied at the Amsterdam Conservatory and himself taught composition at the conservatories of Amsterdam, Utrecht and The Hague. Writing in a broad symphonic style with modal features of French character, he produced much Catholic church music, but his large output also includes symphonies and concertos, organ works and a wide variety of small instrumental pieces. [Donemus]

Andriessen, Jurriaan (1925-) Dutch composer, son of Hendrik Andriessen, who taught him at the Amsterdam Conservatory. His music, in an eclectic style having some affinity with Milhaud's, includes various symphonies and concertante pieces, some notable incidental scores and ballets, and chamber works. [Donemus]

Andriessen, Louis (1939-) Dutch composer, son of Hendrik Andriessen, who taught him at the Utrecht Conservatory. He was also a pupil of Van Baaren. As a leader of the Dutch avant-garde he took part in the collaborative opera *Reconstruction* (1970) and in musical-political endeavours of that period, out of which came his involvement with minimalism, as director of the Hoquetus ensemble of loudly amplified instruments, and as composer of such works as *De Staat* for voices and orchestra (1972-6). [Donemus; Composers' Voice]

Ansermet, Ernest (1883-1969) Swiss conductor. Virtually self-taught, he began conducting in Lausanne and Montreux in 1910, and in 1915 was recommended by Stravinsky to Dyagilev, whose principal conductor he became. He was then founder-director of the Orchestre de la Suisse Romande (1918-66), with whom he made many recordings, particularly of French music from Lalo to Ravel. These show the natural clarity of sound

and articulation that made him one of Stravinsky's favourite conductors, though there was a rift in 1937 when he insisted on making cuts in *Jeu de cartes*. He also disapproved Stravinsky's revisions and opposed serialism in his treatise *Les fondements de la musique dans la conscience humaine* (Neuchâtel, 1961), though he promoted Martin as well as Honegger among his compatriots.
□ I. Stravinsky, *Selected Correspondence* vol. 1 (1982)

Antheil, George (1900-59) American composer. Studied privately with Bloch in 1920, and in 1922 moved to Europe, where that year the Berlin Philharmonic played his First Symphony (1920-22), with its jazz-tinged finale. Jazz, noise and ostinato then became his specialities, worked into brutally simplistic if startling designs in such works as the *Airplane Sonata* (1922) and *Sonata sauvage* (1923) for piano, or the first two violin sonatas (1923). These last were written after he had moved to Paris in June 1923 and caused a furore with his piano recital at the Champs-Elysées on 4 Oct: they were commissioned by Pound, who played the part for drums in the second.

After this came a collaboration with Léger and the film maker Dudley Murphy on the *Ballet mécanique* (1923-5), for which Antheil composed a score for eight pianos, pianola, four xylophones, two electric bells, two propellers, tam-tam, four bass drums and siren. The work was performed in Paris on 19 Jun 1926 and in New York the next year. In 1952-3 it was revised for a gramophone recording (Columbia AML 4956), bearing a note in which Antheil drew attention to the structuring of his piece in lengths of time rather than harmonic processes. He claims this as an original discovery, though his work was obviously marked, in its scoring as well as in its rhythmic construction, by Stravinsky's then new *Les noces*.

In 1926 he turned to neoclassicism, and then to opera: *Transatlantic* (1927-8), with his own libretto caricaturing American political life, was staged at Frankfurt on 25 May 1930. In 1936 he settled in Los Angeles, where he enjoyed a colourful career as film-score orchestrator, inventor and journalist, while also producing a large output of operas, symphonies, songs and chamber music. The form now was conventional; the content as belligerent as it had been in the early 1920s.
□ E. Pound, *Antheil and the Treatise on Harmony* (1927, 1968); G. Antheil, *Bad Boy of Music* (1945, r1981); L. Whitesitt, *The Life and Music of George Antheil* (1983).

Antill, John (1904-) Australian composer. Studied with Alfred Hill at the NSW State Conservatorium and worked for the Australian Broadcasting Commission as conductor and administrator. His *Corroboree* (★1947), influenced by aborigine dance, was one of the first works to show a specifically Australian tone, and was followed by other orchestra pieces, operas and ballets.

antiphony Music for groups of performers in different places, normally implying two groups and a question-response kind of musical argument, as in Bartók's *Music for Strings, Percussion and Celesta* or Boulez's *Domaines*. See also SPATIAL MUSIC.

Aperghis, Georges (1945-) Greek composer working since 1963 in France. His many works are mostly of a theatrical character, influenced by Kagel.

Apollo Ballet by Stravinsky, choreographed by Balanchine: this was their first collaboration. The title was originally *Apollon musagète*, and the work concerns the birth of Apollo and his consorting with three of the Muses; the score is for string orchestra. ★Library of Congress, Washington, 27 Apr 1928 (Bolm choreography); Ballets Russes, Paris, 12 Jun 1928 (Balanchine choreography).

Apostel, Hans Erich (1901-72) German–Austrian composer. Moved to Vienna in 1921 and studied with Schoenberg and Berg, whom he followed in a long-lasting phase of atonal Expressionism (*Kubiniana* for piano, 1945-50), not adopting 12-note serialism until 1957: then he became as absolute a serialist as Webern. His works from this later period include several orchestral pieces but consist mostly of chamber music, sometimes with voice. [Universal, Doblinger]

Appalachian Spring Ballet by Copland, choreographed by Graham: it is a *Les noces* of the American pioneers, musically worked around a Shaker hymntune. The original score was for 13 solo instruments. ★Library of Congress, Washington, 30 Oct 1944.

Arab music Bartók visited Algeria in 1913 and used his findings in his Piano Suite, Dance Suite and other works, but – by contrast with the situation at the time of the Crusades – Arab music has not been a common source for western musicians in the 20th c. Communication in the other direction has also been sparse. The Egyptian composer Yusef Greiss (1899-1961) is credited with the first Arab work for western orchestra, his symphonic poem *Egypt* (1932), and he has had some successors in Cairo: notably Gamal 'Abd al-Rahīm (1924-), professor of composition at the Cairo Conservatory and the çomposer of orchestral works, cantatas and instrumental pieces in a folksong-influenced style. Outside Egypt, however, there would appear to be little composition in the western manner.

Arabella Opera by Strauss and Hofmannsthal, a sophisticated, musically sumptuous love story set in 19th c. Vienna. *Dresden, 1 Jul 1933.

Arcana Work by Varèse for large orchestra, inscribed with an arcane quotation from Paracelsus and working through the powerful collision of sound blocks to a still conclusion added in 1960. *Philadelphia/Stokowski, Philadelphia, 8 Apr 1927.

Archer, Violet (1913-) Canadian composer. Studied at the McGill Conservatorium and in the USA with Bartók and Hindemith, both of whom influenced her strenuous, disciplined style. Her vocal works sometimes use folk material, but they are outnumbered by orchestral and chamber pieces in standard forms.

Arditti Quartet String quartet formed in London in 1974 to specialize in 20th c. music. They have recorded works by Carter, Ferneyhough, Harvey, Ligeti and Xenakis.

Argento, Dominick (1927-) American composer. Studied at the Peabody Conservatory and the Eastman School, and privately with Weisgall, who fostered his leanings towards opera. In 1959 he was appointed professor of composition at the University of Minnesota, and in 1964 he was joint founder of Minnesota Opera. His operas include *Sicilian Lives* (*1954), *The Boor* (*1967), *Colonel Jonathan the Saint* (*1961), *Christopher Sly* (*1963), *The Masque of Angels* (*Minneapolis, 1964), *The Shoemaker's Holiday* (*1967), *Postcard from Morocco* (*Minneapolis, 1971), *A Waterbird Talk* (*1975), *The Voyage of Edgar Allan Poe* (*Minneapolis, 1976), *Miss Havisham's Fire* (*1979) and *Casanova's Homecoming* (*1985). Other works include choral music and songs.

arhythmic An unfortunate term. It ought to be applicable only to music without change (Cage's *4' 33"* might qualify) but has been used to denote the absence of a single, regular pulse, for which purpose 'ametric' is preferable.

Ariadne auf Naxos (Ariadne on Naxos) Opera by Strauss and Hofmannsthal. The first version (*Stuttgart, 25 Oct 1912) was a telling of the myth with *commedia dell'arte* interruptions and psychological exploration; the second (*Vienna, 4 Oct 1916) added to this a prologue showing preparations for the operatic performance in a noble household, replacing the version of Molière's *Le bourgeois gentilhomme* that had formed a double bill with the first version.

Ariane et Barbe-Bleue (Ariane and Bluebeard) Opera by Dukas and Maeterlinck in which Bluebeard's new wife Ariane countermands his orders, opens 7 locked doors and discovers his former consorts, whom she unsuccessfully tries to persuade to flee with her. *Paris, 10 May 1907.

Arnell, Richard (1917-) English composer. Pupil of Ireland at the Royal College of Music, he made a reputation immediately after the second world war with such works as his ballet *Punch and the Child* (1947). His output also includes symphonies, concertos, string quartets and film scores.

Arnold, Malcolm (1921-) English composer. Studied with Jacob at the Royal College of Music and first worked as an orchestral trumpeter, until the success of his concert and film scores enabled him to live from composing. His works, decisively tonal, include 7 symphonies, numerous concertos and other orchestral pieces.

arrangement An art seen in the 18th and 19th c. as a means of disseminating music more widely, e.g. by publishing symphonies in versions for piano duet. 20th c. musicians, less confident that arrangement is a neutral process, have tended to undertake it consciously in order to make some point about a work, as in Webern's motif-enhancing orchestration of BACH's 6-part ricercare or Schoenberg's attempt to discover a hidden symphony in Brahms's G minor Piano Quartet. In some cases – that of Stravinsky's *Pulcinella*, for instance, or Davies' versions of Purcell – the arrangement purposely destroys the original to make something new (or the destruction may be unintended, as in Schoenberg's Cello Concerto after Monn).

Arrieu, Claude (1903-) French composer. Studied with Dukas and others at the Paris Conservatoire, and in a large, varied output has employed a neoclassical style of elegance and seriousness. Among her works are numerous operas, including a setting of *Cymbeline*, as well as concertos and chamber pieces.

Arrigo, Girolamo (1930-) Italian composer. Studied with Deutsch in Paris, and remained there, being influenced first by Boulez and from 1969 by an engagement in left-wing politics. His opera *Orden* (★Avignon, 1969) is a passionate protest against Spanish fascism, the 'musical epic' *Addio Garibaldi* (★Paris, 1972) a political satire.

Asafyev, Boris (1884-1949) Russian composer and critic. Studied under Rimsky-Korsakov and Lyadov at the St Petersburg Conservatory, and spent most of his career as a student of 19th and 20th c. Russian music at institutions in Leningrad and Moscow, publishing his writings as 'Igor Glebov'. His compositions include many operas and ballets, and 5 symphonies.

Ashley, Robert (1930-) American composer. Studied at the University of Michigan and the Manhattan School of Music, but was more influenced by Cage than by any teacher. Working almost exclusively with electronics, he was co-founder with Mumma of the Cooperative Studio for Electronic Music at Ann Arbor (1958-66) and of the ONCE FESTIVAL (1961-8); the two then joined with Behrman and Lucier in the Sonic Arts Union (1966-73), performing live electronic music. The most celebrated of his works from this period was *The Wolfman* for his own amplified voice and tape (1964). In many of them there had been a dramatic component, and this came out into the open when in the 1970s he began working in video opera: *Perfect Lives*, in 7 half-hour episodes, was completed in 1983.

Association for Contemporary Music (Assotsiatsiya Sovremennoy Muzïki) Russian organization founded in 1924 in order to propagate the new music coming from the west; it collapsed in 1931. (*see* POLITICS).

athematic Lacking a melodic theme where one would be expected. The earliest examples are the first atonal instrumental works of Schoenberg and his pupils.

Atmen gibt das Leben (Breathing Gives Life) Choral piece by Stockhausen (1974) extended in 1976-7 to make a 'choral opera' on the coming of Christ.

Atmosphères Orchestral work by Ligeti composed of sustained sound in gradual change, hugely influential on the TEXTURE MUSIC of the 1960s. ★SWF SO/Rosbaud, Donaueschingen, 22 Oct 1961.

atonality The absence of tonality: hence a term embracing all music which is not tonal. More commonly it is restricted to music which is not serial either, and most commonly of all to the post-tonal pre-serial music of Schoenberg and his pupils, along with other music of similar period and style (e.g. certain works by Skryabin, Ives and Stravinsky). This most exclusive definition at least gives the term some useful meaning: Schoenberg himself disliked the word, feeling that the stated absence of tonality implied an absence of music; he preferred 'pantonality'.

The term is indeed fraught with controversy. Some writers, perhaps responding to an implication in Schoenberg's preference, have argued that apparent atonality is merely the result of a rapidly changing and deeply obscured tonality. This may be plausible in much of Schoenberg and certainly in Berg, where tonal features are never missing for long, but it encounters problems in Webern, where the music seems to have a much slower harmonic rhythm than would be necessitated by any analysis in terms of key.

A contrary point of view is that atonal means of ordering may be distinguished as far back as Mozart: one *locus classicus* is the Commendatore's grim statement in the penultimate scene of *Don Giovanni* (1787), where in 7 bars he touches 11 of the 12 notes. Still more striking is the opening of Liszt's *Faust Symphony* (1853-7), where the unharmonized theme strikes the 12 different notes within its first 13. However, these are isolated instances and can be resolved to more normal harmonic features: the Liszt is simply a chain of augmented triads slipping down in semitone steps. One may say there is here the threat of atonality, but the threat does not begin to be carried out until dissonant harmonies are sustained over a longer period, as they are in several of Liszt's late piano pieces (1880-86). Even then, the suspension of tonality is normally achieved once more by recourse to some symmetrical division of the octave: the whole-tone scale, the diminished 7th chord or the augmented triad.

The use of more unconventional harmonies, with the strenuous avoidance of any tonal perspective, began with Schoenberg's and Webern's settings of Stefan George in 1908; the first atonal instrumental pieces came the next year from both composers. In this repertory known chords have no special place, and analysis of the music becomes exceedingly problematic. Some principles have been suggested – the wish to complete the set of 12 notes within the smallest space, the background use of symmetrical octave divisions, the guiding presence of some motif or SET – but analytical methods that work for one piece may not work for another, even within the output of a single composer during a short period.

Schoenberg and Webern shared their analysts' sense of working in the dark, and searched for the means of some new constructive order: SERIALISM. After 1923 they never returned to non-serial atonality, though Berg did: his atonality had never been so adrift from tonal convention in the first place. To compose music which really does dispense with all the rules is decidedly difficult, which may be why instances of complete atonality are so rare and their understanding so uncertain.

□ G. Perle, *Serial Composition and Atonality* (1962, 4/1977); A. Forte, *The Structure of Atonal Music* (1973)

Atterberg, Kurt (1887-1974) Swedish composer. Largely self-taught, he held positions of authority in Swedish musical life as administrator and critic from the 1920s to the 1950s. His music, including 5 operas, ballets, 9 symphonies and much else, is in a Swedish Romantic style stemming from Alfvén.

...au delà du hasard (...beyond chance) The first to be completed of Barraqué's works on Broch's *The Death of Virgil*, scored for women's chorus with solo soprano played off against 4 instrumental groups: brass plus vibraphone, tuned percussion sextet (the piano a soloist), noise percussion trio and 4 clarinets (the first a soloist). ★Edith Semser (soprano), Yvonne Loriod (piano), Hubert Rostaing (clarinet), Jazz Group de Paris/Boulez, Paris, 26 Jan 1960.

Auden, Wystan Hugh (1907-74) English–American poet. He was close to Britten in the 1930s, working with him on films, plays and songs; in the USA in 1941 they collaborated on the opera *Paul Bunyan* and the choral *Hymn to St Cecilia*. Auden continued to live in the USA for at least a part of each year until shortly before his death, and

worked with Chester Kallman on librettos for Stravinsky's *The Rake's Progress*, Henze's *Elegy for Young Lovers* and *The Bassarids*, and Nabokov's *Love's Labour's Lost*, as well as on translations for operas by Mozart, Weill and Dittersdorf. He also wrote the words for Stravinsky's *Elegy for J.F.K.* and Walton's *The Twelve*.

□ W.H. Auden, *The Dyer's Hand* (1962); D. Mitchell, *Britten and Auden in the Thirties* (1980); I. Stravinsky, *Selected Correspondence*, vol I (1982)

Auric, Georges (1899-1983) French composer. Studied at the Paris Conservatoire and under d'Indy at the Schola Cantorum (1914-16), becoming acquainted meanwhile, young though he was, with the leading composers in Paris at the time. He was duly recruited into Les SIX, and showed something of Poulenc's sophistication in the ballets he wrote for Dyagilev (*Les fâcheux*, 1923; *Les matelots*, 1924). Then he provided scores for Cocteau's films *Le sang d'un poète* (1930), *L'éternel retour* (1943), *La belle et la bête* (1946), *L'aigle à deux têtes* (1947) and *Orphée* (1949). His late works, the series of *Imaginées* for solo instrument and piano (1968-73) and the *Doubles-jeux* for 2 pianos (1970-71), bring elements of Boulezian nervosity into his style.

Aus den sieben Tagen (From the Seven Days) Book of 15 compositions by Stockhausen expressed as verbal encouragements. They were written in fact during 5, not 7, days of meditative withdrawal (7-11 May 1968), and were intended to stimulate performances of INTUITIVE MUSIC by musicians close to Stockhausen: the available recordings, including a collection of twelve pieces (DG 2720 073), suggest his influence was profound. The pieces are *Richtige Dauern* (Right Durations), *Unbegrenzt* (Unlimited), *Verbindung* (Union), *Treffpunkt* (Meeting Point), *Nachtmusik* (Night Music), *Abwärts* (Downwards), *Aufwärts* (Upwards), *Oben und Unten* (Above and Below: theatre piece), *Intensität* (Intensity), *Setz die Segel zur Sonne* (Set Sail for the Sun), *Kommunion* (Communion), *Litanei* (Litany), *Es* (It), *Goldstaub* (Gold Dust) and *Ankunft* (Arrival).

avant garde (French for 'vanguard') The notion of the artist forging ahead in advance of public taste probably dates from Baudelaire's time, but the term became widely used in a musical context only after the second world war (before then the vogue word had been MODERNISM). Since most composers in the 1970s became less sure of themselves as representing advance, the term has gained some historical usefulness in distinguishing the music of Boulez, Stockhausen, Berio, Nono and others in the quarter-century 1945-70 from that of, say, Shostakovich during the same period. American composers fit the scheme less neatly. The works of Cage and his followers normally invite the description EXPERIMENTAL MUSIC, and those of Carter or Babbitt scarcely attracted the glamour proper to an avant garde.

Aventures Work by Ligeti for 3 singers and 7 instrumentalists, consisting of short wordless dramatic scenes assembled in strip-cartoon fashion. ★Gertie Charlent, Marie-Thérèse Cahn, William Pearson, Die Reihe/Cerha, Hamburg, 4 Apr 1963. Ligeti added *Nouvelles aventures* (★same vocalists/Markowski, Hamburg, 26 May 1966) and made a theatre piece from the 2 works (★same vocalists/Cerha, Stuttgart, 19 Oct 1966).

Avni, Tzvi (1927-) German–Israeli composer. Studied at the Tel-Aviv Academy of Music and in North America. Early works essay an oriental Impressionism influenced by his teacher Ben Haim; since 1964 he has used modernisms and electronic means.

B

Baaren, Kees van (1906-70) Dutch composer. Studied in Berlin and with Pijper, whom he succeeded as the most influential composition teacher in the Netherlands, directing the conservatories at Utrecht (1953-8) and the The Hague (1958-70). After two works in Pijper's germ-cell technique, the Piano Concertino (1934) and the Woodwind Trio (1936), he wrote nothing until 1947, when he began to integrate Pijperism with 12-note methods, using symmetrical all-interval series and closely controlled forms. His main works are a cantata setting Eliot's *The Hollow Men* (1948), a *Muzikaal zelfportret* for piano (1954), the *Variazioni per orchestra* (1959), the Piano Concerto (1964) and the *Musica per orchestra* (1966). [Donemus]

Babbitt, Milton (1916-) American composer, outstanding for the consistency with which he has developed 12-NOTE COMPOSITION. He studied at New York University and with Sessions at Princeton, where he joined the music faculty in 1938. Through his teaching, as through his theoretical writings and his compositions, he has had a great influence on the seriousness with which 12-note composition is studied and practised in the USA.

His own thinking has been much influenced by Schoenberg, and in particular by his analyses of Schoenberg's later serial works. There he found at work the principle of COMBINATORIALITY; there he found too the use of serial relations to underpin large musical structures as coherently as diatonic relations had done in the past. With the addition of a notion of DERIVED SET taken from Webern, and of his own intuition that the twelve-note system ought to govern elements other than pitch, the theoretical framework was complete: that much was achieved by the time of his first published work, the 3 Compositions for piano (1947).

Subsequent compositions have sustained a constant refinement of his musical world, embracing logical improvements in his organization of rhythm and timbre, extensions into electronic music as a medium able to 'perform' fine detail faultlessly, an increasing command of large structures, and a decreasing amount of obvious motivic connections on the surface (this may make his music of 1947-64 easier to understand than later works). In the sphere of rhythm, he evolved from a relatively simple-minded use of sets of durations (units of 1, 2, 4 and 5 in the 3 Compositions for piano) to the TIME POINT system. On the level of colour, he moved from the splashing of twelve different timbres (COMPOSITION for 12 Instruments) to a complex interrelationship of orchestral dodecets (*Relata I*), an eschewal of special effects (String Quartet no. 3), or the invention in his electronic works of 'instruments' to suit the occasion, using the RCA SYNTHESIZER at the COLUMBIA-PRINCETON ELECTRONIC MUSIC CENTER.

The cogency of Babbitt's system, and his readiness to write and lecture about it, have sometimes led to charges of dryness, as if the works were merely music examples to a treatise. And to be sure, he is attracted by the abstract: many of his works are instrumental, with titles that are either neutral (Composition, String Quartet) or hint more or less wittily at 12-note mechanics (*All Set, Partitions, Ensembles, Reflections*). Nevertheless, his work contains purely musical qualities of humour and drama rare in the 20th c. – qualities that depend precisely on context, and therefore on the systematic nature of his art.

This makes such qualities difficult to define briefly, but one may point to the cool wit of his stream-lined jittery rhythm (by no means confined to *All Set* for jazz group, though found there in exemplary fashion), to the ironic pride with which the Second Quartet goes through its single process of serially unfolding its series, or to the nocturnal disquiet of PHILOMEL for soprano and tape.

Orchestral: Relata I, 1965; Correspondences, str, tape, 1967; Relata II, 1968; Concerti, vn, small orch, tape, 1974; Ars combinatoria, 1981

Vocal: The Widow's Lament in Springtime, S, pf, 1950; Du (Stramm), S, pf, 1951; Two Sonnets (Hopkins), Bar, cl, va, vc, 1955; Sounds and Words (Babbitt), S, pf, 1960; Composition for Tenor and 6 Instruments (Babbitt), 1960; Vision and Prayer (Dylan Thomas), S, tape, 1961; Philomel (Hollander), S, tape, 1964; Phonemena (Babbitt), S, pf, 1970, S, tape, 1974; A Solo Requiem, S, 2 pf, 1976-7; More Phonemena (Babbitt), chorus, 1978

Chamber: Composition for 4 Instruments, fl, cl, vn, vc, 1948; Composition for 12 Instruments, 1948; Str Qt no. 1, 1948; Composition for Viola and Piano, 1950; Woodwind Qt, 1953; Str Qt no. 2, 1954; All Set, jazz octet, 1957; Sextets, vn, pf, 1966; Str Qt no. 3, 1969; Str Qt no. 4, 1970; Arie da capo, qnt, 1973-4; My End is My Beginning, cl, 1978; Images, sax, tape, 1979; Dual, vc, tape, 1980; Composition, gui, 1984

Piano: 3 Compositions, 1947; Duet, 1956; Semi-simple Variations, 1956; Partitions, 1957; Post-Partitions, 1966; Tableaux, 1973; Reflections, pf, tape, 1974

Tape: Composition for Synthesizer, 1961; Ensembles for Synthesizer, 1962-4; Occasional Variations, 1969

□ Special no. of *Perspective of New Music* (1976)
[Peters, AMP, Boelke; CRI, Nonesuch, Columbia, Acoustic Research, Turnabout, New World]

Bacewicz, Grażyna (1909-69) Polish composer. Studied with Sikorski at the Warsaw Conservatory and with Boulanger in Paris, after which she returned to Poland as a violinist, composer and teacher. Most of her works are neoclassical in the way of the Boulanger school, though in the 1960s she bravely opened herself to the new techniques then entering Poland. Her large output includes much violin music: 7 concertos, 5 sonatas with piano, 2 solo sonatas, etc.

Bach, Johann Sebastian (1685-1750) German composer, and arguably the most disputed intel-lectual property of the musical 20th c.: invoked as an examplar by Schoenberg and Stravinsky, worked as a CIPHER into compositions by Webern (String Quartet) and again Schoenberg (Variations op.31), quoted by Berg (in his Violin Concerto) and arranged, with varying degrees of faithfulness, by: Birtwistle: 5 Chorale Preludes, S, cl, basset hn, b cl, 1975; Britten: 5 Spiritual songs, S/T, pf, 1969; Busoni: 7 vols of pf transcriptions, 1892-1919; Carlos: various works, Moog synthesizer, 1969; Davies: Two Preludes and Fugues, 6 insts, 1972-4; Elgar: Fantasy and Fugue in c, orch, 1921-2; Mahler: Suite after movements from orchestral suites, 1910; Reger: reorchestrations of suites and concertos, Suite in g for orch after kbd pieces, arrangements of Brandenburg Concertos, Orchestral Suites and organ works for pf duet; Schnebel: Bach-Bearbeitung (Contrapunctus I from The Art of Fugue), 20 vv, hpd, 1973; Schoenberg: 2 chorale preludes, orch, 1922, Prelude and Fugue in E♭, orch, 1928; Stokowski: various organ works, orch; Stravinsky: Chorale Variations on 'Vom Himmel hoch', chorus, orch, 1955-6; Webern: Ricercare in 6 parts, orch, 1934-5.

Bäck, Sven-Erik (1919-) Swedish composer. Studied privately with Rosenberg and joined with other Rosenberg pupils in examining new music. Hindemith was important to him, and then in the 1950s Webern (*A Game around a Game* for orchestra, 1959). Other works include operas, ballets and much chamber music, besides an important series of motets (some on tape).

Badings, Henk (1907-) Dutch composer. Studied with Pijper in the early 1930s and then taught at institutions in the Netherlands and in Stuttgart. Works from the 1930s, including his first 3 symphonies, tend to be in a sombre polytonal style, often based on non-diatonic modes. These continued to be important, but around 1940 the harmonic textures became lighter: among major works of this period are the ballet *Orpheus en Euridike* (1941) and the next 3 symphonies, no.6 being choral. Then in 1952 he began working with electronic music, which had an effect on his instrumental works leading him to use unconventional tunings (Double Violin Concerto in 31-note scale, 1969). His later works include many other symphonies and concertos, pieces on tape (radio opera *Orestes*, 1954) and much chamber music. [Donemus; Philips]

Bainbridge, Simon (1952-) English composer. Studied with John Lambert at the Royal College of

Music and with Schuller in Tanglewood. Early works like *Spirogyra* for chamber orchestra (1970) and his String Quartet (1972) are in blocks of luminous texture, giving way to a more developed form in the Viola Concerto (1975). A visit to the USA in 1978-9 increased his interest in repetitive heterophonies, to be found in his *Concertante in moto perpetuo* for oboe and ensemble (1982) and Fantasia for two orchestras (1983-4). [United; Unicorn]

Baird, Tadeusz (1928-81) Polish composer. Studied at the Warsaw Conservatory with Rytel and Perkowski, and began by following the party ideology in producing uncomplicated music. Then in 1956 came a turn towards 12-note composition in a lyrical and dramatic, richly textured style close to Berg. The important later works are mostly for orchestra (*4 Essays*, 1958; *Psychodrama*, 1972), sometimes with female voice (*Erotica*, 1961).

Baiser de la fée, Le Ballet by Stravinsky, choreographed by Nijinska for Ida Rubinstein: it is an Andersen fairytale, with music gently adapted out of Tchaikovsky. *Paris Opéra, 27 Nov 1928.

Baker, David (1931-) American composer. Studied at Indiana University and has taught jazz studies there since 1966, also teaching at Tanglewood. His large output includes many works for jazz and brass ensembles.

Balanchine, George (1904-83) Russian-American choreographer. Left Russia in 1924 and was engaged by Dyagilev, for whom he choreographed *Chant du rossignol* (1925) and *Apollon musagète* (1928), beginning his long association with Stravinsky. In 1934 he went to the USA, where he was co-founder and artistic director of the New York City Ballet (1946-, originally Ballet Society). He made ballets to many Stravinsky scores (including several concert works), the composer approving his preference for pure classical dancing over expressive gesture or narrative. He was responsible for the first production of *Jeu de cartes* (1937), the *Circus Polka* (1942), *Scènes de ballet* (1944), *Orpheus* (1948), *Agon* (1957) and *The Flood* (1962).

Balassa, Sándor (1935-) Hungarian composer. Studied with Szervánszky at the Budapest Academy (1960-65) and began to make an international reputation for large, beautifully scored works of sure expressive aim, such as the *Requiem for Lajos Kassák* (1969), *Cantata Y* with solo soprano (1971) and *Iris* for large orchestra (also 1971).

But he is capable too of the stark post-*Wozzeck* drama of his opera *The Man Outside* (1977), written for Hungarian radio, where he works as a music producer, but staged at the Budapest Opera in 1978. [Editio Musica; Hungaroton]

ballet A vastly more important genre for composers of the 20th c. than it was for those of any earlier time, thanks largely to the example of Stravinsky and others who wrote for the Ballets Russes. There is the point too that ballet, presupposing an interest in rhythm and small forms, has proved more congenial to 20th c. composers than the narrative continuities of opera. Apart from Dyagilev's musicians, important composers of ballet scores have included Bartók, Berio, Bernstein, Birtwistle, Blacher, Bliss, Britten, Cage, Carter, Copland, Davies, Dukas, Dutilleux, Harvey, Henze, Hindemith, Holst, Honegger, Nørgård, Osborne, Roussel, Schmitt, Shostakovich, Stockhausen, Vaughan Williams and Walton. *See also* BALANCHINE, CUNNINGHAM, GRAHAM.

Ballets Russes Company brought from Russia by DYAGILEV to give seasons of ballet and occasionally opera in Paris and London (1909-14). Their repertory began with flamboyant Russian spectacle (*Polovtsian Dances*, 1909; *Shéhérazade,* 1910; *The Firebird*, 1910), but quickly developed in other directions in response to Stravinsky's later scores (*Petrushka*, 1911; *The Rite of Spring*, 1913; *The Nightingale*, 1914) and to music commissioned from other composers (Ravel's *Daphnis et Chloé*, 1912; Debussy's *Jeux*, 1913; Strauss's *Josephslegende*, 1914). The war curtailed activities, but from 1917 until Dyagilev's death in 1929 the company, now of permanently exiled Russians, appeared regularly in Paris, Rome and London, presenting most of Stravinsky's stage works from this period (*Chant du rossignol, Renard, Pulcinella, Mavra, Les noces, Oedipus rex, Apollo*) as well as works by Satie (*Parade*, 1917), Falla (*El sombrero de tres picos*, 1919), Prokofiev (*Chout*, 1921; *Le pas d'acier*, 1927; *L'enfant prodigue*, 1929), Milhaud (*Le train bleu*, 1924), Poulenc (*Les biches*, 1924), Auric (*Les fâcheux*, 1924; *Les matelots*, 1925), Berners (*The Triumph of Neptune*, 1926), Lambert (*Romeo and Juliet*, 1926) and Sauguet (*La chatte*, 1927). Choreographers associated with the company included Fokine, Nijinsky, Massine, Nijinska and BALANCHINE; designs were by Bakst, Benois, Picasso, Matisse and others.

□ C. W. Beaumont, *The Diaghilev Ballet in London*, (1940); A. Benois, *Reminiscences of the Russian Ballet*

Ballets Suédois

(1941); S.L. Grigoriev, *The Diaghilev Ballet 1909-1929* (1953)

Ballets Suédois Company founded by Rolf de Maré, a Swedish Dyagilev, employing leading composers and artists in Paris (1920-25). Scores commissioned included Milhaud's *L'homme et son désir* and *La création du monde*, Honegger's *Skating-Rink* and Satie's *Relâche*.

banjo Low-born instrument rarely admitted to classical music, but found in Davies's *Blind Man's Buff* and *The Lighthouse*, and works by Kagel.

Banks, Don (1923-80) Australian composer. Studied in Melbourne, moved to London in 1950 and had lessons with Seiber, Babbitt, Dallapiccola and Nono. During the 1950s he wrote little, but developed a serial style of strong, bold gestures held in lean textures and motivated by a forward-urging rhythm. Then in the late 1960s came a rush of works: concertos for horn (1965) and violin (1968), other orchestral works (*Assemblies*, 1966; *Intersections* with tape, 1969), works for jazz and straight ensembles (*Equations 1-3*, 1963-72; *Meeting Place*, 1970; *Nexus*, 1971) and solo vocal works (*Tirade*, 1968). In 1973 he returned to Australia; later works included his String Quartet (1975). [Schott; Argo]

Bantock, Granville (1868-1946) English composer. A figure of remarkable energy, both as composer and as conductor, he did much to promote the music of his English contemporaries. His own music was influenced variously by early Wagner, a taste for the exotic, and Hebridean folksong. The output is colossal, in all genres except chamber music.
□ M. Bantock, *Granville Bantock* (1972)

Barber, Samuel (1910-81) American composer. Studied at the Curtis Institute in Philadelphia (1924-32) and immediately began to win esteem for the curiously unforced Romanticism of such works as *Dover Beach* for voice and string quartet (written for his own baritone, 1931) and the overture *The School for Scandal*, played by the Philadelphia Orchestra in 1933. His Adagio for strings (originally the second movement of his String Quartet) was conducted by Toscanini in 1938, its elegiacal lyricism making it at once a popular classic. More ambitious works followed readily in the 1940s, less readily thereafter (the operas were not well received).
Operas: Vanessa (Menotti), 1957, *New York, 15 Jan 1958; A Hand of Bridge, 1958, *Spoleto, 17 Jun 1959; Antony and Cleopatra (Zeffirelli, after Shakespeare), 1965-6, *New York, 16 Sep 1966
Ballets: Medea (Cave of the Heart), 1946; Souvenirs, 1952
Orchestral: The School for Scandal, overture, 1931-3; Music for a Scene from Shelley, 1933; Sym no.1, 1935-6; Adagio, str, 1936; Essay, 1937; Vn Conc, 1939-40; Second Essay, 1942; Sym no.2, 1944; Capricorn Conc, fl, ob, tpt, str, 1944; Vc Conc, 1945; Pf Conc, 1962; Fadograph of a Yestern Scene, 1971
Chamber and instrumental: Sonata, vc, pf, 1932; Str Qt, 1936; Excursions, pf, 1944; Pf Sonata, 1949; Summer Music, wind qnt, 1956
Songs: Dover Beach, Mez/Bar, str qt, 1931; 3 Songs (Joyce), v, pf, 1936; Knoxville: Summer of 1915, S, orch, 1947; Hermit Songs, v, pf, 1952-3; many others, also choral works
[G. Schirmer]
□ N. Broder, *Samuel Barber* (1954).

Barraqué, Jean (1928-73) French composer, unique in his use of the highly variegated materials of post-1945 serialism within structures of large span and grand rhetoric. He studied at the Paris Conservatoire with Langlais and with Messiaen (1948-51), beginning there his first two acknowledged works: the Piano Sonata (1950-52) and *Séquence* for soprano and ensemble (1950-55). The Sonata, playing continuously for about 40 minutes, is an immense achievement, even with the example of Boulez's Second Sonata behind it (and behind that Beethoven's *Hammerklavier*). It is a strenuous argument of 2 styles – one formed from groupings of clearly marked rhythmic cells, the other moving more freely – leading to climaxes of cold, violent destructiveness and, in the generally slow second part, to a growing invasion of silence. *Séquence*, related to the Sonata in substance and mood, again has a big part for the piano, rivalling the dramatic soprano in eloquent expression of turbulent creativity and despair. This same pairing of soloists was to occur again in the 3 parts Barraqué completed of his potentially vast network of commentaries on Hermann Broch's novel *The Death of Virgil*, an examination of the artist's urge to destroy what he has made, though before that there was a short *Etude* in *musique concrète* (1954), the sole product of three years' work in Schaeffer's studio.

The Broch works, all setting fragments from the novel infiltrated with Barraqué's own poetic glosses, began with ... AU DELÀ DU HASARD (1958-9), for soprano, women's chorus and four instrumental ensembles. Then came CHANT APRÈS CHANT for soprano, piano and percussion sextet (1966) and *Le* TEMPS RESTITUÉ for soprano, chorus and orchestra (1957, orchestrated 1968). All are works of powerful, urgent development despite their chopped and circuitous forms; the command of a Romantic largeness of gesture is as sure as in the earlier works, and there is the same tension between extremes of beauty and negativity, the latter represented by silence or by fierce but complex outbursts from noise percussion. Barraqué contemplated and even planned several more parts of *La mort de Virgile*, but his last work was an offshoot from the project, the Concerto for clarinet, vibraphone and 6 instrumental trios, again achieving a strong continuity in conflict with pressures to diversify and dilute. [Bruzzichelli; Valois, Unicorn]

Bartók, Béla (1881-1945) Hungarian composer and pianist. His 6 string quartets and other works, mostly instrumental, count among the highest achievements in 20th c. music. Not only did they help establish a vigorous tradition of composition in Hungary, they also have the strength and lucidity of a musical mind at once analytic and creative. Bartók recognized in his twenties that the most adventurous new music (Debussy) and the ancient Hungarian FOLK MUSIC he was studying in the field were both teaching him the same lesson: that the old modes offered a way to redefine key, that rhythms could be counted in something other than 2 and 3, and that satisfying forms could be built from the constant variation of a small number of motifs. He spent the rest of his life exploring the implications of this discovery while also continuing his intensive studies of the folk music of the Magyars and other eastern European peoples.

At the time of Bartók's childhood Hungary was part of the Habsburg empire, within which he travelled widely in the company of his widowed mother and his aunts. He was born in Nagyszentmiklós, a small town now in Romania, and went to secondary school in Bratislava. Intended then to go to the conservatory in Vienna, he instead followed his elder schoolfellow DOHNÁNYI to Budapest, where he studied piano and composition at the academy (1899-1903). Dohnányi was the great hope of Hungarian music, and Bartók at first imitated him in emulating Brahms. But then he felt the force of Strauss, as is manifest in his symphonic poem *Kossuth* (1903), based on the life of the patriotic leader of the Hungarian uprising of 1848.

His nationalist intentions were thus already clear, and wanted only an apt musical embodi-

ment. That Bartók discovered in Hungarian folksong, which he began collecting in 1904, joined the next year by Kodály. In 1907 he came upon pentatonic melodies surviving among primitive Hungarian communities in Transylvania, and the same year he first saw Debussy's music, brought back from Paris by Kodály. These influences were entwined in his first mature works: the First Quartet (1908) and several small volumes of piano pieces. In 1909 he married a teenage pupil, Márta Ziegler, to whom he dedicated his 1-act opera BLUEBEARD'S CASTLE (1911), a parable of the inevitable separateness of human beings. It was followed by his other stage works, the ballet *The* WOODEN PRINCE (1914-17) and the mimed and danced play *The* MIRACULOUS MANDARIN (1918-23).

The decade of these two works was one of further expansion. Bartók was impressed by the rhythmic outburst of *The Rite of Spring* and by Schoenberg's atonality, and as he reacted to these influences he produced his most exuberantly unchecked works: the *Mandarin*, with its driving rhythms and extraordinary orchestral effects, the Second Quartet and a pair of violin sonatas. The orchestral Dance Suite (1923) brought a new clarification on the basis of dance forms characteristic of diverse peoples: the vision of human brotherhood was dear to him, and he reacted sharply against the Nazis' notions of racial purity. In his view, the strength and richness of a culture depended on the absorption and imparting of influences. These processes he had found at work in the music of the Magyars and their neighbours, and he welcomed them in his own music.

Thus Stravinsky's neoclassicism and Schoenberg's serialism both impinged on his works of the later 1920s and 1930s, which include piano music he wrote for himself to perform: the first 2 concertos, the Sonata, and the Sonata for 2 pianos and percussion. This last he wrote for himself and his second wife Ditta, another young pupil whom he had married in 1923 on his divorce from Márta (there was one son of each marriage). Whether with Ditta or, more frequently, alone, he appeared widely as a pianist between the wars, visiting Britain, the USA and the USSR, and making some gramophone records.

Meanwhile his music became ever more marked by clear structure and symmetry. His single-movement Third Quartet, perhaps his knottiest work, was succeeded by a Fourth in five movements on an ABCBA pattern, an ideal of structure to which he returned in his Second Piano Concerto and Fifth Quartet. The substance, though, was changing. The tight chromatic motifs of the Third Quartet, which has little sense of tonality, were opening out into figures more obviously anchored to a root pitch, even to a key. This is a development celebrated in the MUSIC FOR STRINGS, PERCUSSION AND CELESTA, where the chromatic theme of the first movement becomes openly diatonic in the finale.

Such a large-scale view of variation led on to the commanding Second Violin Concerto and to the Sixth Quartet (1939), where each movement begins with a variation of the beginning of the one before, and where thematic change tips over into parody: there is evidence here of the depression Bartók felt that year at the outbreak of war and the death of his mother. In 1940 he moved to New York, where, despite failing health, he continued the outward bravura of the Second Violin Concerto in his Concerto for Orchestra, and the inward circumspection of the Sixth Quartet in his Sonata for solo violin.

Stage: BLUEBEARD'S CASTLE, opera, 1911; The WOODEN PRINCE, ballet, 1914-17; The MIRACULOUS MANDARIN, pantomime, 1918-23

Concertos: for vn, no.1 1907-8, no.2 1937-8; for pf, no.1 1926, no.2 1930-31, no.3 1945; for 2 pf and perc (after Sonata), 1940; for Orch, ? 1942-3; for va, 1945, unfinished

Other orchestral: Kossuth, 1903; Rhapsody, pf, orch, 1904; Scherzo, pf, orch, 1904; Suite no. 1, 1905; Suite no.2, 1905-7; 2 Portraits, 1907-11; 2 Pictures, 1910; 4 Pieces, 1912-21; Dance Suite, 1923; Rhapsodies nos 1-2, with vn, 1928; MUSIC FOR STRINGS, PERCUSSION AND CELESTA, 1936; Divertimento, str, 1939

Chamber: Str Qts no. 1 1908, no. 2 1915-17, no.3 1927, no.4 1928, no.5 1934, no.6 1939; Sonatas for vn, pf, no.1 1921, no.2 1922; Rhapsodies nos1-2, vn, pf, 1928; 44 Duos, 2 vn, 1931; Sonata for 2 pf and perc, 1937; Contrasts, vn, cl, pf, 1938; Sonata, vn, 1944

Piano: Rhapsody, 1904; 3 Hungarian Folksongs, 1907; 14 Bagatelles, 1908; 10 Easy Pieces, 1908; 2 Elegies, 1908-9; For Children, 85 pieces, 1908-9; 2 Romanian Dances, 1909-10; Sketches, 1908-10; 4 Dirges, 1909-10; 3 Burlesques, 1908-11; Allegro barbaro, 1911; Sonatina, 1915; Romanian Folkdances, 1915; Romanian Christmas Carols, 1915; Suite, 1916; 15 Hungarian Peasant Songs, 1914-18; 3 Studies, 1918; 8 Improvisations on Hungarian Peasant Songs, 1920; Sonata, 1926; Out of Doors, 1926; 9 Little Pieces, 1926; Three Rondos, 1916-27; MIROKOSMOS, 6 books, 1926-39

Choral: Village Scenes, female chorus, chamber orch, 1926; Cantata profana (Bartók, after Roma-

nian ballad), T, Bar, chorus, orch, 1930; From Olden Times (folksong words), men's chorus, 1935; 2-and 3-Part Choruses (folksong words), children's/women's chorus, 1935; several sets of folksong arrangements

Songs: 5 Songs op. 15, 1916; 5 Songs op. 16 (Ady), 1916; 8 Hungarian Folksongs, 1907-c. 1917; Village Scenes, 1924; 20 Hungarian Folksongs, 1929 [Boosey, Editio Musica; Hungaroton]

□ H. Stevens: *The Life and Music of Béla Bartók* (New York, 1953, 2/1964; B. Bartók, *Letters* (1971), *Essays* (1976); P. Griffiths, *Bartók* (1984)

Bartolozzi, Bruno (1911-) Italian composer and pioneer of new instrumental techniques. His *New Sounds for Woodwind* (London, New York and Toronto, 1967) has been widely influential, and some of its prescriptions, e.g. chords, described as 'Bartolozzi sounds'.

Bassarids, The Opera by Henze, Auden and Kallman based on the *Bacchae* of Euripides. *Salzburg, 6 Aug 1966.

bass clarinet Instrument in B♭, an octave below the usual clarinet. It is frequent in 20th c. orchestral scores, occasional in ensemble pieces (*Pierrot lunaire*, Webern's opp. 14-17) and rare as a soloist, though the Dutch virtuoso Harry Sparnaay has commissioned works for it by Berio, Ferneyhough and others.

basset horn Clarinet-type instrument in F, extending down a major 3rd below the B♭ clarinet. Favoured by Mozart but rarely used in the 20th c. except by Strauss, in several operas and the 2 wind-band sonatinas, and by Stockhausen.

bassoon Ubiquitous in the orchestra and ensemble, used notably to initiate *The Rite of Spring*. Solo works with orchestra include Elgar's Romance, Villa-Lobos's *Ciranda das sete notas*, Strauss's Duet Concertino (with clarinet) and Hindemith's Concerto (with trumpet). Other repertory: Prokofiev's Scherzo for 4 bassoons, sonatas with piano by Saint-Saëns, Hindemith and Skalkottas, Dutilleux's *Sarabande et cortège* with piano, and Wellesz's unaccompanied Suite.

Baudrier, Yves (1906-) French composer. Trained as a lawyer before taking lessons with the organist at the Sacré Coeur, and then received advice from Messiaen, with whom in 1936 he was a joint founder of the group La Jeune France; he also had counterpoint lessons from another member, Daniel-Lesur. The cinema was important to him: he taught at a college for film studies and wrote film scores, besides the orchestral piece composed for an imaginary film, *Le musicien dans la cité* (1937), which is his most important work, describing the musician's nocturnal wandering through twelve situations. Persistent ill health restricted his later activities.

Bax, Arnold (1883-1953) English composer, the most productive artist of Celtic Impressionism in his earlier years, and later a distinguished symphonist. He studied at the Royal Academy of Music (1900-05), but was most influenced by his encounter with the works of Yeats. Though born in the London borough of Streatham, he adopted Ireland as his spiritual home: he published several novels in Dublin under the pseudonym Dermot O'Byrne, and died in Cork. Moreover, his first successful works were all tone poems rhapsodizing about Celtic legends and landscapes in a style indebted to Strauss, Delius, Debussy and Ravel: there are long lyrical themes supported by a lush and richly scored harmony. In the 1920s his music began to become more contrapuntal and more intensely wrought, which made possible the cycle of 7 symphonies (no.6 is the most remarkable), besides several concertos, much chamber music and a great deal else. He was made Master of the King's Music in succession to Elgar.

Orchestral: In the Faery Hills, 1909; Spring Fire, 1913; The Garden of Fand, 1913-16; November Woods, 1917; Tintagel, 1917-19; The Happy Forest, 1914-21; Sym no.1 1922, no.2 1926, no.3 1929; no.4 1931, no.5 1932, no.6 1934, no.7 1939; Vc Conc, 1932; Vn Conc, 1938

Piano: Sonata no.1 1910, no.2 1919; no.3 1926, no.4 1932; many other works

Much chamber music, various choral works and songs

[Chappell; Lyrita]

□ A. Bax, *Farewell My Youth* (1943); C. Scott-Sutherland, *Arnold Bax* (1973)

Bayle, François (1932-) French composer. Studied with Stockhausen at Darmstadt and Messiaen in Paris. In 1960 he joined the GROUPE DE RECHER-CHES MUSICALES, of which he became director in 1966. Most of his works are composed on tape.

BBC (British Broadcasting Corporation) Institution founded in 1927, providing most of the radio and half the television BROADCASTING in the UK.

The corporation has been musically active through its orchestras (notably the BBC SO, whose conductors have included Boult, Sargent, Davis, Boulez and Rozhdestvensky), its commissioning of new works and its electronic music studio (the BBC Radiophonic Workshop, founded in 1956). Notable commissions have included Britten's OWEN WINGRAVE and works by Vaughan Williams, Birtwistle, Davies, Goehr, and many others.

beat 1. The unit of pulse: e.g. in 4/4 time there are 4 beats to a bar. 2. Phenomenon encountered when neighbouring frequencies are sounded. There is an effect of tremolo, because the frequencies reinforce one another at a rate equal to their difference: e.g. frequencies of 440 Hz and 442 Hz will produce 2 beats per second. 3. Term of approbation more than definition in the field of jazz and popular music, indicating a strong pulse.

Beck, Conrad (1901-) Swiss composer. Studied at the Zurich Conservatory and then moved to Paris (1923-32), where he was influenced by Honegger and Roussel. Later he settled in Basle as music director of the radio station. Many of his most important works, including his 5 symphonies and 2 of his 4 string quartets, date from his time in Paris; later works are mostly in orchestral and chamber genres. [Schott]

Becker, John (1886-1961) American composer. Studied at the Cincinnati Conservatory and spent most of his professional life teaching at Catholic colleges in the mid-west. In the 1930s he began to be known as a modernist, along with Ives, Ruggles, Cowell and Riegger, for though he had begun in a Romantic tonal style, his mature works are in dissonant counterpoint, often in Baroque forms: his *Symphonia brevis* (1929), the third of 7 symphonies, marks the change. Other works include *Abongo* (ballet for large percussion ensemble, 1933), *A Marriage with Space* (ballet for speaking chorus and orchestra, 1935) and pieces making a vehement social protest. He produced little after the mid-1940s. [Peters, Presser]

Beckwith, John (1927-) Canadian composer. Studied in Toronto and with Boulanger in Paris (1950-52), returning then to teach at Toronto University. His output is large and diverse, often deliberately seeking a confusion of means.

Bedford, David (1937-) English composer. Studied with Lennox Berkeley at the Royal Academy

29

of Music and with Nono in Venice, though has been influenced too by his experience of hearing, playing and arranging pop music. Early works, such as *Music for Albion Moonlight* for soprano and mixed sextet (1965), show a strikingly fresh feeling for sonority in a freely atonal context. Then in the mid-1970s he began to dwell on simple harmonies in the manner of American minimalism, as in *Star's End* for rock group and orchestra (1974). [UE; Virgin]

Beecham, Thomas (1879-1961) English conductor. Self-taught as a conductor, he drew on family money (his father was a manufacturing pharmacist) to present orchestral concerts and opera in London from 1905 onwards. He was renowned for his zest, brilliance and exactitude, and though not sympathetic to much music of his time, he was responsible for bringing Strauss's operas to London and championed Delius.
□ T. Beecham, *A Mingled Chime* (1944, r1976 as *The Lyric Stage*); H. Procter-Gregg, ed. *Beecham Remembered* (1977)

Beeson, Jack (1921-) American composer. Studied at the Eastman School and privately with Bartók in New York in 1944, joining the music faculty at Columbia University the next year. His operas, following those of Douglas Moore in Americanness of style and subject, include *Jonah* (1950), *Hello Out There* (1953), *The Sweet Bye and Bye* (1956), *Lizzie Borden* (1965, ★New York, 1965), *My Heart's in the Highlands* (1969), *Captain Jinks of the Horse Marines* (1973) and *Dr Heidegger's Fountain of Youth* (★New York, 1978).

bell Instrument usually encountered in the orchestra in the form of tubular bells, or more rarely sleighbells (e.g. in Mahler's Fourth Symphony), or cowbells (e.g. in Mahler's Sixth Symphony; *see also* CENCERROS). Where single bells are indicated, e.g. in other Mahler works and in *Les noces*, tubular bells are normally used, though Davies has written for handbells in various works. *See also* CHANGE RINGING.

Ben Haim, Paul (1897-) German–Israeli composer. Studied in Munich and worked in Germany as a conductor before emigrating to Tel-Aviv in 1933. There he established himself as the new nation's leading composer, bringing the character of Middle Eastern music into a German Romantic style. His works include 2 symphonies, other orchestral scores, chamber music and sacred choral pieces.

Benjamin, Arthur (1893-1960) Australian–English composer. Studied with Stanford at the Royal College of Music and spent most of the rest of his life in London as a composer, teacher and pianist. Much of his music is light-hearted, somtimes with Caribbean tinges, as in his *Jamaican Rumba* for 2 pianos or orchestra (1938). His other works include 5 operas: three one-acters (*The Devil Take Her*, 1931; *Prima donna*, 1933; *Mañana*, ★BBC TV, 1956), a full-length Dickens adaptation (*The Tale of Two Cities*, 1949-50) and a setting of *Tartuffe* (1959-60). [Boosey]

Benjamin, George (1960-) English composer. Studied with Messiaen in Paris and Goehr in Cambridge, and made an early reputation with his Piano Sonata (1977-8) and orchestral piece *Ringed by the Flat Horizon* (1980), mature in their working of keenly featured gestures into supple forms. [Faber]

Bennett, Richard Rodney (1936-) English composer. Studied at the Royal Academy of Music and with Boulez in Paris (1957-8), the latter briefly influential on such works as *Calendar* for ensemble (1960). Back in England he returned to more conventional kinds of drama and lyricism, sophisticatedly scored; he has also produced much film music, and worked as pianist and arranger with American popular music of the 1920s-1940s. Since the mid-1970s he has spent most of his time in the USA.
Operas: The Ledge, 1961, ★London, 1961; The Mines of Sulphur, 1963, ★London, 1965; A Penny for a Song, 1966, ★London, 1967; Victory, 1968-9, ★Covent Garden, 1970; The Eagle has Two Heads, in progress
Many concs, choral works, songs, chamber music
[Novello, UE]

Bentzon, Niels Viggo (1919-) Danish composer, of vast output. Studied at the Copenhagen Conservatory and has taught there since 1949. His music is forcefully presented in a Hindemithian style.

Berberian, Cathy (?1928-83) American singer. From 1950 to 1966 she was married to Berio, who wrote for her distinctively characterful and flexible voice in his *Circles, Epifanie, Visage, Sequenza III* and *Recital I*. She also gave the first performances of Cage's Aria and of works by Bussotti and others.

Berg, Alban (1885-1935) Austrian composer. The most gifted of Schoenberg's pupils, he felt a passionate loyalty to Schoenberg both personally and creatively. He followed Schoenberg's ideal of a music of constant development, and followed too his teacher's venturings into atonality and serialism; 4 of his dozen mature works he dedicated to Schoenberg. But at the same time he felt the lure of tonal late Romanticism, as expressed in the music of Mahler, Strauss and Schreker. His music throve from this tension, as it throve too from the tension between his taste for secret patterns (structures built on arithmetical proportions, as well as instances of palindrome and CIPHER) and his abundant expressiveness. His 2 operas, WOZZECK and LULU, must count among the most elaborate musical structures ever conceived, and yet they impress themselves in the theatre as immediate, dramatic and shocking stories of exploitation and sexuality.

He was born into the minor gentry: the family had a summer estate, where he took part in play readings and composed songs like any aesthetic young man. Before his first lessons with Schoenberg, in October 1904, he had had almost no musical training, yet his development then was rapid: by 1908 he had written a single-movement Piano Sonata, besides a number of songs reaching far beyond the pastiche of his earlier efforts. The Sonata is a slowish movement in the Schoenbergian key of D minor, though also recalling Mahler. Its rich supply of lyrical themes within a complex sonata form is typical of Mahler and was to be equally typical of Berg.

After this came the 4 Songs op.2 (?1909-10), a nocturnal cycle drifting off into the atonality Schoenberg had recently broached. Next there was the fully atonal String Quartet (1910), in 2 movements more thoroughly developed than anything in Schoenberg at this time, and more completely removed from tonality than anything in later Berg. The Altenberg Songs for soprano and orchestra (1912) and the 4 Pieces for clarinet and piano (1913) are on a smaller scale. The songs set poems by Peter Altenberg of oriental brevity and Viennese bitterness, to music looking both to the pure white of the whole-tone scale and the rich confusion of atonality, which it begins to attempt to order: there is a passacaglia departing from a theme of 12 different notes. Erotic, fascinatingly new and yet also world-weary, the work was Berg's orchestral début and his first wholly characteristic expression.

The 3 Pieces op.6 (1914-15) are again larger and also more heavily scored, using the orchestra of Mahler's Sixth Symphony. The first is a symmetrical prelude of advance from and recession into the hazy noise of untuned percussion; the second is a dance fantasy more in the sensual style of the Altenberg Songs; and the third is an enormous march, reaching to extraordinary violence and textural elaboration. Echoes of it can be heard in *Wozzeck* (1917-22), which Berg wrote after military experience himself (1915-17). After the war he returned to Vienna, which was his home until his death: he remained close to Schoenberg while the latter was in the city, and travelled widely only to attend productions of *Wozzeck*, whose success brought him financial security.

Before embarking on a second opera he wrote his Chamber Concerto for piano, violin and 13 wind (1923-5), a celebration of the threesome of Schoenberg, himself and Webern, and a work riddled with cryptograms and numerical proportions based on 3. The LYRIC SUITE (1925-6) is similar in being both highly wrought and generously expressive: it has a secret programme concerning Berg's feelings for Hanna Fuchs-Robettin, which coloured too his opera *Lulu* (1929-35) as much as his love for his wife Helene had coloured earlier works (they were married in 1911, and he dedicated to her his String Quartet and a group of 7 Early Songs he orchestrated in 1928). Work on *Lulu* was delayed by the composition of the big Baudelaire aria for soprano *Der Wein* (1929) and the Violin Concerto (1935), the latter an instrumental requiem for Mahler's widow's teenage daughter and Berg's last work.

Operas: WOZZECK, 1917-22; LULU, 1929-35
Orchestral: 3 Pieces op.6, 1914-15; Chamber Conc, pf, vn, 13 wind, 1923-5; 3 Pieces from the Lyric Suite, str, 1928; Vn Conc, 1935
Orchestral with voice: Altenberg Songs op.4, 1912; 3 Fragments from Wozzeck, 1924; 7 Early Songs, 1905-8, orch 1928; Der Wein (Baudelaire/George), 1929; 5 Symphonic Pieces from Lulu, 1934
Songs with piano: 7 Early Songs, 1905-8, rev. 1928; 4 Songs op.2 (Hebbel, Mombert), ?1909-10; Schliesse mir die Augen beide (Storm), paired settings of 1907 and 1925
Chamber: Pf Sonata op.1, ?1907-8; Str Qt op.3, 1910; 4 Pieces op. 5, cl, pf, 1913; Adagio from Chamber Conc, vn, cl, pf; LYRIC SUITE, str qt, 1925-6
[UE]
□ A. Berg, *Letters to his Wife*, ed. H. Berg (1971); M. Carner, *Alban Berg* (1975); D. Jarman, *The Music of Alban Berg* (1979); G. Perle, *The Operas of Alban Berg* (1980-84)

Berger, Arthur (1912-) American composer. Studied with Piston at Harvard and Milhaud at Mills College, then embarking on a career as teacher, critic and composer. His music is diatonic up to 1957 and 12-note thereafter, though marked in both periods by spareness and openness of texture. His output is small, and almost exclusively instrumental.

Berio, Luciano (1925-) Italian composer, the most imaginatively fluent of his generation. Much of his work has sprung from a structuralist conception of music as a language of gestures in sound, and he has used the expanded resources of his time in musically examining other languages: verbal languages in his many vocal works, languages of non-verbal communication in solo vocal and instrumental works, historical musical languages (those of concerto form, for instance), languages of theatrical convention and even the languages of his own earlier works (the *Sequenze*, for example, are probed in the *Chemins*). In all this he has been influenced by Italian writers of his generation, notably Eduardo Sanguineti, Umberto Eco and Italo Calvino.

Early musical influences included his teacher Ghedini and Stravinsky; then, following his marriage to Cathy Berberian in 1950, he made frequent visits to the USA, where he encountered Dallapiccola and electronic music. From 1954 to 1959 he was regularly at Darmstadt: he reacted against the prevailing ernestness with his *Serenata I*, but this was also the period of his most complicated conceptions, notably *Tempi concertati* for flute, violin, 2 pianos and 4 instrumental groups. Among his electronic works, *Thema (Omaggio a Joyce)* became an early classic of the genre, being created from a recording of Berberian reading from *Ulysses*. Her voice was also involved in the fully individual works he composed around 1960: the imaginary drama *Visage* (on tape), EPIFANIE and CIRCLES.

During the next decade his work focussed in two directions, sometimes linked: those of solo performance and the theatre. A 1958 *Sequenza* for flute became the first in a series of virtuoso concert pieces, while after the protest drama *Passaggio* he gave his social critique a more dream-like Dantesque form in *Laborintus II*, and in his opera *Opera* found parallels between the crisis in the genre and that in western capitalism. *Recital I* (1972) is both a display vehicle (once more for Berberian) and a theatre piece, presenting the distorted and dismembered contents of a singer's mind on the edge of collapse.

Later works have continued to explore these interests. A concern with different kinds of vocal expression, evident in EPIFANIE and the SINFONIA, was continued in CORO. Other pieces have worked with subtle, shifting variations of a melody (*Linea* and the later *Sequenze* for violin and clarinet), and in his operas *La vera storia* and *Un re in ascolto* the aim is characteristically not to tell a story but rather to examine ways in which, musically and dramatically, stories can be told.

Operas: Opera, 1969-70, *Sante Fe, 1970; La vera storia (Calvino), *Florence, 1982; Un re in ascolto, *Salzburg, 1984

Music theatre: Passaggio, 1961-2, *Milan, 1963; Laborintus II, 1965, *Paris, 1965; Recital I, 1972, *Lisbon, 1972

Orchestral: Concertino, 1951; Nones, 1954; Allelujah I, 1955, rev. as Allelujah II, 1956-8; Serenata I, fl, 14 insts, 1957; Tempi concertati, 1958-9; Chemins I, harp, orch, 1965; Chemins III, va, orch, 1967; Chemins IIb, small orch 1969; Bewegung, 1971; Chemins IIc, b cl, small orch, 1972; Conc for 2 pf, 1972-3; Still, 1973; Eindrücke, 1973-4; Points on the Curve to Find . . ., pf, small orch, 1974; Chemins IV, ob, str, 1975; Quattro versioni, 1975; Il ritorno degli Snovidenia, vc, small orch, 1976-7; Encore, 1978; Entrata, 1980; Corale, vn, orch, 1981-2

Vocal orchestral: Magnificat, 2S, chorus, small orch, 1949; EPIFANIE, S, orch, 1959-61, rev. 1965; SINFONIA, 8 vv, orch, 1968-9; Questo vuol dire che, vv, insts, tape, 1970 ; Bewegung II, Bar, orch, 1971; Ora. vv, orch, 1971; CORO, chorus, orch, 1975-6

Other vocal: Quattro canzoni popolari, female v, pf, 1946-7; El mar la mar, S, Mez, 7 insts, 1950, rev. 1969; Opus Number Zoo, speaker, wind qnt, 1952, rev. 1970; Chamber Music (Joyce), female v, cl, harp, vc, 1953; CIRCLES, female v, harp, 2 perc, 1960; O King, v, 5 insts, 1967; Agnus, 2 female vv, 3 cl, drone, 1971; E vo', insts, 1972; Cries, 6/8 vv, 1973-4; Calmo, S, insts, 1974; A-ronne, 8 vv, 1974-5

Chamber: Due pezzi, vn, pf, 1951; Str Qt, 1956; Différences, 5 insts, tape, 1958-9; Sincronie, str qt, 1963-4; Chemins II, va, 9 insts, 1967, Memory, 2 pf, perc, 1970, rev. 1973; Linea, 2 pf, mar, vib, 1974; Musica leggera, fl, va, vc, 1974

Sequenze: I, fl, 1958; II, harp, 1963; III female v, 1966: IV, pf, 1966; V, trbn, 1966; VI, va, 1967; VII, ob, 1969; VIII, vn, 1975-7; IX, cl, 1980, arr. sax, 1981; X, tpt, 1985

Other instrumental: Cinque variazioni, pf, 1952-3, rev. 1966; Wasserklavier, pf, 1964; Gesti, rec,

1965; Rounds, hpd, 1965, arr. pf, 1967; Erdenkla-
vier, pf, 1970; Chemins V, cl, electronics, 1980;
Duetti, 2vn, vol. 1 1979-83
Tape: Mutazioni, 1955; Perspectives, 1957; Thema
(Omaggio a Joyce), 1958; Momenti, 1960; Visage,
1961; Chants parallèles, 1974-5
Arrangements: Folk Songs, S, 7 insts, 1964, with
orch, 1973; also works by Monteverdi, Falla,
Weill, Lennon and McCartney, etc
[UE, Suvini Zerboni; RCA, Philips, Harmonia
Mundi, Turnabout, Decca, DG]

Berkeley, Lennox (1903-) English composer.
Studied at Oxford and with Boulanger in Paris
(1927-32), the latter guiding him towards a cool,
fluent and elegant technique that takes Stravinsky's
neoclassicism as a model. He himself taught at the
Royal Academy of Music (1946-68). His works include the full-scale opera *Nelson* (★Sadler's Wells,
1954), and three chamber operas: *A Dinner Engagement* (★Aldeburgh, 1954), *Ruth* (★London, 1956)
and *Castaway* (★Aldeburgh, 1967), besides 4 symphonies, several concertos, choral music, songs,
chamber works and piano pieces. [Chester]

Berkeley, Michael (1948-) English composer.
Son and pupil of Lennox Berkeley, he has composed various orchestral and chamber works besides the peace oratorio *Or Shall We Die?* (1982).
[OUP]

Berlin Between the wars a site of feverish artistic
activity, musically expressed in CABARET culture,
in scores composed for the plays of BRECHT and
other writers, in the work of the KROLL OPERA, and
in the compositions of musicians living in Berlin,
notably Schoenberg (1926-33), Hindemith (1927-
38), Schreker (1920-34), Weill (1918-33), Blacher
(1922-38) and Eisler (1925-33). After the war these
last two held central positions in West and East
Berlin respectively as composers and teachers.

Berners, Lord (Gerald Hugh Tyrwhitt-Wilson,
1883-1950) English composer. He was a diplomat
in Rome (1911-19), where he made the acquaintance of Stravinsky and Casella; later he lived the life
of a gentleman dilettante. His early pieces are
mostly small-scale and satirical in Satie's manner
(*Trois petites marches funèbres* for piano, 1914). The
main ones after 1920 are ballets including *The
Triumph of Neptune* (★Ballets Russes, London,
1926) and *A Wedding Bouquet* (★London, 1936).
[Chester]
□ I. Stravinsky, *Selected Correspondence*, vol.2
(1984)

Bernstein, Leonard (1918-) American composer
and conductor. Studied at Harvard and the Curtis
Institute. In his mid-20s he rapidly made a reputation as both composer and conductor, his first
works ranging from the musical *On the Town* to the
Jeremiah Symphony. The divergence is not so extreme, though, since he has always found it possible to use the language of American jazz and popular music in serious works, and to compose light
music while retaining all his care, skill and wit.
In the late 1940s and 1950s he wrote much:
another symphony in the form of a piano concerto
('The Age of Anxiety'), a 1-act opera and more
musicals, notably *West Side Story*. But his appointment as musical director of the New York Philharmonic (1958-69) reduced his output, resumed
thereafter with *Mass*, which unashamedly parades
his tastes for high Romanticism (in Bach as well as
Mahler), theatrical spectacle and popular art.
Operas: Trouble in Tahiti, ★Waltham, Mass.,
1952; A Quiet Place, ★Houston, 1983
Ballets: Fancy Free, ★New York, 1944; Facsimile,
★New York, 1946; Dybbuk, ★New York, 1974
Musicals: On the Town, ★New York, 1944;
Wonderful Town, ★New York, 1953; Candide,
★New York, 1956; West Side Story, ★New York,
1957; 1600 Pennsylvania Avenue, ★New York,
1976
Other dramatic works: On the Waterfront, film
score, 1954; Mass, ★Washington, DC, 1971
Symphonies: no.1 'Jeremiah', Mez, orch, 1943;
no.2 'The Age of Anxiety', pf, orch, 1949; no.3
'Kaddish', S, speaker, chorus, boys' chorus, orch,
1961-3
Other orchestral and choral: Serenade, vn, str, perc,
1954; Chichester Psalms, treble, chorus, orch,
1965; Slava, vc, orch, 1976
Instrumental: Sonata, cl, pf, 1941-2; Seven
Anniversaries, pf, 1942-3; Four Anniversaries, pf,
1947-8
Song cycles: I Hate Music, 1943; La bonne cuisine,
1947
[G. Schirmer; CBS, DG]
□ L. Bernstein, *The Unanswered Question* (1976)

Biches, Les (The Dears) Ballet by Poulenc,
choreography by Nijinska: it is set at a house party
in southern France. ★Ballets Russes, Monte Carlo,
6 Jan 1924.

Billy Budd Opera by Britten, E.M. Forster and
Eric Crozier after the Melville story of an innocent
sailor's destruction. Set on an 18th c. man-o'-war
at sea, the work is entirely for male voices. ★Cov-
ent Garden, 1 Dec 1951

Birtwistle, Harrison (1934-) English composer. He studied with Hall at the Royal Manchester College of Music (1952-5), where with Davies and Goehr he interested himself in the newest European music and in medieval techniques. Something of the latter survived in his conception of music as monody with elaboration, but the most significant influences on him were those of Stravinsky, Varèse and Messiaen; his first published work, *Refrains and Choruses* for wind quintet (1957), is already characteristic in its violent sonorities, its shaping in dissimilar blocks and its ritual character brought about by objectivity and repetitiveness.

However, he composed little until the breakthrough of *Tragoedia* (1965), which took violence and splintering much further, opening the way to PUNCH AND JUDY. Much of this work was written during a year at Princeton (1966), from which he returned to found the Pierrot Players. The period of Varèsian sound drama then ended with *Verses for Ensembles* (1969), for groups of wind and percussion players taking different stations about the platform. *Nenia* opened a new phase of relative quiet and processional slowness, represented on the largest scale by *The Triumph of Time*: many works of this later period relate to the opera *The Mask of Orpheus*. Others since the mid-1970s have been concerned with pulse, and in particular with textures of ensembles in different ticking rhythms.

Operas: PUNCH AND JUDY, 1966-7; The Mask of Orpheus, 1973-83; Yan Tan Tethera, 1984

Other theatrical: Down by the Greenwood Side, S, 5 actors, 9 insts, 1969; Pulse Field, ballet, 1977; Bow Down, 5 actors, 4 insts, 1977; music for National Theatre, London, 1976-83

Orchestral: Chorales, 1962-3; Tragoedia, 10 insts, 1965; Nomos, 1968; Verses for Ensembles, 12 insts, 1969; An Imaginary Landscape, 1971; The Triumph of Time, 1972; Grimethorpe Aria, brass band, 1973; Melencolia I, cl, harp, str, 1976; Silbury Air, 15 insts, 1977; Carmen arcadiae mechanicae perpetuum, 14 insts, 1977; Still Movement, str, 1984; Secret Theatre, 14 insts, 1984

Vocal: Monody for Corpus Christi, S, fl, hn, vn, 1959; Entr'actes and Sappho Fragments, S, 6, insts, 1964; Ring a Dumb Carillon, S, cl, perc, 1964-5; Cantata, S, 6 insts, 1969; Nenia: the Death of Orpheus, S, 5 insts, 1970; Meridian, Mez, S chorus, 13 insts, 1970-71; The Fields of Sorrow, 2 S, chorus, 16 insts, 1971; La plage, S, 5 insts, 1972; ...agm..., chorus, small orch, 1978-9; On the Sheer Threshold of the Night, 16 vv, 1980; Deowa, S, cl, 1983; Songs by Myself, S, insts, 1984

Other works: Refrains and Choruses, wind qnt, 1957; Précis, pf, 1960; Verses, cl, pf, 1965; Chronometer, tape, 1971-2; For O, for O, the Hobby-horse is Forgot, 6 perc, 1976; Cl Qnt, 1980; Pulse Sampler, ob, claves, 1981; Duets for Storab, 2 fl, 1983

[UE; Decca, Argo, HMV, Erato, Philips, Mainstream]

□ M. Hall, *Harrison Birtwistle* (1984)

bitonality The phenomenon of 2 keys present at once. One classic example is the clarinet duet near the start of the second scene of *Petrushka* (1911), where C major and F♯ major are superimposed. Subtler forms of bitonality are common in Stravinsky's neoclassical scores, and the practice was very much pursued by Milhaud, among others.

Bittner, Julius (1874-1939) Austrian composer. Largely self-taught, he practised the law while writing operas to his own librettos based on Austrian folk legends. These enjoyed success in Vienna around the time of the first world war.

Operas: Die rote Gred, ★1907; Der Musikant, ★1909; Der Bergsee, ★1910; Die arme Narren, ★1911; Der Abenteuerer, ★1912; Das höllisch Gold, ★1916; Die Kohlhaymerin, ★1920; Das Rosengärtlein, ★1922; Mondnacht, ★1926; Das Veilchen, ★1934

Other works: operettas, 2 syms, 2 str qts, etc

Blacher, Boris (1903-75) German composer. Born in China, he arrived in Berlin in 1922, studied at the university and remained in the city as a composer, arranger and teacher, except for a period of retirement during the Nazi rule. His music is usually ironic in tone, crisp in its rhythm and clear in its scoring, influenced much less by German traditions than by the Parisian musical culture of the 1920s: Stravinsky, Satie, Milhaud and jazz. After the war he began to use 12-note methods, and to look for rhythmic correspondences, which he found in VARIABLE METRES (first used in *Ornamente* for piano, 1950).

Operas: Romeo und Julia, 1943, ★Berlin, 1947; Die Flut, 1946, ★Dresden, 1947; Abstrakte Oper no.1 ('abstract' in using non-verbal communication), 1953, ★Hesse Radio, 1953; Rosamunde Floris, 1960, ★Berlin, 1960; Zwischenfälle bei einer Notlandung, 1965, ★Hamburg, 1966; Zweihunderttausend Taler, 1969, ★Berlin, 1969; Yvonne, 1972, ★Wuppertal, 1973; Das Geheimnis des entwendeten Briefes, ★Berlin, 1975

Ballets: Hamlet, 1949, ★Munich, 1950; Lysistrata,

1950, *Berlin, 1951; Der Mohr von Venedig, 1955, *Vienna, 1955; Demeter, 1963, *Schwetzingen, 1964; Tristan, 1965, *Berlin, 1965
Orchestral: Concertante Musik, 1937; Paganini Variations, 1947; Pf Conc no. 1 1947; no. 2, 1952; Orchester-Ornament, 1953; Clementi Variations, pf, orch, 1961; many other works
Choral works, chamber music, songs, pf, pieces, tapes
[Bote & Bock; Wergo]

Black Mountain College Institution in North Carolina, where Cage and other artists taught at summer courses in the late 1940s and 1950s. The stimulus of the place encouraged Cage's move into indeterminacy; one event he staged there in 1952 is generally regarded as the first HAPPENING.

Blake, David (1936–) English composer. Studied at Cambridge and with Eisler in East Berlin. Since 1963 he has taught at York University, from 1982 as professor. His music is of Schoenbergian seriousness, though influenced too by the music of the Far East (e.g. in the Pound cantata *Lumina*, 1968-9) and the Caribbean (notably in the opera *Toussaint*, 1974-6, *London Coliseum, 1977). [Schott]

Bliss, Arthur (1891-1975) English composer. Studied at Cambridge and at the Royal College of Music before serving in the first world war. After the war he was briefly the *enfant terrible* of English music, influenced by Stravinsky and Les Six (*Rout* for soprano and 10 players, 1920), but then he gradually moderated his adventurousness with an Elgarian manner: the transformation begins in *A Colour Symphony* (1921-2) and is completed in the orchestral Introduction and Allegro (1926). Subsequent works include the opera *The Olympians* (1948-9, libretto by J.B. Priestley, *Covent Garden, 1949), the ballets *Checkmate* (1937), *Miracle in the Gorbals* (1944) and *Adam Zero* (1946), music for the film *Things to Come* (1934-5) and much else in all genres. [Novello]

Blitzstein, Marc (1905-64) American composer. Studied in the USA and, in 1926-8, with Boulanger in Paris and Schoenberg in Berlin. In 1935, in New York, he heard Eisler lecture and saw a production of the Brecht–Eisler *Die Mutter*, which convinced him that art must concern itself with radical POLITICS: the result was his 'play in music' *The Cradle will Rock* (1936-7, *New York, 1937), to his own text about a boss–union conflict. During the war he

wrote patriotic music, and afterwards returned to his work in the theatre, with original works and a highly successful adaptation of *The Threepenny Opera* (*1952). [Chappell]

Bloch, Ernest (1880-1959) Swiss–American composer. Studied in Brussels and Germany, and then returned to Switzerland as a conductor and teacher. After 1916 he spent most of his time in California, teaching and composing. His early works are in a heady Romantic style influenced by Richard Strauss and Debussy: the biggest of them is the opera *Macbeth* (1904-9, *Paris, Opéra-Comique, 1910), a work whose darkness and turbulence also owe much to Musorgsky. During the next 15 years there were many works of Jewish inspiration, including the symphony *Israel* (with 5 solo voices, 1912-16) and *Schelomo* for cello and orchestra (1915-16). Then in the mid-1920s his music became neoclassical (Concerto grosso no. 1 for strings and piano, 1924-5), though in the 1930s he returned to a broader scale and again to Jewish subject matter, notably in the Sacred Service for baritone, chorus and orchestra (1930-33).
□ S. Bloch and I. Heskes, *Ernest Bloch, Creative Spirit* (1976); R. Strassburg, *Ernest Bloch, Voice in the Wilderness* (1977)

block Portion of music that is to a large degree closed, not leading into something else. Composition in blocks is wholly antithetical to the 19th c. symphonic tradition but is common in Stravinsky, Messiaen, etc.

Blomdahl, Karl-Birger (1916-68) Swedish composer. Studied with Rosenberg and in the 1940s began teaching composition. Though he never lost the vigour of his early Hindemithian works, he was influenced in the 1950s by the patterning and expressiveness of Berg: key works of this period include his Third Symphony (1950) and the ballets *Sisyphos* (1954) and *Minotauros* (1957). Then came his opera *Aniara* (1957-8, *Stockholm, 1959), which caused great excitement both by its spaceship setting and by its stylistic diversity, including episodes of electronic music. Later works include *Fioriture* (1960) and *Forma ferritonans* (1961) for orchestra, and the ballet *Game for Eight* (1962). [Schott]

Bluebeard's Castle (A Kékszakállú herceg vára) Opera by Bartók and Béla Balázs in one act, showing Judith's arrival in the castle of her new husband, her insistence on opening 7 locked doors, and her imprisonment within the castle once she knows his secrets. *Budapest Opera, 24 May 1918.

blue note Note of a diatonic scale commonly lowered in jazz, blues and associated traditions. The effect is usually felt at the 3rd and 7th degrees, but may be also at the 5th and elsewhere, and the lowering may be by a semitone or less.

blues Song tradition of American Blacks, distinguished by a tone of lament, a structure in three phrases each of four bars, and the use of blue notes. The blues has had an enormous influence on jazz and rock, and has occasionally been used by 'classical' composers: Ravel called the slow movement of his Violin Sonata (1923-7) 'Blues', and the style has been essayed too by Copland and Tippett.

Boehmer, Konrad (1941-) German composer. Studied with Koenig in Cologne and settled in Amsterdam in 1967, working as a teacher and composer. Influenced briefly by Stockhausen, he took a radical position in the late 1960s, following on from Eisler and Adorno. His works include the opera *Docteur Faustus* (*Paris Opera, 1985).

Boesmans, Philippe (1936-) Belgian composer. Studied with Froidebise and Pousseur, but has been influenced too by Boulez and Berio in his creation of a music of strong gestures that are constantly being explored in a state of dreamlike continuity, where simple intervallic shapes may echo across wide-spread sustained harmonies.
Opera: La passion de Gilles, *Brussels, 1983
Music theatre: Attitudes, singer, actors, 2 pf, synthesizer, perc., 1977
Orchestral: Corrélations, c1, 2 ensembles, 1967; Explosives, harp, ensemble, 1968, Intervalles I, 1972; Intervalles II, 1973; Multiples, 2 pf, orch 1974, rev. 1978; Ring, electric org, ensemble, 1975; Eléments-Extensions, pf, small orch, 1976; Doublures, harp, pf, perc, 4 ensembles, 1977; Pf Conc, 1978; Vn Conc, 1979; Conversions, 1980
Vocal: Upon la mi, S, hn, ensemble, electronics, 1970; Intervalles III, Mez, orch, 1975
Other: Fanfare I, 2 pf (1 player), 1971-2; Fanfare II, org 1972; La résurrection altérée, wind qnt, 1972; Sur mi, 2 pf, electric org, perc, 1974; Intrusions, gui, 1977; Ricercar sconvolto, org, 1983
[Jobert; Musica Magna, Ricercare]

Boeuf sur le toit, Le (The Ox on the Roof) Ballet by Milhaud and Cocteau set in an American bar and coloured by the CABARET music of its period. *Paris, 21 Feb 1920.

Bolcom, William (1938-) American composer. Studied at the University of Washington, in Paris with Milhaud and Messiaen, and at Stanford with Leland Smith; since 1965 has worked as a university teacher, besides appearing as a pianist. Eclectic in his tastes, he played a large part in the ragtime revival, composing some rags himself, and has produced lurid religious works (*Black Host* for organ, percussion and tape, 1967) as well as an entertaining excursion out of 18th c. disciplines in *Commedia* for chamber orchestra (1971). [AMP; Nonesuch]

Boretz, Benjamin (1934-) American composer and theorist. Studied with Fine and Berger at Brandeis, and Sessions and Babbitt at Princeton. In 1962 he became founder-editor of *Perspectives of New Music*, where he has published major theoretical articles. His works include *Group Variations* for chamber orchestra (1964-7) or computer-synthesized tape (1968-72). [CRI]

Boucourechliev, André (1925-) Bulgarian–French composer. Studied in Sofia and in Paris (1949-51), where he remained as a piano teacher while also starting to compose and attending the Darmstadt courses. He has written books on Schumann, Chopin, Beethoven and Stravinsky, besides works of Boulezian form but often more solid gesture. In *Ombres* for eleven strings (1970) he worked over quotations from Beethoven's quartets; the *Archipel* series, for various instrumental combinations (1967-), provides 'archipelagos' of material to be visited by the performers at will. [Leduc, UE; Erato, Philips]

Boughton, Rutland (1878-1960) English composer. Studied with Stanford and Walford Davies at the Royal College of Music, and in 1914 founded the Glastonbury Festival on the Bayreuth model. There were produced his *The Immortal Hour* (*1914) and other works before the venture collapsed in 1927; in 1922-3 *The Immortal Hour* enjoyed a hugely successful run in London, endearing itself to audiences with its simple tunefulness and tale of mystic enchantment. 5 of his other operas form an Arthurian cycle.
□ M. Hurd, *Immortal Hour* (1962)

Boulanger, Nadia (1887-1979) French teacher. Was born into a musical Franco-Russian family: her father taught at the Paris Conservatoire, where she herself studied, and her sister Lili (1893-1918) was a composer of great promise (she wrote several psalm settings, including the large-scale *Du fond de l'abîme*, 1914–17). Nadia also composed, but quickly concentrated her attentions on teaching composition, at the Conservatoire, at the Ecole Normale de Musique and at the American Conservatory in Fontainebleau. She was close to Stravinsky, whose neoclassical music provided her with a measure of clarity she demanded of her pupils. These included Lennox Berkeley, Carter, Copland, Françaix, Harris, Piston, Thomson and many others.

□ A. Kendall, *The Tender Tyrant* (1976)

Boulevard Solitude Opera by Henze and Grete Weil, telling the story of Manon Lescaut with the emphasis on des Grieux; its heterogeneous style ranges from jazz and *La bohème* to serialism. *Hanover, 17 Feb 1952

Boulez, Pierre (1925-) French composer and conductor. His music has known decisive periods of change, but he has been consistent in demanding of himself that his imagination travel always in new directions, at once bounded and encouraged by a fearsome armoury of rules and aesthetic prejudices. The tension between freedom and restraint has resulted in phases of hectic activity alternating with years of creative impotence: the 1960s and early 1970s, for instance, saw little achieved. However, he has filled such gaps through his parallel activity as a conductor, unrivalled in his performances of music in which he can detect his own mix of imaginative daring and close but hidden structure: Debussy, early Stravinsky, late Webern, Berg and some Bartók.

Born in Montbrison, he went to Paris in 1942 to study music, against his father's wishes, and became Messiaen's pupil at the Conservatoire (1944-5), then learned his Schoenberg from René Leibowitz (1945-6). There followed a rapid succession of works in which he combined 12-note methods with Messiaen's influence, and either worked against the background of standard forms (Flute Sonatina, Piano Sonatas nos 1–2) or else set the highly charged poetry of René Char (*Le visage nuptial, Le soleil des eaux*). During this period of the late 1940s he was influenced also by Artaud, and by a wish to liberate music from the restraints of western culture: with rare exceptions (the first movement of *Le soleil des eaux*) his music was rapid and intemperate, possessed with Char's 'fury and mystery'.

But at the same time he was searching for new means of order. In particular, following on from Messiaen, he pursued the idea of rhythmic parallels for 12-note serialism: there are signs of this in the Second Piano Sonata and even more so in the *Livre pour quatuor*, where feverish rhythmic activity often takes place in a harmonic calm. Then in 1951-2 he discovered means of achieving a TOTAL SERIALISM of duration, timbre and loudness as well as pitch in *Polyphonie X*, the first book of STRUCTURES for 2 pianos and 2 *Etudes* in *musique concrète*. These works were of enormous importance to his colleagues internationally, and for the next decade he was at the head of the European avant garde, teaching regularly at Darmstadt.

After the abstract works of 1951-2 he used his new-found technique to set more fragmentary verses of Char in *Le* MARTEAU SANS MAÎTRE (1953-5), the first undisputed masterpiece of the new music. After this his thoughts turned more to Mallarmé, whose conceptions of aleatory form lay behind his Third Piano Sonata, and whose words he set in 2 *Improvisations* which eventually grew into PLI SELON PLI. The sonata is in 5 'formants' (only 2 are published) which can be arranged in various orders, and which offer the performer various choices of speed, dynamic and formal connection. A second book of *Structures* extended such openness to the 2-piano medium, but there were also more completely composed works: *Figures-Doubles-Prismes* for a large and unusually disposed orchestra, and *Poésie pour pouvoir* for orchestra with tape.

The last works benefited from his experience as a conductor, notably at the Domaine Musical concerts he had founded in Paris in 1954 as a forum for new music and new ways of hearing old. His work as a conductor rapidly increased, culminating in his appointments as chief conductor of the BBC Symphony Orchestra (1971-4) and the New York Philharmonic (1971-8). At the same time, his compositional output declined, and there began a tendency, no doubt stimulated by aleatory considerations, for works to be left 'in progress'. *Eclat/multiples*, begun as a piece for glittering percussion ensemble and associated instruments in 1965, has remained in this state; so too have most of his later works, with the notable exception of the unusually monumental *Rituel*.

Since the mid-1970s he has been involved in setting up and then directing the INSTITUT DE RECHERCHE ET DE COORDINATION ACOUSTIQUE/MUSIQUE in Paris, a computer music studio. The creative result of this has been *Répons*, using a characteristic array of tuned percussion instruments as well as electronic adjuncts, and marking a further stage in his view of serial music, unlike tonal music, as 'a universe perpetually in expansion'.

Orchestral: Le visage nuptial, S, A, female chorus, orch, 1946-7, rev. 1951-2; Le soleil des eaux, S, chorus, orch, 1948, rev. 1958, rev. 1965; Polyphonie X, 18 insts, 1951; PLI SELON PLI, S, orch, 1957-62; Figures-Doubles-Prismes, 1957-68; Poésie pour pouvoir, orch, tape, 1958; Eclat, 15 insts, 1965, became first section of Eclat/multiples, orch, 1965-; Domaines, cl, 21 insts, 1961-8; Livre pour cordes, 1968-; 'Cummings ist der Dichter...', 16 vv, 24 insts, 1970-; Rituel, 1974-5; Notations, 1977-; Répons, 6 soloists, small orch, electronics, 1980-

Chamber: Livre pour quatuor, str qt, 1948-9, rev. as Livre pour cordes; Le MARTEAU SANS MAÎTRE, A, 6 insts, 1953-5; Messagesquisse, 7 vc, 1976; Dérive, 6 insts, 1983

Instrumental: Sonatina, fl, pf, 1946; Pf Sonata no.1, 1946; Pf Sonata no.2, 1947-8; STRUCTURES, 2 pf, book 1 1951-2, book 2 1956-61; Pf Sonata no.3, 1956-7

Tape: Etude sur un son, Etude sur sept sons, 1951-2

[UE, Heugel, Amphion; CBS, Erato, Véga, Wergo]

□ P. Boulez, *Notes of an Apprenticeship* (1968), *Boulez on Music Today* (1971), *Conversations with Célestin Deliège* (1977), *Orientations: Collected Writings* (1986); P. Griffiths, *Boulez* (1978).

Bozay, Attila (1939-) Hungarian composer. Studied with Farkas at the Budapest Academy (1958-62) and began writing strict serial pieces, chiefly in small instrumental genres. A 6-month stay in Paris in 1967 led him to a looser style, and to larger gestures. [Editio Musica]

Brand, Max (1896-) Polish-American composer. Studied with Schreker in Vienna and Berlin, and gained success with his *Maschinist Hopkins* (*Duisburg, 1929), at once a ZEITOPER and a surrealist fantasy: the machines are among the singing characters. With the coming of Nazi rule he fled via Switzerland and Rio de Janeiro to the United States, where he arrived in 1940, and where he continued to compose, especially for theatrical media.

Brant, Henry (1913-) Canadian–American composer. Studied at the McGill Conservatorium before settling in 1929 in New York, where he continued formal studies besides taking private lessons with Riegger and Antheil. He earned his living as an arranger, and later also as a college teacher, while writing works for unconventional forces. Early works include *Angels and Devils* for solo flute and 10 members of the flute family (1931), and *Music for a Five and Dime Store* for violin, piano and kitchen hardware (1932). Since *Antiphony 1* (1953) he has been concerned with SPATIAL MUSIC for ensembles separated in space and in style.

brass band Ensemble of two dozen or so brass players, usually with percussion, thriving particularly in the north of England and there having its own strong working-class traditions. Works for it have been composed, however, by general composers, including Elgar, Holst, Vaughan Williams, Birtwistle and Henze.

Brecht, Bertolt (1898-1956) German playwright and poet. Reversing the normal relationship between composer and librettist, he saw music as a way of adding bite to particular moments in a play, the spoken drama remaining pre-eminent, and usually presenting a parable of acute social meaning. WEILL and HINDEMITH, with whom he worked in the late 1920s and early 1930s, were not quite of the same artistic and political mind: he worked more productively in later years with EISLER and DESSAU.

Brian, Havergal (1876-1972) English composer. Mainly self-taught, he made a mark before the first world war as a composer of choral and orchestral music, but thereafter disappeared from public notice except as a writer for the magazine *Musical Opinion*. He continued nevertheless to compose large-scale operas and symphonies in a brusquely individual Romantic style, until in the 1960s interest was revived by SIMPSON and other champions: his *Gothic* Symphony (designated no.1) for large vocal and orchestral forces (1919-27) had its first performance in 1961. More symphonies followed, the last, no.32, written when he was 92.

□ M. Macdonald, *The Symphonies of Havergal Brian*, 3 vols (1974-83); R. Nettel, *Havergal Brian and his Music* (1976)

Bridge, Frank (1879-1941) English composer. Studied with Stanford at the Royal College of Music, and began as a composer within the English school represented also by Bax and Ireland. But then in his Piano Sonata (1921-4) he began to explore a more purposefully dissonant though still refined harmonic style, approaching Berg in his Third and Fourth Quartets. Britten was his private pupil.

Orchestral: The Sea, 1910-11; Summer, 1914; Enter Spring, 1927; Oration, vc, orch, 1930; Phantasm, pf, orch, 1931; Rebus Overture, 1940
String quartets: Phantasie Qt, f, 1905; e, 1906; g, 1915; no.3, 1926; no.4, 1937
Other chamber works: Pf qnt, 1904-12; Vn sonata, 1932
Choral works, many songs, piano music [Boosey, Faber; Argo, EMI]
☐ A. Payne, *Frank Bridge* (1984)

Britten, Benjamin (1913-76) English composer. He was the outstanding English composer of his time, reacting against the prevalent pastoral tradition in order to draw encouragement from the English past (especially Purcell) and the European present (especially Stravinsky and Bartók). He contributed more operas to the international repertory than any other composer since the generation of Strauss and Puccini, and won wide admiration for his songs and choral works, though his relatively smaller number of orchestral and chamber scores, most of them written before 1945, are perhaps still more remarkable.

He was born in Lowestoft, not far from his eventual home at ALDEBURGH, and composed copiously from the age of 5. At 13 he began studies with Bridge, and then in 1930 he entered the Royal College of Music, studying piano and composition. After hearing *Wozzeck* in 1934 he visited Vienna and formed the plan of studying with Berg, but this came to nothing. Instead he began work in 1935 writing music for documentary films made by the General Post Office: Auden was in the same team, and became his collaborator on concert works as well, notably the 'symphonic cycle' *Our Hunting Fathers*. This and other works of the late 1930s, such as the Bridge Variations for strings, gained him the reputation of an *enfant terrible*, alive to dangerous Continental influences and with a gift for sharp musical satire.

In 1939 he left for the USA with the tenor Peter Pears, his companion for the rest of his life and the destined singer of many of his songs and leading operatic roles: the flamboyant set of Michelangelo Sonnets (1940) was the first of these Pears works, marking a confidence that is evident too in the *Sinfonia da requiem* and the First Quartet. But though the American period was creatively productive, Britten felt the wish to return home when a magazine article turned his attention to the Suffolk poet George Crabbe. He recrossed the Atlantic in 1942, and in 1944 began his Crabbe opera PETER GRIMES.

That work at once established his gift for opera, which depended on word setting that is both extravagant and apt in the manner of Purcell, on the creation of atmosphere through orchestral interludes, on the ability to create distinct musical characters in even the tiniest roles, and on a deep personal engagement with the central figure. In most of his later operas too there is an evident community of feeling between the composer and his main character (Lucretia, Billy Budd, the Governess in TURN OF THE SCREW, Owen Wingrave, Aschenbach in DEATH IN VENICE), and it is this that creates a sense of personal, almost confessional intimacy rare in opera.

Perhaps because it assisted that intimacy, Britten preferred the genre of chamber opera, for a few singers and an orchestra of about a dozen: the English Opera Group grew out of his first such work, RAPE OF LUCRETIA (1946), and for them he wrote ALBERT HERRING, *The Little Sweep*, TURN OF THE SCREW, MIDSUMMER NIGHT'S DREAM and the 3 PARABLES FOR CHURCH PERFORMANCE. In 1948 he created another closed environment for himself in the Aldeburgh Festival, where many of his works had their first performances.

However, he was also active in larger forms and in larger arenas. Beside the chamber operas there were full-scale works for Covent Garden, BILLY BUDD and GLORIANA; there was also the massive WAR REQUIEM, the chief expression of his pacifism. Nor was he deaf to new developments in music. In its essence his musical personality changed little after his very earliest works, but he explored possibilities of 12-note composition within a diatonic context in TURN OF THE SCREW and other works of that period, and the church parables show his own response to the vogue for mixed ensembles. His last work, the Third Quartet, found him looking anew at the challenges of large-scale instrumental composition, which had perforce been neglected during 30 years of concentration on opera and song; it was one of his finest achievements.

Operas: Paul Bunyan, 1941; PETER GRIMES, 1944-5; The RAPE OF LUCRETIA, 1946; ALBERT HERRING, 1947; The Beggar's Opera (after Gay), 1948; The Little Sweep, 1949; BILLY BUDD, 1951; GLORIANA, 1953; The TURN OF THE SCREW, 1954; Noye's Fludde, 1957; A MIDSUMMER NIGHT'S DREAM, 1960; Curlew River, 1964; The Burning Fiery Furnace, 1966; The Prodigal Son, 1968; OWEN WINGRAVE, 1970; DEATH IN VENICE, 1973
Vocal orchestral: Our Hunting Fathers, S/T, orch, 1936; Ballad of Heroes, T/S, chorus, orch, 1939; Les illuminations (Rimbaud), S/T, str, 1939; Sere-

nade, T, hn, str, 1943; St Nicolas, soloists, chorus, orch, 1948; Spring Symphony, S, A, T, boys' vv, chorus, orch, 1949; Nocturne, T, orch, 1958; Cantata academica, S, A, T, B, chorus, orch, 1959; WAR REQUIEM, S, T, Bar, boys' vv, chorus, orch, 1961; Cantata misericordium, T, Bar, chorus, orch, 1963; Phaedra, Mez, orch, 1975

Orchestral: Sinfonietta, chamber orch, 1932; Simple Sym, str, 1933-4; Bridge Variations, str, 1937; Pf Conc, 1938; Vn Conc, 1939; Diversions, pf (left hand), orch, 1940; Sinfonia da requiem, 1940; Prelude and Fugue, str, 1943; The Young Person's Guide to the Orchestra, 1946; The Prince of the Pagodas, ballet, 1956; Cello Sym, vc, orch, 1963

Choral: A Boy was Born, 1933; Hymn to St Cecilia, 1942; A Ceremony of Carols, boys' vv, harp, 1942; Rejoice in the Lamb, chorus, org, 1943; Festival Te Deum, chorus, org, 1944; Five Flower Songs, 1950; Missa brevis, boys' vv, org, 1959; Voices for Today, 1965; The Golden Vanity, boys' vv, pf, 1966; Children's Crusade, children's vv, insts, 1968

Chamber: Str Qt in D, 1931, rev, 1974; Phantasy, ob qt, 1932; Str Qt no.1, D, 1941; Str Qt no.2, C, 1945; Lachrymae, va, pf, 1950; Six Metamorphoses after Ovid, ob, 1951; Sonata, C, vc, pf, 1961; Suites nos 1-3, vc, 1964, 1967, 1972; Suite, harp, 1969; Str Qt no.3, 1975

Song cycles with piano: On this Island (Auden), 1937; Seven Sonnets of Michelangelo, 1940; The Holy Sonnets of John Donne, 1945; A Charm of Lullabies, 1947; Winter Words (Hardy), 1953; Sechs Hölderlin-Fragmente, 1958; Gemini Variations, vn, fl, 2 pf, 1965; Songs and Proverbs of William Blake, 1965; The Poet's Echo (Pushkin), 1965; Who are these Children?, 1969

Canticles: I My Beloved is Mine (Quarles), S/T, pf, 1947; II ABRAHAM AND ISAAC, A, T, pf, 1952; III Still Falls the Rain (E. Sitwell), T, hn, pf, 1954; IV The Journey of the Magi (Eliot), Ct, T, Bar, pf, 1971; V The Death of St Narcissus (Eliot), T, harp, 1974 [Boosey; Faber; Decca]

□ P. Evans, *The Music of Benjamin Britten* (1979); M. Kennedy, *Britten* (1981)

broadcasting The first radio stations opened at the start of the 1920s, and music inevitably figured largely in programmes from the first. In the 1920s and 1930s orchestras were established by, among others, the BBC in London, the NBC in New York, and stations in France, Germany and Italy. Efforts were made to present contemporary music, especially in Europe. Schoenberg and Webern conducted their music for the BBC, for in-

stance, and Britten wrote music for broadcast plays; special radio works were written by Hindemith and Weill (*Der Lindberghflug*, Berlin, 1929), and by Honegger (*Les 12 coups de minuit*, Paris, 1933). In the USA radio patronage was less generous, though in 1936 CBS commissioned orchestral works from Copland, Gruenberg, Hanson, Harris, Piston and Still, while in 1933 NBC had broadcast one of the first radio operas, Cadman's *The Willow Tree* (the distinction is shared with Egk's *Columbus*, Munich, 1933).

Later radio operas include Martinů's *Comedy on the Bridge* (Prague, 1937), Menotti's *The Old Maid and the Thief* (NBC, 1939), and Henze's *Ein Landarzt* (Hamburg, 1951) and *Das Ende einer Welt* (Hamburg, 1953). Radio stations have also encouraged electronic music: Cage was able to work with oscillators and other equipment in Chicago (*Imaginary Landscape no.3,* 1942) and Schaeffer initiated MUSIQUE CONCRÈTE in Paris in 1948. Studios for electronic music were set up in the 1950s by broadcasting authorities in Paris, Cologne, Milan, London, Brussels, Tokyo and elsewhere. At the same time radio organizations have promoted live new music through festivals (notably in Cologne, Munich and Hamburg) and commissions: many works by Stockhausen, Tippett, Boulez, Berio and others have been commissioned for radio audiences to share, though again this has been less a feature of American broadcasting.

Music commissioned for television represents a much smaller repertory. Menotti's *Amahl and the Night Visitors* (NBC, 1952) was the first television opera, followed by Martinů's *The Marriage* (New York, 1953), Stravinsky's *The Flood* (CBS, 1962) and Britten's *Owen Wingrave* (BBC, 1971). The potential of the video medium has been exploited almost exclusively by rock and pop musicians.

Brouwer, Leo (1939-) Cuban composer and guitarist. Studied in the USA, though was more marked by the music he heard at the 1961 Warsaw Autumn Festival. Since his return to Havana later that year he has taught composition, been influenced by composers who have visited Cuba (Nono in 1967, Henze in 1969-70) and written works of an adventurousness felt to be in keeping with his position as an artist in a revolutionary society.

Brown, Earle (1926-) American composer. Studied at the Schillinger School in Boston, and in the early 1950s was a close associate of Cage's. During this period he was a pioneer of GRAPHIC NOTATION (*Folio*, 1952-3), TIME-SPACE NOTATION and MOBILE

FORM (*Twenty-Five Pages*, 1953). Later works are generally more fully composed, though still with aleatory elements; most of them are for instrumental ensembles, ranging from 2 or 3 pianos (*Corroboree*, 1964) to orchestra (*Available Forms II*, 1961-2; *Modules I-III*, 1967-9; *Time Spans*, 1972-3; *Cross Sections and Color Fields*, 1973-5) [AMP, Schott, UE; Mainstream]

bruitism Originally a French term, 'bruitisme' (from 'bruit' = 'noise'), denoting the use of noise, as in the music of FUTURISM, etc.

Bruneau, Alfred (1857-1934) French composer. A Massenet pupil at the Paris Conservatoire, he worked with Zola on several operas influenced by verismo, Wagner's orchestra and the lyricism of his teacher. New works by him appeared regularly at the Paris Opera and the Opéra-Comique from the 1890s to the 1930s, but they did not spread or last.

Bryars, Gavin (1943-) English composer. Read philosophy at Sheffield University and worked at the University of Illinois in 1968. An admirer of Satie, low art and American iconoclasm, he is one of the foremost experimental composers in England: his works are often slow, repetitive and done with a whimsical wit. They include *The Sinking of the Titanic* for variable forces and the opera *Medea* (★Lyons, 1984). [Experimental Music Catalogue; Obscure]

Buch der hängenden Gärten, Das (The Book of the Hanging Gardens) Cycle of 15 songs by Schoenberg to poems of Stefan George evocative of erotic love in a fantastic landscape. These and the Second String Quartet were the works in which Schoenberg first dispensed with tonality; the songs were begun in March 1908. ★Martha Winternitz Dorda, Etta Werndorff, Vienna, 14 Jan 1910.

Buller, John (1927-) English composer. Did not start composition studies until 1959, with Milner, and began to gain attention only in the early 1970s when he produced a sequence of Berio-like commentaries on *Finnegans Wake*, notably *The Mime of Mick, Nick and the Maggies* for soloists, chorus and ensemble (1977). Later works include *Proença* for mezzo-soprano, electric guitar and orchestra (1977), an exalted love song and lament addressed to Provençal civilization. [G. Schirmer; Unicorn]

Burgon, Geoffrey (1941-) English composer. Studied with Wishart and Berkeley, and has had success as a composer of theme music for television. Other works, in a broad-spanned diatonic style, include a Requiem (1976).

Burian, Emil František (1904-59) Czech composer. Studied with Foerster at the Prague Conservatory and wrote his first operas in a Straussian style. In 1925, though, he fell under the influence of jazz, dada and Les Six: his Voice Band, active from 1927 until the war, gave performances of non-verbal utterance supported by piano, percussion and jazz group. Meanwhile his operas *The War* (1935) and *Maryša* (1938, ★Brno, 1940) were showing Janáček's influence. After the war he adopted SOCIALIST REALISM.

Burkhard, Willy (1900-55) Swiss composer. Studied in Berne, Leipzig, Munich and Paris, and then returned to Switzerland as a teacher and composer. Influenced by Hindemith and Bartók, he developed a stark polyphonic style, often based on church modes and appealing to Bachian principles of form: many of his most important works were of oratorio character, including *Das Gesicht Jesajas* (1933-5), *Das Jahr* (1942) and the Mass (1951). Other works include the opera *Die schwarze Spinne* (1948, ★Zurich, 1949) and orchestral and chamber music in standard genres. [Bärenreiter, UE, Schott, Hug]

Bush, Alan (1900-) English composer. Studied at the Royal Academy of Music, with Ireland, and at the University of Berlin (1929-31). In 1925 he had begun teaching at the RAM; he also founded the Workers' Music Association in 1936. His earlier works, notably *Dialectic* for string quartet (1929), are distinguished by consistent thematic working in a dissonant contrapuntal style aware of Schoenberg, Bartók and Hindemith. After the war he deliberately simplified his style and produced a series of operas which, vigorously conveying his communist sympathies, had more success in East Germany than in Britain. They include *Wat Tyler* (★Leipzig, 1953), *Men of Blackmoor* (★Oxford, 1960), *The Sugar Reapers* (★Leipzig, 1966) and *Joe Hill* (★Berlin, 1970).
□ A. Bush, *In my Seventh Decade* (1970), *In my Eighth Decade* (1980)

Busoni, Ferruccio (1866-1924) German–Italian composer and pianist. Enjoying a successful career as a pianist from the age of 7 (and composer from the age of 11), he travelled widely before settling in Berlin in 1894. There he taught at the Prussian

41

Academy, conducted concerts of contemporary music, wrote an exceedingly forward-looking *Sketch for a New Aesthetic of Music* (1907, English translation in *Three Classics in the Aesthetic of Music*, New York, 1962), continued a monumental sequence of BACH adaptations, and composed operas, orchestral works and piano music.

His output is as diverse as that of Liszt, whom he greatly admired. At first his horizons were bounded by Mendelssohn, Schumann and Brahms, but in his *Konzertstück* for piano and orchestra (1890) he began to aim at neoclassicism (his term was 'junge Klassizität'), taking Bach and Mozart as models of clarity. However, the Classical aspects of his art tend to be imposed on music that looks in many different directions: back to the 19th c., forward with Debussy and Schoenberg, across to Reger. He was interested in everything – even, in the *Sketch*, in the very new possibility of electronic music – and instead of combining his interests freely as his contemporary Ives was doing, he used one to balance another. Fittingly his greatest work was a study of the thirst for knowledge in its most celebrated mythical form, the Faust legend. Many of his later works, including the almost atonal Sonatina no.2, are satellites of this opera.

Operas: Die Brautwahl, 1908-10, *Hamburg 1912; Arlecchino, 1914-16, *Zurich, 1917; Turandot, 1917, *Zurich, 1917; DOKTOR FAUST, 1916-24
Orchestral: Konzertstück, pf, orch, 1890; Pf Conc, 1903-4; Berceuse elegiaque, 1909; Nocturne symphonique, 1912; Indianische Fantasie, pf, orch, 1913; Indianisches Tagebuch, book 2, 1915; Cl Concertino, 1919; Divertimento, fl, orch, 1920
Piano: Elegien, 1907; Fantasia contrappuntistica, 1910-12, also versions for 2 pf and org; Sonatinas: no.1 1910, no.2 1912, no.3 1916, no.4 1917, no.5 1919, no.6 1920; Indianisches Tagebuch, book 1, 1915; Toccata, 1921
[Breitkopf]
□ E.J. Dent, *Ferruccio Busoni* (1933, r1974)

Bussotti, Sylvano (1931-) Italian composer. Studied at the Florence Conservatory as a boy, then studied composition independently before taking lessons with Deutsch in Paris (1957). Boulez and Cage were important to him too, generating a clash of interests vividly expressed in his first publications, the *Sette fogli* and the 5 Pieces for David Tudor (both 1959): this is music of fragile beauty and grand gesture, intense violence and caressing warmth, and extreme virtuosity. Later works have continued to expose a personality of glamorous self-indulgence.

Stage: La passion selon Sade, *Stockholm 1969; Lorenzaccio, opera, *Venice, 1972; Bergkristall, ballet, *Rome, 1974; Nottetempo, opera, *Milan, 1976; Le racine, 1980
Other works: Sette fogli (Couple, fl, pf; Coeur, perc; Per tre sul piano; Lettura di Braibanti, v; Mobilestabile, v, pf, guis; Manifesto per Kalinowski, ensemble; Sensitivo, string soloist), 1959; Five Pieces for David Tudor, pf, 1959; Memoria, vv, orch, 1962; The Rara Requiem, vv, orch, 1969-70
[Bruzzichelli, Moeck, Ricordi, UE; DG, Italia]

Butterley, Nigel (1935-) Australian composer. Studied at the New South Wales State Conservatorium (where he later joined the staff) and with Rainier in London. *In the Head of the Fire* for radio (1966) was an early success in its dramatic treatment of religious texts with all the resources of vocal, instrumental and studio electronic music. Later works are mostly for orchestra or small ensemble.

Butterworth, George (1885-1916) English composer. A close associate of Vaughan Williams, whom he accompanied on folk music expeditions. His small published output – including an orchestral rhapsody *A Shropshire Lad* after Housman, 2 sets of songs to words by the same poet, and 3 orchestral idylls on folk tunes – dates from 1911-13. In 1914 he abandoned music to join the army; he died in action.

C

cabaret Provocative entertainment offered in night clubs from the 1880s to the 1930s, especially in Paris and Berlin. The first cabaret milieu was that of the 'Chat Noir' in Paris, which opened in 1881 as a place for avant-garde artists to meet and create sophisticated entertainment: Satie was a regular pianist, and wrote piano pieces and songs for the ambience. In Berlin the lead was taken by the 'Überbrettl', which opened in 1901 with Schoenberg as one of its first musicians (he wrote 7 *Brettllieder* before returning to Vienna in 1903). After the war, cabarets provided a natural home for imported and indigenous jazz. In Paris the main venue was 'Le Boeuf sur le Toit', which may have given its name to Milhaud's ballet or vice versa; in any event, the place fertilized the absorption of jazz by Milhaud, Poulenc and others. Meanwhile in Berlin and Munich cabaret art was becoming increasingly political, providing an essential part of the background for Brecht, Weill and Eisler.

□ L. Appignanesi, *The Cabaret* (1976)

Cadman, Charles (1881-1946) American composer. Began collecting American Indian music in 1909, and used it, within a firmly 19th c. style, in his music, which includes the opera *Shanewis* (*New York, 1918).

Cage, John (1912-) American composer. By one simple step, the denial of intention as necessary to composition, he has changed the perceived nature of music more radically than any other musician of the century. Allowing decisions to be made by CHANCE OPERATIONS, admitting INDETERMINACY into the acts of composition and performance, and opening his music to all manner of materials have produced a body of work of remarkable variety, and yet the very freedom of his art has given most of it the profile of a distinctive personality: candid, open and happily disposed. His work has been enormously influential.

Born in Los Angeles, he travelled in Europe in 1930-31 and then studied with Cowell in New York and with Schoenberg in California (1934). From this period date his first compositions, which were essays in non-serial 12-note composition. In 1937 he moved to Seattle, where he organized a percussion orchestra, as he did again in San Francisco (1939-41), Chicago (1941-2) and New York (his home since 1942). Most of his music now consisted of pieces for percussion ensemble, and his 12-note methods gave way to constructive principles based on rhythmic proportions. The *First Construction (in Metal)* for 6 players (1939), for example, has a rhythmic structure of $4 + 3 + 2 + 3 + 4$ units, with the whole form thus marked out in units of 16 bars, and each 16-bar section similarly divided. Pulsation, heterophony and percussive scoring all make for a suggestion of gamelan music, though the influence may have come too from ANTHEIL.

In their materials the percussion pieces already show Cage's willingness to accept the unorthodox: there are tin cans besides the more usual instruments; there are also electrical devices used for the first time in composed works (frequency recordings on variable-speed turntables in *Imaginary Landscape no. 1* of 1939; these together with oscilla-

tors, a buzzer and an amplified coil of wire in no. 3 of the series). Another innovation was the PREPARED PIANO, which was effectively a percussion orchestra for limited spaces. In the 1940s this was Cage's chief resource, used in dance scores (he has worked often with ballet companies, especially that of Merce Cunningham) and in the major concert works that culminated in the Sonatas and Interludes, influenced by Indian thought. The prepared piano's confinement to a relatively small number of sonorities also had an effect on the austere, mesmeric String Quartet.

His enthusiasm for Asian philosophies led in the late 1940s to a close study of Zen. This in turn led him to the art of non-intention which he practised by tossing coins to make choices about pitches, durations and attacks (*Music of Changes*, 1951), by writing for the unpredictable sounds of radio receivers (*Imaginary Landscape no. 4*, 1951) or by providing just SILENCE (*4' 33"*, 1952). The door was opened to a wide range of chance operations, brought together in the masterpiece of indeterminacy, the Concert for Piano and Orchestra (1957-8).

During the 1960s he was most concerned with live electronics, notably in *Cartridge Music* for amplified small sounds, in the *Variations* sequence (which are exceedingly non-committal, but which have often been used, e.g. by his long-standing associate David Tudor, as cues to electronic performance). He also developed a wish to include as much as possible in MIXED MEDIA pieces, extending to 7 amplified harpsichords, multiple tapes and lighting effects in *HPSCHD*. Subsequent works have drawn on the whole range of his experience, from chance composition in conventional notation (*Etudes australes* for piano, *Chorals* for violin) to graphic notation for orchestra (*Renga*) and the verbal description of experiments with natural materials (*Branches* for amplified plant materials, *Inlets* for water-filled conch shells).

Chromatic pieces: Solo and 6 Short Inventions, 3 or more insts, 1933; Sonata, cl, 1933; Sonata for 2 Voices, 1933; Composition for 3 Voices, 1934

Percussion ensemble: Qt, 1935; Trio, 1936; First Construction (in Metal), 6 players, 1939; Imaginary Landscape no. 1, 4 players, 1939; Living Room Music, 4 player-speakers, 1940; Second Construction, 4 players, 1940; Double Music, with Lou Harrison, 4 players, 1941; Third Construction, 4 players, 1941; Credo in Us, 4 players, 1942; Imaginary Landscape no. 2, 5 players, 1942; Imaginary Landscape no. 3, 6 players, 1942; Amores, 3 players, 1943

Prepared piano: Bacchanale, 1940; And the Earth Shall Bear Again, 1942; In the Name of the Holocaust, 1942; Tossed as it is Untroubled, 1943; Totem Ancestor, 1943; The Perilous Night, 1943-4; A Book of Music, 2 prepared pfs, 1944; Prelude for Meditation, 1944; Root of an Unfocus, 1944; Spontaneous Earth, 1944; The Unavailable Memory of, 1944; A Valentine out of Season, 1944; Three Dances, 2 prepared pfs, 1944-5; Daughters of the Lonesome Isle, 1945; Mysterious Adventure, 1945; Music for Marcel Duchamp, 1947; Sonatas and Interludes, 1946-8

Other works of 1938-48: Metamorphosis, pf, 1938; 5 Songs (Cummings), A, pf, 1938; Music for Wind Instruments, qnt, 1938; Forever and Sunsmell (Cummings), v, 2 perc, 1942; Primitive, strings of pf, 1942; The Wonderful Widow of Eighteen Springs (Joyce), v, closed pf, 1942; Our Spring will Come, pf, 1943; She is Asleep (Qt, 12 tom-toms; Duet, v, pf; A Room, pf/prepared pf), 1943; Experiences no. 1, 2 pf, 1945; Ophelia, pf, 1946; Two Pieces, pf, 1946; Nocturne, vn, pf, 1947; The Seasons, orch/pf, 1947; Dream, pf, 1948; Experiences no. 2 (Cummings), v, 1948; In a Landscape, harp/pf, 1948; Suite for Toy Piano, 1948

Works of 1949-52: Str Qt, 1949-50; 6 Melodies, vn, pf, 1950; A Flower, v, closed pf, 1950; Concerto, prepared pf, chamber orch, 1950-51; 16 Dances, 9 insts, 1951; Imaginary Landscape no.4, 12 radios, 1951; Music of Changes, pf, 1951; Two Pastorales, prepared pf, 1951-2; Waiting, pf, 1952; Imaginary Landscape no.5, any 42 recordings, 1952; Seven Haiku, pf, 1952; Water Music, pianist, 1952; Williams Mix, tape, 1952; For M.C. and D.T., pf, 1952; 4′ 33″, any inst/ensemble, 1952

Later works (selection): Music for piano 1-84, 1952-6; 31′ 57.9864″, pf, 1954; 34′ 46.776″, pf, 1954; 26′1.1499″, str player, 1953-5; 27′ 10.554″, perc, 1956; Winter Music, 1-20 pfs, 1957; Concert for Piano and Orchestra, 1957-8; Variations I, any means, 1958; Fontana Mix, any means, 1958; Aria, v, 1958; Water Walk, solo TV performance, 1959; Theatre Piece, 1960; Cartridge Music, amplified sounds, 1960; Variations II, any means, 1961; Atlas eclipticalis, orch, 1961-2; Variations III, any means, 1962-3; Variations IV, any means, 1963; Variations V, audio-visual performance, 1965; Variations VI, plurality of sound systems, 1966; HPSCHD, 1-7 hpds, 1-51 tapes, other means ad lib, 1967-9; Cheap Imitation, pf, 1969, orch, 1972; Song Books, v, 1970; Etudes australes, pf, 1974-5; Branches, amplified plant materials, 1976; Renga, orch, 1976; Inlets, conches, fire, 1977; Chorals, vn, 1978; Variations VIII, no music, 1978; Hymns and Variations, 12 vv, 1978; 30 Pieces for Five Orchestras, 1981; 30 Movements, str qt, 1983
[Peters]

□ J. Cage, *Silence* (1961), *A Year from Monday* (1967), *M* (1973), *Empty Words* (1980), *For the Birds* (1981); R. Kostelanetz, ed., *John Cage* (1970); P. Griffiths, *Cage* (1981)

Campo, Conrado del (1878-1953) Spanish composer. He studied at the Madrid Conservatory, where he taught from 1915. His works include many tone poems influenced by Spanish folk music and Strauss.

canon Music in which 1 melodic part follows another at a short distance in time. Normally regarded as a test of skill, the art was reintroduced into creative works around the turn of the century by composers who looked to Bach as a model, notably Reger and Busoni. Later Schoenberg and his followers found it a useful technique in the handling of SERIALISM: Webern's serial music is practically all in canon, and Schoenberg was in the habit of writing short canons, serial and tonal, as occasional pieces. Neoclassical tendencies also encouraged the outbreak of canon in the music of Stravinsky, Bartók and Hindemith, while Messiaen would seem to have been influenced by medieval music in his practice of mensural canon (called by him 'rhythmic canon'), which can also be found in Boulez and Davies.

cantata Used as title by Webern, Stravinsky and others. Webern's two cantatas are distantly Bachian, with solo recitatives and arias and choral movements, setting poems of intimate mystical piety by Jone. ★no.1 Hooke, BBC forces/Rankl, London 12 Jul 1946; no.2 Steingruber, Wiener, Belgian radio forces/Häfner, Brussels, 23 Jun 1950. Stravinsky's interleaves stanzas of the 'Lyke-Wake Dirge', set for women's choir and instrumental quintet, with canonic arias and a duet for solo soprano and tenor, these also setting medieval English poems. ★cond Stravinsky, Los Angeles, 11 Nov 1952.

Canticum sacrum ad honorem Sancti Marci nominis (Sacred Song to Honour the Name of St Mark) Work by Stravinsky for tenor and baritone soloists with choir and a stark orchestra omitting violins, cellos, clarinets and horns. It is a short Marcian liturgy of a declamatory power enhanced by proto-serial machinations. ★cond Stravinsky, San Marco, Venice, 13 Sep 1956.

Caplet, André (1878-1925) French composer. He studied at the Paris Conservatoire and became a friend of Debussy, whom he helped on the orchestration of *Le martyre de Saint-Sébastien*. His own works include a cello concerto *Epiphanie* (1923) and *Le miroir de Jésus* for women's voices, harp and strings (also 1923). [Durand]

Capriccio Opera by Strauss and Clemens Krauss: it is the story of a countess's divided love for a poet and a composer, and thereby a parable of the rival arts engaged in opera. *Munich, 28 Oct 1942.

Cardew, Cornelius (1936-81) English composer. Studied at the Royal Academy of Music (later taught there) and with Stockhausen in Cologne, remaining there to assist in the realization of CARRÉ. His first works had been in the line of Stockhausen and Boulez, but then in 1958 he moved towards Cage, Brown and Feldman. He returned to England in 1961 and became the centre of EX-PERIMENTAL MUSIC there: he played improvised music with AMM and wrote 2 enormous works, the 193-page score in GRAPHIC NOTATION *Treatise* and *The Great Learning*. A performance of part of the latter in 1969 led to the formation of the Scratch Orchestra, a group of professional and amateur musicians who gathered to perform libertarian pieces by themselves and others. In 1971 the Scratch Orchestra began to adopt a Maoist stance, and Cardew repudiated Cage, Stockhausen and his own past work, turning to arrangements of Chinese Revolutionary songs and large-scale instrumental works based on protest songs.
Works of 1955-62: 3 pf sonatas, 1955-8; 2 Books of Study for Pianists, 2 pf, 1958; Octet 1959, 8 insts, 1959; Autumn '60, any insts, 1960; February Pieces, pf, 1959-61; Octet '61, any insts, 1961; Movement, orch, 1962
Works of 1963-70: Solo with Accompaniment, 2 performers, 1964; Volo Solo, virtuoso performance, 1964; 2 Buns, orch, 1964-5; Three Winter Potatoes, pf, 1961-5; Treatise, graphic score, 1963-7; The Great Learning, 7 paragraphs for diverse groupings, 1968-70
Works of 1971-81: numerous protest songs and arrs of Chinese material; Piano Album 1973; Piano Album 1974; Thälmann Variations, pf, 1974; Vietnam Sonata, pf, 1976; Boolavogue, 2 pf, 1981; We Sing for the Future, pf, 1981
[Peters, UE, Experimental Musical Catalogue; DG, Cramps]
☐ C. Cardew, *Scratch Music* (1972), *Stockhausen Serves Imperialism* (1974)

Cardillac Opera by Hindemith and Ferdinand Lion, after E. T. A. Hoffmann, set as a sequence of musical numbers in strict form: Cardillac is a jeweller who murders to regain his creations. *Dresden, 9 Nov 1926, rev. Zurich, 20 Jun 1952.

Carpenter, John Alden (1876-1951) American composer. Studied with Paine at Harvard and then joined the family firm. He wrote a charming Ravelian suite *Adventures in a Perambulator* (1914), and then gained renown for his use of jazz in the ballets *Krazy Kat* (1921) and *Skyscrapers* (1923-4). Later works include 2 symphonies and the tone poem *Sea Drift* (1933). [G. Schirmer]

Carré Work by Stockhausen, assisted by Cardew, for 4 spaced groups of instrumentalists and singers, concerned mostly with sounds of long duration. *Hamburg, 28 Oct 1960

Carrillo, Julian (1875-1965) Mexican composer. Studied violin and composition in Mexico City, Ghent and Leipzig. In 1924 he began to work with MICROTONES, for which he used the term 'sonido 13' (i.e. adding to the normal 12). His Concertino for mixed microtonal sextet and orchestra (1927) was commissioned by Stokowski and aroused much interest through performances in several American cities. In the 1930s he toured Mexico with a microtonal ensemble, the Orquesta Sonido 13; he also made plans for pianos in third tones, quarter tones, etc up to sixteenth tones, and these were built and exhibited at the 1958 Brussels Exposition. He continued until his death to write microtonal and semitonal works in various media, though the unusual sounds did not alter the broadly Romantic, diatonic nature of his music.

Carter, Elliott (1908-) American composer. Stravinsky's commendation of his Double Concerto (in *Dialogues and a Diary*, 1968) came as the emblem of a wider appreciation of him as a composer whose inventive energy sounds boldly through music of great textural and metrical complication – indeed as one of the most important composers still working after Stravinsky himself had ceased composing.

This late recognition was true to his late development. Born in New York, he had studied at Harvard and with Boulanger in Paris (1932-5); he had also enjoyed the friendship of Ives from the time he was 16. But he published nothing important before the ballet *Pocahontas* (1936-9), and then spent the next decade removing himself from Stravinsky-style neoclassicism in order to let his contrapuntal lines carry themselves through atonal regions with the robust independence of his First Quartet (1951). Important works along the way included the lithe, clear-toned Piano Sonata, fitting itself to natural resonance, the ballet *The Minotaur*, which was a farewell to Stravinsky (and in particular to the Symphony in Three Movements) and the Cello Sonata, displaying what was to become a typical casting of the instruments as characters in an abstract drama.

This conception, coming perhaps from Ives's Second Quartet, is fully embodied in Carter's First, where the argument of the 4 players continues even across the boundaries of the underlying 4 movements. The urge for constant change is expressed too in METRIC MODULATION. During the next quarter century Carter explored the new style in a sequence of works, all in substantial instrumental forms. The notion of dialogue remained important: the Second Quartet is scored for 4 individuals, the Third for 2 duos, and the conversational element is obvious in the concertos. At the same time, Carter began to establish his instrumental characters by more conscious means than had seemed to be operating in the First Quartet, working with particularly selected harmonic frameworks and in more tightly constructed forms. This is exemplified by the Double Concerto, where the solo piano and harpsichord are given different intervallic and rhythmic units, and differently scored accompaniments. The effect is to remove the last traces of 19th c. rhetoric (still remaining in the orchestral Variations) and let the soloists speak in a new, brilliantly mobile language of their own.

The achievement of the Double Concerto is somewhat opened to doubt by the unusually dark and enclosed Piano Concerto, but the liveliness of Carter's orchestral imagination is unsuppressed again in the Concerto for Orchestra and A Symphony of Three Orchestras (1976-7), the latter composed during a period when he had returned to vocal composition. However, the late vocal works, all accompanied by exuberant instrumental ensembles, show no lessening in his pressure for movement and activity: rather do the words – simultaneously in Greek and English in *Syringa* – encourage a characteristic racing exultation in minutiae.

Ballets: Pocahontas, 1936-9, *Ballet Caravan, New York, 24 May 1939; The Minotaur, 1947, *Ballet Society, New York, 26 March 1947
Orchestral: Sym no.1, 1942; Holiday Overture, 1944; Variations, 1953-5; Double Conc, hpd, pf, 2 chamber orchs, 1961; Pf Conc, 1965; Conc for Orch, 1969; A Sym of 3 Orchs, 1976-7; Penthode, chamber orch, 1985
Choral: Tarantella, TTBB, pf duet, 1936; To Music, SSAATTBB, 1937; Heart not so Heavy as Mine, SATB, 1938; The Defense of Corinth, speaker, men's vv, pf, duet, 1941; The Harmony of Morning, SSAA, chamber orch, 1944; Musicians Wrestle Everywhere, SSATB, str ad lib, 1945; Emblems, TTBB, pf, 1947
Solo vocal: Tell me where is fancy bred, A, gui, 1938; Three Poems by Robert Frost, v, pf, 1942; Warble for Lilac Time, S/T, pf/small orch, 1943; Voyage, Mez/Bar, pf, 1943, with orch, 1975; A Mirror on Which to Dwell, S, small orch, 1975; Syringa, Mez, B, small orch, 1978; In sleep, in thunder, T, small orch, 1981
Chamber: Canonic Suite, 4 alto sax, 1939, rev. 4 cl, 1955-6; Pastoral, va/ca/cl, pf, 1940; Elegy, vc, pf, ?1942, arrs for str qt, str orch and va, pf; Pf Sonata, 1946; Wind Qnt, 1948; Sonata, vc, pf, 1948; 8 Etudes and a Fantasy, fl, ob, cl, bn, 1949; 8 Pieces, timp, 1950, rev, 1966; Str Qt no.1, 1951; Sonata, fl, ob, vc, hpd, 1952; Str Qt no.2, 1959; Str Qt no.3, 1971; Canon for 3, 1971; Duo, vn, pf, 1974; Brass Qnt, 1974; A Fantasy on Purcell's Fantasia on One Note, brass qnt, 1974; Night Fantasies, pf, 1980; Triple Duo, fl, cl, pf, perc, vn, vc, 1982-3; Changes, gui, 1983; Riconoscenza per Goffredo Petrassi, vn, 1984
[AMP; Columbia, Nonesuch]
□ *The Writings of Elliott Carter*, ed. E. and K. Stone (1977); D. Schiff, *The Music of Elliott Carter* (1983)

Casella, Alfredo (1883-1947) Italian composer. Studied at the Paris Conservatoire (1896-1902) and remained in the city, associated with Ravel, Stravinsky and others. In 1915 he returned to Italy, where he began campaigning on behalf of contemporary music, as he continued to do in later years. His early works were wildly eclectic; then in 1913-20 he developed a highly chromatic style influenced by Stravinsky, Bartók and Schoenberg, following this with Stravinskian neoclassicism.
Operas: La donna serpente, 1928-31, *Rome, 1932; 2 others
Orchestral: Notte di maggio, v, orch, 1913; Pagine di guerra, 1918; Pupazzetti, 1920; A notte alta, pf, orch, 1921; Partita, pf, orch, 1924-5; Conc romano, org, brass, timp, str, 1926; Scarlattiana, 1926; Vn Conc, 1928; Triple Conc, 1933; Vc Conc, 1934-5; Conc for Orch, 1937; Conc, pf, perc, str, 1943
Other works: 9 Pf Pieces, 1914; Pupazzetti, pf duet,

1915; Pf Sonatina, 1916; 5 Pieces, str qt, 1920; Conc, str, qt, 1923-4; Serenata, 5 insts, 1927

Casken, John (1949-) English composer. Studied at Birmingham University and with Dobrowolski in Warsaw, where he absorbed Lutoslawski's influence (two mixed quartets *Music for the Crabbing Sun*, 1974, and *Music for a Tawny-Gold Day*, 1975-6). Later works, notably his String Quartet (1980) and *Orion over Farne* for orchestra (1984), show a more strongly personal voice exercised in structures of symphonic range. [Schott; Wergo]

Castelnuovo-Tedesco, Mario (1895-1968) Italian composer. Studied with Pizzetti at the Florence Conservatory and gained Casella's support before his move to the USA in 1939. He is best known for the charm of his guitar music, including 2 concertos, but his output of over 200 works with opus numbers also included operas on *The Merchant of Venice* and *All's Well that Ends Well*, and settings of all Shakespeare's songs.

Castiglioni, Niccolò (1932-) Italian composer. Studied at Milan, Salzburg and Darmstadt, but held himself aloof from the international avant garde of the 1950s and 1960s. Instead he took a then unfashionable interest in late Romanticism (*Après-lude*): the subsequent Boulezian tendency of such works as *A Solemn Music* and *Aleph* was in retrospect only a stage in his development of a music of very precise artifices, typically of elaborate structures working themselves out in the high treble and of wilfully heterogeneous doublings.
Operas: Attraverso lo specchio, radio, 1961; The Lords' Masque (Campion), *Venice, 1980; Oberon (Jonson), *Venice, 1980
Orchestral: Concertino per la notte di Natale, 1952; Impromptus 1-4, 1957-8; Movimento continuato, pf, 11 insts, 1958-9; Sequenze, 1959; Aprèslude, 1959; Eine kleine Weihnachtsmusik, 1959-60; Disegni, 1960; Rondels, 1961; Conc, 1962; Consonante, fl, chamber orch, 1962; Décors, 1962; Synchromie, 1963; Caractères, 1963; Ode, 2 pf, orch, 1966; Masques, 12 insts, 1967; Arabeschi, fl, pf, orch, 1971; Inverno In Ver, 1972; Quodlibet, pf, chamber orch, 1976; Sinfonia con giardino, 1977-8; Doppio coro, 10 wind, 1978; Mottetto, 10 wind, 1978; Couplets, hpd, orch, 1978-9; Morceaux lyriques, ob, orch, 1983
Vocal orchestral: Gyro, chorus, 9 insts, 1963; A Solemn Music (Milton), S, orch, 1963, rev, 1965; Figure, S, orch, 1965; Canzoni, S, chamber orch, 1966; Sym in C, chorus, orch, 1968; Dickinson-

Lieder, S, orch, 1977; Le favole di Esopo, chorus, orch, 1979; Sinfonietta, S, small orch, 1980; Psalm 19, 2 S, chorus, orch, 1980
Other works: Inizio di movimento, pf, 1958; Tropi, 6 insts, 1959; Cangianti, pf, 1959; Gymel, fl, pf, 1960; Divertimento, tape, 1960; Aleph, ob, 1964; Sinfonie guerriere et amorose, org, 1967; 3 Pieces, pf, 1978; Beth, cl, 5 insts, 1979; Daleth, cl, pf, 1979; Cosi parlo Baldassare, S, 1980-81; Musica Vneukokvhaja, pic, 1981; Omaggio a Edvard Grieg, 2 pf, 1982
[Ricordi, Schott, Suvini Zerboni; Fonit Cetra]

Catalogue d'oiseaux (Bird Catalogue) Cycle of 13 piano pieces by Messiaen, each descriptive of a French bird in its habitat. The pieces are *Le chocard des alpes* (Alpine Chough), *Le loriot* (Golden Oriole), *Le merle bleu* (Blue Rock Thrush), *Le traquet stapazin* (Black-Eared Wheatear), *La chouette hulotte* (Tawny Owl), *L'alouette lulu* (Wood Lark), *La rousserolle éffarvatte* (Reed Warbler), *L'alouette calandrelle* (Short-Toed Lark), *La bouscarle* (Cetti's Warbler), *Le merle de roche* (Rock Thrush), *La buse variable* (Buzzard), *Le traquet rieur* (Black Wheatear) and *Le courlis cendré* (Curlew). *Loriod, Paris, 15 Apr 1959.

celesta Small piano-style instrument in which the hammers hit metal plates instead of strings. Common in 20th c. orchestras and ensembles, pinpointed in Bartók's Music for Strings, Percussion and Celesta.

cell Small group of notes, MOTIF. Pijper developed a technique of composing with cells.

cello The repertory has been much expanded through works written for Casals, Piatigorsky, Rostropovich, Tortelier, Palm and others. Important concertos include those by Schoenberg, Prokofiev (two), Shostakovich (two), Britten (Cello Symphony), Honegger, Ligeti and Dutilleux. The recital repertory includes works by Debussy, Webern, Hindemith, Kodály, Poulenc, Shostakovich, Honegger and Zimmermann.

cencerros Cowbells of Cuban origin used in Latin American dance music and Messiaen.

Cerha, Friedrich (1926-) Austrian composer and conductor. Studied in Vienna and in 1958 founded there the ensemble Die REIHE. He completed the third act of LULU; his own works include an operatic setting of Brecht's *Baal* (1974-9). [UE]

Chadwick, George (1854-1931) American composer. Studied in Leipzig and Munich, then returned to Boston in 1880 as composer and teacher. Influenced by French as well as German music, and showing some emergent Americanism, he composed freely in all genres.

chamber music Music for a small group of performers, classically between 3 and 6, performing without a conductor. The 20th c. has seen 2 main developments in this area: a revival of such conventional genres as the string quartet after a period of creative neglect during much of the 19th c. and a breakdown of the barrier between chamber and orchestral music brought about by an increased size and variety of ensemble.

The link between these phenomena is a decline in the intimacy of medium and expression that had been a chief characteristic of chamber music. No longer were quartets written literally for the domestic chamber: most have been composed for the many outstanding professional quartets who have proliferated in the 20th c. as never before. Chamber music has moved therefore into the public arena, and the great growth in music for mixed ensemble has followed naturally from this. The prototypes are Schoenberg's Chamber Symphony no. 1 and his *Pierrot lunaire*, and though it may have been his intention to foster chamber-musical qualities of discourse within more colourful ensembles, the necessity of a conductor strikes against this.

A conductor is similarly required for much of the ensemble music of Stravinsky, Webern and later composers, which therefore is not really chamber music at all. However, some regularly performing ensembles, such as the FIRES OF LONDON or Stockhausen's live electronic group, have recovered the art of musical conversation essential to chamber music.

chamber opera Opera for a small number of singers and instrumentalists: e.g. Blacher's *Romeo und Julia*, Britten's *The Rape of Lucretia* and *The Turn of the Screw*, and Birtwistle's *Punch and Judy*.

Chamber Symphony Coinage of Schoenberg's for 2 works of large symphonic scope but diminished scoring: no. 1 for 15 players (1906) and no. 2 for 17 (begun 1906, finished 1939). The example stimulated Schreker (Chamber Symphony, 1916), Milhaud (6 chamber symphonies, 1917-23), Berg (use of Schoenberg's quindecet in *Wozzeck*; also Chamber Concerto for 15, 1923-5) and others.

chance operations Term used by Cage for compositional methods dependent largely on chance, the aim being to eliminate as far as possible the composer's exercise of choice. Examples of such operations include picking and placing notes according to dice throws (*Music of Changes*) and inscribing notes where there are imperfections in the music paper (Music for Piano). These may be combined with other sorts of INDETERMINACY.

change ringing English art of ringing bells in changing orders according to a cyclical scheme. For instance, a 'plain course' of Grandsire Doubles involves a sequence of 30 different orderings before the original order of the 5 bells is restored. Parallels with serialism (though change ringing goes back to the 17th c.) stimulated English composers in the 1950s and 1960s: notably Davies, whose *Stedman Doubles* and *Stedman Caters* are named after ringing patterns.

Chanler, Theodore (1902-61) American composer. Studied in New York, Cleveland, Oxford and with Boulanger in Paris, then worked as a teacher and critic. His works are modest in number and scale; the songs are best remembered. [AMP, G. Schirmer]

Chant après chant (Song after Song) Work in Barraqué's cycle on Broch's *The Death of Virgil*, scored for soprano, piano and 6 percussionists on a large array of instruments. ★Kal, Krist, Percussions de Strasbourg/Bruck, Strasbourg 23 Jun 1966.

Chávez, Carlos (1899-1978) Mexican composer. Studied with Ponce as a pianist (1910-14) but was mainly self-taught in composition. He first made a mark with 2 ballets for voices and orchestra on Aztec subjects, *El fuego nuevo* (1921) and *Los cuatro soles* (1925). Then came a period in New York (1926-8), where he associated with Copland, Cowell, Varèse and others. On his return to Mexico he became founder-conductor of the Mexico Symphony Orchestra (1928-48), with whom he gave many first performances. In his own music he developed a modern-primitive style influenced by Varèse and sometimes incorporating Indian themes (*Sinfonía india*, 1935-6, the second of his 7 symphonies) or indigenous percussion instruments (*Xochipili* for 4 wind and 6 percussion, 1940). [Mills, G. Schirmer, Boosey]

Cheltenham Festival Started in 1945 as festival of contemporary British music, its commissioning policy giving rise to the pejorative term 'Cheltenham symphony' for a work of modest conservative substance. Since the 1960s has become somewhat less provincial. Composers featured have included Lennox Berkeley, Fricker and Crosse.

Chihara, Paul (1938-) American composer of Japanese extraction. Studied at Cornell and with Schuller at Tanglewood, Boulanger in Paris and Pepping in Berlin; then joined the faculty at UCLA. His music shows an oriental feeling for subtleties of colouring within a static harmony.

Chinese music The use of pentatony and much percussion to suggest a Chinese ambience is a commonplace of the Romantic picturesque, to be found, for example, in *Das Lied von der Erde* and *Turandot*, though it is doubtful whether Mahler or Puccini had any first-hand knowledge of Chinese music. Indeed, the difficulties of western access to China, the paucity of recordings and the extreme irregularity of Chinese musical exports have all limited communication, so that composers in Europe and the USA have been much more influenced by Japanese, Indian and Indonesian music than by Chinese. The exceptions include of course those few composers who have emigrated from China, such as Chou Wen-chung. As for the practice of western composition in China, information is scanty: apart from the *Yellow River Concerto* for piano and orchestra (adapted from a *Yellow River Cantata* by Hsien Hsing-hai, 1905-45), the main works exported from China on record have been operas, ballets and songs of revolutionary intention but often conservative musical content, in a broad diatonic style touched by the old 'Chinese' gestures of a Mahler or Puccini. Nevertheless, Chinese music of the Mao period had an influence on western composers sympathetic to Maoism, such as Cardew and Wolff.

Chou Wen-chung (1923-) American composer. Emigrated from China to the USA in 1946 and studied at the New England Conservatory, Columbia University and privately with Varèse (1949-54). He bacame Varèse's musical executor, and completed the unfinished *Nocturnal* besides editing corrected scores of other works; in 1972 he was appointed professor at Columbia. His own works combine Varèsian and Chinese traits.

Chowning, John (1934-) American composer. Studied at Stanford University and in Paris with Boulanger. In 1975 he became director of the Center for Computer Research in Music and Acoustics at Stanford, where he has worked with fine timbral discriminations obtainable through computer sound synthesis. His works include *Stria* (1977) and *Phoné* (1981).

Christou, Jani (1926-70) Greek composer. Brought up and educated in Alexandria, he studied at Cambridge (England) and settled in Greece in 1960; his early death was in a car crash. Influenced by Jungian psychology, he moved from an eclectic early phase into a frenzied post-serial style (oratorio *Tongues of Fire*, 1964) and then into a prolific final period when most of his works had the title 'anaparastasis' (re-enactment) and were exercises in group therapy for the performers.

chromatic Based on a scale of 12 semitones to the octave; hence used of music which includes notes other than those of the major or minor scale, though normally with the implication that the sensation of a major or minor tonality remains (hence such phrases as 'the work opens in a highly chromatic E minor'). Where this is not the case one may be dealing with ATONALITY, SERIALISM or 12-NOTE COMPOSITION.

church music Genre of uneven history in the 20th c. Often the writing of masses, anthems, hymns and organ music has been the province of specialist composers who have ventured little into other fields or beyond the norms of taste established by the end of the 19th c. On the other hand, many composers of the first rank have contributed nothing (Debussy, Bartók, Berg) or practically nothing to this field. Even composers whose concert music bespeaks a strong Christian faith, such as Messiaen or Webern, have not composed for the liturgy, and at least in Messiaen's case the decision was deliberate, being founded on the view that plainsong is the only proper church music. In its turn, the church has through liturgical reform encouraged the view that church music must be ephemeral. Probably the most important work written for the Christian liturgy this century is Stravinsky's Mass, which however is rarely performed as such owing to its wind decet accompaniment.

Cikker, Ján (1911-) Slovak composer. Studied with Novák at the Prague Conservatory, and then taught in Bratislava. He is one of the most successful opera composers of his time in eastern Europe, working in a fiercely expressive, free 12-note style. His operas include *Resurrection* (1962) and *Coriolanus* (1972).

Cilea, Francesco (1866-1950) Italian composer. Studied at the Naples Conservatory, of which he was later director. He wrote nothing of consequence apart from the grand dramatic opera *Adriana Lecouvreur* (*Milan, 1902).

cimbalom Hungarian instrument of the dulcimer type, a trapezoidal box of strings struck with hand-held hammers. A ubiquitous feature of the café ensemble, it has been used by Hungarian composers (Kodály in *Háry János*, Bartók in his Second Violin Rhapsody) and sometimes others (Stravinsky in *Rag-Time* and *Renard*, Boulez in *Eclat*, Davies in *Image, Reflection, Shadow*).

Cinderella Ballet by Prokofiev, choreography originally by Rotislav Zakharov, though Ashton's version is best known in the west. *Moscow, Bolshoy, 21 Nov 1945

cipher The translation of words into music, usually on the basis of pitch names, has often been associated in the 20th c. with homages addressed by one composer to another e.g. the BACH motif in Schoenberg and Webern, or with authorial signatures, e.g. Shostakovich's use of his German-transliterated initials DSCH in his Tenth Symphony and other works, the second letter being rendered as E♭ (German 'Es'). Other instances of ciphering using this system of 9 letters (A-H, where B = B♭ and H = B♮, plus S) include Berg's Chamber Concerto, where he encodes the names SCHoEnBERg, wEBErn and BErg, and his Lyric Suite, where he introduces his initials along with those of his lover Hanna Fuchs-Robettin. Musgrave's Third Chamber Concerto uses Berg's equivalences for the 3 composers' names, and Bussotti appeals to a different intellectual patron in the D-E-E♭-A-D-E cipher of his *La passion selon Sade*. The addition of pitch names from French usage can extend the alphabet, as in Boulez's *Messagesquisse* on the name of Sacher (E♭-A-C-B-E-D where D corresponds to Ré).

More comprehensive ciphers become possible if pitch equivalents are found for all the letters, as they may be by cycling the usual 7 or 8 notes through the alphabet (i.e. the pitches A-G represent A-G, H-N, etc, or else A-H represent A-H, I-P, etc). These systems were used by various Parisian composers in commemorations of Haydn's death centenary (Debussy, Ravel, Dukas, Hahn, d'Indy), Fauré's death and Roussel's death. Honegger's Roussel tribute is based on an alphabet of 26 stipulated pitches (not pitch classes), and Messiaen used a rather similar alphabet, though defining durations as well, in order to inscribe lines from Aquinas across his *Méditations sur le mystère de la Sainte Trinité* and *Des canyons aux étoiles. . .*

Circles Work by Berio for female singer, harpist and two percussionists, on poems by Cummings. The singer moves to different positions between movements to indicate and assure a greater or lesser identification with the instrumentalists, and hence a greater or lesser identification of verbal with musical sound. A circling on the platform thus coincides with a circling from comprehensible language to disjointed vocal sound and back again.

clarinet The standard clarinet is in B♭ ; the clarinet in A is also common in 20th c. music, as is the high clarinet in E♭ (a favourite of Mahler's) and the bass clarinet in B♭ or more rarely A. Less common members of the family include the high clarinet in D (frequent in Strauss), the clarinet in C (also to be found in Strauss), the alto clarinet (in the original version of Stravinsky's Symphonies of Wind Instruments and his *Threni*), the BASSET HORN and the contrabass clarinet (an octave below the bass clarinet, used e.g. in Stravinsky's *The Flood*). Birtwistle has used even rarer instruments, including the Mozartian basset clarinet, the clarinet in A♭ and an 18th c. B♭ clarinet of high pitch.

Important concertos include those of Nielsen, Stravinsky (*Ebony Concerto*), Copland, Hindemith, Martino (Triple Concerto with bass and contrabass clarinets) and Birtwistle (*Melencolia I*); the chamber repertory includes 3 notable works with violin and piano (Stravinsky's *Soldier's Tale* suite, Berg's Adagio adapted from his Chamber Concerto and Bartók's *Contrasts*) as well as much music with piano (by Berg, Poulenc, Davies, etc), clarinet quintets (by Bliss, Birtwistle, etc) and unaccompanied solos (Stravinsky's Three Pieces, Martino's *B, a, b, b, it, t*, Goehr's *Paraphrase*, Boulez's *Domaines*). The clarinet has proved itself specially adept at BARTOLOZZI sounds and other new effects.

Clementi, Aldo (1925-) Italian composer. Studied with the Schoenberg pupil Sangiorgi, with Petrassi and at Darmstadt. In a sequence of three *Informels* he began to work with tangled textures of extreme density and essential changelessness, often caught up on repetitions and quotations within particular lines, though the general flow is continuous. His view is that music's only subject is its own ending, achieved in his own work by an overload that negates the meaning of any detail.

Stage: Collage, ★Rome, 1961; Blitz, 1973, Collage 4, 1979; ES, ★Venice, 1981

Orchestral: Informel no. 1, 12 perc and kbd, 1961; Informel no. 2, 15 insts, 1962; Informel no. 3, 1961-3; Variante A, chorus, orch, 1964; Variante B, 1964; Reticolo: 11, 11 insts, 1966; Conc, 2 pf, 40 wind, 1967; Conc, pf, 7 insts, 1970; Reticolo: 12, 12 str, 1970; Conc, pf, 24 insts, 1975; Conc, db, insts, carillons, 1976; Conc, vn, 40 insts, carillons, 1977; Capriccio, va, 24 insts, 1979-80

Vocal, chamber, keyboard and tape works

[Suvini Zerboni; Fonit Cetra]

cluster Band of several adjacent notes played simultaneously. Clusters can easily be played on the piano by depressing consecutive keys all at once with the hand or forearm or some other part of the body, choosing white notes, black notes or the lot: Cowell seems to have been the first to have written for the technique in his *The Tides of Manaunaun* (?1912). Narrow clusters are used in Bartók's Piano Sonata, broader ones in Stockhausen's *Klavierstück X* and Ligeti's *Volumina* for organ. Stockhausen and Ligeti also pioneered orchestral clusters in the 1950s.

Cocteau, Jean (1889-1963) French poet. Bowled over by the Ballets Russes, he tried unsuccessfully to collaborate with Stravinsky (on *David*, 1914), then turned his attention to Satie (scenario for *Parade*, 1916-17) and the group of young composers he encouraged to be Les Six: his manifesto *The Cock and the Harlequin* (1918) asked for music to be simple, clear, up-to-date and French. Later he worked successfully with Stravinsky (*Oedipus rex*, 1926-27), Honegger (*Antigone*, 1922-7), Milhaud and Auric. Poems by him were set by Satie, Les Six and others in the 1920s.

☐ I. Stravinsky, *Selected Correspondence*, vol. 1 1982)

collage Term (Fr. 'necklace') used in the visual arts to denote an assembly of various heterogeneous materials used to make a picture, as in Picasso's works with snippets of newspapers. In music the term is applied to similar constructions of the unexpected and inharmonious, the elements usually referring to other music. Ives's orchestral works, for instance, often incorporate collages of marches, dances, etc, but these remained isolated examples until after the second world war, when magnetic tape made collage as easy to achieve in music as it had been in visual media. Varèse's POÈME ÉLECTRONIQUE is the classic of the category; Stockhausen has insisted that works of his like TELEMUSIK and HYMNEN are not collages because the components are subject to intermodulation. They are, though, quite as heterogeneous as such contemporary works for live performance as Berio's SINFONIA and Davies's EIGHT SONGS FOR A MAD KING. The word has been used in titles by Gerhard (Symphony no. 3 'Collages' for tape and orchestra) and Clementi (*Collage* series).

colour 1. Synonym for sound quality, or timbre. 2. Phenomenon of importance to some composers as a creative resource (Skryabin, Schoenberg) or stimulus (Messiaen). The notion of a correspondence between colour and sound was widely entertained in the 19th c., by writers as diverse as E. T. A. Hoffmann and Rimbaud; some 'colour organs' were even built, for the performance of light with or without music. However, the only important composer to write for such an instrument was Skryabin, in his *Prometheus* (1908-10), though the 'light keyboard' part here was not realized until after his death. His ideas were taken up by some of his followers, notably Vishnegradsky. Schoenberg's use of detailed colour lighting in *Die glückliche Hand* (1910-13) probably owes more to Strindberg than to Russian parallels. Later composers interested in a marriage of colour and music found readier means in film.

Messiaen's interest has been less in colour-music performance (except in his opera) than in composing music which corresponds intuitively with his imaginings of celestial colours (*Couleurs de la cité céleste*), light on desert rock (*Des canyons aux étoiles...*), Japanese scenes (*Sept haïkai*) or the plumage of birds (*Catalogue d'oiseaux*). In all these works the intended colour effects are notated: occasionally the correspondence is on the level of tonality, as it was for Skryabin, though the equivalences differ (bright blue is A major for Messiaen, F♯ for Skryabin); but Messiaen has insisted that the colouring is a matter also of mode, register and instrumentation. His statements, though not quite unequivocal on this point, would seem to suggest that he regards the colour as a personal sensation, not necessarily to be shared by his listeners unless they train their imaginations.

Working in the reverse direction, music has been a stimulus to some painters, especially composer-painters like Luigi Russolo, Mikolajus Čiurlionis and Edward Cowie.

Columbia–Princeton Electronic Music Center Studios at Columbia University operating since 1960, distinguished by the presence of the unique RCA Sound Synthesizer and a personnel including Babbitt, Luening and Ussachevsky. Selection of output on CRI 268.

combinatoriality Property of a SET that all the elements of it are to be found in a combination of analogous segments from different set forms. For example, the theme of Schoenberg's orchestral Variations opens with 12-note sets exhibiting this property, a prime form (S_1) and a retrograde inversion (S_2):

S_1 Bb–E–F#–Eb–F–A   D–C#–G–G#–B–C
S_2 F–F#–A–Bb–E–Eb   Ab–C–D–B–C#–G

The first hexachord of S_1 includes the same pitch classes as that of S_2 (but in a different order), and the same goes for the second hexachords. Hence the second hexachord of S_1 and the first hexachord of S_2 (i.e. notes 7–18 of the theme) form a 12-note aggregate, sometimes known as a secondary set.

This sort of combinatoriality is inversional hexachordal combinatoriality, and was the only kind exploited by Schoenberg (in many works). But sets may also be combinatorial with retrograde forms (they are then 'all-combinatorial', since inversional combinatoriality necessarily follows as well), and the property may also be displayed by tetrachords of 3 set forms, trichords of 4 or dyads of 6. The resulting invitations to set linkage in 12-NOTE COMPOSITION have been most welcomed by Babbitt.

Composers Quartet American ensemble founded in 1965 and specializing in 20th c. American music. They have recorded quartets by Babbitt, Perle and others.

composition The art of musical composition in the 20th c. has been so much diversified by new assumptions and methods (see AESTHETICS, ALEATORY, ATONALITY, COMPUTERS, ELECTRONIC MUSIC, MODE, POLITICS, SERIALISM, SOCIETY, 12-NOTE COMPOSITION, etc) that no brief statement of composition's meaning or purpose is at all possible. The only generalization that can be made with some certainty is that in the 20th c. composition has been more widely and abundantly essayed than ever before, which may account for, or perhaps be accounted for by, the diversity of means and techniques at large. Despite this, the word has pleased Babbitt with its connotations of 'abstractness and "formalism"': hence his use of it to name several works.

computers Digital equipment can be useful to composers in 3 main ways: in the calculation of details to be included in a score, in the storage of information and in the production of sound. The first application arrived earliest, when in the mid-1950s Hiller and Isaacson produced an *Illiac Suite* for string quartet composed by a computer in accordance, of course, with programmed rules, and Xenakis used a computer to save the immense labour of STOCHASTIC composition.

Much more subtle and far-reaching have been the uses of computers in sound generation, pioneered by Mathews in the late 1950s. Coupled to a SYNTHESIZER, a computer is notionally capable of specifying with exactitude all qualities of a sound, and capable therefore of providing composers with complete control of their material. But this is not so straightforward. Because sounds change rapidly in time, a considerable amount of information is needed to program even the simplest sound. This effectively limits computer sound synthesis to the production of music on tape, though Ussachevsky used computers in LIVE ELECTRONIC MUSIC in 1971. The other result of this thirst for information is that sounds tend to be lifeless if the information for change is lacking. It was perhaps partly to obviate this that many composers turned to the use of recorded sounds, which a computer might then be instructed to analyse and re-synthesize with some difference (at another pitch level, for instance); also, programs began to be introduced not only for sound generation but for creating logical chains of sounds. Important work during this early period, following on from Mathews, was done at Columbia and Princeton Universities by Randall, Dodge, Winham and others, and at Stanford by Chowning, Risset and others.

In the mid-1970s the opening of the INSTITUT DE RECHERCHE ET DE COORDINATION ACOUSTIQUE/MUSIQUE brought sophisticated computer music to Europe, where work has been done on increasingly subtle sound generation and on the use of digital technology to effect real-time transformations on sounds: changing the timbre, adding programmed embellishment (for instance, a chain of sounds sparked off by the input), etc. The subsequent spread of the technology may make composition with or by computers an amateur pursuit as common as playing the piano.

Recordings: Decca DL 9103 (pioneering studies of 1963), Nonesuch H 71245 (Randall, Dodge, Vercoe, 1970), CRI 348 (Dodge, 1976), IRCAM 0001 (anthology, 1983)

☐ H. von Foerster and J.W. Beauchamp, ed., *Music by Computers* (1969); H.B. Lincoln, ed., *The Computer and Music* (1970)

concert Some dissatisfaction with 19th c. patterns of concert-giving established itself early in the century, precisely when concert audiences began to express dissatisfaction with 20th c. patterns of composition. One answer seemed to be the founding of special concert series devoted to new music, such as in New York the INTERNATIONAL COMPOSERS' GUILD, the LEAGUE OF COMPOSERS and the Copland–Sessions Concerts, in Vienna the SOCIETY FOR PRIVATE MUSICAL PERFORMANCES, and in Paris a variety of organizations. All these had their heyday in the 1920s, which also saw the founding of the INTERNATIONAL SOCIETY FOR CONTEMPORARY MUSIC and the first regular FESTIVAL for contemporary music at Donaueschingen. However, the same spirit has animated such later ventures as the DOMAINE MUSICAL and the LONDON SINFONIETTA. The obvious drawback is that specialization may foster only a specialized audience, but on the other hand there are problems, too, in the programming of a modern work between a Beethoven concerto and a Tchaikovsky symphony.

It may be that the very concept of concert needs to be more radically challenged, as it has been in many performances by Cage, working as happily in art galleries as concert halls, or by Stockhausen, whose venues have ranged from a cave in the Lebanon to a park in West Berlin and a specially constructed auditorium in Osaka. It may be, too, that the ubiquity of sound reproduction has made concerts distinctly secondary as avenues for the communication of new music.

concert band American ensemble of wind and percussion, for which Schoenberg wrote his Theme and Variations (1943), Hindemith his Symphony in B♭ (1951) and Stockhausen his *Luzifers Tanz* (1983)

concerto As common a form in the 20th c. as before, but with some interesting developments. Most simply, concertos have been written for a greater range of instruments (e.g. Milhaud's for percussion, Jolivet's for ondes martenot, Cage's for prepared piano). On a structural level, it has become common for cadenzas to be brought into the musical continuity by being accompanied, instead of being left outside the main body of the work as moments of solo display (see the violin concertos of Elgar, Berg and Schoenberg). Old forms rediscovered in the 20th c. include the concerto grosso (by Bloch, Martinů, Vaughan Williams), while the main new genre is the Concerto for Orchestra, seemingly invented by Hindemith (1925) and imitated as a vehicle for virtuoso orchestral playing and orchestration by Bartók, Petrassi, Lutosławki, Gerhard, Tippett and others.

'Concord' Sonata Ives's Second Piano Sonata, named after the town in Massachusetts which was the home of New England literary life in the mid-19th c. The movements honour the writers of that milieu: Emerson, Hawthorne, the Alcotts, Thoreau. Ives published the work himself in 1919-20 along with his *Essays before a Sonata*.

Cone, Edward (1917-) American composer and theorist. Studied with Sessions at Princeton, where he began teaching in 1947. A literate, provocative and acute observer of contemporary analysis, he has written on Stravinsky, Webern and Schoenberg among others. His own works are mostly chamber music (String Sextet, 1966) and orchestral.

Constant, Marius (1925-) Romanian–French composer and conductor. Studied in Bucharest and with Messiaen and Boulanger in Paris, where he has remained. His works include ballet scores and pieces for large orchestra (*Turner*, 1961). As a conductor he has worked mostly with his own Ars Nova ensemble, founded in 1963 and specializing in modern music.

constructivism Style of painting in simple geometrical shapes, associated with artists in Russia (e.g. Malevich) and later the Netherlands (e.g. Mondrian). The term has been used in connection with music displaying a high degree of evident STRUCTURE, such as Webern's.

Contemporary Chamber Ensemble New York orchestra for modern music founded by Arthur Weisberg in 1960 and conducted by him. They have recorded works by Schoenberg, Varèse, Babbitt, etc.

Converse, Frederick (1871-1940) American composer. Studied with Paine at Harvard and Rheinberger in Munich, then worked as teacher (at the New England Conservatory, 1900-02 and 1920-38) and opera administrator. His *The Pipe of Desire* (★Boston, 1906) was the first American opera staged at the Metropolitan, in 1910; other works include 5 symphonies and many tone poems.

Conyngham, Barry (1944-) Australian composer. Early experience as composer and pianist was in jazz; then in his early 20s he began studies with Raymond Hanson and Sculthorpe, followed in 1970 by lessons with Takemitsu in Japan. This brought an oriental fragility and delicacy into his music (*Ice Carving* for violin and 4 string groups, 1970), but he is also capable of vivid drama, particularly in his theatre works (*Edward John Eyre*, 1971; *Ned Mark II*, 1974-6). [UE]

Copland, Aaron (1900-) American composer. Throughout the half century of his composing life he retained, despite several Stravinskian shifts of manner, a strong and clear individuality of sound as well as a consistent affirmation of Americanness. On the level of sound, his transparency depends on lean, sparingly doubled instrumentation and an approximation of harmony to overtone structure (as in his characteristic open 5ths). His music usually has too a singleness of movement, whether in melody with accompaniment or homophony. Such features of openness and space have often been taken as relating to the American landscape, and though Copland has lived most of his life in New York it is to the west that he appealed in his ballet scores, imitated in countless scores for cowboy movies. However, this is only one aspect of his Americanism: he has also used jazz and Latin American music, and occasionally made big rhetorical statements to his countrymen and women that his unrivalled stature as an American composer have justified. This has been enhanced by his vigorous activities as a champion of other composers, teacher, broadcaster and conductor.

Born in Brooklyn, into the first generation of Americans in a prosperous Jewish family, he studied in New York with Goldmark (1917-21) and in Paris with Boulanger (1921-4), as one of her first American pupils. She encouraged his Stravinskian orientation (he was already an admirer of Debussy), which provided a very apt technical foundation when, back in New York in 1925, he determined to make his music more American by incorporating elements of jazz. This brief episode produced the *Music for the Theatre* and the Piano Concerto, but in 1930 he turned aside from jazz to explore a personal world of hard-edged sonorities and compact form in the Piano Variations, whose growth out of a 7-note theme suggests parallels with the serial style of his 50s and 60s.

In the interim, though, he moved away from the esoteric towards the emphatically popular, even if works like *El salón Mexico* and the two cowboy ballets are composed quite as individually and perspicaciously as more serious pieces. There was therefore no barrier to merging the popular and the personal in APPALACHIAN SPRING, the Third Symphony and the Dickinson songs. At the start of the 1950s, however, the gap began to widen. The Piano Quartet showed a return towards serialism, continued in the Piano Fantasy and 2 brief but bold orchestral scores of the 1960s, *Connotations* and *Inscape*. But the arrangements of Old American Songs were done with the simplest harmonies, and such later works as the *Dance Panels*, the Nonet for strings and the Duo for flute and piano show the old ability to make diatonic tonality anew.

Opera: The Tender Land, 1952-4, ★New York, 1954, rev. 1954, 1955

Ballets: Billy the Kid, 1938; Rodeo, 1942; APPALACHIAN SPRING, 1943-4; Dance Panels, 1959, rev. 1962.

Symphonies: Sym, org, orch, 1924, rev. without org as Sym no.1, 1928; Dance Sym, 1930; Short Sym (Sym no.2) 1932-3, Sym no.3, 1944-6

Other orchestral: Cortège macabre, 1922-3; Music for the Theatre, 1925; Pf Conc, 1926; Sym Ode, 1927-9; Statements, 1932-5; El salón Mexico, 1933-6; Music for Radio, 1937; An Outdoor Overture, 1938; Quiet City, 1939; John Henry, 1940 rev. 1952; Lincoln Portrait, speaker, orch, 1942; Fanfare for the Common Man, 1942; Letter from Home, 1944, rev. 1962; Danzón cubano, 1944; Cl Conc, 1947-8; Preamble for a Solemn Occasion, speaker, orch, 1949; Orch Variations (arr. of Pf Variations), 1957; Two Mexican Pieces, 1959; Connotations, 1962; Music for a Great City, 1964; Emblems, 1964; Inscape, 1967; Three Latin American Sketches, 1972

Chamber: Two Pieces, str qt, 1923; Two Pieces, vn, pf, 1926; Vitebsk, pf trio, 1928; Sextet (arr. of Short Sym), cl, pf, str qt, 1937; Sonata, vn, pf, 1942-3; Pf Qt, 1950; Nonet, str, 1960; Duo, fl, pf, 1971; Two Threnodies, fl, str trio, 1971-3

Piano: Pf Variations, 1930; Sonata, 1939-41; Four Pf Blues, 1926-48; Pf Fantasy, 1952-7; Night Thoughts, 1972; several early pieces

Two pianos: Danzón cubano, 1942; Danza de Jalisco, 1963
Songs: As it fell upon a day, S, fl, cl, 1923; Poet's Song, 1927; Vocalise, 1928; Twelve Poems of Emily Dickinson, 1949-50; Old American Songs, 1950-52; Dirge in Woods, 1954
Few choral and org pieces
[Boosey; Columbia]
□ A. Copland, *Copland on Music* (1960), *Copland*, vol. 1 (1984); A. Berger, *Aaron Copland* (1953)

Coro (Chorus) Work by Berio for a chorus of 40 singers, each placed next to an instrumentalist of corresponding range. There are massive tuttis on words by Neruda, interspersed with memories of folksong and folk singing for smaller groupings.
*Cologne, 1977

Cowell, Henry (1897-1965) American composer, pioneer in his youth of EXPERIMENTAL MUSIC and later the composer of much orchestral music influenced by diverse American and exotic traditions. Born and largely raised in California, he began as a boy to try new ways of playing the piano: he had already introduced clusters, in *The Tides of Manaunaun*, by the time he made his début as a composer–pianist in San Francisco on 5 March 1914, just 6 days before his seventeenth birthday. He then studied with Seeger at Berkeley (1914-16) and briefly in New York (1916), but mostly explored alone, gathering material for his book *New Musical Resources* (New York, 1930, r1969), which ranges over clusters, atonality, polytonality and rhythmic construction.

During the 1920s and early 1930s he appeared throughout the USA and Europe playing his own music, which by now included experiments with the STRING PIANO: brushing unstopped strings by hand (*Aeolian Harp, The Banshee*) and stopping strings with the fingers (*Sinister Resonance*). He also worked with extremely complex rhythms, for which in 1931 he engaged Thérémin's assistance in the construction of a special performing machine, the rhythmicon (*Rhythmicana*, a concerto for the new instrument, remained unrealized until 1971). The *Quartet Romantic* and the *Quartet Euphometric* work with durational ratios derived from frequency ratios among overtones; the *Mosaic Quartet* was an early instance of what he called 'elastic form', providing fragments for the performers to assemble (*see* ALEATORY and MOBILE FORM).

While producing a vast and Protean output, Cowell was also active as teacher (Cage and Gershwin were pupils) and as a promoter of new American music through his New Music Edition, which began publishing in 1927.

Piano: The Tides of Manaunaun, ?1912; Dynamic Motion, 1914; What's This, 1914; Advertisement, 1914; Anger Dance, 1914; Antimony, 1914; 7-Ings, 1916; Episode, 1916; Amiable Conversation, 1917; Fabric, ?1917; Exultation, 1919; Voice of Lir, 1919; Vestiges, 1920; Snows of Fujiyama, 1922; The Hero Sun, 1922; Aeolian Harp, 1923; Harp of Life, 1924; Pièce pour piano avec cordes, 1924; The Trumpet of Angus Og, 1924; Lilt of the Reel, 1924; The Banshee, 1925; Tiger, ?1928; Fairy Answer, 1929; Maestoso, 1929; Sinister Resonance, ?1930; Two Woofs, 1930; Irishman Dances, 1934; Harper Minstrel Sings, 1934; Rhythmicana, 1938; later pieces
Chamber: Qt Romantic, 2 fl, vn, va, 1915-17; Qt Euphometric, str qt, 1916-19; Mosaic Qt, str qt, 1935; United Qt, str qt, 1936; many other pieces
21 syms, much other orch music, choral pieces, songs
□ B. Saylor, *The Writings of Henry Cowell* (1977)

Cowie, Edward (1943-) English composer. Studied with Fricker at Morley College, with Goehr and in Poland, then worked at the universities of Leeds (1971-3), Lancaster (1973-83) and Wollongong, New South Wales (1983-). In his music, as in his paintings, he has attempted to convey a tangle of impressions from nature, as observed in wilder English landscapes. His works include the opera *Commedia* (1976-8) and several large orchestral scores. [Schott; Hyperion]

Craft, Robert (1923-) American writer and conductor. Studied at the Juilliard School and began career as a conductor before in 1948 he became Stravinsky's close associate. The relationship produced numerous recordings, several conversation books, and posthumous memoirs and works of documentation.

Crawford Seeger, Ruth (1901-53) American composer. Studied in Jacksonville, in Chicago and in New York with Charles Seeger, whom she married in 1931, after a year in Berlin and Paris. Her few works show a delight in abstract pattern-making, applying serial and numerical systems to duration as well as pitch (String Quartet). In later years she joined her husband in working on American folk music.
9 Preludes, pf, 1924-8; Etude in Mixed Accents, pf, 1930; 4 Diaphonic Suites, 2 insts, 1930; Str Qt, 1931; 3 Songs, A, ob, perc, pf, orch ostinato ad lib,

1930-32; 2 Ricercari, v, pf, 1932 [New Music; Nonesuch, CRI]

Création du monde, La (The Creation of the World) Ballet by Milhaud, scenario by Cendrars, choreography by Jean Börlin, designs by Léger: it was an early example of jazz influence in European music, being an imagined African creation myth. *Ballets Suédois, Paris, 25 Oct 1923.

Creston, Paul (1906-) American composer. Born (as Giuseppe Guttoveggio) into a poor Italian family, he was self-taught in composition and began to make a mark only in his late 20s. His music, ebullient and jazzy, includes 5 symphonies, much else for orchestra, settings of the Catholic mass and chamber pieces. [G. Schirmer]

Crosse, Gordon (1937-) English composer. Studied at Oxford with Wellesz and in Rome with Petrassi. His early works were close to Davies in their Renaissance and serial interests, but since his powerful setting of Yeats's duodrama *Purgatory* (1966) his music has been broader and much more eclectic in style, with Britten's influence rivalling several others. He has worked in all genres, including music for children, and taught at the universities of Birmingham and Essex. [OUP]

crotales Small cymbals of definite pitch, also called 'antique cymbals', used by Debussy, Ravel, Messiaen, etc.

Crumb, George (1929-) American composer. Studied with Finney at the University of Michigan, and then taught at the universities of Colorado (1959-65) and Pennsylvania. His *Ancient Voices of Children* for soprano, treble and ensemble (1970) brought him wide attention, being a Lorca setting of fierce drama achieved through a bold handling of sound effect and quotation. Other works similarly depend on the strangeness of particular sonorities, and include chamber and orchestral pieces besides more Lorca settings. [Peters; Nonesuch, CRI]

cryptogram *See* CIPHER.

Cunningham, Merce (1919-) American choreographer and dancer. Was a member of the Graham company, with whom he danced in the first *Appalachian Spring*. In the late 1940s he began association with CAGE, and in 1952 he started his own company, taking an open, experimental attitude to dance and releasing the interdependence of music and movement. He has continued to work with Cage, and also with Feldman, Mumma and others, as well as with such painters as Rauschenberg and Johns.

Cunning Little Vixen, The (Příhody Lišky Bystroušky) Opera by Janáček after novel by Rudolf Těsnohlídek, being a sharp, unsentimental fable of mostly animal characters. *Brno, 6 Nov 1924.

D

dada The iconoclastic movement that flourished briefly around 1917-20 was almost exclusively a phenomenon of the literary and visual arts, though it did spill over towards the musical, or antimusical, in the work of Jef GOLISHEV and Kurt Schwitters, whose *Sonata in Urlauten* (Sonata in Primitive Sounds) is a phonetic text for vocal performance. Very possibly this had an influence on the musical use of speech by Vogel and other composers in the 1920s, though Schwitters' other innovation of MIXED MEDIA composition was not followed up until the 1950s. Since the explosion of EXPERIMENTAL MUSIC at that time, the term 'dada' has sometimes been applied to the work of Cage in particular, and indeed there is a tangible link in the person of Marcel Duchamp, the dadaist who became one of Cage's adoptive spriritual godfathers. The word has also been used in connection with Satie's music of the dada epoch (though Satie would seem to have arrived at his absurdities quite independently) and with such later manifestations as the FLUXUS movements.

Dahl, Ingolf (1912-70) German–American composer. Studied in Cologne, Zurich and California, where he settled in 1938, and where he taught at USC (1945-70). He was close to Stravinsky, and this is reflected in his music. His European works had been dense and fraught in the manner of German Expressionism, but in the USA his music became clearer and more diatonic, until in his Piano Quartet (1957) he began to use serial methods. Most of his small output is instrumental. [A. Broude, Boosey, Presser, Southern]

Dallapiccola, Luigi (1904-75) Italian composer, the most distinguished of his generation. He was one of the first composers outside German-speaking Europe to take a creative interest in Schoenbergian serialism, which he did from the mid-1930s. His example was important to younger Italian composers, many of whom were his pupils at the Florence Conservatory (where he taught 1930–67). But still more crucially, his understanding of serialism within the context of an Italianate voice-centred lyricism produced an individual body of music, marked also by his highly civilized mind and his taste for economy.

Born in Istria, then part of the Habsburg Empire, he was confined with his family in Graz during the last 18 months of the first world war. Back in Italy, he studied in Florence and was powerfully impressed by *Pelléas* and *Pierrot lunaire*, though everything he wrote in the 1920s was later withdrawn. His official career as a composer began in the mid-1930s, with the Michelangelo choruses, which look partly to Busoni, partly to Berg and Webern. Gradually the latter influences came to predominate, and with them the use of 12-note methods: this is apparent in the *Tre laudi* and the 1-act opera *Volo di notte* (Night Flight). However, it was in the music associated with another 1-act opera, *Il prigioniero* (The Prisoner, 1944–8), that he took a decisive step forward. His loathing of fascism was expressed first in a choral work, the *Canti di prigionia* for chorus and a percussive ensemble recalling *Les Noces*, though the harmonic style is much closer to Berg than Stravinsky. *Il prigioniero* continues this style (the *Liriche greche* meanwhile had seen his first ventures into strict 12-note serialism) and makes it more personal, just as the theme of imprisonment is treated in a more philosophical, enquiring spirit. Immediately after *Il prigioniero* his music became sparer in texture and more refined in its gestures, as if Berg's influence had been replaced by Webern's: indeed, his admiration for the latter is evident in such works as the *Goethe Lieder* for mezzo and 3 clarinets (1953), though his preference was for all-interval series. Most of his works were now in this form of vocal chamber music, and yet there were also larger compositions, most notably the full-length opera *Ulisse*. Quite unlike the other operas, this is more a lyrical than a dramatic work, using the exquisiteness and subtlety of Dallapiccola's late style in following the hero's restless exploration of inner dilemmas.

Operas: Volo di notte, 1937–9, ★Florence, 1940; Il prigioniero, 1944–8, ★RAI, 1949; Job, 1950, ★Rome, 1950; Ulisse, 1960–68, ★Berlin, 1968
Ballet: Marsia, 1942–3, ★Venice, 1948
Orchestral: Piccolo conc per Muriel Couvreux, pf,

chamber orch, 1939–41; Due pezzi, 1947; Tartiniana, vn, orch, 1951; Variazioni, 1954; Piccola musica notturna, 1954; Tartiniana seconda, vn, orch, 1955–6; Dialoghi, vc, orch, 1959–60; 3 Questions with 2 Answers, 1962
Choral: 6 cori di Michelangelo, nos 1–2, chorus, 1933, nos 3–4, boys'/womens' vv, 17 insts, 1934–5, nos 5–6, chorus, orch, 1935–6; Canti di prigionia, chorus, 2 pf, 2 harp, perc, 1938–41; Canti di liberazione, chorus, orch, 1951–5; Requiescant, chorus, orch, 1957–8; Tempus destruendi–Tempus aedificandi, chorus, 1970–71
Solo vocal: 3 laudi, S/T, 13 insts, 1936–7; Liriche greche, no. 1 Cinque frammenti di Saffo, v, 15 insts, 1942, no. 2 6 carmina Alcaei, v, 11 insts, 1943, no. 3 2 liriche di Anacreonte, v, 4 insts, 1944–5; Rencesvals, Mez/Bar, pf, 1946; 4 liriche di Machado, S, pf, 1948, arr. S, chamber orch, 1964; 3 poemi, S, 14 insts, 1949; Goethe Lieder, Mez, 3 cl, 1953; An Mathilde, S, orch, 1955; 5 canti, Bar, 8 insts, 1956; Conc per la notte di Natale dell'anno 1956, S, chamber orch, 1957, rev. 1958; Preghiere, Bar, chamber orch, 1962; Parole di San Paolo, Mez/boy, 11 insts, 1964; Sicut umbra, Mez, 12 insts, 1970; Commiato, S, 15 insts, 1972
Instrumental: Musica per 3 pf, 1935; Sonatina canonica, pf, 1942–3; Ciaccona, intermezzo e adagio, vc, 1945; 2 studi, vn, pf, 1946–7; Quaderno musicale di Annalibera, pf, 1952
[Suvini Zerboni, UE; Argo, Fonit Cetra]

Daniel-Lesur (1908–) French composer. Studied at the Conservatoire and then taught at the Schola Cantorum (1935–64). In 1936 he was a founder of La JEUNE FRANCE, and around that time he seemed likely to prove as adventurous an organist–composer as another member of the group, Messiaen. However, his music is generally closer in style to their common teacher Dukas. His works include the opera *Andrea del Sarto* (1961–8, ★Marseilles, 1969), orchestral pieces, sacred choral music, songs and a few instrumental pieces.
[Choudens, Ricordi, Durand]

Daphne Opera by Strauss and Josef Gregor, intended to form a double bill with their *Friedenstag:* it is one of Strauss's marriages of myth and modern psychology, fitted with a radiant and serene score. ★Dresden, 15 Oct 1938.

Daphnis et Chloé Ballet by Ravel, choreography by Fokine, a Greek pastoral of the young lovers' discovery of their feelings. The score, which Ravel called a 'choreographic symphony', is his biggest and most sumptuous. The 2 suites consist of the first and last thirds of the work. *Ballets Russes, Paris, 8 Jun 1912.

Darmstadt Site of the Internationale Ferienkurse für Neue Musik (International Summer Courses for New Music) established in 1946 by Wolfgang Steinecke. In 1948 the teachers included René Leibowitz and Peter Stadlen, and the pupils Henze; Schoenberg's music was also performed and discussed. Then between 1949 and 1951 Messiaen was regularly present. He planned his MODE DE VALEURS ET D'INTENSITÉS there in 1949, and this piece was the main talking point in 1951, when the students included Stockhausen, Nono, Goeyvaerts and Maderna. Thenceforward Darmstadt belonged to the new generation. In 1953 Stockhausen began giving lectures there, followed in 1955 by Boulez; Maderna, Nono, Berio and Pousseur were also regular teachers throughout the second half of the 1950s, when young composers arrived from all over the world to learn the latest serial developments. There was an atmosphere of confident optimism in a common endeavour, though the seeds of discord were already there in the widely different aims and assumptions of the teachers. Cage's arrival in 1958 was more the symbol than the cause of a failure of faith that a new language could be created – the faith with which the word 'Darmstadt' is commonly associated.

Boulez and Pousseur continued teaching at Darmstadt until the mid-1960s; Stockhausen was there until the early 1970s (from 1970 the courses were biennial); and Maderna, who had settled in the town, remained to conduct the ensemble. At the end of the 1970s, however, responsibility for instruction passed to a new generation led by Ferneyhough. Proceedings at the courses have been published annually since 1958 as *Darmstädter Beiträge zur Neuen Musik*.

David, Johann Nepomuk (1895-1977) Austrian composer. Received early musical education at St Florian, then studied with Joseph Marx at the Vienna Academy. Afterwards he worked as a schoolteacher and church musician, and as professor of composition at Stuttgart (1948-63). His roots in church music inclined him to a Hindemith-like style of learned counterpoint moving with strong purpose through dissonant harmonic regions: much of his large output consists of organ music (including the 21 volumes of *Das Choralwerk*, 1932-74), motets, cantatas and masses. However, he also, particularly in later years, pro-duced many orchestral works (8 symphonies, various concertos, etc), and in these he began in the 1950s to use serial methods, sometimes in association with esoteric principles from Dürer and Goethe. [Breitkopf]

Davidenko, Alexander (1899-1934) Russian composer. Studied with Glier at the Moscow Conservatory and threw himself into the production of revolutionary songs for mass singing.

Davidovsky, Mario (1934-) Argentinian–American composer. Studied in Buenos Aires and moved to the USA in 1960, working at the Columbia–Princeton Electronic Music Center and teaching at City College. His best known works are the fluent, characterful *Synchronisms* that create blendings and dialogues for instruments and tape.
Synchronism no.1, fl, 1962; no.2, fl, cl, vn, vc, 1964; no.3, vc, 1964; no.4, chorus, 1966; no.5, perc, 1969; no.6, pf, 1970; no.7, orch, 1974; no.8, wind qnt, 1974
Other works: orch pieces, chamber music, tape studies
[McGinnis & Marx; CRI]

Davies, Peter Maxwell (1934-) English composer. His music theatre works of the 1960s, taking Schoenbergian expressionism into the disturbing borderlands of self-parody, his sombre reflections on the landscape of the Orkney islands and his ambitious symphonic works of the late 1970s and 1980s bear witness to a personality of abundant and diverse creativeness. His output is extensive; his antecedents range from the English Renaissance through Beethoven to Boulez; and his musical manners (good and bad) are similarly various.

He was born and studied in Manchester, where his colleagues at the Royal Manchester College of Music (1952-6) included Birtwistle and Goehr. All shared in the discovery of Indian and medieval music, and of the European avant garde (Davies went to Darmstadt in 1956): the result was an assured synthesis in his first acknowledged works (1955-7), which already display characteristic features of instrumental brilliance verging towards violence, and slow, troubled contemplation. Medieval techniques, especially isorhythm, gave him an essentially static, repetitive framework; they also encouraged him towards contorted rhythms. But on the other hand there is an urge for sure forward motion and development: Stravinsky is contradicted by Schoenberg.

Further studies with Petrassi in Rome (1957-9) gave him the means to control larger forms, and then a period of teaching at Cirencester Grammar School (1959–62) provided him with the stimulus not only to revitalize school music (he has continued to write for children, and his work in this area has been widely followed) but to welcome spontaneity and effect in his own art. The major works of this period were O magnum mysterium (a sequence of modal carols interspersed with more adventurous meditations for school orchestra and capped by an organ fantasia of eerie flamboyance), the Leopardi Fragments and the String Quartet. Then he went to Princeton (1962–4) for studies with Sessions and Kim, and while there he began his opera TAVERNER.

Work on Taverner led him into areas of extreme experience (madness, blasphemy, self-betrayal) which prompted repeated forays into the world of PIERROT LUNAIRE: in the Trakl setting Revelation and Fall, in the EIGHT SONGS FOR A MAD KING and in VESA-LII ICONES, all of which were first performed by the Pierrot Players (later FIRES OF LONDON). There were also instrumental works of similar ferocity, notably Hymnos for clarinet and piano, or the orchestral St Thomas Wake which, in common with several works of this period, swerves from high complexity into the seductive banality of the fox-trot. Another orchestral work, Worldes Blis, channels expressive intemperateness into a continuous 40-minute form, looking forward to the later symphonies.

At the beginning of the 1970s he took up residence in the Orkneys, and his music became on the surface more calm. There were more music theatre pieces, but there were also settings of the island poetry of George Mackay Brown, concerned with ancient myth, ritual and pastoral (From Stone to Thorn, Dark Angels, The Blind Fiddler). In 1977 he helped set up the St Magnus Festival on Orkney, composing his Viking chamber opera The Martyr-dom of St Magnus for the first festival. Other works, including the operas The Two Fiddlers and Cinderella, were written for local children.

During the same period he returned to large-scale instrumental composition with his First Symphony and Ave maris stella, these to be rapidly followed by more symphonies, symphonic works for chamber orchestra and solo sonatas. All these grew out of his understanding that tonal forces of long range but deep ambiguity might be created by a modal gloss on major–minor harmony: he has described his Second Symphony, for instance, as being in B minor but with F as its dominant, and the conflict between 'real' and traditional dominants is perhaps one source of his music's strange-

ness, tension and energy. Here, as in most if not all his compositions, the basic material comes from plainsong, but only very rarely does this produce an open show of modality (it does in his ballet Salome, for instance): instead the transformations produce music where dynamic tonality is at odds with tendencies towards disintegration.

Operas: TAVERNER, 1962–8, The Martyrdom of St Magnus, 1976, ★Kirkwall, 1977; The Lighthouse, 1979, ★Edinburgh, 1980

Music theatre: Missa super L'homme armé, 1968, rev. 1971; EIGHT SONGS FOR A MAD KING, 1969; VESA-LII ICONES, 1969; Blind Man's Buff, 1972; Miss Donnithorne's Maggot, 1974; Le jongleur de Notre Dame, 1978; The Medium, 1981; The No. 11 Bus, 1984

Orchestral: St Michael, 17 wind, 1957; Prolation, 1957–8; 5 Klee Pictures, 1960, rev. 1976; First Taverner Fantasia, 1962; Sinfonia, chamber orch, 1962; Second Taverner Fantasia, 1964; Worldes Blis, 1966–9; St Thomas Wake, 1969; Sym no. 1, 1973–6; A Mirror of Whitening Light, 14 insts, 1976–7; Salome (ballet), 1978; Sym no. 2, 1980; Sinfonia concertante, 1982; Sinfonietta accademica, 1983; Sym no. 3, 1984; Vn Conc, 1985

Vocal orchestral: 5 Motets, soloists, chorus, 16 insts, 1959, rev. 1962; Veni Sancte Spiritus, soloists, chorus, orch, 1963; Ecce manus tradentis, soloists, chorus, wind, bells, harp, 1964; Revelation and Fall, v, 16 insts, 1966, rev. 1980; Stone Litany, Mez, orch, 1973; Black Pentecost, Mez, Bar, orch, 1979; Into the Labyrinth, T, chamber orch, 1982

Works for Fires ensemble with voice: Also hat Gott die Welt geliebet (after Buxtehude), 1971; From Stone to Thorn, 1971; Hymn to St Magnus, 1972; Tene-brae super Gesualdo, 1972; Fiddlers at the Wedding, 1973–4; The Blind Fiddler, 1975; Anakreon-tika, 1976

Works for Fires ensemble without voice: Stedman Caters, 1958, rev. 1968; Antechrist, 1967; Fantasia on a Ground and Two Pavans (after Purcell), 1968; Veni Sancte Spiritus/Veni Creator Spiritus (after Dunstable), 1972; Fantasia on One Note (after Purcell), 1973; Renaissance Scottish Dances, 1973; 4 Instrumental Motets (after Scottish originals), 1973–7; Ave maris stella, 1975; Kinloche his Fantassie, 1976; Runes from a Holy Island, 1977; Image, Reflection, Shadow, 1982

Other chamber: Sonata, tpt, pf, 1955; Stedman Doubles, cl, perc, 1955, rev. 1968; Alma redemptoris mater, 6 wind, 1957; Ricercar and Doubles on 'To Many a Well', 8 insts, 1959; Leopardi Fragments, S, A, 8 insts, 1961; Str Qt, 1961; 7 In Nomine, 10 insts, 1963–4; Shakespeare Music, 11 insts 1964;

Hymnos, cl, pf, 1967; Dark Angels, v, gui, 1973; Brass Qnt, 1981

Instrumental: 5 Pieces, pf, 1955–6; 5 Little Pieces, pf, 1960–64; Sub tuam protectionem, pf, 1969; Solita, fl, 1969, rev. 1972; Ut re mi, pf, 1971; The Door of the Sun, va, 1975; The Kestrel Paced Round the Sun, fl, 1975; The 7 Brightnesses, cl, 1975; 3 Voluntaries, org, 1976; Pf Sonata, 1980–81; Hill Runes, gui, 1981; Org Sonata, 1981

Choral: Westerlings, SATB, 1976–7; Solstice of Light, T, SATB, org, 1979; carols

Children's music: O magnum mysterium, 1960; Te lucis ante terminum, 1961; The Shepherd's Calendar, 1965; The 2 Fiddlers, 1978; Cinderella, 1979–80

Film scores: The Devils, 1970; The Boy Friend, 1971 [Boosey, Chester, Schott; Unicorn, Decca, Nonesuch]

□ S. Pruslin, ed,. *Peter Maxwell Davies* (1979); P. Griffiths, *Peter Maxwell Davies* (1982)

Death in Venice Opera by Britten and Myfanwy Piper after Thomas Mann's novella about a distinguished writer charmed by a boy. The central role was the last written for Pears; the boy, his friends and his mother are dancers. ★English Opera Group, Snape, 16 Jun 1973.

Debussy, Claude (1862–1918) French composer. Though he belonged to no school and looked with distaste on his imitators, his music has been enormously influential, since even before the 19th c. was over he was freeing music from the norms of continuous forward movement, thematic working and coherent diatonic harmony. This last he subverted by using the old modes (often stimulated or excused by an ancient Greek or ecclesiastical subject) and the whole-tone scale. The resultant weakening of harmonic impetus went with forms of an improvisatory character, where thematic developments tended increasingly to be momentary affairs in music of generally less logical progress, and where subtleties of orchestration took on primary importance. If all this made music a more static art than hitherto, it was perhaps inevitable that he should have been so attracted to visual subjects, though the poetry of Verlaine and others was certainly of equal importance in his fashioning of a new sensibility.

He was born at St Germain-en-Laye and studied at the Paris Conservatoire (1872–84) with Marmontel for the piano and Guiraud for composition. The Prix de Rome took him to Italy until 1887, but he was unhappy there and completed little of consequence. Back in Paris, though, he began to compose freely in all genres, especially after his visits to Bayreuth in 1888 and 1889. The Baudelaire settings of 1887–9 were of Wagnerian opulence, but the Verlaine songs of 1891 show a crisper, more fantastical style, with a freer use of unrelated triads and a lingering on dominant discords. 2 instrumental masterpieces followed: the String Quartet in a G minor expanded by the Phrygian mode as well as by some oriental ostinato structures in the scherzo (he had heard Indonesian and Indochinese music in Paris in 1889), and the orchestral *Prélude à 'L'après-midi d'un faune'* (Prelude to 'A Faun's Afternoon'). Around this time too he began work on his opera PELLÉAS ET MÉLISANDE.

The middle 1890s were less productive, partly because of difficulties in his personal life; his marriage in 1899 was succeeded swiftly by the long-delayed completion of the *Nocturnes* for orchestra. The marriage, however, did not last long. In 1903 he met Emma Bardac, dedicatee of Fauré's *La bonne chanson*, and in 1904 he left his wife for her; a daughter was born to them in 1905, and later given the present of the *Children's Corner* suite. With Bardac his creative confidence suddenly bloomed, for the years 1903–5 saw the composition of *La* MER, another important group of Verlaine songs, and of piano works that at last brought his music for his own instrument into the world he had discovered through song, opera and orchestral music.

Then again there was a lull, until in 1908 he started a new opera on Poe's *The Fall of the House of Usher* and completed the orchestral *Ibéria*. In 1909 he began to show painful symptoms of a rectal cancer that was to kill him, but during the next few years he composed copiously, and variously. *Ibéria* gained 2 companions to make the set of orchestral IMAGES; smaller vignettes went into the 2 books of piano PRELUDES. There were also 4 stage works, on some of which he sought collaborators' help in orchestration, though not on the ballet JEUX, the most individual of his orchestral works in its succession of waves and flurries of motivic development within a general unpredictability, and in its fine orchestration. Here, more than in any other work, there is a lack of repetition, even an avoidance of repeating the same timbre. Yet in *Le* MARTYRE DE ST SÉBASTIEN, the mystery of d'Annunzio's which he provided with music, there is a quite different style of modal homophony matched by a colouring in large blocks. *Jeux* points towards Boulez and Stockhausen, as they were quick to acknowledge; *Sébastien* foreshadows Messiaen (though not in its heretical mixture of Christianity and erotic paganism: Debussy himself was agnostic).

His last years were devoted to the *Usher* project, never finished, and to chamber and piano music. The first world war intensified his sense of himself as a French musician, and he embarked on an intended set of 6 sonatas in imitation of 18th c. masters, though in form and content the 3 completed works are entirely his own. That for flute, viola and harp employs the quintessence of his orchestra in pursuit of ideas as momentary as those of *Jeux*, while the cello and violin sonatas have more in common with the teasing artificiality of his Verlaine songs. At the same time, he was very aware of Stravinsky's arrival in Paris, for there is the echo of *Petrushka* in both *En blanc et noir* for 2 pianos and the last of the solo piano ETUDES, a remarkable collection which surveys also the enormous range of sounds he had obtained from the piano by exploiting its resonances, and the fluidity he had brought to the way music moves.

Opera: PELLÉAS ET MÉLISANDE, 1893–1902
Other stage works: LE MARTYRE DE ST SÉBASTIEN, 1911; Khamma, ballet, 1911–12; JEUX, ballet, 1912–13; La boîte à joujoux, ballet, 1913
Orchestral: Printemps, 1887, rev. 1912; Fantaisie, pf, orch, 1889–90; Prélude à 'L'après-midi d'un faune', 1892–4; Marche écossaise, arr. 1894–1908; Nocturnes (Nuages, Fêtes, Sirènes), 1897–9; La MER, 1903–5; Danse sacrée et danse profane, harp, str, 1904; IMAGES (Gigues, Ibéria, Rondes de printemps), 1905–12; Première rapsodie, arr. 1911
Vocal orchestral: Salut printemps, women's vv, orch, 1882; Invocation, men's vv, orch, 1883; L'enfant prodigue, 3 solo vv, orch, 1884, rev. 1906–8; La damoiselle élue, S, women's vv, orch, 1887–8, rev. 1902; Le jet d'eau (arr.), 1907; 3 ballades de Villon (arr.), 1910
Choral: 3 chansons de Charles d'Orléans, 1898–1908
Songs: Ariettes oubliées (Verlaine), 1885–8; 5 poèmes (Baudelaire), 1887–9; 3 mélodies (Verlaine), 1891; Fêtes galantes (Verlaine), first set 1891, second set 1904; Proses lyriques (Debussy), 1892–3; Chansons de Bilitis (Louÿs), 1897–8; 3 chansons de France, 1904; Le promenoir des 2 amants (Lhermite), 1904–10; 3 ballades de Villon, 1910; 3 poèmes de Mallarmé, 1913
Chamber: Str Qt, 1893; Rapsodie, a sax, pf, 1901–8; Première rapsodie, cl, pf, 1909–10; Petite pièce, cl, pf, 1910; Syrinx, fl, 1913; Sonata, vc, pf, 1915; Sonata, fl, va, harp, 1915; Sonata, vn, pf, 1916–17
Piano: Suite bergamasque, 1890, rev. 1905; Pour le

piano, suite, 1894–1901; D'un cahier d'esquisses, 1903; Estampes, 1903; L'isle joyeuse, 1904; Masques, 1904; IMAGES, first set 1905, second set 1907; Children's Corner, suite, 1906–8; Hommage à Haydn, 1909; The Little Nigar, 1909; PRELUDES, first book 1909–10, second book 1912–13; La plus que lente, 1910; Berceuse héroïque, 1914; Six épigraphes antiques, 1914; ETUDES, 1915
Piano duet: Petite suite, 1886–9; Marche écossaise, 1891; Six épigraphes antiques, 1914
Two pianos: Lindaraja, 1901; En blanc et noir, 1915
Many early songs and pf pieces, unfinished operas, etc

□ C. Debussy, *Debussy on Music* (1976); E. Lockspeiser, *Debussy* (1962–5)

decay The process of a sound's extinction, subject as part of the ENVELOPE to electronic change.

Delius, Frederick (1862–1934) English composer, though of German extraction and resident most of his life in France. His musical world, too, was cosmopolitan: he used English folksong on occasion (notably in *Brigg Fair*), but the composers most important to him were Wagner as a model of continuous flow, Grieg for an untroubled handling of chromaticism, and Debussy for orchestral finesse. He wrote little that was not for the orchestra, nor strayed far from a manner of rhapsodic celebration undercut by elegy and nostalgia: his expanded harmonic vocabulary is not stabilized in non-progressive forms as in Debussy, but directed rather to an often sonata-type movement towards resolution, and it is the exquisite delay of such resolution (which may not arrive even at the end) that gives his music its poignancy.

He studied with Thomas Ward in Florida while working there as an orange planter (1884–5). In 1886 he went to the Leipzig Conservatory, where he met Grieg, and then he moved to Paris. His friends there included Gauguin, Strindberg and Munch, as well as a young Norwegian painter, Jelka Rosen, with whom he settled at Grez-sur-Loing in 1897. Most of his music was written there, often in his adored garden, for the move was soon followed by his achievement of the mature style in the orchestral *Paris* and the opera *A Village Romeo and Juliet*. These works had their first performance in Germany, but around 1907 he began to be more performed in England, especially by Beecham, who directed the first complete performance of his *A Mass of Life*, a statement of exuberant Nietzschean affirmation. Later, during the war (when he retreated to England) and for some years afterwards, he concentrated on traditional forms while keeping his music's rhapsodic flow. After 1923 he fell virtually silent, blinded and paralysed by syphilis, but the services of Eric Fenby as amanuensis enabled him to resume composition in his last years.

Operas: Irmelin, 1890-92, ★Oxford, 1953; The Magic Fountain, 1893-5; Koanga, 1895-7, ★Elberfeld, 1904; A Village Romeo and Juliet, 1900-01, ★Berlin, 1907; Margot la rouge, 1902; Fennimore and Gerda, 1909-10, ★Frankfurt, 1919; Hassan (incidental music), 1920-23, ★London, 1923

Orchestral: Pf Conc, 1897, rev. 1906; Life's Dance, 1899, rev. 1901; Paris, 1899; Brigg Fair, 1907; In a Summer Garden, 1908; Dance Rhapsody no.1, 1908, no.2, 1916; Summer Night on the River, 1911; On Hearing the First Cuckoo in Spring, 1912; North Country Sketches, 1913-14; Air and Dance, str, 1915; Double Conc, vn, vc, orch, 1915-16; Vn Conc, 1916; Eventyr, 1917; A Song before Sunrise, 1918; Vc Conc, 1921; A Song of Summer, 1929-30; Caprice and Elegy, vc, orch, 1930; Fantastic Dance, 1931

Vocal orchestral: Mitternachtslied, Bar, men's vv, orch, 1898; Appalachia, chorus, orch, 1898-1903; Sea Drift, Bar, chorus, orch, 1903-4; A Mass of Life, 4 solo vv, chorus, orch, 1904-5; Songs of Sunset, Mez, Bar, chorus, orch, 1906-8; Cynara, Bar, orch, 1907, rev. 1928-9; An Arabesk, Bar, chorus, orch, 1911; A Song of the High Hills, chorus, orch, 1911; Requiem, S, Bar, chorus, orch, 1914-16; A Late Lark, v, orch, 1925; Songs of Farewell, chorus, orch, 1930; Idyll, S, Bar, orch, 1930-32

Choral: On Craig Dhu, SATTBB, pf, 1907; Two Songs to be Sung of a Summer Night on the Water, SATTBB, 1917

Chamber: Vn Sonata no.1, 1905-14, no.2, 1923, no.3, 1930; Str Qt, 1916

Few instrumental pieces, many songs, some with orch

[Boosey]

□ E. Fenby, *Delius as I knew him* (1936, 3/1966); C. Redwood, ed., *A Delius Companion* (1976)

Dello Joio, Norman (1913-) American composer. Followed his father as a Catholic church organist, then studied with Wagenaar at the Juilliard School (1939-41) and Hindemith at Yale (1941). His music is strong in gesture and large in melody, influenced by plainsong, Italian opera and American popular music of the 1920s and 1930s. Among his works are operas (*The Triumph of St Joan*, 1951), ballets (*Seraphic Dialogue*, 1948, choreographed by

Graham), sacred choral works, orchestral and chamber pieces. [Fischer, Marks, G. Schirmer]

Del Tredici, David (1937-) American composer. Studied at Berkeley and with Sessions at Princeton. In 1968 he began a long series of works based on Carroll's *Alice* books, often employing large-scale and diverse resources to the ends of surrealist whimsy. These include *The Final Alice* for amplified speaking and singing soprano, folk group and orchestra (1976). [Boosey; Decca, Nonesuch]

Denisov, Edison (1929-) Russian composer. Studied as mathematician in Tomsk and then as composer with Shebalin and others at the Moscow Conservatory (1951-6), where in 1960 he began teaching. Around the same time he began to interest himself in serialism, from which followed works that cross the Boulez of *Pli selon pli* with the Stravinsky of *Les noces*: notably *The Sun of the Incas* for soprano and mixed nonet (1964). Later works, in a luminous style of intricate motivic continuity, have been more performed in western Europe than in the USSR.

Stage: L'écume des jours (opera), 1981; Confession (ballet), 1984

Orchestral: Peinture, 1970; Concs for vc, 1972, pf, 1974, fl, 1975, vn, 1977, fl and ob, 1979, bn and vc, 1982; Chamber Sym, 12 insts, 1982

Vocal: The Sun of the Incas, S, 10 insts, 1964; Laments, S, pf, perc, 1965; La vie en rouge, v, 6 insts, 1973; Requiem, S, T, chorus, orch, 1980; The Blue Notebook, S, narrator, 5 insts, 1984

Much chamber and instrumental music, songs, choruses

[UE, Peters, Gerig, Leduc]

Density 21.5 Solo flute piece by Varèse, written to inaugurate an instrument made of platinum, which has this density. ★Barrère, New York, 16 Feb 1936.

derived set 12-note set derived from a smaller set by applying the usual serial transformations of inversion, retrogression and transposition. Many of Webern's sets are constructed in this way, the classic example being that of his Concerto op.24:

| original subset | retrograde inversion | retrograde | inversion |

In Webern this is the set for the whole work: Babbitt, who introduced the term, has used derived sets built from units of his principal set, as for example in his Second Quartet.

Déserts Work by Varèse, his first with recorded sound, and the first by anyone for orchestra and tape. It is, however, essentially an orchestral composition (for wind and percussion), and can be played without the 3 'interpolations' of 'electronically organized sound'. ★RTF Orchestra/ Scherchen, Paris, 2 Dec 1954.

Deshevov, Vladimir (1889-1955) Russian composer. Studied with Shteynberg and others at the St Petersburg Conservatory. He belonged to the progressive wing of Soviet music in the 1920s, being influenced by Honegger and Prokofiev; his machine piece for piano *Rails* (1926) has survived to typify the period. Later he wrote mostly incidental music and film scores.

Dessau, Paul (1894-1979) German composer. Studied at the Klindworth-Scharwenka Conservatory in Berlin (1910-12), then worked as a theatre conductor in Bremen, Hamburg, Cologne, Mainz and Berlin (Städtische Oper, 1925-33). As a Jew he moved to Paris in 1933, and there studied 12-note music with Leibowitz. He then moved to the USA (1939-48), where in 1942 he met and began his collaboration with Brecht (he had already written an incidental score for Paris). The 2 returned together to East Berlin, and Dessau became the leading figure in East German music.
Operas: Die Verurteilung des Lukullus (Brecht), 1949, ★Berlin, 1951; Puntila (after Brecht), 1957-9, ★Berlin, 1966; Lanzelot, 1967-9, ★Berlin, 1969; Einstein, 1971-3, ★Berlin, 1973
Incidental scores for Brecht: Furcht und Elend des Dritten Reiches, 1938; Mutter Courage und ihre Kinder, 1946; Der gute Mensch von Sezuan, 1947; Herr Puntila und sein Knecht Matti, 1949; Mann ist Mann, 1951; Der kaukasische Kreidekreis, 1953-4 Numberless choral works, songs, orch pieces, chamber music
[Deutscher Verlag für Musik]

Deutsch, Max (1892-) Austrian-French composer and teacher. Studied at Vienna University and with Schoenberg (1913-20), then worked as a theatre conductor and composer for Pabst films. In 1924 he settled in Paris, where he introduced works by Schoenberg, Berg and Webern, worked as a pianist and cabaret composer, and taught 12-note composition.

Diaghilev *See* DYAGILEV.

Diamond, David (1915-) American composer. Studied at the Eastman School, with Sessions in New York (1935) and with Boulanger in Paris (1936-7). He lived in Italy from 1951 to 1965, then returned to New York. His music is in a clear, lithe contrapuntal style, influenced by the composers with whom he associated in Paris: Ravel, Stravinsky and Roussel. Among his works are ballets and theatre scores, symphonies and concertos, many songs and a series of string quartets. [Southern]

Diepenbrock, Alphons (1862-1921) Dutch composer, the first of importance since the 17th c. Self-taught, he was influenced by Wagner and in his last years by Debussy; Mahler was a friend and admirer. His biggest works are tone poems with solo voice (*Zwei Hymnen an die Nacht*, 1899; *Im grossen Schweigen*, 1906; *Die Nacht*, 1911) and incidental scores (*Marsyas*, 1910; *Electra*, 1920). [Alphons Diepenbrock Fonds]

Dieren, Bernard van (1887-1936) English composer of French–Dutch extraction. Settled in England in 1909 and was mostly self-taught, except for studies in Germany (1912). His music was praised by a circle of artistic friends including the Sitwells, Warlock and the sculptor Epstein (on whom he wrote a book), and has periodically been revived, particularly the 6 string quartets and the *Chinese Symphony* for soloists, chorus and orchestra (1914), which has more of Delius than Mahler in it.
□ B. van Dieren, *Down among the Dead Men* (1935)

d'Indy, Vincent (1851-1931) French composer and teacher. Studied with Franck and became his staunchest advocate, though less in his music than in his writings and his teaching at the Schola Cantorum, of which in 1894 he was a founder. His works lighten academic craftsmanship with exoticism (symphonic variations *Istar*, 1896), Catholic piety and long diatonic folksong themes (*Symphonie sur un chant montagnard français* with piano, 1886); they cover all genres.

Distler, Hugo (1908-42) German composer. Studied at the Leipzig Conservatory with Grabner and Högner, who pointed him towards the organ tradition of Bach and his predecessors. He was then organist at the Jakobkirche in Lübeck (1931-7) and a teacher in Stuttgart (1937-40) and Berlin (1940-42), though he suffered harassment from the authorities and eventually committed suicide. His works consist mostly of choral and organ music. [Bärenreiter]

dodecaphony Inelegant and imprecise term whose meanings are covered by ATONALITY, SERIALISM and 12-NOTE COMPOSITION.

Dodge, Charles (1942-) American composer. Studied with Luening at Columbia University and Ussachevsky (1964-70), and at Princeton with Winham (1966-7), then taught at these universities. His works show wit in the handling of computer resources.
Changes, tape, 1967-70; Earth's Magnetic Field, tape, 1970; Humming, tape, 1971; Extensions, tpt, tape, 1973; Speech Songs, tape, 1973; The Story of our Lives, tape, 1974; In Celebration, tape, 1975; Cascando, tape, 1979 [American Composers Alliance; Nonesuch, CRI]

Dohnányi, Ernő (1877-1960) Hungarian composer. Studied with Thomán and Koessler at the Budapest Academy (1894-7), then appeared widely as a composer-pianist: Brahms had approved his C minor Piano Quintet (1895), and this was followed by more works in solid German instrumental forms, besides the popular *Variationen über ein Kinderlied* for piano and orchestra (1914). In 1915 he returned to Hungary, where he taught and worked vigorously as a conductor (he directed several Bartók premieres). His activity as a composer declined until the 1940s, when he took up his old style with little change. In 1949 he moved to Tallahassee, Florida.

Doktor Faust Opera by Busoni to his own libretto after an old puppet play, though aware of other treatments of the subject as it is aware of diverse musical styles: abstract models of form from the German tradition, Italian lyricism, atonality. The last scene was finished by Jarnach. *Dresden, 21 May 1925.

Domaine Musical Organization founded by Boulez, originally as the Concerts du Petit Marigny, under the patronage of the Renaud-Barrault Company (Boulez was their music director). They began in 1954 with concerts bringing together pre-Classical music, 20th c. masterpieces and new works: the first programme, conducted by Scherchen, consisted of Bach's *Musical Offering*, Stravinsky's *Renard*, Webern's Concerto, Nono's *Polifonia-Monodia-Ritmica* and Stockhausen's *Kontra-Punkte*. From 1957 onwards most of the concerts were conducted by Boulez, until in 1967 direction passed to Amy; the organization disbanded in 1973. Among the works it presented for the first time were Messiaen's *Oiseaux exotiques*, *Couleurs de la cité céleste*, *Sept haïkaï* and *Et exspecto*, Stockhausen's *Zeitmasze*, Barraqué's *Séquence*, *...au delà du hasard* and *Le temps restitué*, and compositions by Henze, Philippot, Nono, Maderna and others.

Donatoni, Franco (1927-) Italian composer. Studied in Milan, Bologna and with Pizzetti in Rome (1952-3), but was most influenced by his meeting with Maderna (1953) and subsequent attendance at the Darmstadt courses. Since 1953 he has taught at various Italian institutions. His works of the 1950s show a gradual adherence to the methods and styles of Boulez and Stockhausen, followed in the septet *For Grilly* (1960) by an objective creation of crisp musical objects, sometimes mechanically set out in dense textures: other works of this crucial period include the orchestral *Puppenspiel* (1961) and *Per orchestra* (1962). Then came a period of Cageian indeterminacy (in the Fourth Quartet of 1963 the players react to what they read in newspapers), though this soon gave way to a return to traditional notation and objective craftsmanship. [Suvini Zerboni]

Donaueschingen Festival Started in 1921 as a summer festival of new music under the patronage of Prince Max Egon zu Fürstenberg, featuring the first performances of Hindemith's *Kammermusik no.1* (1922), Webern's Trakl songs op.14 (1924) and other works. The festival moved in 1927 to Baden-Baden, where it included the premieres of Weill's *Mahagonny* 'Songspiel', Hindemith's *Hin und zurück* and Milhaud's *L'enlèvement d'Europe* (all in 1927) and the Hindemith-Weill version of *Der Lindberghflug* (1929). In 1930 the last festival took place in Berlin.
Attempts to revive the festival in Donaueschingen before and after the war were unsuccessful, but in 1950 the occasion recommenced as an October weekend of new music under the aegis of the Sudwestfunk. It then played an important part in promoting the new avant garde, giving the first performances of Stockhausen's *Spiel* (1952), *Momente* (1964 version, 1965), *Mantra* (1970), *Trans* (1971), *Inori* (1974) and *Michaels Reise um die Erde* (1978), and Boulez's *Polyphonie X* (1951), *Livre pour quatuor* (1955), *Poésie pour pouvoir*

(1958), second book of *Structures* (1961), *Pli selon pli* (1962) and *Répons* (1981). The death of Prince Max Egon in 1959 was marked by memorial tributes from Stravinsky (*Epitaphium*), Boulez (*Tombeau*) and Fortner.

Donnerstag aus Licht (Thursday from Light) Opera by Stockhausen to his own libretto, the first completed of his seven-evening cycle *Licht*. It is in 3 separately performable acts: *Michaels Jugend* (Michael's Youth), concerning the artistic and sexual awakening of the hero Michael, *Michaels Reise um die Erde* (Michael's Journey Round the Earth), a trumpet concerto in which Michael is in musical dialogue with different cultures, and *Michaels Heimkehr* (Michael's Homecoming), which is his celestial triumph and visionary account of himself. There is also an overture *Donnerstags-Gruss* (Thursday's Greeting) for brass and percussion, and a closing *Donnerstags-Abschied* (Thursday's Farewell) for 5 trumpeters stationed on roofs outside the theatre. *Milan, 15 Mar 1981.

double bass The conductor Kusevitsky was a bassist and wrote a concerto for the instrument (*Moscow, 1905), but the repertory was not much expanded until the arrival of several virtuoso bass players in the 1960s, notably Bertram Turetzky, Gary Karr, Barry Guy and Fernando Grillo. Karr commissioned concertos from Henze, Schuller and others; Guy has featured the double bass in several of his own works, often with jazz-style amplification (there is also an amplified bass in Boulez's *Domaines*).

Druckman, Jacob (1928-) American composer. Studied with Persichetti and Mennin at the Juilliard School (1949-56), with Copland at Tanglewood (1949-50) and in Paris, later teaching at the Juilliard School and at Brooklyn College (from 1972). He also worked at the Columbia-Princeton Electronic Music Center, where he composed a series of dramatic encounters for live musicians and tape: *Animus I* for trombonist (1966), *Animus II* for female singer and two percussionists (1968) and *Animus III* for clarinettist (1969). Later works are no less strongly figured but often on a larger scale: they include the orchestral pieces *Windows* (1972), *Lamia* (with soprano, 1974), *Chiaroscuro* (1976-7), *Aureole* (1979) and *Prism* (1980). [AMP; Nonesuch]

Dufourt, Hugues (1943-) French composer. Studied at the Geneva Conservatory and then with Guyonnet while also training as a philosopher at Geneva University. In 1967 he graduated and began teaching philosophy in Lyons, but he later moved to Paris and concentrated on composition and electronic research. His works show a Varèsian sense of sound mass and a command of slow, long-range formal manoeuvres.

Mura della città di dite, 17 insts, 1969; Erewhon, 6 perc, 1972-6; Antiphysis, fl, chamber orch, 1978; Saturne, wind, perc, electronic insts, 1979 [Jobert; Sappho, Erato]

Dukas, Paul (1865-1935) French composer and teacher. Holding to a noble vision of artistic integrity, he published only a few works, and in the biggest of them, the opera ARIANE ET BARBE-BLEUE, dramatized the clear, purposeful search after truth that he felt to be his own responsibility. His career ran parallel with Debussy's, and the two admired and influenced each other, though Dukas inclined to the more solid and conservative, in particular to Wagner and Beethoven.

He studied at the Paris Conservatoire with Guiraud (1882-9), and first gained notice with his Wagnerian overture *Polyeucte*; in 1892 he started work as a critic, in which capacity he showed wide sympathies and discernment. His Symphony in C was his most powerfully Beethovenian work, and not unsuccessfully so, but the scherzo *L'apprenti sorcier* (The Sorcerer's Apprentice) was much more popular and much more influential in its brilliant orchestration and its symmetrical harmonies (diminished 7th chord and augmented triad): Stravinsky practically quotes it in his *Fireworks*. After this came 2 big symphonic works for the piano, the Sonata and the Rameau Variations, both profitting from late Beethoven and Franck, and both displaying a vigour of variation technique that is also shown by the contemporary *Ariane* and the later ballet *La péri*, an exercise in diaphanous orientalism. This was followed by almost a quarter century of SILENCE, broken only by two contributions to the *Revue musicale*: a tribute to Debussy and a Ronsard setting. Meanwhile he worked as an inspector of provincial conservatories and teacher at that of Paris (1928-35), where his pupils included Messiaen.

Stage: ARIANE ET BARBE-BLEUE, 1899-1906; La péri, 1911-12, *Paris, 1912

Orchestral: Polyeucte, overture, 1891; Sym, C, 1895-6; L'apprenti sorcier, 1897

Piano: Sonata, E♭, 1899-1901; Variations, interlude et final sur un thème de Rameau, ?1899-1902; Prélude élégiaque, 1908; La plainte, au loin, du faune..., 1920

Other works: Villanelle, hn, pf, 1906; Vocalise-étude, v, pf, 1909; Sonnet de Ronsard, v, pf, 1924 [Durand; Erato, Arion, EMI, Columbia]

Dumbarton Oaks Residence in Washington DC of Mr and Mrs Robert Woods Bliss, who commissioned Stravinsky's Concerto in E flat: the work was first performed there, and has gained the appellation as a nickname.

Dupré, Marcel (1886-1971) French composer and organist. The son and grandson of organists, he took his first appointment, at St Vivien in his home town of Rouen, when he was 12. He then studied at the Paris Conservatoire with Guilmant, Vierne and Widor (1902-14), and in 1920 began an international career as a recital organist; he was also Widor's successor at St Sulpice in Paris (1934-71). Famed as an improviser, he produced too a large quantity of notated organ music, often of a virtuoso character. His pupil Messiaen aptly called him 'the Liszt of the organ', drawing attention to his use of staccato chords in rapid toccata motion. Notable among his works are 2 sets of 3 Preludes and Fugues, op.7 (1912) and op.36 (1938). [Leduc, Bornemann]
□ M. Dupré, *Recollections* (1975)

duration 1. The length of a sound, either in notational value or clock time. This may be of particular concern in music where the principles of 12-note composition are applied to rhythm; it may also be a matter of interest when a single sound is held for an unusually long time, as in many early works by Young. 2. The length in clock time of a composition or movement. In 20th c. music this has been unusually variable: some of Webern's movements in his opp.9-11 last for only about a quarter of a minute, whereas some experimental works are notionally of infinite duration. Cage's *4' 33"*, which may be given any time limit, can be taken as embracing all the sounds one will hear in a lifetime. The record for the longest notated composition is obviously always subject to assailment, but among the works of important composers, Stockhausen's *Licht* seems likely to overtake Wagner's *Ring*.

Durey, Louis (1888-1979) French composer. Studied at the Schola Cantorum until 1914 and then, as an admirer of Satie and Stravinsky, became involved in Les six. He set Cocteau in *Le printemps au fond de la mer* for voice and wind decet (1920), but his earnestness soon led him away from the group.

In the 1940s and 1950s he was closely associated with left-wing organizations and wrote settings of Mao, Mayakovsky and Ho-Chi-Minh. [Chester]

Durkó, Zsolt (1934-) Hungarian composer. Studied with Farkas at the Budapest Academy and with Petrassi in Rome (1961-3). He then returned to Budapest and immediately established himself as a leader of the avant garde, working with small cells in incessant variation and with broad sweeps of colour. Most of his works are for large resources or else chamber ensemble. [Editio Musica; Hungaroton]

Duruflé, Maurice (1902-) French composer and organist. Studied with Tournemire and with Gigout and Dukas at the Paris Conservatoire (1920-28). In 1930 he was appointed organist of St Etienne-du-Mont; he has also appeared internationally as a recitalist. His few works, in a colourful modal style, include a Requiem for soloists, chorus, orchestra and organ (1947), other choral works, organ music, *3 danses* for orchestra (1932) and instrumental pieces. [Durand]

Dutilleux, Henri (1916-) French composer, the foremost representative of the French symphonic tradition in the age of Messiaen and Boulez, though by no means opposed to learning from both. He studied at the Paris Conservatoire with the Gallons and Büsser (1933-8), worked at French radio (1943-63) and took teaching appointments at the Ecole Normale de Musique (1961) and the Conservatoire (1970). Rather like Carter, he arrived at an independent, intuitive style around 1950 after a period of sophisticated achievement in a more conventional manner (in his case a Ravelian manner: most of the early works have been destroyed or repudiated). Ravel is still important in his mature works, though they breathe an airy spirit of freedom: thematic processes tend to be subtle and indirect in music of fluid movement and tenuous, constantly varying texture. This search for perpetual renewal has led him gradually away from the Ravelian diatonicism of his First Symphony, though not away from its rhetorical punch.
Orchestral: Sym no.1 1949-51; Le loup (ballet), 1953; Sym no.2 'Le double', 1956-9; Métaboles, 1962-5; 'Tout un monde lointain...', vc, orch, 1968-70; Timbres, Espace, Mouvement, 1977
Chamber: Sonàtina, fl, pf, 1942; Sarabande et cortège, bn, pf, 1942; Sonata, ob, pf, 1947; Choral, cadence et fugato, trbn, pf, 1950; Ainsi la nuit, str qt, 1975-6

Piano: Au gré des ondes, 1946; Bergerie, 1947; Sonata, 1947; Résonances, 1965; 2 figures de résonance, 2 pf, 1970; 2 préludes, 1974 [Heugel, Amphion, Durand; Calliope]

dyad Group of 2 pitch classes, normally with reference to a 12-note set.

Dyagilev, Sergey (1872-1929) Russian impresario. Studied law in St Petersburg, but soon moved into theatrical and artistic circles. In 1907 he promoted 5 concerts of Russian music in Paris, followed in 1908 by performances of *Boris Godunov* for the first time outside Russia and in 1909 by the first appearance of what became the BALLETS RUSSES. He gave Stravinsky his first important commission (*The Firebird*) and worked with numerous other leading composers, choreographers and painters. Stravinsky sketched his portrait in a Polka for piano duet (in Three Easy Pieces, 1914-15) and dedicated *Les noces* to him.
□ J. Percival, *The World of Diaghilev* (1971)

Dzerzhinsky, Ivan (1909-78) Russian composer. Studied in Leningrad with Popov, Ryazanov and Asafyev, all associated with the progressive ACM, though his music was always highly conservative. His bland opera *Quiet flows the Don* (1932-4, *Leningrad, 1935) was in 1936 held up as a model of SOCIALIST REALISM in contrast with Shostakovich's *Lady Macbeth*. He wrote more operas, including another 2 after Sholokhov, but his music has not outlasted its Stalinist heyday.

E

Eaton, John (1935-) American composer. Studied with Babbitt, Cone and Sessions at Princeton (1953-9). He had a career as a jazz pianist, and then in 1964 began to work with electronic instruments, especially the SYNKET, in music of violent Expressionist intent. In 1971 he was appointed associate professor at Indiana University, where he has developed as a composer of opera (*The Tempest*, *Santa Fe, 1985). [Carisch, Malcolm, Shawnee; CRI]

Eben, Petr (1929-) Czech composer, organist and pianist. Imprisoned at Buchenwald during the war, then studied with Bořkovec at the Prague Academy (1948-54). He has worked in music education and as a performer of his own works, most of which evince a concern with philosophical speculation conducted through a synthesis of Bachian counterpoint with modern resources. His output includes the oratorio *Apologia Sokrates* (1961-7) and *Faust* for organ (1982).

Ecuatorial Work by Varèse for unison bass chorus (or soloist), brass, piano, organ, 2 ondes martenot and percussion, setting a Maya prayer in Spanish translation. One of the first works with electronic instruments. *New York, 15 Apr 1934.

Edinburgh Festival Annual event held since 1947 for 3 weeks in August-September, presenting concerts, opera, ballet, drama and exhibitions. New music has appeared occasionally in the proceedings, notably in performances of indigenous works by Scottish Opera (Musgrave's *Mary, Queen of Scots*, 1977), in concerts conducted by Boulez and in chamber recitals.

Egk, Werner (1901-83) German composer. Studied with Orff in the early 1920s, but owed most to Stravinsky in the dissonant bite, rhythmic élan and irony of his music. His relationship with the Nazi régime was equivocal: he received a medal for his *Olympische Festmusik* for the Berlin games, but his satirical opera *Peer Gynt* was banned, and yet he remained in Germany through the war. Afterwards he directed the Berlin Hochschule für Musik (1950-53).
Operas: Columbus, *Bavarian Radio, 1933; Die Zaubergeige, *Frankfurt, 1935; Peer Gynt, *Berlin, 1938; Circle, *Berlin, 1948; Irische Legende, *Salzburg, 1955; Der Revisor, *Schwetzingen, 1957; Die Verlobung in San Domingo, *Munich, 1963; Die Abraxas, 1979
Ballets: Joan von Zarissa, *Berlin, 1940; Abraxas, *Munich, 1948; Ein Sommertag, *Berlin, 1950; Die chinesische Nachtigall, *Munich, 1953; Casanova in London, *Munich, 1969
Orchestral and vocal orchestral works, few others [Schott; DG]

Eight Songs for a Mad King Music theatre piece by Davies and Randolph Stow. A vocalist of uncanny range presents himself as George III, on a stage occupied also by 6 instrumentalists. *Hart, Pierrot Players, London, 22 Apr 1969.

Eimert, Herbert (1897-1972) German composer. Studied as a musicologist at the conservatory

(1919-24) and university (1924-30) in Cologne, and joined the radio there in 1927. During the war he worked as a music critic, then in 1945 returned to the WESTDEUTSCHER RUNDFUNK, where he was founder-director of the studio for electronic music (1951-62). He had earlier worked with atonality (5 Pieces for string quartet, 1923-5), mechanical instruments (ballet *Der weisse Schwann*, 1926) and serialism; now, in his 4 Pieces (1952-3), he produced one of the first works in purely electronic sound. This was followed by other tape compositions: *Struktur 8* (1953), *Glockenspiel* (1953), *Etüde über Tongemische* (1953-4), Five Pieces (1955), *Zu Ehren von Igor Stravinsky* (1957), *Selektion 1* (1959-60), *Epitaph für Aikichi Kuboyama* (1958-62) and 6 Studies (1962). With Stockhausen he also edited *Die* REIHE. From 1965 to 1971 he taught electronic music at the Cologne Hochschule für Musik. [Wergo]

Einem, Gottfried von (1918-) Austrian composer. Worked as coach at the Berlin Staatsoper and at Bayreuth before studying composition with Blacher (1941-3), who influenced him deeply and wrote 4 librettos for him. His first 2 operas, though, were in an Expressionist style nearer Berg and early Hindemith; only in the comedy *Der Zerrissene* did a more playful, diatonic style emerge. Later works show a command of various inheritances from the 1920s (from Stravinsky to Schoenberg) at the service of genre or, in the stage pieces, dramatic effect.

Operas: Dantons Tod, ★Salzburg, 1947; Der Prozess, ★Salzburg, 1953; Der Zerrissene, ★Hamburg, 1964; Der Besuch der alten Dame, ★Vienna, 1971; Kabale und Liebe, ★Vienna, 1976; Jesu Hochzeit, ★Vienna, 1980

Ballets, orch and vocal orch works, songs, few chamber pieces

[UE, Schott, Boosey]

Eisler, Hanns (1898-1962) German composer. Studied at the New Vienna Conservatory and privately with Schoenberg (1919-23), who influenced such early works as *Palmström* for PIERROT LUNAIRE ensemble without piano (1924). But in 1926 his political activism led him to the Communist Party and he became critical of Schoenberg and of his own early music. He turned to writing political songs in a diatonic style, though without obliterating all trace of his erstwhile modernism; he was now in Berlin, where in 1925 he had taken an appointment at the Klindworth-Scharwenka Conservatory. In 1930 he met Brecht and started a long collaboration with the Lehrstück *Die*

Massnahme. He spent most of the Hitler period in the USA, latterly in Los Angeles teaching at USC and writing FILM MUSIC, until in 1947 he was brought before McCarthy's committee. In 1948 he returned to Vienna and in 1950 to Berlin, where he taught at the German Academy and the Hochschule für Musik. He produced numerous songs, incidental music and film scores, following his belief that music in a socialist country must be objective and generally useful, but he met official objection when he tried to be more ambitious: his 3-act libretto *Johann Faustus* was published but not composed.

Brecht settings: Die Massnahme (Lehrstück), solo vv, chorus, orch, 1930; Die Mutter (play/cantata), solo vv, chorus, orch, 1931; Kuhle Wampe (film), 1931; Rote Revue (play), 1932; Die Rundköpfe und die Spitzköpfe (play), 1934-6; Deutsche Sinfonie, solo vv, chorus, orch, 1936-9; Hangmen also Die (film), 1942; Furcht und Elend des dritten Reiches (play), 1945; Galileo Galilei (play), 1947; Tage der Kommune (play), 1950; Herr Puntila und sein Knecht Matti (film), 1956; Die Gesichte der Simone Machard (play), 1957; Die Teppichweber von Kujan-Baluk (cantata), S, orch, 1957; Schweyk im zweiten Weltkrieg (play), 1943-59; numerous independent songs

Chamber music: Palmström, reciter, 4 insts, 1924; Str Qt, 1938; Nonet no.1, 1939, no.2, 1941; Septet no.1, 1940, no.2, 1947; 14 Arten, den Regen zu beschreiben, 5 insts, 1940

Enormous output of songs and music for the theatre and cinema

[Breitkopf, Deutscher Verlag für Musik, UE]

□ M. Grabs, ed., *Hanns Eisler: A Rebel in Music* (selected writings of Eisler) (1978); A. Betz, *Hanns Eisler Political Musician* (1982).

electric guitar Instrument manufactured from 1936-7 and used in Stockhausen's *Gruppen*, Boulez's *Domaines* and Buller's *Proença*, for example.

electrochord Instrument invented by Peter Eötvös for performances with Stockhausen's ensemble (1968-72): it consisted of a 15-string Hungarian peasant zither whose sounds could be altered by a VCS-3 synthesizer. 'Electrochord' is also the name of a manufactured electric keyboard instrument.

electronic (electric) instruments Those specially built for music include the ONDES MARTENOT, the SPHAEROPHON, the THEREMIN and the TRAUTONIUM, as well as adaptations of existing instruments, such as the ELECTRIC GUITAR and ELECTRONIC ORGAN.

There are also ad hoc arrangements such as the ELECTROCHORD and ELECTRONIUM, or natural instruments joined to electronic equipment (e.g. the 'electric viola' played by Johannes G. Fritsch in Stockhausen's ensemble, 1967-70).

electronic music Music whose playing requires electronic means. Often the term is restricted to music on tape, the rest being LIVE ELECTRONIC MUSIC or music for ELECTRONIC INSTRUMENTS: another usage would confine it to tape music created without natural sounds (STOCKHAUSEN and EIMERT used the term 'Elektronische Musik' in the early 1950s to distinguish their work from MUSIQUE CONCRÈTE).

The 200-ton telharmonium, exhibited by Thaddeus Cahill in Holyoke, Massachusetts, in 1906, is usually counted the ancestor of electronic music, since it was the first instrument to make music by electrical means, but viable electronic instruments did not arrive until the 1930s. SCHAEFFER'S *musique concrète* followed in 1948, at first using disc techniques, and then the arrival of the commercial tape recorder around 1950 made possible the creation of electronically generated sound: this seems to have been first achieved by Stockhausen and Eimert at the studios of WESTDEUTSCHER RUNDFUNK in 1952-3. Similar studios were founded in Paris (GROUPE DE RECHERCHES MUSICALES), New York (COLUMBIA-PRINCETON ELECTRONIC MUSIC CENTER), Milan, London, Toronto and many other cities during the next decade, and important works were created by BERIO, BABBITT, LUENING, USSACHEVSKY, VARÈSE and others.

However, studio techniques for electronic composition were tedious, and some composers shared Boulez's aesthetic bafflement with a world where, notionally, anything was possible, but where in practice the results seemed rather meagre and predictable. The arrival of the SYNTHESIZER in the mid-1960s provided composers with machines made for the creation of music, instead of the test equipment that had been used earlier, and at the same time the development of compositional programs for COMPUTERS made it easier and quicker to control sound generation, as well as store information about the parameters of individual sounds and musical structures. Sophisticated facilities for computer composition became available at the Universities of Stanford, Princeton and Columbia, and in Europe at the INSTITUT DE RECHERCHE ET DE COORDINATION ACOUSTIQUE/MUSIQUE. In the mid-1980s digital equipment for sound synthesis began to be marketed, bringing electronic music within the range of the composer working privately.

□ H. Davies, ed., *International Electronic Music Catalog* (1968); J. Appleton and R. Perera, ed., *The Development and Practice of Electronic Music* (1975); P. Griffiths, *A Guide to Electronic Music* (1979); P. Manning, *Electronic and Computer Music* (1985)

electronic organ Instrument manufactured from 1935 by Laurens Hammond, from 1946 by the Wurlitzer Company and from the 1960s by Yamaha. There are 2 electronic organs in Stockhausen's *Momente* and one in his *Mikrophonie II*.

electronium Instrument invented by Harald Bojé for performances with Stockhausen's ensemble (1967-72): it was a synthesizer controlled by a keyboard or potentiometer.

Elegy for Young Lovers Opera by Henze, Auden and Kallman on an invented story of counterpointed obsessions among 6 characters in an Austrian mountain resort. ★Schwetzingen, 20 May 1961.

Elektra Opera by Strauss and Hofmannsthal, their first collaboration: the Classical myth of revenge is set to Strauss's most strained and discordant score. ★Dresden, 25 Jan 1909.

Elgar, Edward (1857-1934) English composer. One of the last great exponents of the diatonic symphonic tradition, he effected, like Schoenberg at the same time, a powerful synthesis of Brahmsian developing form with Wagnerian enriched harmony, the difference being that he was conservative in his inclinations: his major works are symphonies, concertos and oratorios that look back as far as Mendelssohn and Schumann for models.

His musical education took place largely in his father's music shop in Worcester, enabling him from his late teens to find local work as a teacher, conductor and instrumentalist. In 1889 he married and moved to London, but expected opportunities did not arrive, and in 1891 the Elgars returned to the Midlands. During the next few years he began to make a name as a composer of cantatas for choral societies, but the real breakthrough came in 1899 with the *Enigma* Variations. He then returned to choral music with his setting of Newman's *The Dream of Gerontius*, a defiantly Catholic work (he had been born a Roman Catholic, but did not regularly practise his religion), followed by the first 2 parts of a never completed trilogy of oratorios. Most of his large instrumental works date from the next dozen years, 1907-19: he wrote very little after his wife's death in 1920.

Of his orchestral works, *Falstaff* is his masterpiece of instrumentation and rivals Strauss as a character study created by thematic metamorphosis, but he preferred the standard forms, even if his means of achieving them were new. Like Tchaikovsky, he interpreted the dynamism of sonata form as a searching after some ideal, which may be presented at the outset in straightforward diatonicism (Symphony no.1), to be succeeded by music of more restless character: themes often begin with wide upward leaps, rarely return to an accented tonic, and move in accented rhythmic figures within the metre of a march or dance. The speed and nature of his harmony are Wagnerian, but the music is always strongly tied to thematic symphonic working.

Oratorios: The Dream of Gerontius, 1899-1900; The Apostles, 1902-3; The Kingdom, 1901-6

Orchestral: Froissart, overture, 1890; Serenade, e, str, 1892; 'Enigma' Variations, 1899; Cockaigne, overture, 1900-01; In the South, overture, 1903-4; Introduction and Allegro, str, 1904-5; The Wand of Youth, 2 suites, 1907-8; Sym no.1, A♭, 1907-8; Vn Conc, b, 1909-10; Sym no.2, E♭, 1909-11; Falstaff, 1913; The Sanguine Fan (ballet), 1917; Vc Conc, e, 1919

Chamber: Sonata, e, vn, pf, 1918; Str Qt, e, 1918; Pf Qnt, a, 1918-19

Many other choral and orch works, songs, instrumental pieces

[Novello]

□ J. N. Moore, *Edward Elgar: A Creative Life* (1984)

Eloy, Jean-Claude (1938-) French composer, Studied with Milhaud at the Paris Conservatoire (1950-61), with Scherchen and Pousseur at Darmstadt (1957), and with Boulez at the Basle Academy (1961-2). His *Equivalences* for wind and percussion (1963) shows him an inventive and purposeful pupil of the last, and he has retained a Boulezian exactness of sonority and gesture even in those later works whose slowness, as in *Kamakala* for 3 choral-orchestral groups (1971), is one outward sign of an immersion in oriental cultures. [Heugel, UE; Everest]

Emmanuel, Maurice (1862-1938) French composer and teacher. Studied at the Paris Conservatoire with Bourgault-Ducoudray, who prompted his interest in Greek modality, and with Delibes, who disapproved. He used modes from his Phrygian Cello Sonata (1887) onwards, sometimes in folksong arrangements (*30 chansons bourguignonnes*, 1913) or Aeschylean operas (*Prométhée enchaîné*, 1916-18; *Salamine*, 1921-8), and also interested himself in Greek rhythm. Messiaen was among his pupils at the Conservatoire (1909-36).

Enescu, George (Enesco, Georges; 1881-1955) Romanian composer and violinist. Studied in Vienna and with Massenet and Fauré at the Paris Conservatoire (1895-9). Thereafter he divided his time between Paris, where his career as a performer was centred, and Bucharest, where he encouraged younger composers. His own music is in a late Romantic style coloured by Romanian folk music, especially in the *2 rhapsodies roumaines* for orchestra (1901). Other works include the opera *Oedipe* (1921-31, ★Paris, 1936), 5 symphonies and chamber music. [Enoch, Salabert; Electrecord]

Enfant et les sortilèges, L' (The Child and the Enchantments) Opera by Ravel and Colette in which a naughty boy is alarmed by household objects that come to life and animals that talk, both providing opportunities for exquisite musical fantasy. ★Monte Carlo, 21 Mar 1925.

Ensemble InterContemporain Chamber orchestra founded at the Institut de Recherche et de Coordination Acoustique/Musique in 1976, conducted by Boulez and Peter Eötvös, and specializing in 20th c. music. They have given the premières of works by Boulez, Birtwistle, etc, and recorded for DG and Erato.

envelope The shape of the change in a sound's amplitude over time. It is an important determinant of sound quality, and therefore of interest to composers of electronic music.

epic theatre Concept introduced by Piscator and developed by Brecht to signify the kind of drama he was practising: not self-sufficient but distinctly to be observed as a parable, offered objectively by its authors, whose aim should be more to intensify their dramatic statement than to offer some interpretation of it; stylistic unity was therefore a low priority, even counterproductive. Epic opera was the musical department, first essayed in Brecht and Weill's MAHAGONNY and THREEPENNY OPERA.

Epifanie (Epiphanies) Work by Berio for female voice and orchestra, using different texts (by Proust, Machado, Joyce, Sanguineti, Simon and

Brecht) in a mobile form of different ways of setting words to music.

Erwartung (Awaiting) Schoenberg's 'monodrama', or opera for 1 singer, with a libretto by Marie Pappenheim charting the emotions of a woman seeking her dead or departed lover in a forest. The music responds to the changing situation without much obvious linkage of theme, harmony or instrumentation: it is a key work of atonality. ★Prague, 6 Jun 1924.

Etudes Volume of 12 piano pieces by Debussy which run beyond didactic intention to explore, in miniature, whole musical worlds. They are 1. 'Pour les cinq doigts', 2. 'Pour les tierces', 3. 'Pour les quartes', 4. 'Pour les sixtes', 5. 'Pour les octaves', 6. 'Pour les huit doigts', 7. 'Pour les degrés chromatiques', 8. 'Pour les agréments', 9. 'Pour les notes répétées', 10. 'Pour les sonorités opposées', 11. 'Pour les arpèges composés', 12. 'Pour les accords'. ★Walter Morse Rummel, 14 Dec 1916.

experimental music Any work of art is an experiment in thought, but the term 'experimental' is normally used of music which departs significantly from the expectations of style, form and genre enshrined in tradition – except in the experimental tradition. Some writers, particularly in the late 1960s and early 1970s when experimental music was at its height, drew a useful distinction between the avant garde, working within the tradition and within accepted channels of communication (opera houses, orchestral concerts, universities, broadcasting corporations, record companies), and experimental composers, who preferred to work in other ways. The great prototype is unavoidably Ives, who worked as an iconoclast and took no care for furthering his music, though Satie's naivety too makes him a major progenitor. Other composers whose work has often been considered experimental include Cowell, Cage, Brant and Cardew, and indeed experimental work has been much more a feature of American and English music than of mainland European.
□ M. Nyman, *Experimental Music* (1974)

Expressionism Quality of art which expresses extreme, intense and immediate emotion. The term was first applied to the paintings of Kandinsky, Nolde and others in 1910-11, and then quickly spread to the discussion of the music of Schoenberg and his pupils, as was perhaps inevitable when Schoenberg was so much associated with Kandinsky and other 'Blaue Reiter' painters. The assumption is that Expressionism results from the urge to give voice to some innermost reality, often identified with the Freudian unconscious. Fiercely personal, therefore, it inevitably involves the rejection as far as possible of extra-personal aspects (traditional forms and techniques): hence the ready equation of atonality with Expressionism – an equation that Schoenberg did not dismiss. The term is, indeed, normally used in connection with Schoenberg's atonal, pre-serial music (ERWARTUNG, PIERROT LUNAIRE, etc), with works that point towards a similar departure from the norms (ELEKTRA, some Mahler) and with works that look back to the Schoenbergian examples (by Davies, Henze and others).

F

Falla, Manuel de (1876-1946) Spanish composer. Studied as a pianist at the Madrid Conservatory, wrote 5 zarzuelas (Spanish light operas, 1901-3) and took composition lessons with Pedrell (1902-5). In 1907 he left for Paris, where he enjoyed fruitful contacts with Debussy, Ravel, Dukas and Albéniz: all had their influences on him, though most important was Pedrell's teaching about the value of folk music. He used the passionate song of Andalusia, the *cante jondo*, in his ballet *El amor brujo* (Love the Magician), and piano concerto *Noches en los jardines de España* (Nights in the Gardens of Spain), and again in his ballet for Dyagilev *El sombrero de tres picos* (The Three-Cornered Hat), other aspects of style coming from the colourful orchestral styles of Debussy, Ravel and Stravinsky. In 1919 he settled in Granada, though his links with Paris remained strong. Following Stravinsky, most notably, he moved away from his earlier flamboyance to music of smaller scale and sparer harmony; he also, in his Harpsichord Concerto, inspected features of Spanish Renaissance and Baroque music. In 1939 he moved to Buenos Aires, where he continued to work on the choral orchestral *Atlántida* that occupied him for 2 decades and remained unfinished.
Stage: La vida breve (opera), 1904-5, ★Nice, 1913; El amor brujo (ballet), 1914-15, ★Madrid, 1915; El

sombrero de tres picos (ballet), 1918–19, *London, 1919; El retablo de maese Pedro (puppet opera), 1919–22, *Paris, 1923; Atlántida (scenic cantata), 1926–46, unfinished, completed by E. Halffter, *Milan, 1962
Orchestral: Noches en los jardines de España, pf, orch, 1911–15; Homenajes, 1920–39
Vocal: 3 mélodies, v, pf, 1909; 7 canciones populares españolas, v, pf, 1914–15; Psyché, v, fl, harp, str trio, 1924; Soneto a Cordoba, v, harp/pf, 1927
Chamber and instrumental: Pièces espagnoles, pf, 1902–8; Fantasia bética, pf, 1919; Le tombeau de Claude Debussy, gui, 1920; Conc, hpd/pf, 5 insts, 1923–6; Pour le tombeau de Paul Dukas, pf, 1935 [Chester, Eschig, Ricordi]
□ R. Crichton, *Manuel de Falla: Descriptive Catalogue of his Works* (1976)

Fanciulla del West, La (The Girl of the Golden West) Opera by Puccini, Civinini and Zangarini after cowboy play by Belasco. *New York, 10 Dec 1910.

Fano, Michel (1929–) French composer. Studied with Boulanger and Messiaen at the Paris Conservatoire (1948–53). In 1950 he met Boulez and shared in the adventure of TOTAL SERIALISM, his Sonata for 2 pianos (1952) being important to the background of *Structures*. In 1954 he abandoned abstract composition to work in films.

Fate (Osud) Opera by Janáček concerning a composer's ill-fated marriage and the opera that comes out of it: the self-reflection points to the work's partly autobiographical genesis. *Brno Radio, 18 Sep 1934.

Fauré, Gabriel (1845–1924) French composer. Studied at the Ecole Niedermeyer in Paris with Saint-Saëns, who became a lifelong friend. He worked as an organist and choirmaster, and later as a professor of composition at the Paris Conservatoire (1896–1920), where his pupils included Ravel, Schmitt, Koechlin and Boulanger. By the start of the 20th c. he was well established as a master of French song and of the piano miniature; his works in the new century include his restrained, lyrical opera *Pénélope* and a group of late pieces in which his music became more rarefied in harmony and texture. Only 20th c. works noted below.
Opera: Pénélope, 1907–13, *Monte Carlo, 1913
Song cycles: La chanson d'Eve, 1906–10; Le jardin clos, 1914; Mirages, 1919; L'horizon chimérique, 1921

Chamber: Pf Qnt no.1, d, 1887–1905, no.2, c, 1919–21; Vn Sonata no.2, e, 1916–17; Vc Sonata no.1, d, 1917, no.2, g, 1921; Pf Trio, d, 1922–3; Str Qt, e, 1923–4
Piano: Barcarolle no.7, d, 1905, no.8, D♭, 1906, no.9, a, 1909, no.10, a, 1913, no.11, g, 1913, no.12, E♭, 1915, no.13, C, 1921; Impromptu, no.4, D♭, 1905–6, no.5, f♯, 1909; Nocturne no.9, b, 1908, no.10, e, 1908, no.11, f♯, 1913, no.12, e, 1915, no.13, b, 1921; 9 Preludes, 1909–10
□ R. Orledge, *Gabriel Fauré* (1979); J.M. Nectoux, ed., *Gabriel Fauré: his Life through his Letters* (1984)

Feldman, Morton (1926–) American composer. Studied with Riegger and Wolpe, and in 1950 met Cage. For the next few years he was associated with Cage's circle and with painters working in New York at the time, and it was to the painters he owed his concept of music as a colouring of time with strands of different pigment: his music is typically slow and quiet, operating with sounds of imperceptible attack and long duration. In the *Projection* series (1950–51) he made this spatial character plain by notating the music as a simple graph (*see* GRAPHIC NOTATION). Later works return more or less to conventional notation, but the nature of the music does not change, which makes it difficult to distinguish outstanding compositions. Representative ones, though, might include *The King of Denmark* for percussion (1964), the 4 *The Viola in my Life* pieces for viola with other instruments (1970–71) and the 4-hour String Quartet no.2 (1983). [Peters, UE; CRI]

Felciano, Richard (1930–) American composer. Studied with Milhaud at Mills College and the Paris Conservatoire, and with Dallapiccola in Florence, since when he has taught at Lone Mountain College and Berkeley. His large output includes many works with tape or other electronic adjuncts.

Ferne Klang, Der (The Distant Sound) Opera by Schreker to his own libretto concerning a woman's decline into prostitution. Berg made the vocal score, and perhaps learned something in the handling of large operatic resources and the expression of the erotic. *Frankfurt, 18 Aug 1912.

Ferneyhough, Brian (1943–) English composer. Studied at the Royal Academy of Music, in Holland with Ton de Leeuw (1968–9) and in Basle with Huber (1969–71). In 1973 he began teaching at the Musikhochschule in Freiburg; he has also taught regularly at Darmstadt. His first works were stimulated by Boulez's TOTAL SERIALISM, and all his music is exceedingly complex in its notation, the intention being to encourage a desperate virtuosity in performance. His interest in the limits of the feasible has also led him to explore areas of arcane thought.

Orchestral: Epicycle, 20 str, 1968; Firecycle Beta, 1969-71; La terre est un homme, 1976-9; Carceri d'invenzione I, 16 insts, 1982, II, fl, chamber orch, 1984

Vocal: Missa brevis, 12 vv, 1969; Time and Motion Study III, 16 vv, perc, electronics, 1974; Transit, 6 vv, chamber orch, electronics, 1972-5; Etudes transcendantales, v, fl, ob, vc, hpd, 1984

Chamber: Sonatina, 3 cl, bn, 1963; 4 Miniatures, fl, pf, 1965; Coloratura, ob, pf, 1966; Prometheus, 6 wind, 1967; Sonatas, str qt, 1967; Funérailles I-II, 7 str, harp, 1969-80; Str Qt no.2, 1980; Adagissimo, str qt, 1983

Piano: Epigrams, 1966; Sonata, 2 pf, 1966; 3 Pieces, 1966-7; Lemma-Icon-Epigram, 1981

Other instrumental: Cassandra's Dream Song, fl, 1970; Sieben Sterne, org, 1970; Unity Capsule, fl, 1975-6; Time and Motion Study I, b cl, 1971-7; Time and Motion Study II, vc, 1973-6; Superscriptio, pic, 1981; Kurze Schatten II, gui, 1985 [Peters; RCA, Decca]

festival A striking feature of European musical life, particularly since the second world war, has been the importance of festivals in promoting new music. Those which have been most active include the ALDEBURGH, CHELTENHAM, DONAUESCHINGEN, HOLLAND, HUDDERSFIELD, LA ROCHELLE, METZ, MUSICA NOVA, MUSICA VIVA, ROYAN, WARSAW AUTUMN and ZAGREB festivals; *see also* EDINBURGH FESTIVAL and SALZBURG. Often the paying audience at festivals of contemporary music is modest, but the attendance of publishers, radio administrators and critics makes them significant occasions in determining what contemporary music shall receive publicity and dissemination.

Fibonacci series Sequence of numbers in which each is the sum of the preceding pair: . . . 2, 3, 5, 8, 13, 21, . . . Neighbouring pairs approximate ever more closely to the GOLDEN SECTION, which may be why the series was used by Corbusier in his 'modulor' system. That was probably the source for Stockhausen's use of Fibonacci numbers in the temporal proportioning of his *Klavierstück XI* (1956) and many later works.

Fiery Angel, The (Ognennïy angel) Opera by Prokofiev to his own libretto after Bryusov's novel of religious obsession, passionate love and madness. It occupied him for nearly a decade but was never staged during his lifetime; he drew material from it for his Third Symphony. *Paris, 25 Nov 1954 (concert), Venice, 14 Sep 1955 (staged)

film music Silent films were commonly accompanied by a pianist or small orchestra, but the music they played was either improvised or taken from popular classics and light music. This was inevitable: a special score would have had to be distributed with the film and rehearsed by each cinema's musicians for a short run. Some, nevertheless, were composed. Saint-Saëns' score for Lavedan's *L'assassinat du Duc de Guise* (1908) would seem to have been the first; other notable scores included Strauss's unbelievable bowdlerization of *Der Rosenkavalier* for cinema band (1924), Edmund Meisel's up-to-date music for Eisenstein's *Battleship Potemkin* (1925) and Honegger's accompaniment for Gance's *Napoléon* (1927).

The arrival of film soundtrack in the late 1920s immediately made such ventures more viable, and by the mid-1930s it was well established that feature films needed some or even continuous musical accompaniment (films entirely without music remain extraordinarily rare). Typically music is required for the opening titles (often being based here on a 'title theme') and for sequences where musical rhythm can support regular motion (moving trains, galloping horses, speeding cars, etc) or where musical expression can intensify the emotional character. These criteria have tended to keep film music within the stylistic ambit of late Romanticism, whether the subject be Robin Hood or intergalactic warfare, though there have been exceptions where the action has been so bizarre as to justify some musical venturesomeness (Herrmann's score for *Psycho* and Davies's for *The Devils* (1970); possibilities of this sort were also discerned by Schreker and Schoenberg in their music for imaginary films). The absurdity of lavish orchestral music being fitted to all manner of cinematic scenes has been pointed out by Randall, who instead used computer synthesis in making music for *Eakins* (1972); but the absurdity is no grander than opera's. Obviously there is a special case when music is justified by the nature of the film, as it is in filmed musicals or in biographies of real or imagined composers (e.g. the *Warsaw Concerto* written by Richard Addinsell for the hero of *Dangerous Moonlight* (1941) to thump out). Otherwise the effectiveness of film music, and certainly the success of the visual–aural blend, must be measured by the degree to which the music is not heard as such.

This would seem to make film music a rather limited genre, even without the practical limitations of composing to a given plan of time-lengths, tempos and moods. Nevertheless, it has engaged the interest of recognized composers as well as specialists. Among the former must count Auric (Cocteau films, 1930-49), Richard Rodney Bennett, Bernstein (*On the Waterfront*, 1954), Bliss (*Things to come*, 1934-5), Copland, Davies, Honegger, Prokofiev (*Alexander Nevsky*, 1938; *Ivan the Terrible*, 1942-4), Shostakovich and Walton (*Henry V*, 1944; *Hamlet*, 1947; *Richard III*, 1955); Stravinsky showed interest, but all his intended film music had to be diverted into concert works. Specialist composers of film music have included Bernard Herrmann (*Citizen Kane*, 1940; *The Magnificent Ambersons*, 1942; *Psycho*, 1959; *Fahrenheit 451*, 1966), Maurice Jarre (*Dr Zhivago*, 1965), Erich Wolfgang Korngold (*The Adventures of Robin Hood*, 1937), Michel Legrand (*Les parapluies de Cherbourg*, 1964), Miklós Rózsa (*The Thief of Bagdad*, 1940), Dimitri Tiomkin (*The Guns of Navarone*, 1961) and John Williams (*Star Wars* series). There have also been notable uses of pre-existing music in films, notably of Bach, Beethoven, Dukas, Stravinsky and others in Disney's *Fantasia* (1940) and of Richard Strauss, Johann Strauss II, Khachaturian and Ligeti in Kubrick's *2001* (1968). The opposite case of music composed for a pre-existing film is exemplified by Carl Davis's score for Gance's *Napoléon*.

Film soundtrack has been used as a creative medium analogous to magnetic tape: one simply draws on designs. The results are not altogether predictable, but the technique has been used by Norman MacLaren and the Whitney brothers.
□ H. Eisler and T. W. Adorno, *Composing for the Films* (1947, 2/1971); I. Bazelon, *Knowing the Score* (1975); K. Gough-Yates and M. Tarratt, *The Film Music Book* (1978)

Fine, Irving (1914-62) American composer. Studied at Harvard with Piston (1933-8) and in Paris with Boulanger, then taught at Harvard (1939-50) and Brandeis. He wrote in a lean, elegant, Stravinskian style, adopting 12-note techniques in 1952. His modest output includes a Symphony (1960-62) but otherwise consists mostly of smaller works: songs, choral pieces and chamber music.

Fine, Vivian (1913-) American composer. Studied with Crawford at the American Conservatory in Chicago (1925-31) and with Sessions in New York (1934-42), then worked as a teacher, notably at Bennington College (from 1964). Her earliest works, including the 4 Songs for voice and strings (1933, New Music Edition), were strenuously dissonant and contrapuntal, but in New York she fell more under the influence of Copland; later works include the opera *The Women in the Garden* (★San Francisco, 1978).

Finney, Ross Lee (1906-) American composer. Studied with Boulanger in Paris (1927-8), with Sessions at Harvard (1928-9) and with Berg in Vienna (1931-2), and taught at the University of Michigan (1949-74). His music exhibits strong rhythmic propulsion and a passion for dialectic, together with techniques of hexachordal composition from the 1950s. A large output includes symphonies and concertos, large-scale choral works, 8 quartets and much other chamber music. [Peters, New Valley]

Finnissy, Michael (1946-) English composer. Studied with Stevens and Searle at the Royal College of Music, and with Vlad in Italy. His large output includes music theatre pieces, much else for ensembles of voices and instruments, and a great deal of piano music conceived for his own hectic virtuosity. [UE, United]

Finzi, Gerald (1901-56) English composer. Studied with Bairstow in York (1917-22) and R.O. Morris in London (1925), where he taught at the Royal Academy of Music (1930-33) before retiring with his wife to the country. His music too was pastoral, meandering in the region of Vaughan Williams and best when quietly fastened to the poetry of Hardy in particular.
Orchestral: Dies natalis, S/T, str, 1926-39; Intimations of Immortality, T, chorus, orch, 1936-50; Conc, cl, str, 1948-9
Hardy song cycles: A Young Man's Exhortation, 1926-9; Earth and Air and Rain, 1928-32; Before and After Summer, 1938-49; Till Earth Outwears, 1927-56; I said to love, 1928-56
[Boosey; Lyrita]

Firebird, The (Zhar'-Ptitsa, L'oiseau de feu) Ballet by Stravinsky, choreography originally by Fokine: the magical Firebird helps Prince Ivan save his princess from a wizard monster. The score shows Stravinsky still influenced by Rimsky-Korsakov in his orchestral sumptuousness, folksong themes (for Prince Ivan) and chromatic glitter (for the Firebird), but there are signs too of Skryabin. ★Ballets Russes, Paris, 25 Jun 1910. Stravinsky made a suite in 1911, another in 1919 for a reduced orchestra, and again another in 1945 for the same ensemble, continuously refining but also moderating the flamboyance of the original.

Fires of London Ensemble based on the personnel of *Pierrot lunaire* plus percussionist, originally founded in 1967 by Davies and Birtwistle as the Pierrot Players, and then reformed in 1970 as the Fires of London with Davies as sole musical director. They have been closely associated with Davies's works, of which over 50 have been conceived for them, but they have also had pieces written for them by Carter (Triple Duo), Henze and many younger British composers; they have recorded for Decca, Nonesuch and Unicorn. Over the years the membership has changed many times, but the group has maintained its character of brilliant virtuosity and searching expressiveness.

flexatone Instrument similar to the musical saw introduced in the first half of the 1920s as a jazz novelty, but adopted into the orchestra by Honegger (*Antigone*) and Schoenberg (Variations, *Von heute auf morgen*, *Moses und Aron*). Khachaturian's Piano Concerto had a flexatone solo in the original version; the instrument also occurs in the orchestra of Henze, Penderecki and Davies.

Flood, The 'Musical play' by Stravinsky for television, with words from Genesis and English miracle plays, relating the Noah story in dance, sung and spoken drama, and spoken narrative. ★CBS TV, 14 Jun 1962.

Floyd, Carlisle (1926-) American composer. Studied with Ernest Bacon at Syracuse University (1945-9) and started teaching at Florida State University in 1947. His opera *Susannah* (★Tallahasee, 1955), telling the Biblical story in a Tennessee context and with a smooth folksong lyricism, won great success. Later operas include *Wuthering Heights* (★Sante Fe, 1958), *Of Mice and Men* (★Seattle, 1970), *Bilby's Doll* (★Houston, 1976) and *Willie Stark* (★Houston, 1981). [Boosey]

flugelhorn Bugle-type instrument found in brass and military bands, and in some orchestral scores, e.g. Stravinsky's *Threni* and Vaughan Williams's Ninth Symphony.

flute An important repertory for the unaccompanied instrument was initiated by Debussy's *Syrinx*, followed by works by Varèse, Berio, Ferneyhough and others, these adding percussive key-taps and sometimes BARTOLOZZI sounds to the flute's range. Works with piano have appeared from Boulez, Henze, Hindemith, Poulenc and Prokofiev, concertos from Nielsen and Ligeti (Double Concerto with oboe). The alto flute is common in 20th c. orchestral works (e.g. Ravel's *Daphnis et Chloé*) and ensemble pieces (e.g. *Le marteau sans maître*). Holst uses the term 'bass flute' for alto flute in *The Planets*: a real bass flute is required in Zimmermann's *Tempus loquendi* and Ligeti's Double Concerto.

Fluxus Movement active in New York (1960-65), presenting concerts of experimental events of a musical–theatrical and often humorous–earnest nature. An example might be George Brecht's *Drip Music (Drip Event)*, which instructs simply that: 'A source of dripping water and an empty vessel are arranged so that the water falls into the vessel.' Brecht took a leading part in the movement; others associated with it included Young and (briefly) Ligeti.

Foerster, Josef Bohuslav (1859-1951) Czech composer. Studied at the Prague Organ School (1879-82), moving with his singer wife to Hamburg (1893), where he met Mahler. In 1903 they followed Mahler to Vienna, and then in 1918 returned to Prague, where he taught composition. He himself composed abundantly in an eminently Czech style: he produced almost 200 works with opus numbers, including 6 operas, 5 symphonies, much choral music, songs and chamber pieces.

folk music A subject of study and creative stimulus for a large number of composers in the 20th c., notably Stravinsky, Bartók, Kodály, Copland, Vaughan Williams, Falla, Skalkottas, Stockhausen and Berio. The reasons have been basically 3: an awareness that folk music was dying out, an intuition that its modal and other characteristics might help in imagining new kinds of music, and a desire to create a national style. The first and third of these might seem mutually opposed, since something moribund is unlikely to foster something new. However, since most folk music is song, an intimate connection exists between a country's folk music and its language: for instance, the common first-syllable stress of the Magyar language is honoured in the short falling phrases that are frequent in Hungarian folksong. A folksong-based style, therefore, might be able to retain features that identify its national origin as surely as those of a spoken language. That, certainly, was the aim and the achievement of most of the composers mentioned above. However, Bartók for one was opposed to a narrow nationalism and extended his research to the music of other countries. Berio and Stockhausen have interested themselves in music from all over the world, and particular non-European traditions, of art as well as folk music, have given suggestions to a great many composers (*see* AFRICAN MUSIC, CHINESE MUSIC, INDIAN MUSIC, INDONESIAN MUSIC, JAPANESE MUSIC).

Bartók usefully distinguished 3 ways in which a composer might treat folk music: first, in simple arrangement, whether to fit it for the concert hall, school or drawing room; second, as material for imitation; and third, as subject for analysis, the results then to be used in the composition of entirely original works (such as his own Third Quartet, wholly unfolksy but imbued with motivic, rhythmic, timbral and variational ideas that sprang from his work on folk music). One might add to these a fourth – the use of folk themes in large-scale forms (e.g. Kodály's 'Peacock' Variations) – and a fifth arising after Bartók's time – the interpolation of folk music directly into composed music through recordings (e.g. Stockhausen's *Telemusik*). Arrangement obviously serves the function of conservation, extended in Stockhausen's *Herbstmusik* to the conservation of rural activities. Analysis has made possible not only the modal languages of Bartók and Vaughan Williams but also the survey of vocal styles and musical-poetic fusions in Berio's *Coro*.

form Large-scale musical forms became possible only with the arrival of the diatonic system; their achievement in non-diatonic music has been a matter of confusion and controversy. This is not surprising. The diatonic system provided 2 persuasive criteria of form: a limited range of possibilities, and a network of relationships among those possibilities. So persuasive have these criteria proved that many composers have sought to retain them in non-diatonic music – quite apart from the great number who have continued to work with the diatonic system and the kinds of form natural to it.

Schoenberg most powerfully exemplifies formal conservatism, in his serial as well as his diatonic works. It even seems clear that the formal imperative was a primary incentive towards his development of serialism: 'one uses the series and then one composes as before'. By contrast with the atonality of 1908-9, serialism limited the possibilities, and COMBINATORIALITY opened up the networks. Schoenberg could thus compose sonata forms, variations, ternary dance movements, etc 'as before', and his example has been widely followed, both by composers who have shared his sense of the inevitability of the traditional ways of making musical forms (e.g. Davies) and by composers who have abstracted his methods to different ends (e.g. Babbitt).

If the old patterns are not to be taken as guiding form, there are essentially 4 alternatives. First, the dynamic of diatonic music can be obtained in other ways, towards other goals through other forms. Or consistent goal-direction can be abandoned: the form can then be a continuum, or else a kaleidoscope of different objects which may most usually generate a sense of form by symmetry and repetition. Finally, the composer may give no thought to form at all, or give his thought only to avoiding the internal consistency and completeness that a sensation of form normally implies.

Goal-directed forms without diatonic harmony have normally been executed in 1 of 2 ways: either by setting up some process or else by obtaining forward motion through rhythmic pulsation (hence, perhaps, the favouring of toccata by composers otherwise as different as Hindemith and Boulez). Process forms include several examples in Bartók (e.g. the canonic entries in the first movement of the Music for Strings, Percussion and Celesta, each a 5th displaced from the last), various kinds thrown up by 12-note composition (e.g. Babbitt's gradual unfolding of a 12-note set in his Second Quartet) and many instances of stepwise alteration in ostinato patterns (e.g. in early Cage, Reich, Glass, etc).

The ideal of continuum form – where, notionally, all change is formally meaningless within a basic sameness – is perhaps most nearly approached in various works by Ligeti, such as his *Atmosphères*: Ligeti has himself spoken of such compositions as segments from a potential music without beginning or end. Kaleidoscopic form can give the same impression. Here the classic example is Stravinsky's Symphonies of Wind Instruments, which requires a substantial slow coda to bring it to an end. And one may regard Stockhausen's moment form as an extension of this, gaining consistency in most cases from a very individual choice of sounding means (e.g. the solo soprano, chorus, brass, percussion and electronic organs of *Momente*) but proceeding by a concatenation of episodes that is theoretically without beginning or end (though the 1973 version of *Momente* very definitely has both).

If music without dynamism, consistency, process or repetition is to be regarded as formless, then a great deal of 20th c. music has no form. Perhaps such a view is justified with respect to much of Cage, for example, but it seems patently absurd in the face of, say, Boulez's *Pli selon pli*. The difficulty is one of definition. Musical form is normally regarded as something which can be given expression in space, in such formulations of forms as 'exposition-development-recapitulation' or 'ABCBA'. But this is only rarely adequate. There are composers, notably Messiaen, who appear to be thinking in such terms in their construction of kaleidoscopic forms, and in Messiaen's case the spatial metaphor is entirely apt to music that looks to timelessness as its proper domain. Most music, however, is conceived to unfold in time, so that the understanding of form ought to embrace not only what events are placed where but what is happening to them at the time: how they may be affected by context and even by reference to other music. Nevertheless, it seems clear that the 20th c. has been as typified by composers who have avoided describable form (Debussy, Ives, Stockhausen, Boulez) as it has by composers who have revelled in the symmetries and repetitions that bring form decisively to the surface (Bartók, Webern, Messiaen, Reich). *See also* CANON, FUGUE, PALINDROME, SONATA, STRUCTURE, SYMPHONY, TIME.

formalism Pejorative term used by authorities in the USSR to anathematize the music of Shostakovich, Prokofiev and others in the 1930s and 1940s (*see* POLITICS). It had little to do with form: nothing could be more formal than the music that was approved. Instead the implication was intended to be that the offending music was artificial, aware as it was of Stravinsky, Hindemith and Krenek.

formant A characteristic of timbre. The formant of an instrument, or of the mouth cavity readied to produce a vowel sound, is the variation it produces in amplitude over the range of frequencies: regardless of the pitch played or sung, some regions of higher frequencies will be stronger than others. Boulez used the word of the movements of his Third Piano Sonata, perhaps to suggest that these 5 formants are the responses of different imaginary instruments to the same input.

formula Term used by Stockhausen for the melody (or small number of melodies) that provides a composition's basic material. He has used such melodies in all his major works since *Mantra*, as well as in the early *Formel* (Formula).

Fortner, Wolfgang (1907-) German composer. Born and educated in Leipzig, where he grew up in the Bach tradition and studied composition with Grabner at the conservatory. He taught at the Heidelberg Institute of Church Music (1931-54), Darmstadt (from 1946), Detmold (1954-7) and the Freiburg Musikhochschule (1957-72). His early works were in a post-Bachian contrapuntal style influenced by Hindemith and Stravinsky. In 1945 he began to work with 12-note series, and to become more productive, as well as more expansive in his gestures.

Operas: Die Bluthochzeit, 1957; In seinem Garten liebt Don Perlimplin Belisa, chamber opera, 1962; Elisabeth Tudor, 1972
Orch and vocal orch works, chamber music [Schott]

Foss, Lukas (1922-) German-American composer. Studied in Berlin and Paris (1933-7) before the family moved to the USA, where he was a pupil of Thompson at the Curtis Institute and Hindemith at Yale (1939-40). He started out as a neoclassicist, inclining towards the popular manner of Copland in such works as his Sandburg cantata *Prairie* (1944). Then in 1956 he began to improvise with students at UCLA, where he was professor of composition (1951-62): this led to the formation of the Improvisation Chamber Ensemble (1957-62), consisting of clarinet, cello, piano and percussion. For this grouping he wrote *Echoi* (1961-3), an aleatory score followed by others of this sort; *Baroque Variations* for orchestra (1967), in 3 movements based on pieces by Handel, Scarlatti and Bach, is a fantasy of distortion, multiple image and 'composition by deletion' (i.e. composing holes into the originals). He has also worked as a conductor with the Buffalo Philharmonic (1962-70) and Jerusalem Symphony orchestras. [Fischer, Schott, G. Schirmer; Nonesuch]

Foulds, John (1880-1939) English composer. Played the cello in the Hallé orchestra under Richter (1900-11), then moved to London as a teacher and conductor. His enormous *A World Requiem* was sung annually in the Albert Hall from 1923 to 1926 for the dead of the first world war; he then worked in Paris as a cinema pianist, returned to London (1930-35) and finally went to India, where he worked for the radio. He also wrote pieces for Indian instruments, though he had long been influenced by INDIAN MUSIC, as well as by other modalities (even using quarter tones, *see* MICROTONES); within an ample Romantic style. His output was enormous and diverse, but includes at least one outstanding work in his *Quartetto intimo* (1931, Pearl).

☐ M. Macdonald, *John Foulds* (1975)

Français, Jean (1912-) French composer. Studied the piano with Philipp at the Paris Conservatoire and composition with Boulanger. He has produced a large quantity of music in all forms, in a style that has changed little in a composing career of over half a century, being indebted to Ravel and Poulenc for its grace, charm and lightheartedness. [Schott]

Frankel, Benjamin (1906-73) English composer. Studied with Orlando Morgan at the Guildhall School while working as a jazz violinist, later making his living as an arranger and conductor for the theatre and composer of film scores. His works up to the mid-1950s are tonal; the later works, created in rapid succession, use 12-note serialism, though still with diatonic elements and within large-scale symphonic forms.
Opera: Marching Song, 1971-2
Orchestral: Vn Conc, 1951; Sym no.1, 1958, no.2, 1962, no.3, 1964, no.4, 1966, no.5, 1967, no.6, 1969, no.7, 1970, no.8, 1971
Chamber: Str Qt no.1, 1944, no.2, 1944, no.3, 1947, no.4, 1948, no.5, 1965; Pf Qt, 1953; Cl Qnt, 1956
[Novello, Chester]

Frau ohne Schatten, Die (The Woman with no Shadow) Opera by Strauss and Hofmannsthal, an invented symbolist myth supported by an enormous colourful score. ★Vienna, 10 Oct 1919.

frequency Rate of vibration. The frequency of a sound wave determines the pitch that is experienced (e.g. concert A is defined as 440 cycles per second).

frequency modulation Change to the frequency of a wave. By means of such changes information can be put into an electromagnetic wave (hence FM radio).

Fricker, Peter Racine (1920-) English composer. Studied at the Royal College of Music (1937-41) and with Seiber (1946-8). In the 1950s, when he was teaching at the RCM and Morley College, he was the most prominent English composer of European outlook, influenced by Bartók, Hindemith, Schoenberg and Berg in creating music whose diatonic underpinning is compromised by

high dissonance in vigorous counterpoint (12-note serialism is rare). Major works of this period, when nearly all his music was instrumental, include the first 3 symphonies (1948-9, 1950-51, 1960), 2 violin concertos (1949-50, 1953-4), the Viola Concerto (1951-3) and the Piano Concerto (1952-4). In 1964 he took an appointment at the University of California at Santa Barbara. [Schott]

Friedenstag (Day of Peace) Opera by Strauss and Josef Gregor, intended to form a double bill with *Daphne*, with which it contrasts in its stark strength and soldierly setting, in a fortress during the Thirty Years' War. ★Munich, 24 Jul 1938.

From the House of the Dead (Z mrtvého domu) Opera by Janáček after Dostoyevsky's novel of prison life, which it compacts into 3 short acts scored almost exclusively for male voices. ★Brno, 12 Apr 1930.

fugue The fugal sonata of Beethoven and Brahms is the ideal behind Reger's fugues, appearing at the ends of large-scale variation movements, or else, with a nod also to Bach, in pairings with preludes or fantasias for the organ. There is the shadow of the former kind behind the finale of Schoenberg's orchestral Variations, but much commoner is the Regerian homage to Bach, conducted by Busoni in the fugues within his *Fantasia contrappuntistica*, by Hindemith in those of his *Ludus tonalis*, by Shostakovich in his 24 Preludes and Fugues, and by many organist-composers (e.g. David, Dupré, Pepping). Bach has also been important to composers who have been more radical in their interpretation of fugue, such as Stravinsky in the double fugue of his Symphony of Psalms, which is a marriage of fugue and chorale prelude, or Bartók in the opening movement of his Music for Strings, Percussion and Celesta: in neither of these cases is there real development, but rather a wandering of the theme from one entry to the next, closed in both cases by symmetrical return followed by a coda, which in the Stravinsky is massive and in the Bartók minute. Another way of adapting fugue is to conceal it, as Berg does in Act 2 scene ii of *Wozzeck* and Webern does in the middle of the finale of his String Quartet op.28. Or fugue can be implied by the choice and repetition of a subject, only for all contrapuntal possibilities to be annihilated in toccata-style heterophony: this is the case in Messiaen's 'Par lui tout a été fait' from his *Vingt regards*, which, along with the finale of the 'Hammerklavier', influenced the pseudo-fugue that ends Boulez's Second Piano Sonata.

furniture music Concept introduced by Satie (as 'musique d'ameublement'), indicating music written to be a background. Honegger apparently wrote the first such in 1919, followed the next year by the *Musique d'ameublement* for small ensemble composed jointly by Satie and Milhaud.

Furtwängler, Wilhelm (1886-1954) German conductor and composer. Studied composition with Rheinberger and von Schillings, and began career as conductor in 1906, first in provincial opera houses, then with the Berlin Philharmonic (1922-54). He brought to his work a deep seriousness (he regularly consulted Schenker on his scores until the latter's death), together with a fullness of tone and breadth of rubato that gave him impressive command over big symphonic forms. He conducted the first performances of Schoenberg's Variations and of Hindemith's *Konzertmusik* op. 48, *Philharmonisches Konzert* and *Mathis der Maler* symphony. His own works included symphonies in B minor (1938-41), E minor (1944-5) and C♯ minor (1947-54).

Futurism Italian artistic movement initiated by Marinetti in 1909 and expressing itself most dynamically in the painting and sculpture of Balla, Boccioni and Severini. Marinetti's statement that 'a roaring motor car...is more beautiful that the Victory of Samothrace' gave the movement its aggressive, up-to-date aesthetic, musically embodied in the manifestos of Pratella and the noise compositions of Russolo. Debussy was impressed by the aesthetic; so too, to more creative purpose, were Varèse, Honegger and such Russian composers as Prokofiev, Mosolov and Deshevov.

☐ U. Apollonio, ed., *Futurist Manifestos* (1973)

G

Gaburo, Kenneth (1926-) American composer. Studied with Rogers at the Eastman School (1946-9), Petrassi in Rome (1954-5) and Phillips at the University of Illinois (1955-62), where he remained to teach before moving to the University of California at San Diego (1968-75). Studies of phonetics and linguistics have been important to his music, much of which is for choral and/or electronic resources, sometimes with theatrical elements.

Antiphony I, 3 str groups, tape, 1957, II, chorus, tape, 1962, III (Pearl White Moments), chorus, electronics, 1962, IV (Poised), pic, trbn, db, electronics, 1966, V, pf, tape, slides, 1971, VI (Cogito), str qt, tape, slides, 1971; Lingua, mixed media, 1965-70 [Lingua, Presser; Heliodor, Nonesuch]

gagaku The court orchestral music of Japan; *see* JAPANESE MUSIC.

Gambler, The (Igrok) Opera by Prokofiev after Dostoyevsky's novella, a study of manic obsession. ★Brussels, 29 Apr 1929.

gamelan Ensemble of metal percussion in INDONESIAN MUSIC.

gamut Term used loosely for scale or pitch range, but more precisely by Cage for the collection of sounds available to a composition. The prepared piano seems to have given him the idea that such collections could be limited, and he used deliberately restricted collections in his String Quartet and other works.

Garant, Serge (1929-) Canadian composer. Studied with Champagne and in Paris with Messiaen (1951-2), returning fascinated by Webern, Boulez and Stockhausen. His works include *Anerca* for soprano singing Eskimo texts and ensemble (1961) and a group of compositions on the royal theme of Bach's *Musical Offering*. In 1966 he became professor of composition at the University of Montreal and musical director of the Society for Contemporary Music in Quebec.

Gaspard de la nuit Piano triptych by Ravel after fantastic prose poems by Bertrand and in musical terms after Liszt: 'Ondine', 'Le gibet', 'Scarbo'. ★Viñes, Paris, 9 Jan 1909.

Gebrauchsmusik (Utility Music) Term used by Besseler in 1925 for music designed to be generally useful: music for the cinema and radio, political music, music for amateurs. The term answered to a tendency in German music at the time, represented by Hindemith, Weill, Eisler, Orff and others, but the ethos was more widespread: Copland, Britten and Tippett, for instance, similarly felt an obligation to SOCIETY. In English writing the term is most associated with Hindemith and his copious productions for amateur and professional musicians, though he himself rejected it.

Gentle Fire English ensemble active from 1968 into the early 1970s, performing LIVE ELECTRONIC MUSIC: works by American experimental composers and Stockhausen, and their own group compositions, often featuring their own constructed instruments. They recorded music by Cage, Brown and Wolff (EMI Electrola 1 C 065-02 469) and were involved in performances of Stockhausen's *Sternklang*.

Genzmer, Harald (1909-) German composer. Studied with Hindemith in Berlin (1928-34), then taught in Berlin while working with Sala and Trautwein on electronic instruments: he composed two concertos for trautonium (1939, 1952). After the war he taught at the Musikhochschulen in Freiburg (1946-57) and Munich. His works, covering all genres except opera, are Hindemithian. [Schott, Peters]

Gerhard, Roberto (1896-1970) Spanish-British composer. Studied with Granados and Pedrell, and then with Schoenberg (1923-8), under whose influence he wrote his Wind Quintet. He then returned to Spain in 1929 as a teacher, and after the fall of the Republican government in 1939 settled in Cambridge. In England he began to compose more abundantly, though in a Spanish manner, his major works being ballets and an opera. However, the Violin Concerto of this period showed a revitalization of dormant 12-note interest, though still with some Spanishness and also with the first signs of a freedom of percussion scoring that recalls Varèse. In his First Quartet he moved towards an individual kind of hexachordal serialism: the hexachords can be reordered (the music becomes athematic), and their interval contents may be used to generate rhythmic sets. His Second Quartet shows him taking note of the new string effects introduced by Xenakis and Penderecki, and there is the same lively responsiveness to sound in the other chamber and orchestral works of his highly creative last decade.

Opera: The Duenna, 1945-7
Ballets: Ariel, 1934, ★Barcelona, 1936; Soirées de Barcelone, 1936-8; Don Quixote, 1940-41; Alegrias, 1942; Pandora, 1943-5
Orchestral: Albada, 1936; Sym 'Homenaje a Pedrell', 1941; Vn Conc, 1942-3; Pf Conc, 1951; Sym no.1, 1952-3; Hpd Conc, 1955-6; Sym no.2, 1957-9; Sym no.3 'Collages', with tape, 1960; Conc for Orch, 1965; Epithalamion, 1966; Sym no.4, 1967
Choral: L'alta naixença del rei en jaume, S, Bar, chorus, orch, 1932; The Plague, speaker, chorus, orch, 1963-4

Chamber: 2 Sardanas, 11 insts, 1928; Wind Qnt, 1928; Str Qt no.1, 1950-55; Sonata, vc, pf, 1956; Nonet, 1956-7; Str Qt no.2, 1960-62; Concert for 8, 1962; Hymnody, 11 insts, 1963; Gemini, vn, pf, 1966; Libra, 6 insts, 1968; Leo, 10 insts, 1969
Instrumental: 2 apunts, pf, 1921-2; Capriccio, fl, 1949; 3 Impromptus, pf, 1950; Fantasia, gui, 1957; Chaconne, vn, 1959
Songs: 7 Haiku, S/T, 5 insts, 1922; Cancionero de Pedrell, S/T, pf, 1941; Por do passare la sierra, S/T, pf, 1942; 6 Tonadillas, S/T, pf, 1942; Sevillanas, S/T, pf, 1943; The Akond of Swat, Mez/Bar, 2 perc, 1954; Cantares, S/T, gui, 1956
Tape pieces, incidental music for films, plays, broadcast drama
[OUP, Belwin-Mills, Prowse; Decca]

Gershwin, George (1898-1937) American composer. Learned to play the piano only in 1910, but by 1914 was working in popular music and in 1916 had his first song published. He later studied briefly with Goldmark, Cowell, Schillinger and others, more from feelings of inadequacy than from actual need. For similar reasons he was drawn to write large-scale concert works, alongside a large quantity of popular songs in jazz style.

Opera: Porgy and Bess, ★New York, 1935
Orchestral: Rhapsody in Blue, pf, jazz band, 1924, orchestrated by Grofe, Pf Conc, F, 1925; An American in Paris, 1928; Second Rhapsody, pf, orch, 1931; Cuban Overture, 1932; 'I got rhythm' Variations, pf, orch, 1934
Piano: Preludes, 1926; George Gershwin Song-Book, 1932; Two Waltzes, 1933
[New World]
□ C. Schwartz, *Gershwin* (1973)

Gesang der Jünglinge (Song of the Youths) Tape piece by Stockhausen created from recordings of electronic sounds and a boy singing from the *Benedicite omnia* opera. Originally devised for 5 groups of loudspeakers, it was later adapted to 4-track tape and 2-channel disc. ★Cologne, 30 May 1956.

Ghedini, Giorgio Federico (1892-1965) Italian composer. Studied privately with Cravero and with Bossi at the Liceo Musicale in Bologna, then worked as a conductor (1909-20) and teacher in Turin (1918-38), Parma (1938-41) and Milan (1941-62), where his pupils included Berio. His music is steeped in the Baroque and, to a lesser extent, plainsong, and is marked too by imaginative colouring. Among his works are 8 operas, large-scale vocal works (Concerto del'albatro for orchestra with voice speaking words from *Moby Dick*, 1945), orchestral pieces (*Architetture*, 1940) and relatively fewer smaller compositions. [Ricordi, Suvini Zerboni]

Gilbert, Anthony (1934-) English composer. Came to music late, studying at Trinity College (1952-5), with Seiber, and at Morley College with Milner and Goehr (1959-63). His early works featured bold, colourful musical objects in a style indebted to Varèse, Messiaen and Birtwistle (*Brighton Piece* for ensemble, 1967), but in the early 1970s his style became more continuous and intimate as he moved towards the clear influence of Indian modality and thought in such pieces as his radio drama *The Chakravaka Bird* (1976-7). [Schott]

Gilbert, Henry Franklin (1868-1928) American composer. Studied at the New England Conservatory (1886-7) and with MacDowell (1889-92), though did not devote himself to composition until after seeing *Louise* in Paris (1901). He used spirituals, ragtime and American Indian music in his compositions, which include orchestral works (*Comedy Overture on Negro Themes*, c.1906; *The Dance in Place Congo*, c.1908), piano pieces and songs. [Wa-Wan Press]

Gilson, Paul (1865-1942) Belgian composer. Mainly self-taught, stimulated by seeing the *Ring* (1883) and hearing concerts of the Russian 'Five' (1886). His most successful work was the symphony *La mer* (1892), one of many large-scale compositions from the period before 1906, including the opera *Prinses Zonneschijn* (1901). In later years, disillusioned by the course music was taking, he wrote little, but was an important teacher.

Ginastera, Alberto (1916-83) Argentinian composer. Born and educated in Buenos Aires, at the Williams Conservatory (1928-35) and the National Conservatory (1936-8). A performance of a suite from his ballet *Panambí* in 1937 made him a national figure, and introduced a phase of colourful and energetic nationalism in his work, when he drew on gaucho or, as here, Indian music, influenced in his settings by Bartók, Stravinsky and Falla. In 1941 he became professor of composition at the National Conservatory, and in 1945-7 he paid an extended visit to the USA, where he became acquainted with Copland.

Soon after his return he began to write in a more subjective style, and to work more in chamber forms. Then in 1958, in his Second Quartet, he

began to use 12-note methods, though never strictly: they were part of a wide-ranging vocabulary used to produce music of high exuberance and expressive force, a vocabulary that also included quarter tones, polytonality and extreme vocal and instrumental effects. The climax came in his 3 operas of sexuality and violence. Throughout this period he held important teaching posts in Argentina, until in 1970 he removed to Geneva.

Operas: Don Rodrigo, 1963-4, ★Buenos Aires, 1964; Bomarzo, 1966-7, ★Washington, 1967; Beatrix Cenci, 1971, ★Washington, 1971
Ballets: Panambí, 1934-6; Estancia, 1941
Orchestral: Obertura para el 'Fausto' criollo, 1943; Ollantay, 1947; Variaciones concertantes, 1953; Pampeana no.3, 1954; Harp Conc, 1956; Pf Conc no.1, 1961, no.2, 1972; Vn Conc, 1963; Conc, str, 1965; Estudios sinfónicos, 1967; Vc Conc, 1968; Popol vuh, 1975; Glosses sobre temes de Pau Casals, str qnt, str, 1976
Large vocal: Psalm 150, chorus, orch, 1938; Hieremiae prophetae lamentationes, chorus, 1946; Cantata para América mágica, S, perc orch, 1960; Bomarzo, narrator, T/Bar, chamber orch, 1964; Milena, S, orch, 1971; Serenata, Bar, vc, 9 insts, 1973; Turbae ad passionem gregorianam, soloists, chorus, orch, 1974
Chamber: Duo, fl, ob, 1945; Str Qt no.1, 1948, no.2, 1958, no.3, with S, 1973; Pf Qnt, 1963
Instrumental: Pampeana no.1, vn, pf, 1947, no.2, vc, pf, 1950; Toccata, Villancico and Fugue, org, 1947; Puneña no.1, fl, 1973, no.2, vc, 1976; Sonata, gui, 1976
Piano: Danzas argentinas, 1937; 3 Pieces, 1940; Malambo, 1940; 12 American Preludes, 1944; Suite de danzas criollas, 1946; Rondo sobre temas infantiles argentinos, 1947; Sonata no.1, 1952
Songs 2 canciones, v, pf, 1938; Cantos del Tucuman, v, 4 insts, 1938; 5 canciones populares argentinas, v, pf, 1943; Las horas de una estancia, v, pf, 1943
[Boosey]

Glagolitic Mass (Glagolská mše) Janáček's setting of the mass in Church Slavonic for soloists, chorus, orchestra and organ: the 5 usual parts of the Ordinary are contained within orchestral movements, an Introduction and an Intrada, the latter prefaced by an organ solo. ★Brno, 5 Dec 1927.

Glass, Philip (1937-) American composer. Studied at the University of Chicago, at the Juilliard School, and in Paris with Boulanger. In Paris too he worked with Ravi Shankar, and after his return to New York in 1967 with Alla Rakha. Indian music provided his entry into working with ostinato patterns in forms of slow change, often aggressively amplified in his early work. He formed his own ensemble to perform this music, and has appeared with them internationally while also increasing his scope in operas that work in slow motion, chant and repetition (*see* MINIMAL MUSIC).

Operas: Einstein on the Beach, ★Paris, 1976; Satyagraha, ★Rotterdam, 1980; The Photographer, ★Rotterdam, 1982; Akhnaten, ★Stuttgart, 1984

Ensemble music: Music in Fifths, 1969; Music in Similar Motion, 1969; Music with Changing Parts, 1970; Music in 12 Parts, 1971-4

[Chatham Square, Virgin, CBS]

Glazunov, Alexander (1865-1936) Russian composer. Studied with Rimsky-Korsakov and had his First Symphony conducted by Balakirev when he was 16. He then quickly took his place as the leading Russian nationalist of his generation. In 1905 he was made director of the St Petersburg Conservatory, where he remained while the city twice changed its name, moving to the west only in 1928 after the staff had complained of his conservatism. His works include the ballets *Raymonda* (1896-7) and *The Seasons* (1899), 9 symphonies (1 unfinished), much other orchestral music, 7 quartets, etc. [Belaieff]

Glier, Reyngol'd (1875-1956) Russian composer. Studied with Taneyev, Arensky and Ippolitov-Ivanov at the Moscow Conservatory (1894-1900) and with Conus in Berlin (1905-7), then taught at the conservatories in Kiev (1913-20) and Moscow (1920-41). His music belongs in the Romantic nationalist tradition of Borodin and Glazunov, and includes several operas (among them pioneering efforts in Azerbaijani opera), ballets, 3 symphonies (no. 3 'Il'ya Muromets', 1909-11), concertos (for harp, 1938; for coloratura soprano, 1943), other orchestral works and chamber music.

Globokar, Vinko (1934-) Yugoslav composer and trombonist. Studied in Ljubljana, at the Paris Conservatoire (1955-9), with Leibowitz for conducting (1959-63) and with Berio for composition (1965). His virtuosity and characterful style on the trombone brought him compositions by Berio (*Sequenza V*) and Kagel (*Der Atem*); he also made the official recording of Stockhausen's *Solo*. His own compositions include virtuoso studies for soloist (*Atemstudie* for oboe, 1972; Res/as/ex/ins-pirer for brass instrument, 1973), but he has been concerned too with communication within groups. In 1972 he was a founder member of the quartet New Phonic Art, playing improvisations and compositions which, like his *Correspondences* (1969), invite some creative response from the performers. [Peters; DG]

Gloriana Opera by Britten and Plomer after Strachey's *Elizabeth and Essex*, commissioned for the coronation of Elizabeth II. ★London, 8 Jun 1953.

Glückliche Hand, Die (The Skilled Hand) 'Drama with music' by Schoenberg to his own libretto, a symbolist play of sexual jealousy and urgent creativity set atonally for 3 type characters, men's choir and large orchestra. ★Vienna, 14 Oct 1924.

Gnesin, Mikhail (1883-1957) Russian composer and teacher. Studied with Rimsky-Korsakov and Lyadov at the St Petersburg Conservatory (1901-9). His early works include ecstatically lyrical settings of Balmont and music for Meyerhold's productions of Greek tragedies (1912-16). After 1923 he was most active as a teacher, at institutions in Moscow and Leningrad, though he also wrote chamber music and a few larger works.

Goehr, Alexander (1932-) English composer. Son of the conductor Walter Goehr, he was born in Berlin and taken to England the year after his birth. He studied with Hall at the Royal Manchester College of Music (1952-5), where his colleagues included Davies and Birtwistle, and then in Paris with Messiaen and Loriod (1955-6). Back in England he worked as a producer for the BBC (1960-68), then held visiting appointments at the New England Conservatory (1968-9) and Yale (1969-70), continuing in academic life at the universities of Southampton (1970-71), Leeds (professor, 1971-6) and Cambridge (professor, 1976-).

His first works, like those of Davies, recognize the kinship between serial and medieval techniques, but the first to gain notice were cantatas of a Schoenbergian expressive ferocity: *The Deluge* and *Sutter's Gold*. Then in such works as the Little Symphony (1963) he began to work out a way of controlling long time-spans by harmonic backgrounds derived from the series, an achievement comparable with Perle's 12-note modality. This has given him the means to write developing structures, often stubbornly cast in Classical forms, though in his best works, which include the dramatic pieces and the large *2 études* for orchestra, there is an energy of imagination in balance with his wish for music to be well made.

Operas: Arden Must Die, *Hamburg, 1967; Behold the Sun, *Duisburg, 1985

Music theatre: Naboth's Vineyard, 1968; Shadowplay-2, 1970; Sonata about Jerusalem, 1970; together the three form Triptych, speaker, mime, 5 singers, 9 insts

Orchestral: Fantasia, 1954, rev. 1958; Hecuba's Lament, 1959-61; Vn Conc, 1961-2; Little Sym, 1963; Little Music, str, 1963; Pastorals, 1965; Romanza, vc, orch, 1968; Konzertstück, pf, small orch, 1969; Sym in 1 Movement, 1969-70; Pf Conc, 1971-2; Metamorphosis/Dance, 1973-4; Chaconne, 19 wind, 1974; Fugue and Romanza on Psalm 4, str, 1976; Deux études, 1981

Vocal: The Deluge, S, A, 8 insts, 1957-8; Four Songs from the Japanese, S/T, orch/pf, 1959; Sutter's Gold, B, chorus, orch, 1959-60; A Little Cantata of Proverbs, chorus, pf, 1962; 2 Choruses, 1962; Virtutes, chorus, insts, 1963; 5 Poems and an Epigram of William Blake, chorus, tpt, 1964; Warngedichte, A/B, pf, 1967; Psalm 4, S, A, women's chorus ad lib, va, org, 1976; Babylon the Great is Fallen, chorus, orch, 1979; Das Gesetz der Quadrille, Mez/Bar, pf, 1979; Behold the Sun, aria, S, ensemble, 1981

Chamber: Fantasias, cl, pf, 1954; Variations, fl, pf, 1959; Suite, 6 insts, 1961; Pf Trio, 1966; Str Qt no.2, 1967; Paraphrase, cl, 1969; Conc for 11, 1970; Lyric Pieces, 8 insts, 1974; Str Qt no.3, 1975-6; Prelude and Fugue, 3 cl, 1978; A Musical Offering, ens, 1985

Piano: Sonata, 1951-2; Capriccio, 1957; 3 Pieces, 1964; Nonomiÿa, 1969

[Schott; Wergo, Argo]

Goeyvaerts, Karel (1923-) Belgian composer. Studied in Antwerp and at the Paris Conservatoire with Milhaud and Messiaen (1947-50). Influenced by the latter's *Mode de valeurs* and his own analysis of Webern's op.27 he wrote his sonata for 2 pianos (1951), which provided a model of TOTAL SERIALISM that was important to Stockhausen: the 2 composers met at Darmstadt the same year. He continued in the direction of metaphysical abstraction in *Opus 2* (1951) and *Opus 3* (1952) for instrumental ensemble, and in electronic works, of which he realized *Composition no.5* (1953) and *Composition no.7* (1955) at the WESTDEUTSCHER RUNDFUNK studios. But he then drifted away from the avant garde: he worked as a translator for Sabena (1958-70) and wrote a variety of electronic, theatrical and Christian works.

Golden Cockerel, The (Zolotoy petushok) Opera by Rimsky-Korsakov and Vladimir Bel'sky after Pushkin, a glittering fantastic-satirical fairytale. *Moscow, 7 Oct 1909.

golden section Division of a quantity into 2 parts such that the ratio of the smaller to the larger is the same as that of the larger to the whole (the ratio is 0.618 to 1). The Greeks proportioned temples in this way, and there is circumstantial evidence that Debussy and Bartók used the golden section in shaping their musical forms.

□ E. Lendvai, *Béla Bartók* (1971); R. Howat, *Debussy in Proportion* (1983)

Golishev, Jef (1897-1970) Russian composer. Studied as a violinist with Auer and as a painter with his father. In 1909 he moved to Berlin, where he wrote a String Trio (1914) in '12-note-duration-complexes', each note having a different rhythmic value. After the first world war he was a member of the Berlin dada group, exhibiting as both painter and composer (*Antisymphonie, Keuchmaneuver*, with his own instruments and kitchen utensils). In 1933 he fled Berlin to Portugal, Barcelona, France, São Paulo and Paris.

gongs Sometimes used in tuned groups (e.g. in *Madama Butterfly*), but untuned gongs are commoner, the larger ones being known as 'tam-tams'. Stockhausen makes important use of a single tam-tam in *Kontakte, Momente, Mikrophonie I*, etc; groups of gongs and tam-tams occur notably in Messiaen and Boulez.

Górecki, Henryk (1933-) Polish composer. Studied with Szabelski at the Katowice Conservatory (1955-60) and with Messiaen in Paris, then returned to Katowice to teach. His earliest works were in a Polish brand of Parisian neoclassicism, but the experience of hearing new western music and the first Warsaw Autumn festival (1956) brought an abrupt change to 12-note techniques and a Penderecki-like zest for new sonorities, though in a style of monumental simplicity.

Orchestral: Sym no.1, str, perc, 1959; Monologhi, S, 3 groups, 1960; Scontri, 1960; Choros I, str, 1964; Refrain, 1965; Old Polish Music, 1969; Canticum graduum, 1969; Ad matrem, S, chorus, orch, 1971; 2 Sacred Songs, Bar, orch, 1971; Sym no.2 'Copernicus', S, Bar, chorus, orch, 1972; 3 Dances, 1973; Sym no.3, orch, 1976; Beatus vir, Bar, chorus, orch, 1979; Conc, hpd, str, 1980 Many choral, instrumental and ensemble pieces [PWM]

Gould, Glenn (1932-82) Canadian pianist. Studied with Guerrero at the Toronto Conservatory and enjoyed an international career until 1964, when he retired to concentrate on recording a personal repertory (Bach, Beethoven, Schoenberg) in an intensely purposeful if idiosyncratic manner. He wrote a String Quartet (1953-5) and created adventurous radio programmes.

Gould, Morton (1913-) American composer. Studied with Vincent Jones at the New York Institute of Musical Art, and has worked widely as a composer, conductor and arranger. His brilliantly orchestrated and distinctly American works embrace light music as well as more ambitious genres.

Graham, Martha (1894-) American choreographer. Founded her company in 1929 and soon became the leading practitioner of modern dance in the USA, commissioning scores from Copland (APPALACHIAN SPRING), Hindemith (*Hérodiade*), Barber (*Cave of the Heart*) and many others.
□ M. Graham, *The Notebooks* (1973)

Grainger, Percy (1882-1961) Australian–American composer and pianist. Studied with Knorr and Kwast at the Hoch Conservatory in Frankfurt (1895-9), then settled in London (1901) as a pianist, folksong collector and composer. He continued this variety of occupations after moving to the USA in 1914. His output is enormous and ramshackle, most works having been revised and rescored on at least one occasion. The diversity has its root in his dream of a 'free music', liberated from all norms of harmony, metre, form and instrumentation. Much of his music, comprising original pieces and folksong settings in equal quantities, was written or at least conceived during his London period.
□ J. Bird, *Percy Grainger* (1976)

Granados, Enrique (1867-1916) Spanish composer and pianist. Studied with Pedrell in Barcelona (1883-7), then in Paris before returning to Barcelona in 1889 and making his début there as pianist (1890) and composer (1892). For the next 2 decades he enoyed local success as a pianist, teacher and composer of light operas, but his performance in Paris of his *Goyescas* on 4 April 1914 (performed in Barcelona in 1911) brought him international attention. He used the music in composing an opera, introduced at the Metropolitan on 26 January 1916, and died at sea on his way back to Spain.

The piano *Goyescas* are florid yet acutely sensitive impressions of paintings by Goya, coloured by the Castilian dance, the tonadilla.
Goyescas: Los requiebros, Coloquio en la reja, El fandango del candil, Quejas o la maja y el ruisenor, El amor y la muerte, Epilogo: la serenada del espectro, El pelele
Other works: operas, orch pieces, songs, chamber music.

Grand Macabre, Le (The Great Macabre) Opera by Ligeti and Michael Meschke after Ghelderode, a grand surrealist-erotic comedy of the purported ending of the world. ★Stockholm, 12 Apr 1978.

graphic notation Use in musical scores of something other than the customary symbols and words. Two kinds can be distinguished. First there are notations which answer to quite specific compositional needs not met by conventional symbols: these would include Feldman's systems of squares releasing him from indicating precise pitches (in his *Projection* series of 1950-51, sometimes counted the first instance of graphic notation), Stockhausen's notational language of plus and minus signs, most of Cage's diagram kits coming with rules for interpretation (e.g. *Variations I-II*) and varieties of TIME-SPACE NOTATION. On the other hand there are graphics which are intended not to symbolize but rather to stimulate. Here the pioneer was Brown in his *December 1952*, which offers only an elegant design of slim black rectangles on a white background. The *Ring* of this art is surely Cardew's *Treatise* (1963-7), also one of the last examples.

Griffes, Charles (1884-1920) American composer. Studied in Berlin with Humperdinck and others (1903-7), then worked as a schoolmaster in Tarrytown, NY. His first works were solidly Germanic, but around 1911 he began to be influenced by Debussy and oriental art, and then in his Piano Sonata (1917-18) by the most recent Skryabin. Other piano works include The Pleasure-Dome of Kubla-Khan (1912, orchestrated 1917), the four *Roman Sketches* (1915-16) and the Three Preludes (1919).
□ E.M. Maisel, *Charles T. Griffes* (1943)

Grisey, Gérard (1946-) French composer. Studied at the Paris Conservatoire with Messiaen and at Darmstadt, then taught at Darmstadt (1978-82) and from 1982 at Berkeley. Most of his music is for instrumental groupings (e.g. *Modulations* for 33 players, ★1978), though he has been influenced by electronic work in his creation of large forms based on the growth and collision of sound masses. [Erato]

group Apart from the everyday meaning it has in such expressions as 'instrumental group' or 'rhythmic group', the word acquired the status of a term in Stockhausen's vocabulary in the 1950s. Dissatisfied with the POINT manner of total serialism, he began in *Kontra-Punkte* to work with groups, which were at first short figures in a single instrument. In *Gruppen*, however, the notion of group has been extended to embrace orchestral events unified by some stability of texture, harmony and internal rhythm.

Groupe de Recherches Musicales The electronic music studio of French radio, growing out of Schaeffer's Club d'Essai (1948-51) and founded as the Groupe de Musique Concrète under the direction of Schaeffer and Henry in 1951. In 1957 Henry left and the organization attained its present name; in 1966 Bayle became its director. Other composers who have worked there include Boulez, Stockhausen, Barraqué, Philippot, Xenakis and Parmegiani.

Group for Contemporary Music Ensemble founded in 1962 at Columbia University and directed by Harvey Sollberger, the prototype for similar groups at other American universities.

Gruber, Heinz Karl (1943-) Austrian composer and performer. Studied with Ratz, Jelinek and von Einem at the Vienna Hochschule für Musik, and began career as double bass player. His *Frankenstein!!* (1976-7), written for his own *Sprechgesang* narration with orchestra, is a masterpiece of absurdly horrific musical surrealism; other works, including his Violin Concerto (1977-8), show a similar perfection of technique towards a disquieting recovery of tonality. [Boosey]

Gruenberg, Louis (1884-1964) American composer. Taken from Russia to the USA at the age of 2, he went to Berlin at 19 to study with Busoni and remained in Europe as a pianist and teacher. His works of this period include the opera *The Bride of the Gods* (1913), to a libretto by Busoni. In 1919 he returned to New York, where he was a founder of the League of Composers and a leader of jazz-based modernism, notably expressed in *The Daniel Jazz* for tenor and sextet (1924) and other works. Jazz and Negro spirituals also influenced his opera *The*

Emperor Jones (1931), successful in its time, and his Violin Concerto (1944). In later years he moved to California and wrote film music.

Gruppen (Groups) Work by Stockhausen for 3 small orchestras placed (ideally) around the audience, thus permitting polyphonies of tempo and giving the illusion of sounds moving in space. *cond Maderna, Boulez, Stockhausen, Cologne, 24 Mar 1958.

Guézec, Jean-Pierre (1934-71) French composer. Studied with Messiaen at the Paris Conservatoire (1953-63) and developed a style based on opposed stretches of texture, often with febrile internal movement. His works include *Architectures colorées* for 15 instruments (1964), *Textures enchaînées* for wind and percussion (1967) and *Reliefs polychromés* for voices (1969). Messiaen wrote the horn solo of *Des canyons* in his memory. [Salabert; Erato]

guitar Occasional orchestral instrument for Mahler (Symphony no.7) and Schoenberg (*Von heute auf morgen*) with reference to its current associations with light music (see also Berg's use of it in the tavern ensemble of *Wozzeck* and Kagel's practice *passim*). The appearance of Segovia and other guitar virtuosi restored the instrument's dignity, winning it concertos from Rodrigo and many others. It has also become common in ensembles (e.g. *Le marteau sans maître*) and gained a wide solo repertory (e.g. pieces by Davies and Henze as well as the more Hispanic music of such as Ponce and Villa-Lobos).

Gulbenkian Foundation Established in Lisbon in 1956 in accordance with the will of Calouste Gulbenkian (1869-1955). Contemporary music has been one of its main interests, and it has commissioned for performance in Lisbon works by Messiaen (*La Transfiguration*), Xenakis (*Cendrées*) and others.

Gurney, Ivor (1890-1937) English composer and poet. Studied at the Royal College of Music with Stanford (1911-15) and Vaughan Williams (1918-21), serving meanwhile in the first world war. Gassed and shellshocked during the conflict, he was admitted to mental hospital in 1922, though by then he had produced a large output of songs in a more Brahmsian than folksong style.

Gurrelieder (Songs of Gurra) Work by Schoenberg, a sequence of concert tableaux for soloists, choirs and enormous orchestra, setting a German translation of poems by the Dane J. P. Jacobsen. The subject is erotic love, treated in alternate Wagnerian songs for Waldemar and Tove (who lives at the castle of Gurra), and then the damnation of Waldemar for cursing God on Tove's death. Composed in 1900-01, the work was not fully orchestrated until 1911. *cond Schreker, Vienna, 23 Feb 1913.

H

Hába, Alois (1893-1973) Czech composer. Studied at the teacher-training institute in Kroměříž (1908-12), with Novák in Prague (1914-15) and with Schreker in Vienna (1918-20) and Berlin (1920-22). He began to use quarter tones (*see* MICROTONES) in his Suite for string orchestra (1917), following a newspaper report of a lecture, and was further influenced by his attendance at Schoenberg's private concerts. In 1923 he returned to Prague and the next year began courses in microtonal music at the conservatory. He also produced a large output of music in quarter, fifth and sixth tones, some of it for special instruments (e.g. Suite for quarter-tone clarinet and quarter-tone piano, 1925), and ranging from piano works and string quartets to operas (*The Mother* in quarter tones, 1927-9; *Thy Kingdom Come* in sixth tones, 1939-42).

Hahn, Reynaldo (1875-1947) Venezuelan-French composer. Taken to Paris at the age of 3, he studied at the Conservatoire with Massenet and quickly made a fashionable reputation as composer and performer of his own songs (e.g. 'Si mes vers avaient des ailes'): Proust and Sarah Bernhardt took him up. In later years he wrote mostly for the stage, including the operettas *Ciboulette* (*Paris, 1923) and *Mozart* (*Paris, 1925).

Haieff, Alexei (1914-) Russian-American composer. Moved to the USA in 1932 and studied with Jacobi and Goldmark at the Juilliard School (1934-8), later with Boulanger (1938-9). His music, mostly in standard instrumental forms, owes much to Stravinsky's neoclassicism.

Halffter Spanish family of composers. Rodolfo (1900-) and his brother Ernesto (1905-) both re-

ceived help from Falla, and Ernesto became his disciple, finishing *Atlántida* after his death. Rodolfo settled in Mexico City in 1939, and continued to cultivate a Falla-like style, as did Ernesto, remaining in Spain. Their nephew Cristobal studied with del Campo at the Madrid Conservatory (1947-51), and he too began to compose under the influence of Falla, though in the 1960s he became the chief Spanish representative of the Darmstadt-based avant garde. His works include several for large orchestra with or without voices, 3 quartets and compositions with electronics, all showing a typically Spanish fervour of expression. [UE]

Hall, Richard (1903-82) English composer and teacher. Studied at Cambridge and worked as church musician before teaching at the Royal Manchester College (1938-56) and Dartington (1956-67). At the former institution his pupils included Birtwistle, Davies and Goehr. Some of his own music, including 5 symphonies and 2 quartets, marries Schoenbergian harmony with an English modal mellifluousness.

Hambraeus, Bengt (1928-) Swedish composer. Studied at Uppsala University (1947-56) and at the Darmstadt courses, then worked for Swedish radio before his appointment in 1972 to McGill University. He pioneered new techniques for the organ, his own instrument, in such works as *Konstellationer I* (1958) and *III* (1961).

Hamilton, Iain (1922-) Scottish composer. Studied with Alwyn at the Royal Academy of Music (1947-51) and began to compose large-scale works influenced by Bartók, Berg and Hindemith. His Sinfonia for 2 orchestras (1958) initiated a serial period, continuing after his move to Duke University, North Carolina, in 1961. Then in the mid-1960s his music became again more expansive and he began to write operas: *Agamemnon* (1967-9), *The Royal Hunt of the Sun* (1967-9), *Pharsalia* (1968), *The Catiline Conspiracy* (1972-3), *Tamburlaine* (1976), *Anna Karenina* (1979-80) and *Lancelot* (1985). [Presser, Schott]

Hanson, Howard (1896-) American composer and teacher. Studied with Goetschius at the New York Institute of Musical Art and worked as teacher, notably as director of the Eastman School (1924-64), where he also conducted much American music. His own music, including 7 symphonies, is close to Sibelius. [Fischer]

happening Extraordinary artistic manifestation, often involving a great variety of events in an unusual situation. The first is said to have taken place at Black Mountain College in 1952, stimulated by Cage, but the golden years of the happening were the early 1960s (*see* FLUXUS).

Harawi Cycle of 12 songs by Messiaen, forming a Tristan trilogy with his *Turangalîla-symphonie* and *5 rechants*. Musically and poetically the work is based on Peruvian folksongs (the 'harawi' is a genre of lament). *Bunlet, Messiaen, Mâcon, 24 Jun 1946.

Harbison, John (1938-) American composer. Studied at Harvard (1956-60), Berlin (1960-61) and Princeton with Kim and Sessions (1961-3); has taught at MIT since 1969. His works include operas (*Winter's Tale*, *San Francisco, 1979; *Full Moon in March*, *Cambridge, Mass., 1979) and other vocal music, orchestral pieces and chamber compositions.

Harmonie der Welt, Die (The Harmony of the World) Opera by Hindemith to his own libretto on Kepler's search for the celestial mechanics. *Munich, 11 Aug 1957.

harmonium Instrument given a virtuoso repertory by Karg-Elert and also curiously favoured by Mahler (Symphony no.8), Strauss (*Ariadne auf Naxos*) and Schoenberg (*Herzgewächse* and various arrangements).

harmony A simultaneous sounding of pitches, having in diatonic music a function (e.g. tonic chord, dominant 7th, etc). Where such functions are not intended, some writers, notably Babbitt, have preferred the noncommittal term SIMULTANEITY, and have avoided speaking of harmony in the wider sense of the network of pitch relationships that give a work coherence and movement.

The study of 20th c. harmony, in this wider sense, is not well advanced, except in so far as it concerns music which accepts diatonic functionalism without much alteration. The alternatives are basically two: to adapt diatonic harmony, most usually by introducing some modal understanding of it, or to avoid it through ATONALITY or the elimination of pitch altogether (one might add a third option, that of creating a new system of pitches, whether by adding MICROTONES or by electronically constructing scales based on other intervals, but

it is debatable whether new systems of harmony are so easily made).

Within these possibilities, too, quite different kinds of harmony are possible. At one extreme the harmony may be static, because it changes so rapidly that no harmonic progression is perceptible, or because there are gross textural changes that inhibit any long-term continuity, or because the chords are so dense that their harmonic functions are wholly obscured, or because there is some essential harmonic changelessness. At the other extreme the dynamism of diatonic harmony may be retained. As yet there is no clear evidence that this can be achieved by any harmonic means other than those of the diatonic system, at least over long spans (on the smaller scale goal-directedness is possible when, for example, 11 of the pitch classes are sounded, leaving an expectation of the twelfth, as sometimes in Webern and Boulez). Non-diatonic dynamism, if it is not purely rhythmic (as in Varèse's *Ionisation*), may therefore involve some invocation of diatonic functions (e.g. Bartók's frequent achievement of resolution in moving from greater to lesser dissonance), or, perhaps more commonly, the pretence of such invocation by the retention of rhythmic and gestural features characteristic of diatonic music, as in Schoenberg's serial sonata movements or possibly in Carter. Of course, the former have normally been analysed in terms of COMBINATORIALITY and the latter in terms of his own non-tonal harmonic constructs, but the way this music is perceived, rather than conceived, still remains controversial. Nor can it be said that the dynamic modal diatonicism of such composers as Stravinsky, Copland, Vaughan Williams, Britten or Davies is well understood.

Static harmony naturally presents fewer problems. The classic and perhaps earliest case of changelessness is the third of Schoenberg's 5 Orchestral Pieces, but examples of this sort are uncommon. More usually the constancy is in the background (e.g. the fixing of pitch classes to particular registers at the start of Webern's Symphony), or else the static effect is obtained by rapid cross-cutting of material (e.g. in Stravinsky's Symphonies of Wind Instruments) or sheer chordal density (e.g. the same composer's *Star-Visaged*). A static effect is also produced by the persistent fastening of the music to some symmetrical harmonic feature, whether the whole-tone scale (Debussy, Messiaen), the diminished 7th chord (Messiaen, Skryabin) or the augmented triad (Messiaen). More complex are those cases where the static and the dynamic appear to meet, not simply because static harmony is met by dynamic rhythm (as variously in much of Schoenberg and Messiaen), but rather because the harmony itself is at once static and dynamic. This is particularly a characteristic of Stravinsky, most of all during his neoclassical period, where the ideas may act against rather than within the tonality (e.g. the insistent tonic-dominant step executed by the opening motif of the Symphony in C).

It is difficult to know whether the inadequacy of harmonic theory in the 20th c. is a cause or a symptom of the decline in harmonic purposefulness in 20th c. music: Schoenberg's treatise (1911) marks the point at which practice begins to depart radically from theory. However, harmony has become since the 1970s a subject of renewed conscious concern for composers, whether they have preferred the repetitive stasis of simple chords (Riley, Reich, Glass), a return to the diatonic system, or some recovery of direction in a 12-note system embracing modal and diatonic forces (Perle, Davies, Goehr).
□ A. Schoenberg, *Harmonielehre* (1911; Eng. trs. 1978); V. Persichetti, *Twentieth Century Harmony* (1961)

harp Instrument brought into the forefront of the orchestra by Debussy and Ravel, both of whom wrote works featuring it. The possibilities have been further extended by Berio (*Sequenza II, Circles*) and Boulez (*Improvisations sur Mallarmé*), but the harp's limited dynamic and timbral range have kept its solo repertory small. There are concertos by Glier, Milhaud and others, a sonata by Hindemith, and double concertos with oboe commissioned by Heinz and Ursula Holliger from Henze, Lutosławski and others.

harpsichord The 20th c. revival of the instrument has brought it a substantial repertory by such composers as Falla and Gerhard (concertos), Carter (Double Concerto and Sonata a 4), Davies (many ensemble pieces) and others, assuring the modern instrument a life even though performers of pre-Classical music now prefer original or reproduction models.

Harris, Roy (1898-1979) American composer. Studied at Berkeley, privately with Farwell and in Paris with Boulanger (1926-9), then taught at the Juilliard School (1932-40) and other institutions. His First Symphony, and even more so his Third, made a great impression through their rugged grandeur and long melodies in a diatonic idiom imbibed from folksongs and hymntunes.

Symphonies: no.1, 1933; no.2, 1935; no.3, 1937; no.4, 1940; no.5, 1942; no.6, 1944; no.7, 1952; no.8, 1962; no.9. 1962; no.10, 1965; no.11, 1967; no.12, 1968; no.13, 1969; no.14, 1974; no.15, 1978; no.16, 1979
Other works: concs, choral pieces, 3 quartets, etc [AMP, Mills, G. Schirmer]
□ R. Strassburg, *Roy Harris* (1974)

Harrison, Lou (1917-) American composer. Studied in San Francisco with Cowell (1934-5) and worked with Cage in writing and performing percussion music (1939-41), then had lessons with Schoenberg (1941) before moving to New York in 1943, though he soon returned to the west coast and continued his habit of taking various employments. His music is equally diverse in style, scoring and genre, often using unusual, exotic or invented instruments, and generally modal.

Hartmann, Karl Amadeus (1905-63) German composer. Studied with Haas at the Munich Academy (1924-7), then with Scherchen and Webern (1941-2): he destroyed all he composed before this last study. In 1945 he started the Musica Viva concerts in Munich, which provided a platform for the music that had been banned during the Nazi years, and were imitated in other German cities. His own works include 8 symphonies in a vigorously expressive style drawing on Berg, Bartók, Hindemith and Blacher. [Schott; Wergo]

Harvey, Jonathan (1939-) English composer. Studied at Cambridge, privately with Erwin Stein and Keller, and at Princeton with Babbitt (1969-70), and has taught at the universities of Southampton (1964-77) and Sussex (1977-). His pre-Princeton works exhibit a range of influences from Britten to Stockhausen and Davies, but though these remain important his later music achieves coherence through operations with sets on both large and small scales, motivated by a view of serialism as an apt means for the communication of spiritual experience.
Persephone Dream, orch, 1972; Inner Light 1, 6 insts, tape, 1973; Inner Light 3, orch, tape, 1975; Inner Light 2, 5 solo vv, 12 insts, 1977; Str Qt, 1977; Mortuos plango, vivos voco, tape, 1980; Bhakti, small orch, tape, 1982 [Novello; Erato, RCA]

Haubenstock-Ramati, Roman (1919-) Polish-Austrian composer. Studied with Malawski at the Krakow Conservatory (1934-8) and Koffler at the

Lwow Academy (1939-41). In 1950 he left Poland for Tel Aviv, then in 1957 moved to Vienna, where he worked for Universal Edition. He has worked much with mobile form and graphic notation.

Hauer, Josef Matthias (1883-1959) Austrian composer. Trained as a teacher, self-taught in composition. His first works (1912-19) are freely atonal; he then worked with his own system of 12-note composition, in which the set was considered as a hexachordal trope. Living in Vienna from 1915, he had met Schoenberg in 1917, and the latter had programmed his music within the Verein für Privataufführungen in 1919: it seems inevitable that Schoenberg gained something from the connection but the relationship ended when Hauer insisted 12-note composition was his invention. He produced a large and various output of 12-note pieces (71 opus numbers), including the Hölderlin cantatas *Wandlungen* (1927) and *Der Menschen Weg* (1934), but the Anschluss put an end to his public activities, and he retired to produce about 1000 *Zwölftonspiele*, mechanical operations with his 12-note rules. [UE]

Hauptstimme (Ger. 'chief voice') Schoenberg's term for the main part in polyphony, which he marked with an 'H' in scores from op. 16 onwards. Berg followed this practice, adding the term 'Hauptrhythmus' and the marking 'HR' for the principal metre. See NEBENSTIMME.

heckelphone Oboe-like instrument, pitched an octave lower than the conventional oboe, made by the Biebrich firm of Heckel in 1904. It was used in the orchestra by Strauss (notably in *Salome*) and by Holst and Delius, though they called it 'bass oboe'. Hindemith wrote a Trio for heckelphone, piano and viola (1928).

Heiller, Anton (1923-79) Austrian organist and composer. Studied at the Vienna Academy (1941-2), where he taught from 1945. A renowned Bach performer, he also composed masses, cantatas and organ music in a style akin to David's. [Doblinger, UE]

Heininen, Paavo (1938-) Finnish composer. Studied with Englund and Kokkonen at the Helsinki Academy (1956-60), with Zimmermann at the Cologne Hochschule (1960-61) and with Persichetti at the Juilliard School (1961-2). His music is powerfully expressive, whether in a lyrical or a dramatic tone, reflecting his enthusiasms for Hart-

mann and Strauss as much as Boulez. Among his works are symphonies and concertos, choral and chamber pieces, and the chamber opera *The Silken Drum*, after a nō play (*Helsinki, 1983).

Henry, Pierre (1927-) French composer. Studied with Messiaen and Boulanger at the Paris Conservatoire (1938-48), then joined Schaeffer's *musique concrète* studio in 1949 and collaborated with him on the *Symphonie pour un homme seul* (1950-51), an effective and sometimes humorous montage of recorded sounds in 12 short movements. He remained as co-director with Schaeffer of the Groupe de Musique Concrète (1951-8), then left to found his own studio. His works employ the surrealist possibilities of *musique concrète* and include several compositions for ballets by Béjart, such as *Orphée* (1958), *Messe pour le temps présent* (1967) and *Nijinsky, clown de Dieu* (1971).

Henze, Hans Werner (1926-) German composer. After army service in 1944-5 he studied with Fortner at the Heidelberg Institute for Church Music (1946-8), and with Leibowitz at the 1948 Darmstadt courses and subsequently privately. Very quickly he created an apt synthesis of sprightly Stravinskian neoclassicism with Bergian serialism, sometimes with jazz colouring; he also proved himself an effective man of the theatre, both as composer and as music director at the Wiesbaden State Theatre (1950-53).

Yet he felt himself out of sympathy with Germany, and in 1953 left for the Bay of Naples, where his music became more luxuriant in harmony and rich in orchestral colour: these were the qualities of his first full-length opera, KÖNIG HIRSCH. It was followed by a sequence of operas in quite different theatrical styles, though all elaborated with the same musical largeness, and each surrounded by orchestral and vocal works inhabiting similar worlds of hedonistic fantasy and irony. Meanwhile he moved from Naples to Rome in 1961 and began to appear widely as a teacher, lecturer and conductor of his own music.

This period reached its climax in *The* BASSARIDS, after which he entered a period of self-questioning, charted in his Second Piano Concerto and giving rise to a commitment to revolutionary socialism. There followed a sequence of vivid, often violent political allegories, including *Das Floss der 'Medusa'* (The Raft of the 'Medusa') and *El Cimarrón*, eulogizing the outcast hero and pouring contempt on bourgeois society: the opera WE COME TO THE RIVER brought this intemperate style to its culmination, but by then he had already returned to more personal spheres of ripe orchestral story-telling (in *Tristan* and *Heliogabalus Imperator*) and chamber music. Subsequent works have continued in this manner, even where there has been, as in *The English Cat*, some ostensible political moral.

Operas: Das Wundertheater, 1948, rev. 1964; BOULEVARD SOLITUDE, 1951; Ein Landarzt, 1951, rev. 1964; Das Ende einer Welt, 1953, rev. 1964; KÖNIG HIRSCH, 1952-5; Der PRINZ VON HOMBURG, 1958; ELEGY FOR YOUNG LOVERS, 1959-61; The BASSARIDS, 1965, Moralities, 1967; WE COME TO THE RIVER, 1974-6; The English Cat, 1980-82, *Schwetzingen, 1983

Ballets: 7 early scores; Maratona, 1956; Ondine, 1956-7; L'usignolo dell'imperatore, 1959; Orpheus, 1979

Music theatre: Der langwierige Weg in der Wohnung der Natascha Ungeheuer, 1971; La Cubana, 1973

Orchestral: Chamber Conc, pf, fl, str, 1946; Concertino, pf, wind, perc, 1947; Sym no.1, 1947, rev. 1963, no.2, 1949, no.3, 1949-50, no.4, 1955, no.5, 1962, no.6, 1969, no.7, 1983-4; Vn Conc no.1, 1947, no.2, 1971; Pf Conc no.1, 1950, no.2, 1967; Sym Variations, 1950; Ode to the Westwind, vc, orch, 1953: 4 poemi, 1955; 3 Sinfonische Etüden, 1955, rev. 1964; Sonata, str, 1957-8; 3 Dithyrambs, chamber orch, 1958; Antifone, wind, timp, 1960; Los caprichos, 1963; In memoriam: Die weisse Rose, chamber orch, 1965; Double Conc, ob, harp, str, 1966; Db Conc, 1966; Fantasia, str, 1966; Telemanniana, 1967; Compases para preguntas ensimismadas, va, chamber orch, 1969-70; Heliogabalus Imperator, 1971-2; Tristan, pf, orch, tape, 1974; Ragtimes and Habaneras, brass band, 1975; Aria de la folia espanola, chamber orch, 1977; Il Vitalino raddoppiato, vn, chamber orch, 1977; Barcarola, 1980; Le miracle de la rose, cl, chamber orch, 1981

Vocal orchestral: Chor gefangener Trojer, chorus, orch, 1948, rev. 1964; 5 neapolitanische Lieder, Mez/Bar, orch, 1956; Nachtstücke und Arien, S, orch, 1957; Novae de infinito laudes, 4 solo vv, chorus, small orch, 1962; Ariosi, S, vn, orch, 1963; Cantata della fiaba estrema, S, small chorus, small orch, 1963; Das Floss der 'Medusa', S, Bar, speaker, chorus, orch, 1968; Versuch über Schweine, Bar, orch, 1968; Voices, Mez, T, small orch, 1973

Smaller vocal works: Wiegenlied der Mutter Gottes, boys' vv, 9 insts, 1948; Whispers from Heavenly Death, S/T, 8 insts, 1948; Apollo et Hyazinthus, A, 9 insts, 1948; KAMMERMUSIK, T, gui, 8 insts, 1958; Being Beauteous, S, harp, 4 vc, 1963; Choral

Fantasy, chorus, 7 insts, 1964; Muses of Sicily, chorus, 2 pf, wind, timp, 1966; El Cimarrón, Bar, 3 insts, 1969-70; El Rey de Harlem, S, 8 insts, 1980; König Oedipus, T, gui, 1983

Chamber and instrumental: Sonata, vn, pf, 1946; Str Qt no.1, 1947, no.2, 1952, no.3, 1975-6, no.4, 1976, no.5, 1976-7; Chamber Sonata, pf trio, 1948, rev. 1963; Serenade, vc, 1949; Variations, pf, 1949; Wind Qnt, 1952; Conc per il Marigny, pf, 8 insts, 1956; Pf Sonata, 1959; 6 absences, hpd, 1961; Lucy Escott Variations, hpd/pf, 1963; Divertimenti, 2 pf, 1964; Carillon, Récitatif, Masque, mand, gui, harp, 1974; Royal Winter Music, gui, 1975-6; Sonata, vn, 1976; Amicizia, 5 insts, 1976; L'autunno, wind qnt, 1978; Sonata, va, pf, 1981

Film scores, arrangements
[Schott; DG, Decca]
□ H. W. Henze, *Music and Politics* (1982)

heterophony Term for music in which 2 lines are variations of the same melody, often extended to encompass music in which the simultaneous lines are so distinct – in timbre, rhythmic character and/or pitch contents – as to be perceived as quite separate, not joined by necessary harmonic linkages as they most usually are in the western tradition of POLYPHONY from the Renaissance to Brahms. Heterophony of this latter sort begins to arise in Mahler (e.g. opening of 'Der Abschied') and Debussy (e.g. scherzo of String Quartet), and is exceedingly common in Messiaen and later composers. It is also very common in the music of the Far East.

Heure espagnole, L' (The Spanish Hour) Comic 1-act opera by Ravel and Franc-Nohain on the erotic adventures of a watchmaker's wife during his absence. *Paris, 19 May 1911.

hexachord Set of 6 different pitch classes. Normally the term implies that they form one half, fore or aft, of a 12-note set: there is no connection with the use of the term in medieval theory.

hierarchy A term much affected by European writers on serialism in the 1950s and 1960s, of doubtful meaning. The sense of tiers of importance seems to have been intended to cover, for example, the position of pitch in relation to duration, dynamic and other parameters, or the pyramid of derived forms obtainable from a set.

Hiller, Lejaren (1924-) American composer. Studied chemistry at Princeton and had composition lessons with Babbitt and Sessions, then in 1952 joined the chemistry department at the University of Illinois. There with Leonard Isaacson he produced the first digitally programmed composition, the *Illiac Suite* for string quartet (1957), named after its computer. He duly moved to the music department at the same university (1958-68) and thence to Buffalo, continuing to work on composition with computers. He collaborated with Cage on the programming of *HPSCHD* for harpsichords and tapes (1967-9). [Presser]

Hindemith, Paul (1895-1963) German composer. One of the century's most productive composers, he has achieved the unusual distinction of being given a place among the masters while a very large part of his output remains unknown and unregarded. He is celebrated as the foremost German neoclassicist of the 1920s and 1930s, which he surely was, and as a composer ready to make his art useful to others, which his lengthy catalogue cannot deny. But in his youth he was among the Expressionists, and in later years he created a consistent diatonic style on the basis of his own harmonic theory. His influence from the 1920s to the 1950s was immense and widespread, but his later absence from the family trees of the avant garde has left his whole achievement uncertain.

He studied composition with Arnold Mendelssohn and Bernard Sekles at the Hoch Conservatory in Frankfurt (1909-17), and then served in the army. After the war he returned to places he had held as a violinist since 1915 in Adolf Rebner's string quartet and the Frankfurt Opera orchestra (in 1919 he became the quartet's viola player). In 1921 the premieres at Stuttgart of his first theatre works, *Mörder* and *Das Nusch-Nuschi*, gained him notoriety, the former being a grandiose statement of violence as necessary between the sexes, but in 1922 he presented himself at the Donaueschingen Festival with a very different work: the *Kammermusik no.1* for 12 instruments, which was the first of many suites looking towards Baroque models of form and vigorous polyphonic texture driven by motor rhythm.

The previous year he had formed the Amar Quartet (he was again the violist) in order to play his own Second Quartet, and the success of this ensemble led him to relinquish his post with the Frankfurt Opera in 1923. He and the quartet took a leading part in the Donaueschingen festivals, and he produced a large output of chamber music and other works of neoclassical design, including operas ranging from the full-length CARDILLAC to the

tiny jeu d'esprit *Hin und zurück*, whose action reverses itself half way through. There was also a brief collaboration with Brecht on a LEHRSTÜCK, and he wrote other works which, like this, were designed for amateurs, besides experimenting with mechanical and electronic instruments.

Around 1930 his style began to become broader and less frenetically propelled: the *Kammermusiken* for small orchestras gave place to the larger *Konzertmusiken*, and the deliberate anti-expressive manner of *Cardillac* was replaced by an artistic apologia in MATHIS DER MALER. He was attacked by the new Nazi government, and eventually in 1937 he left Germany, setting in New York in 1940. He taught at Yale, took American citizenship (in 1946) and set about becoming an American composer, writing works for the great American orchestras and composing a Requiem to words by Whitman, *When Lilacs Last in the Door-Yard Bloom'd*. He also, controversially, revised and smoothened some of his earlier works, notably *Cardillac* and his Rilke song cycle *Das Marienleben*, and produced in his *Ludus tonalis* a cycle of piano fugues partly elucidating his view of notes and intervals arranged in definite orders of relationship: 5ths and 4ths were closest, then major and minor 3rds, then major 2nds, then minor 2nds and finally tritones.

In 1953 he moved to Switzerland, where he lived for the rest of his life, bringing to completion his long-standing project for an opera on Kepler, *Die* HARMONIE DER WELT.

Operas: Mörder, Hoffnung der Frauen, 1919; *Stuttgart, 1921; Das Nusch-Nuschi, 1920, *Stuttgart, 1921; Sancta Susanna, 1921, *Frankfurt, 1922; CARDILLAC, 1926; Hin und zurück, 1927, Baden-Baden, 1927; Neues vom Tage, 1928-9, *Berlin, 1929; MATHIS DER MALER, 1934-5; Die HARMONIE DER WELT, 1956-7; The Long Christmas Dinner, 1960, *Mannheim, 1961

Ballets: Der Dämon, 1922; *Darmstadt, 1923; Nobilissima visione, 1938, *London, 1938; Hérodiade, 1944

Works for full orchestra: Conc for Orch, 1925; Konzertmusik op.50, str, wind, 1930; Philharmonic Conc, 1932; Mathis der Maler, sym, 1934; Der Schwanendreher, va, orch, 1935; Symphonic Dances, 1937; Vn Conc, 1939; Vc Conc, 1940; Sym, E♭, 1940; Cupid and Psyche, 1943; Sym Metamorphosis on Themes of Carl Maria von Weber, 1943; PfConc, 1945; Symphonia serena, 1946; Cl Conc, 1947; Conc, woodwind, harp, orch, 1949; Sinfonietta, E, 1949; Hn Conc, 1949; Die Harmonie der Welt, sym, 1951; Pittsburgh Sym, 1958; Org Conc, 1962

Works for reduced orchestra: KAMMERMUSIK no.1, 1921; Kammermusik no.2, pf, 12 insts, 1924; Kammermusik no.3, vc, 10 insts, 1925; Kammermusik no.4, vn, chamber orch, 1925; Konzertmusik op.41, wind, 1926; Kammermusik no.5, va, chamber orch, 1927; Kammermusik no.6, va d'amore, chamber orch, 1927; Kammermusik no.7, org, chamber orch, 1927; Konzertmusik op.48, va, chamber orch, 1930; Konzertmusik op.49, pf, brass, 2 harps, 1930; Trauermusik, va, str, 1936; Theme and Variations 'The 4 Temperaments', pf, str, 1940; Conc, tpt, bn, str, 1949; Sym, B♭, concert band, 1951

Choral: Das Unaufhörliche, 4 solo vv, chorus, orch, 1931; When Lilacs Last in the Door-Yard Bloom'd, Mez, Bar, chorus, orch, 1946; Apparebit repentina dies, chorus, brass, 1947; Ite, angeli veloces, Mez, A, T, chorus, orch, audience, 1953-5; 12 Madrigals, SSATB, 1958; Mass, chorus, 1963; many smaller works

Solo vocal: Die junge Magd, A, fl, cl, str qt, 1922; Das Marienleben, S, pf, 1922-3, rev. 1936-48, orch version 1938-59; Die Serenaden, S, ob, va, vc, 1925; 6 Lieder, T, pf, 1933-5; 9 English songs, S/Mez, pf, 1942-4; 13 Motets, S/T, pf, 1941-60

Chamber: Str Qt no.1, 1919, no.2, 1921, no.3, 1922, no.4, 1923, no.5, 1943, no.6, 1945; Kleine Kammermusik, wind qnt, 1922; Cl Qnt, 1923; Str Trio no.1, 1924, no.2, 1933; 3 Pieces, cl, tpt, pf, vn, db, 1925; Rondo, 3 gui, 1925; Trio, pf, va, heckelphone/t sax, 1928; Qt, cl, vn, vc, pf, 1938; Septet, wind qnt, b cl, tpt, 1948; Sonata, 4 hn, 1952; Octet, cl, bn, hn, vn, 2 va, vc, db, 1957-8

Sonatas with pf: Vn op.11/1, E♭, 1918; Vn op.11/2, D, 1918; Vc op.11/3, 1919; Va op.11/4, F, 1919; Kleine Sonate op.25/2, va d'amore, 1922; Vn, E, 1935; Fl, 1936; Bn, 1938; Ob, 1938; Hn, 1939; Tpt, 1939; Vn, C, 1939; Va, C, 1939; Cl, 1939; Cor Anglais, 1941; Trbn, 1941; A sax/Hn, 1943; Vc, 1948; Db, 1949; Tuba, 1955

Solo sonatas: Va op.11/5, 1919; Va op. 25/1, 1922; Vc op.25/3, 1922; Vn op.31/1, 1924; Vn op.31/2, 1924; Harp, 1939; Org no.1, 1937, no.2, 1937, no.3, 1940

Other instrumental works: 3 Pieces, vc, pf, 1917; Kanonische Sonatine, 2 fl, 1923; 8 Pieces, fl, 1927; 2 kanonische Duette, 2 vn, 1929; 14 easy pieces, 2 vn, 1931; Duet, va, vc, 1934; 3 easy pieces, vc, pf, 1938; Meditation, vn/va/vc, pf, 1938; A frog he went a-courting, vc, pf, 1941; Echo, fl, pf, 1942

Piano: Dance pieces, 1922; Suite '1922', 1922; Piano Music, op.37, 1925-7; Sonatas nos. 1-3, A, G, B♭, 1936; Sonata, 4 hands, 1938; Ludus tonalis, 1942; Sonata, 2 pf, 1942

Lehrstücke, music for amateurs, arrangements, unpublished music for mechanical and electronic instruments [Schott]

□ P. Hindemith, *The Craft of Musical Composition* (1941-2), *A Composer's World* (1952); I. Kemp, *Hindemith* (1970); G. Skelton, *Paul Hindemith* (1975)

history Until the 20th c., music was unique among the arts in having no history, since its products could not be preserved except in the form of written scores, whose relationship with sounded music has always been problematic. Composers have tried to remedy this by making their NOTATION ever more precise; meanwhile RECORDING has provided the art with the history it lacked. This has had serious consequences, but the prominence of recording in contemporary musical life is perhaps only a symptom of a deeper failure of confidence in the present, a nostalgia for the past or for the future (*see* FUTURISM). When music was ahistorical the distant past was a closed book: Beethoven's inspection of Handel (less than 70 years dead at the time) was unusual, and there was hardly any musical counterpart to the medievalizing of 19th c. painting and architecture. In the 20th c., however, history has become one of the composer's chief resources, used to provide particular models of technique (notably by Stravinsky), general concepts of style (*see* NEOCLASSICISM, NEW ROMANTICISM) and sounding means. Remarkably few instruments have been introduced in this century by comparison with the last; the rapid development of the orchestra naturally stopped when music became historical; and the century's major innovation of ELECTRONIC MUSIC, made possible ironically by the same inventions that led to recording, has remained of marginal concern.

Hoddinott, Alun (1929-) Welsh composer. Studied at University College, Cardiff, where he joined the staff in 1959 and was made professor in 1967; he was also a pupil of Arthur Benjamin in London. His works, in a forceful, highly chromatic but essentially tonal style, include operas, many orchestral scores, choral pieces and a diverse output of chamber music [OUP, Novello]

□ B. Deane: *Alun Hoddinott* (Cardiff, 1977)

Holland Festival Annual summer festival of all the arts, instituted in 1947 and with events taking place in all the major Dutch cities. The works of Dutch composers have always been featured alongside new works by foreign composers, including Britten (*Spring Symphony*, 1949) and Stockhausen (*Festival* from *Donnerstag aus Licht*, 1980).

Höller, York (1944-) German composer. Studied with Zimmermann at the Cologne Hochschule für Musik (1963-8) and with Boulez at the 1965 Darmstadt courses. He has been associated with the electronic studios of Westdeutscher Rundfunk and IRCAM, using electronics with live ensembles in music of sure professionalism.
Antiphon, str qt, tape, 1974; Arcus, small orch, tape, 1978; Mythos, orch, tape, 1979-80; Traumspiel, S, orch, tape, 1983; PfConc, 1985 [Schott]

Holliger, Heinz (1939-) Swiss oboist and composer. Studied the oboe in Berne and Paris, and composition in Berne with Veress and Basle with Boulez (1962). His bright-toned, intelligent and inquisitive manner as a performer has brought him new works from Berio (*Sequenza VII*) and many others, and he has introduced BARTOLOZZI sounds and other new techniques in his own oboe works. Other works also demand a virtuoso achievement of new effects, somewhat in the manner of Kagel.
Music theatre: Not I (Beckett), S, electronics, 1980
Orchestral: Siebengesang, ob, women's vv, orch, 1966-7; Pneuma, wind band, radios, org, perc, 1970; Atembogen, 1974-5; Übungen zu Scardanelli, chamber orch, 1975-84
Choral: Dona nobis pacem, 12 vv, 1970; Psalm, 16 vv, 1971
Chamber: h, wind qnt, 1968; Kreis, 4-7 insts, 1971-2; Str Qt, 1973; Duo, vn, vc, 1982; Lieder ohne Worte, vn, pf, 1982-3
Solo instrumental: Cardiophonie, wind inst, electronics, 1971; Lied, fl, 1971; Studie über Mehrklänge, ob, 1971; Chaconne, vc, 1976; 5 Pieces, org, tape, 1980; Trema, va/vc/vn, 1981; (t)air(e), fl, 1983
[Schott; Wergo, DG]

Holloway, Robin (1943-) English composer. Took composition lessons with Goehr and studied at Cambridge (1961-9), where he remained as research fellow and lecturer. His music shows an appreciation of the lyrical spring in German Romanticism from Schumann to Berg: much of his large output consists of songs, and the several orchestral works tend to be richly textured and rhapsodic in style if not in form. They include a vocal symphony drawn from his opera *Clarissa* (1968-76). [Boosey; Chandos]

Holmboe, Vagn (1909-) Danish composer. Studied with Høffding and Jeppesen at the Copenhagen Conservatory (1927-30) and with Toch in Berlin (1931), then taught at the Institute for the Blind and at the Conservatory (1950-65). His large output, influenced by Nielsen, Hindemith and Stravinsky, includes 10 symphonies, numerous concertos and 14 quartets. [Hansen]

Holst, Gustav (1874-1934) English composer. Studied with Stanford at the Royal College of Music (1895-8), where there started a lifelong friendship with Vaughan Williams. He also took lessons in Sanskrit in order to read Hindu sacred books. He made his living as a trombonist and then as a teacher, notably at St Paul's Girls' School in Hammersmith, London (1905-34), and at Morley College (1907-24). Like Vaughan Williams, he took an interest in English folksong and learned from its modality, but he was impressed too by early Stravinsky as well as by his Sanskrit readings: both led him to use unusual metres and an intense richness of orchestral colour which, however, he could moderate to bleakness in *Egdon Heath*.
Operas: Sāvitri, 1908, *London, 1916; The Perfect Fool, 1918-22, *London, 1923; At the Boar's Head, 1924, *Manchester, 1925; The Wandering Scholar, 1929-30, *Liverpool, 1934
Orchestral: Beni Mora, 1909-10; St Paul's Suite, str, 1912-13; The Planets, 1914-16; A Fugal Overture, 1922; A Fugal Conc, fl, ob, str, 1923; Egdon Heath, 1927; A Moorside Suite, brass band, 1928; Double Vn Conc, 1929; Hammersmith, band, 1930, orch version 1931; Brook Green Suite, str, 1933
Choral orchestral: Choral Hymns from the Rig Veda, 1908-12; The Cloud Messenger, 1909-10; The Hymn of Jesus, 1917; Ode to Death, 1919; First Choral Sym, S, chorus, orch, 1923-4; A Choral Fantasia, S, chorus, orch, 1930
Other works: many smaller choral pieces, songs, few inst pieces
[Boosey, Curwen, Faber, Novello, Stainer & Bell]
☐ I. Holst, *Gustav Holst* (1938, 2/1969), *The Music of Gustav Holst* (1951, 3/1975)

Honegger, Arthur (1892-1955) Swiss composer. A serious-minded artist, he expressed his conscientiousness in providing much well-made utility music (for films, radio, etc), in developing a style of strong contrapuntal energy and expanded diatonic harmony, and in applying himself to large instrumental forms as well as to the moral pageants of his operas and oratorios. The early membership of Les six is therefore misleading: it came after a period of study with Gédalge, Widor and d'Indy at the Paris Conservatoire (1911-14), and it lasted only briefly. He remained in Paris, but his musical allegiances were to Beethoven and Bach, even if he learned much too from the music Prokofiev and Stravinsky were composing in the early 1920s. As a creative character he perhaps had most in common with Dukas, except that in his case the pursuit of musical truth led not to silence but to a large body of works in which more questions are posed than answers found.

Operas and staged oratorios: Le roi David, 1921, ★Mézières, 1921, rev. 1923; Impératrice aux rochers, 1925, ★Paris, 1927; Antigone, 1924-7, ★Brussels, 1927; Judith, 1925, ★Monte Carlo, 1926; Jeanne d'Arc au bûcher, 1934-5, ★Basle, 1938; L'aiglon, with Ibert, 1935, ★Monte Carlo, 1937; Charles le téméraire, 1943-4, ★Mézières, 1944

Ballets: Skating Rink, 1921; Amphion, 1929; Sémiramis, 1931; Le cantique des cantiques, 1937; La naissance des couleurs, 1940; L'appel de la montagne, 1945

Oratorios: Les cris du monde, 1930-31; La danse des morts, 1938; Une cantate de Noël, 1953

Orchestral: Pastorale d'été, 1920; Horace victorieux, 1920-21; Chant de joie, 1923; Prélude pour 'La tempête', 1923; Pacific 231 (Mouvement symphonique no. 1), 1923; Pf Concertino, 1924; Rugby (Mouvement symphonique no. 2), 1928; Vc Conc, 1929; Sym no. 1, 1929-30, no. 2, str, tpt, 1941, no. 3, 'Liturgique', 1945-6, no. 4, 'Deliciae Basilienses', 1946, no. 5, 'Di tre re', 1950; Mouvement symphonique no. 3, 1932; Nocturne, 1936; Conc da camera, fl, cor anglais, str, 1948; Monopartita, 1951; Suite archaïque, 1951; Toccata, 1951

Chamber: Str Qt no. 1, 1916-17, no. 2, 1934-6, no. 3, 1936-7; Vn Sonata no. 1, 1916-18; Sonatina, 2 vn, 1920; Vc Sonata, 1920; Sonatina, cl/vc, pf, 1921-2; 3 contrepoints, 4 insts, 1922; Sonatina, vn, vc, 1932; Sonata, vn, 1940; Intrada, tpt, pf, 1947

Piano: 3 Pieces, 1915-19; Le cahier romand, 1921-3; Prelude, Arioso, Fughetta, 1932; Scenic-Railway, 1937; Partita, 2 pf, 1940; 2 esquisses, 1943-4

Many scores for theatre, cinema and radio, songs [Salabert]

□ A. Honegger, *I am a Composer* (1966)

Hopkins, Bill (1943-81) English composer. Studied with Nono at Dartington (1960-61), Rubbra and Wellesz at Oxford (1961-4), and Messiaen and Barraqué in Paris (1964-5). He took occasional work as a critic, translator and teacher before he was appointed in 1979 to Newcastle University. His few works are composed with a rare intensity and density of thought, accepting the challenges of Barraqué's musical example and Beckett's poetic vision.

2 Pomes, S, 4 insts, 1964; Sensation, S, 4 insts, 1965; Etudes en série, 3 books, pf, 1965-72; Pendant, vn, 1968-9, rev. 1973; Nouvelle étude hors série, org, 1974; En attendant, fl, ob, vc, hpd, 1976-7 [Schott, UE]

horn The 20th c. repertory includes concertos by Strauss, Hindemith, Banks and Schuller as well as Britten's Serenade with tenor and strings. There are sonatas for horn quartet by Hindemith and Tippett, chamber works by Britten (*Canticle III*), Hindemith (Sonata) and Ligeti (Trio), and a solo movement in Messiaen's *Des canyons aux étoiles....* This last includes unusual effects, but otherwise the instrument has not been called upon much to enlarge its range of sounds.

Hovhaness, Alan (1911-) American composer. Studied with Converse at the New England Conservatory and with Martinů at Tanglewood (1943). His output is immense, including well over 300 works with opus numbers and covering all genres. The style is one of modal orientalism, sometimes with the use of Asian instruments and often with an awareness of his partly Armenian background. [AMP, Peer, Peters]

Howells, Herbert (1892-1983) English composer. Studied with Stanford at the Royal College of Music (1912-16), where he joined the staff in 1920, also teaching as Holst's successor at St Paul's Girls' School (1936-62). His music is serenely English in a style between Vaughan Williams and Elgar; the first works were mostly orchestral, including 2 piano concertos (in C major, 1913, and C minor, 1924), but after his *Hymnus paradisi* (concert Requiem for soloists, chorus and orchestra, 1938) he wrote mostly Anglican church music. [Novello]

Hubay, Jenő (1858-1937) Hungarian violinist and composer. Studied with his violinist father and in Berlin with Joachim (1871-6), and taught at the Budapest Conservatory from 1886. In 1919 he was appointed director of the Academy, where his conservatism proved irksome to Bartók. His works include 4 violin concertos, 4 symphonies and several operas.

Huber, Klaus (1924-) Swiss composer. Studied with Burkhard at the Zurich Conservatory (1947-

9) and privately, and with Blacher in Berlin (1955-6). He has taught at the conservatories of Zurich, Lucerne and Basle (from 1961). His music springs from a metaphysical background close to Burkhard's, taking texts and images from German Renaissance mysticism, though his musical means are those of a later generation: serialism has a natural place in his arcane science of numbers.

Opera: Jot, oder Wann kommt der Herr zurück ★Berlin, 1973

Vocal orchestral: Soliloquia, 5 solo vv, chorus, orch, 1959-64; ...inwendig voller figur..., chorus, orch, tape, 1970-71; ...ausgespannt..., Bar, insts, tape, 1972; Erniedrigt-Geknechtet-Verlassen-Verachtet, 4 solo vv, chorus, orch, tape, ★Donaueschingen, 1983

Orchestral: Alveare vernat, fl, str, 1965-7; Tenebrae, 1966-7; Tempora, vn, orch, 1969-70; Turnus, orch, tape, 1973-4

Chamber: Noctes intelligibilis lucis, ob, hpd, 1961; Ascensus, fl, vc, pf, 1969

[Schott; Wergo]

Huddersfield Contemporary Music Festival
Founded in 1978 by Richard Steinitz at the Polytechnic of Huddersfield, Yorkshire. The festival takes place annually in November and has included retrospectives of works by Xenakis (1982), Carter and Henze (1983), Davies (1984) and Berio (1985).

Husa, Karel (1921-) Czech-American composer. Studied with Ridky at the Prague Conservatory (1941-5) and with Boulanger and Honegger in Paris (1946-51); in 1954 he moved from Paris to Cornell University. His music is in a strongly rhythmic neoclassical style within the ambit of Honegger and Bartók, imbued latterly with Viennese serialism. Nearly all his works are instrumental: they include pieces for orchestra, concert band and smaller ensembles. [AMP, Schott, Leduc]

Hymnen (Anthems) 2-hour tape composition by Stockhausen based on national anthems from around the world. The tape may be played alone, or with commentary from 4 musicians, or with the addition of an orchestra in the third of the 4 'regions'. ★Cologne, 30 Nov 1967 (with ensemble).

Hyperprism Work by Varèse, his first for a typical compact ensemble of wind and percussion. The title suggests a geometrical object in 4 dimensions – not inappropriately for music of clashing sound objects. ★cond Varèse, New York, 4 Mar 1923.

I

Ibert, Jacques (1890-1962) French composer. Studied with Vidal at the Paris Conservatoire (1909-13) and won the Prix de Rome in 1919. While based in Rome he travelled widely around the Mediterranean and conveyed his Ravelian impressions in the orchestral *Escales* (1922). Later works include the operetta *Angélique* (1926) and the comic *Divertissement* for chamber orchestra (1930). He returned to Rome as director of the Académie de France (1937-60) and composed rather less in these later years. [Leduc, Heugel]

Ichiyanagi, Toshi (1933-) Japanese composer and pianist. Studied with Ikenouchi and, from 1952, at the Juilliard School. He remained in the USA until 1961 and associated himself with Cage's ideas, then returned to Japan, where he has worked as a composer and organizer of concerts of new music. [Peters]

Images (Pictures) Debussy used the title for a set of 3 piano pieces (1894) that he did not publish and for 2 later sets that he did, the first (1905) consisting of 'Reflets dans l'eau', 'Hommage à Rameau' and 'Mouvement', the second (1907) of 'Cloches à travers les feuilles', 'Et la lune descend sur le temple qui fût' and 'Poissons d'or', ★Viñes, Paris, 3 Mar 1906, 21 Feb 1908. He also gave it as title to his orchestral triptych comprising *Gigues, Ibéria* and *Rondes de printemps*. ★Paris, 20 Feb 1910 (*Ibéria*), 2 Mar 1910 (*Rondes* cond Debussy), 26 Jan 1913 (complete).

Imbrie, Andrew (1921-) American composer. Studied with Sessions at Princeton and Berkeley, where he was appointed to the faculty in 1947. His music follows Sessions in being 12-note but driven by harmonic progressions and in being contained within large, strongly shaped forms. His works include 4 quartets, 3 symphonies, a variety of concertos, operas and choral music. [Malcolm]

Impressionism Term originating in art criticism: Louis Leroy sneeringly wrote of 'Impressionists' after attending an exhibition at which Monet's *Impression: soleil levant* was shown in 1874. The group later accepted the name, and soon it was being applied to music, most famously in an official judgment of Debussy's *Printemps* in 1887 as showing dangerous Impressionism. Debussy's titles, such as those of his IMAGES, show how willing he was to be stimulated by, and to let his listeners be stimulated by, pictorial subject matter, and there is some kinship between the indefiniteness produced by his harmony and instrumentation and that produced by Monet's brushwork. To that extent the term is a useful label for a similar style in some works by Ravel, Dukas, Ibert and Bartók, for instance, though its value is undermined by its association too with those intense moments of subjective impression to be found in the atonal miniatures of Schoenberg and Webern.

improvisation An art that had been in decline long before the beginning of the 20th c., with the custom for cadenzas and ornaments to be written out and for extemporization on given themes to be confined to the organ loft. However, improvisation of various kinds began to be practised again in the 1950s with the arrival of ALEATORY composition, GRAPHIC NOTATION and INDETERMINACY, though improvisation in the old sense, allowing the display of virtuosity within a prescribed musical world, is more a characteristic of JAZZ, from which the 'free improvisation' of such groups as Globokar's can be distinguished only in terms of the performer's clichés.

indeterminacy Term introduced by Cage and preferred by him to ALEATORY composition. He has distinguished between works which are 'indeterminate of their composition' (i.e. a conventional score is produced by chance operations) and those which are 'indeterminate of their performance' (i.e. the score leaves a lot of decisions to the performers). The former is exemplified by the *Music of Changes* and other works of the 1950s, the latter by most of Cage's subsequent output, displaying a wide variety of means by which intention may be avoided: graphic notation (*Concert*), instructions conveyed only in words (*Inlets*), the provision of a multitude of options (*HPSCHD*). There is also a lecture by Cage entitled 'Indeterminacy', consisting of an unlinked sequence of anecdotes and published in his *Silence*.

Indian music The rhythmic and melodic formulae of Sanskrit theory have been important to Messiaen since the 1930s, while the sound of present-day Indian music and musical instruments excited

Foulds from even earlier. His initiative, however, has been surprisingly little followed, even though the sitar became almost a *sine qua non* of popular music around the time of the Beatles' *Sergeant Pepper* (1967). There is some influence in early Davies and later Eloy. Similarly, there has been little western-style composition by Indian composers, the main exception being Naresh Sohal (1939–).

Indonesian music No exotic sound has more deeply penetrated western music since the Crusades than that of the Javanese and Balinese gamelan: an orchestra consisting largely of gongs and tuned metallophones. McPhee lived on Bali (1934–6) and came back with scientific studies, transcriptions and material for original compositions, and his work almost certainly had an influence on Cage's pieces for percussion orchestra in the late 1930s and early 1940s. Messiaen heard a Balinese gamelan at the Exposition Coloniale in Paris in 1931, and has written for similar ensembles of vibrating metal instruments in most of his orchestral works since the *Trois petites liturgies* of 1944, influencing his pupils, such as Boulez and Stockhausen, and indeed creating a sensible change in the nature of the orchestra. Britten heard Balinese music on the spot in 1955 and used a tuned percussion ensemble in his ballet *The Prince of the Pagodas* and opera *Death in Venice*.

In memoriam Dylan Thomas Work by Stravinsky, consisting of 'dirge-canons' for quartets of trombones and strings around a setting of the poet's 'Do not go gentle' for tenor and string quartet. It is based on a 5-note set and was the first of several memorials from the composer's last years, written for a man with whom he had hoped to create an opera. ★Los Angeles, 20 Sep 1954.

Inori (Jap. 'Adorations') Work by Stockhausen for orchestra with 1 or 2 mimes who go through gestures of prayer in synchrony with the music's elaboration of a melody. ★cond Stockhausen, Donaueschingen, 20 Oct 1974.

Institut de Recherche et de Coordination Acoustique/Musique Institution attached to the Centre Pompidou in Paris and directed by Boulez. It began its activities in 1977, presenting concerts (notably with the Ensemble InterContemporain) and providing facilities for computer composition and the development of digital machinery in concert performance. Composers who have produced works there include Boulez (*Répons*), Berio (*Che-*

mins V for clarinet and computer), Birtwistle (tape for *The Mask of Orpheus*) and Harvey (*Mortuos plango, Bhakti*).

Intégrales Work by Varèse for wind and percussion, which he later spoke of reinterpreting in electronic terms. ★cond Stokowski, New York, 1 Mar 1925.

Intermezzo Opera by Strauss, a domestic comedy based on an incident of misunderstanding in his own marital life. ★Dresden, 4 Nov 1924.

intermodulation The interference of 2 signals, commonly encountered when a radio is slightly mistuned. Stockhausen adapted the term to cover a range of electronic techniques he used initially in *Telemusik* to make 2 or more musical recordings interfere with one another. For instance, one recording may be given the dynamic envelope of a second and the rhythm of a third. The word was adopted as name by an English live electronic ensemble including Smalley and Souster, active from 1970 to 1976; they took part in the first performances of Stockhausen's *Sternklang*.

International Composers' Guild Concert organization directed by Varèse and Salzedo in New York (1921-7), giving the first performances of Varèse's *Offrandes*, *Hyperprism*, *Octandre* and *Intégrales*, and the American premieres of *Pierrot lunaire*, *Les noces*, Berg's Chamber Concerto and Webern's op.5.

International Society for Contemporary Music (ISCM) Body founded in 1922 and giving annual festivals of contemporary music since the following year. These festivals have included the first performances of Berg's Violin Concerto (Barcelona, 1936), Webern's *Das Augenlicht* (London, 1938) and Second Cantata (Brussels, 1950), Boulez's *Le marteau sans maître* (Baden-Baden, 1955) and Birtwistle's *An Imaginary Landscape* (London, 1971).

Intolleranza 1960 Opera by Nono, on the plight of an immigrant caught in the machine of police surveillance and bourgeois capitalism; it was the first opera by a leader of the postwar European avant garde. ★Venice, 1961. Rev. as *Intolleranza 1970*, ★Florence, 1974.

intonarumori (It. 'noisemakers') Instruments invented by Luigi Russolo from 1913 onwards and demonstrated in Milan, Genoa, London (1914) and Paris (1921). They would seem to have been created as much for visual impact as for newness of sound, but this is difficult to judge, since only one recording survives (of pieces by Luigi's brother Antonio) and the instruments themselves were destroyed in Paris during the second world war. An echo of them may possibly be found, though, in the percussion scoring and mechanical rhythm of composers who were impressed by them, notably Varèse, Antheil, Stravinsky and Honegger.

intuitive music Term preferred by Stockhausen to 'improvisation' for music he has made with chosen musicians in response to verbal texts (*Aus den sieben Tagen*), indeterminate notations (*Prozession*), shortwave radio receptions (*Kurzwellen*) and tape compositions (*Hymnen*).

inversion Standard operation with a 12-note set by which all the intervals are reversed in direction, i.e. a falling minor 3rd in the original form becomes a rising minor 3rd in the inversion. It was introduced by Schoenberg in his first wholly 12-note serial work, the Piano Suite.

Ionisation Work by Varèse for a percussion orchestra of 13 players (though played by Les Percussions de Strasbourg as a sextet), without defined pitch until the chiming of piano, glockenspiel and tubular bells at the end. It is probably the first western work for percussion alone, though anticipated by Milhaud's music for *Les choëphores* and by *Les noces*. ★New York, 6 Mar 1933.

Ippolitov-Ivanov, Mikhail (1859-1935) Russian composer. Studied with Rimsky-Korsakov at St Petersburg Conservatory (1875-82), then led a career as a teacher and conductor. His Russian academicism held him in good stead after the Revolution, when he turned from lyrical orientalism to mass songs and marches.

Ireland, John (1879-1962) English composer. Studied with Stanford at the Royal College of Music (1893-1901), where he returned to teach (1923-39), working also as a church musician. He composed in an aloof style with its roots in Elgar but drawing also on influences from Debussy and Ravel.

Orchestral: The Forgotten Rite, 1913; Mai-Dun, 1920-21; Pf Conc, 1930; Legend, pf, orch, 1933; A London Overture, 1936; Concertino pastorale, str, 1939; Epic March, 1942; Satyricon, overture, 1946

Pf music, songs, choral works, chamber music
□ M. V. Searle, *John Ireland* (1979)

Ives, Charles (1874-1954) American composer. Undoubtedly the most extraordinary discoverer in western music, he was working with polytonality, atonality, ametrical rhythms, unusual ensembles, SPATIAL MUSIC, COLLAGE, etc before he virtually gave up composition in the early 1920s. Priority, though, is a historical criterion, and his historical position is complicated, largely because he composed in isolation, caring little for performance: almost none of his music had been heard before the 1930s, and many major works were not played until after his death.

His father George Ives (1845-94) would seem to have been a hardly less remarkable man: he was a bandmaster in Danbury, Connecticut, where Ives was born, and he encouraged his son to question musical convention. This started early. At the age of 14 he became organist at Danbury Baptist Church, for which he wrote choral and organ music: a setting of Psalm 67 (?1894) is firmly in 2 keys throughout, and there are polytonal interludes in the organ Variations on 'America' (?1891). However, there are again historical difficulties here, for these works were not printed until long afterwards (indeed, nothing of Ives's was published until the 1920s), and Carter, who knew Ives from the 1920s, has wondered how much his scores were altered after the event.

However that may be, he embarked on the training that would have equipped him for a normal musical career: he went to Yale (1894-8) and studied with Parker, composing there such relatively well-behaved works as the First Symphony and First String Quartet, followed by the eminently Parkerian (except for what here definitely sounds like later gingering up) cantata *The Celestial Country*. He did not, however, seek a full-time musical appointment, but instead went into the insurance business, which he understood in utopian fashion as a means for people to gain control over their own lives by providing for unfavourable eventualities; in 1906 he formed his own agency with Julian Myrick, having married Harmony Twichell the year before.

Business left him only the weekends in which to compose, but during the first 15 years of the century he produced an enormous quantity of music: symphonies and other orchestral pieces, chamber works, piano music and a large number of songs. The songs best show the scope and nature of his musical gift: they give the impression of being im-

mediate responses to the words, whether in the form of nostalgic reverie on hymntunes ('At the River'), comic sketch ('Ann Street'), grandly rhetorical atonality ('From "Paracelsus"'), breezy Americana ('Charlie Rutlage') or an extraordinary mixture of the visionary and the commonplace ('General William Booth Enters into Heaven'). Many songs were arranged as instrumental pieces, or derived from instrumental pieces: Ives was in the habit of revising and rescoring his music, so that the whole output forms a network from which only a few adventurous sound pictures, like *The* UNANSWERED QUESTION, escape.

Although the songs set diverse texts, most of the music is centred in the songs and dances, hymns, books, poems and landscapes Ives knew as a boy. His orchestral THREE PLACES IN NEW ENGLAND is a set of personal impressions; so too is the 'Holidays' Symphony, while the 'CONCORD' SONATA considers the writings of 19th c. New England authors, among them Emerson, whose transcendentalism was adopted by Ives as a doctrine of winning vision through muscular self-reliance. That is the message conveyed by his Second Quartet, whose instruments discuss and argue before marching up the mountains in harmony. It is the message too of his colossally various Fourth Symphony and of his whole output.

In 1918 he had a heart attack and was away from work for a year. He had the 'Concord' Sonata, its accompanying *Essays* and a volume of 114 songs privately printed in 1920-22 but composed almost nothing new: nothing at all after 1926. In the 1930s, though, his music began to come to public attention, thanks to publications by Cowell of orchestral movements and songs, orchestral performances under Slonimsky (and Webern in Vienna) and performances of the 'Concord' Sonata by John Kirkpatrick.

Works for full orchestra: Sym no.1, 1895-8; Sym no.2, 1900-01; 'Holidays' Sym (Washington's Birthday, Decoration Day, The Fourth of July, Thanksgiving), 1904-13; Robert Browning Overture, 1908-12; THREE PLACES IN NEW ENGLAND (Orchestral Set no.1) 1908-?14; Orchestral Set no.2, 1909-15; Sym no.4, 1909-16

Works for small orchestra: Overture '1776', 1903; Country Band March, 1903; Sym no.3, 1904; Over the Pavements, 1906-13; The Pond, 1906; Set for Theatre Orch, 1906-11; The UNANSWERED QUESTION, 1906; Central Park in the Dark, 1906; The Gong on the Hook and Ladder, ?1911; The Rainbow, 1914; Tone Roads no.1, 1911, no.3, 1915; Chromâtimelôdtune, ?1919

Choral: Psalm 150, 12 vv, org, ?1894; Psalm 67 8 vv, ?1894; Psalm 54, 6vv, ?1894; Psalm 24, 8vv, ?1894; The Celestial Country, solo vv, SATB, 8 insts, 1898-9; Psalm 100, 12vv, bells ad lib, 1898-?9; Psalm 25, 8vv, org, 1899-?1901; Psalm 135, 8vv, timp, org, ?1900; 3 Harvest Home Chorales, SATB, brass, org, ?1898-1901; Processional, 4vv, org/brass, 1901; The New River, unison, orch, 1911; Lincoln, unison, orch, 1912; December, unison, wind, 1912-13; Psalm 90, 8vv, bells, org, 1894-1924

Chamber: Str Qt no.1, 1896, no.2, 1907-13; From the Steeples and Mountains, tpt, trbn, bells, 1901-?2; Largo, vn, cl, pf, 1902-?3; An Old Song Deranged, cl/cor anglais, harp, str qt, ?1903; Hymn, str qt, db, 1904; Pf Trio, 1904-5; Halloween, pf qnt, 1906; Largo risoluto no.1 and no.3, pf qnt, 1906; All the Way Around and Back, cl, bugle, vn, bells, pf duet, 1906; The Innate, str qt, db, pf, 1908; Holding your own, str qt, 1903-14; In re con moto et al, pf qnt, 1913; Chromâtimelôdtune, brass qt, pf, ?1919

Violin sonatas: Pre-First, 1899-?1903; no.1, 1902-8; no.2, 1907-10; no.3, 1913-?14; no.4, 1906-?16

Piano: 3-Page Sonata, 1905; Set of 5 Take-Offs, 1906-7; The Anti-Abolitionist Riots, 1908; Some Southpaw Pitching, ?1909; Andante maestoso-Allegro vivace, ?1909; Sonata no.1, 1901-9; Waltz-Rondo, 1911; Sonata no.2 'CONCORD', 1910-15; Varied Air and Variations, ?1923; 3 Quarter-Tone Pieces, 2pf, 1923-4

Organ: Variations on 'America', ?1891; Prelude on 'Adeste fideles', ?1897

Songs: around 200 published

[AMP, Mercury, Peer, Southern; Columbia, Nonesuch]

□ C. Ives, *Essays before a Sonata* (1961), *Memos* (1972); H. and S. Cowell, *Charles Ives and his Music* (1955, 2/1969); H. W. Hitchcock, *Ives* (1977)

J

Jacob, Gordon (1895-1984) English composer and teacher. Studied with Stanford and Howells at the Royal College of Music, where he taught (1926-66). He was a fluent composer for the orchestra, his works including concertos for a variety of instruments.

Jacob, Max (1906-77) French composer. Studied at the Paris Conservatoire and privately with Koechlin (1926-7) and Milhaud (1926-30), being associated at the time with the Ecole d'Arcueil around Satie and known as a writer of songs. In 1930 he entered the Benedictine order, and his music became weightier and modal. His later works include liturgical music and cycles of piano sonatas and string quartets. [Jobert, Leduc]

Jahreslauf, Der (The Course of the Year) Work by Stockhausen, a scene from *Dienstag aus Licht*. It is a ballet of the years, decades, centuries and millennia, scored for gagaku ensemble or western equivalent, with tape. ★Tokyo, 31 Oct 1977.

Jakobsleiter, Die (Jacob's Ladder) Oratorio by Schoenberg concerned with the Swedenborgian journey of the soul towards perfection, and with the discovery of serialism. He spoke several times in later years of finishing it, but left only a large fragment to be posthumously orchestrated by Winfried Zillig. ★Vienna, 1961.

Janáček, Leoš (1854-1928) Czech composer. Older than Elgar or Wolf, he belonged musically with the later generation of Bartók and Stravinsky: chronologically because most of his best music came during his last decade, and stylistically because he attuned himself to folk music as they did, rawly. He also followed the natural rhythms and intonations of Moravian speech, producing a Musorgsky-style operatic realism except at those similarly characteristic moments where the emotional situation calls for lyrical splendour. His orchestral writing was equally individual, with its energetic ostinato patterns, its strongly characterized motifs and the presence of unusual combinations and unusual open spacings.

His long apprenticeship had begun in the choir at the Augustinian monastery in Brno, followed by studies at the teachers' training college in Brno (1869-72), the Prague Organ School (1874-5), and the conservatories of Leipzig (1879-80) and Vienna (1880-81). He then returned to Brno as a teacher and wrote his first opera, *Šárka* (1887-8), in a Dvořákian style that gradually gave way, under the influence of Moravian folk music, to the new manner of the cantata *Amarus* and JENŮFA: the intermediate works, including the opera *The Beginning of a Romance*, consist mostly of arrangements of folk music. *Jenůfa* was a success in Brno in 1904, and he went on to finish FATE, begin his only comedy *The Excursions of Mr Brouček* and write some instrumental pieces.

Then 2 things combined to quicken his creativity. *Jenůfa* was successfully staged in Prague in 1916, winning him international renown; and he became passionately attached to a young married woman Kamila Stösslová (his marriage to a young pupil in 1881 had not proved happy). During the 12 remaining years he wrote 4 more operas, strikingly diverse in subject, besides other large-scale works and chamber pieces that, like the operas, convey highly charged feeling through ostinato and vivid eccentricity.

Operas: Šárka, 1887–8, rev. 1918–19, 1924–5, ★Brno, 1925; The Beginning of a Romance, 1891, ★Brno, 1894; JENŮFA, 1894–1903; FATE, 1903–5, rev. 1906–7; The Excursions of Mr Brouček, 1908–17, ★Prague, 1920; KATYA KABANOVA, 1919–21; The CUNNING LITTLE VIXEN, 1921–3; The MAKROPULOS CASE, 1923–5; FROM THE HOUSE OF THE DEAD, 1927–8

Choral: Amarus, S, T, Bar, SATB, orch, *c*.1897, rev. 1901, 1906; GLAGOLITIC MASS, S, A, T, B, SATB, orch, org, 1926; many smaller works

Orchestral: Lachian Dances, 1893; Jealousy, overture, 1894; The Fiddler's Child, 1912; Taras Bulba, 1915–18; The Ballad of Blaník, 1920; Sinfonietta, 1926; The Danube, 1923–8, completed by Chlubna

Chamber: Fairytale, vc, pf, 1910; The Diary of One who Disappeared, T, female vv, pf, 1917–19; Vn Sonata, 1914–21; Str Qt no.1 'The Kreutzer Sonata', 1923, no.2 'Intimate Letters', 1928; Youth (Mládí), 6 wind, 1924; Concertino, pf, 6 insts, 1925; Capriccio, pf left hand, 7 insts, 1926; Nursery Rhymes (Říkadla), 9 vv, 10 insts, 1927

Piano: On the Overgrown Path, 15 pieces, 1901–8; Sonata 1.X.1905, 1905; In the Mists, before 1912; Reminiscence, 1928

[UE; Supraphon, Decca]

□ J. Vogel, *Leoš Janáček* (1962, 2/1980)

Japanese music Since Japanese traditional musicians have not often travelled, it was the poetry and decorative arts of Japan that first stimulated western composers: the goldfish of Debussy's piano *Images* swam on a lacquer box, and Stravinsky set 3 lyrics. Only when composers from Europe and the USA began to visit Japan, after the second world war, did the influence begin to become musical. Cowell wrote 2 concertos for the koto, a sort of zither (1962, 1964–5); Britten adapted a nō play (*Curlew River*, 1964); Varèse in *Nocturnal* (1961) and Messiaen in his 7 *haïkaï* (1962) transferred the sounds of gagaku, the imperial court orchestral music, to western instruments; and Stockhausen, paying a long visit in 1966, was powerfully impressed. He took recordings of Japanese percussion instruments into the work he composed in Tokyo, *Telemusik*, and has used impressions from nō drama and monastic ceremony in *Mantra*, *Inori* and *Licht*. His *Japan* (from *Für kommende Zeiten*) is a text piece with a melody composed in Japan in 1970, when he was performing his music at the Exposition in Osaka; he also composed for gagaku ensemble in *Der Jahreslauf*.

In turn, Japanese composition in the western manner has become a livelier field since 1945, responding particularly to the work of western composers who have learned from Japan: Messiaen, Boulez, Stockhausen and Cage, who is perhaps most Japanese of all in his practice of zen music. *See* ICHIYANIGI; TAKAHASHI; TAKEMITSU.

Jaques-Dalcroze, Emile (1865–1950) Swiss educationist and composer. Studied in Paris with Fauré and Delibes, in Vienna with Bruckner, and in Geneva, then gradually worked out his method of 'eurhythmics': the development of a rhythmic sense through bodily movement in response to music. In 1914 he founded an institute in Geneva; he also wrote a lot of music.

jazz Its influence on 'classical' composers began in the early 1920s, and seems to have been felt simultaneously by Europeans and Americans. Carpenter wrote his jazz ballet *Krazy Kat* in 1921, while Milhaud heard jazz in London in 1920 and Harlem in 1922, and responded in *La création du monde* (1923) and many later works, using characteristic compound rhythms, syncopations, added-note harmonies and instrumental formations. By the end of the decade hardly any notable composer had resisted the influence, and the vogue was sufficient to make a wild success of Krenek's mildly jazzy opera *Jonny spielt auf* (1927). In Europe the new dance music entered the styles of Hindemith, Weill, Poulenc, Martinů and others, besides being used for local colour by Berg (*Der Wein*, *Lulu*); in the USA Carpenter's initiative was followed by Copland and Gruenberg. Some of these composers, notably Copland and Weill, were using jazz partly in the conscientious belief that a jazz-classical fusion might reconcile the contemporary composer with his audience; others found it a useful image of modernity or simply a source of new musical possibilities, though in the 1920s and 1930s these did not include improvisation.

Jazz itself was becoming more composed. Ellington wrote much for his own band; Gershwin contributed to the jazz-classical alliance from the other side (and influenced Ravel and Bartók); and jazz musicians began commissioning composers: Stravinsky wrote his *Ebony Concerto* (1945) for Woody Herman. After the war all these trends continued, Bernstein following the Gershwin-Copland blend, and Liebermann, Banks, Penderecki and Babbit writing for jazz ensemble. At the same time, the revival of improvisation in the 'free jazz' of the 1960s may have encouraged improvisation by groups of classically trained musicians on normal instruments (*see* FOSS, GLOBOKAR) or in electronic ensembles (*see* AMM, INTUITIVE MUSIC, MUSICA ELETTRONICA VIVA). Schuller has approached the field of jazz-classical marriage, or 'THIRD-STREAM MUSIC' in a variety of ways.

Jelinek, Hanns (1901-69) Austrian composer. Studied with Schoenberg (1918-19) and Schmidt (1920-22), and was a friend of Berg's. He worked variously as a pianist and composer in bars and the cinema before his appointment to the Vienna Musikhochschule in 1958, meanwhile adopting serialism in his Second Quartet (1934-5). Soon after this he wrote nothing for a decade; later works include the *Zwölftonfibel* in 12 volumes for piano (1953-4) and a treatise on 12-note composition.

Jenůfa (Její pastorkyňa: Her Foster-Daughter) Opera by Janáček after Preissová's play of jealousy and passion in a Moravian village setting. ★Brno, 21 Jan 1904.

Jeu de cartes (Card Game) Ballet by Stravinsky, choreographed by Balanchine: it is a continuous sequence of short movements in 3 'deals' alluding to other music. ★cond Stravinsky, New York, 27 Apr 1937.

Jeune France, La (Young France) Group comprising Baudrier, Daniel-Lesur, Jolivet and Messiaen, who banded together in 1936 to present concerts and promote a view of music as a challenging and expressive art, in opposition to what they saw as the flippancy of Parisian neoclassicism. The group did not maintain its early impetus – the composers were too individual for that – and did not outlast the start of the war.

Jeux (Games) Ballet by Debussy, choreographed by Nijinsky as a play of encounters on the tennis court. Debussy provided his most subtly invented score, with fine-spun textures and phases of motivic development that spin out of the music without carrying it forward. ★Paris, Ballets Russes, 15 May 1913.

Jirák, Karel Boleslav (1891-1972) Czech composer. Studied with Novák (1909-11) and Foerster (1911-12), then worked as a conductor, teacher and music director for Czech radio (1930-45). In the 1920s he wrote music combining the Czech Romantic tradition with newer styles, but while working on his Third Symphony (1929-38) he completed nothing else, and the symphony turned out to represent a return to diatonic Czech nationalism. This style he continued after his move to Roosevelt College, Chicago, in 1947.

Johnson, Robert Sherlaw (1932-) English composer. Studied at Durham University (1950-53), at the Royal Academy of Music with Alwyn, Bush and Ferguson (1953-7), and in Paris (1957-8), where he attended Messiaen's classes. He is an outstanding Messiaen pianist and author of a book on the composer (London, 1974); much of his own music shows similar concerns with motivic rhythm, resonance, discontinuous form and Catholic doctrine, though he has been influenced too by Varèse, Stockhausen and Boulez. His works include 3 piano sonatas (1963, 1967, 1976) and sacred and secular vocal music. [OUP; Argo]

Johnston, Ben (1926-) American composer. Studied at various institutions and privately with Partch (1950-51) and Cage (1959-60), following the former in using microtonal tunings and just intonation. His works include 4 quartets (1959, 1964, 1966-73, 1973) and compositions for less usual ensembles. In 1951 he began teaching at the University of Illinois.

Jolas, Betsy (1926-) French composer. She studied in the USA (1940-46) and with Messiaen and Milhaud at the Paris Conservatoire (1948-55), then worked for French radio (1955-70) and as Messiaen's deputy at the conservatoire. Her music stands with that of Amy and Boucourechliev in the Boulez tradition. [Heugel]

Jolivet, André (1905-74) French composer. Studied with Le Flem (1928-33) and Varèse (1930-33), of whom the latter strongly influenced the feeling for dissonant sounds, irregular rhythm and incantatory magic in such early works as his String Quartet (1934), piano suite *Mana* (1935, based on 6 totemic objects Varèse gave him), *Cinq incantations* for flute (1936) and *Cinq danses rituelles* for orchestra or piano (1939). He was a member of La Jeune France and shared with Messiaen a taste for exotic modalities, rich orchestration and the ondes martenot: he introduced 2 of these instruments into his *Danse incantatoire* for orchestra (1936), played at the first Jeune France concert, and also wrote an Ondes Martenot Concerto (1947). His later works include other concertos, 3 symphonies, various instrumental and vocal pieces, and music for the Comédie Française, where he was music director (1943-59). [Durand, Heugel, Costallat, Boosey; Erato]

Jongen, Joseph (1873-1953) Belgian composer. Studied at the Liège Conservatory (1881-97) and taught there from 1902 after periods in Germany, Italy and Paris which opened him to a variety of influences: Franck, Brahms, Wagner and Strauss. He spent the first world war in England, then in 1920 was appointed to the Brussels Conservatory. His output consisted mostly of orchestral and chamber music. His brother Léon (1884-1969) was also a composer.

Josephs, Wilfred (1927-) English composer. Studied with Nieman at the Guildhall School (1954-6) and Deutsch in Paris (1958-9). He has produced a large quantity of music in all genres (over 100 opus numbers), though with an emphasis on orchestral and chamber music; there is also an opera *Rebecca* (★Leeds, 1983), benefitting from his expressive force and grasp of large-scale form. [Boosey, Chester, Novello, OUP, Weinberger; Unicorn]

Joyce, James (1882-1941) Irish novelist and poet. Musical allusions and quasi-musical forms are important to his *Ulysses* and *Finnegans Wake*, his formal audacity in particular exciting the interest of Boulez: Joyce's non-directedness was one of the sanctions for his aleatory endeavours. Joyce's words, too, have been noticed by composers, from the 18 who made settings for *The Joyce Book* (London, 1933) to Berio (*Chamber Music, Epifanie*), Machover and Hopkins.

Junge Lord, Der (The Young Lord) Opera by Henze and Bachmann, a satirical comedy in Classical and bel canto numbers on the story of an ape who passes for an English milord in bourgeois society. ★Berlin, 7 Apr 1965.

K

Kabalevsky, Dmitry (1904-) Russian composer. Worked as pianist before studying composition with Catoire and Myaskovsky at the Moscow Conservatory (1925-9), where he taught from 1932. He produced a fair quantity of patriotic oratorios and songs, but also works of fresh Russian lyricism, including his opera *Colas Breugnon* and much of his instrumental music (the 3 concertos of 1948-52 were written for young performers).
Opera: Colas Breugnon, 1936-8, rev, 1953, 1969
Orchestral: Pf Conc no.1, a, 1928, no.2, g, 1935, no.3, D, 1952; Sym no.1, c♯, 1932, no.2, c, 1934, no.3, b♭, with chorus, 1933, no.4, c, 1954; Vn Conc, C, 1948; Vc Conc no.1, g, 1948-9, no.2, C, 1964
Chamber: Str Qt no.1, a, 1928, no.2, g, 1945, Vc Sonata, B♭, 1962
Piano: Sonata no.1, F, 1927, no.2, E♭ 1945, no.3, F, 1946; 24 Preludes, 1943-4; 6 Preludes and Fugues, 1958-9

Kagel, Mauricio (1931-) Argentinian composer. Self-taught in composition, he created music and films in Buenos Aires before moving to Cologne in 1957. Contact with Stockhausen there may have sharpened his technique, but his musical world is entirely his own: a world in which defunct, patchy, banal and absurd materials are treated to sophisticated and elegant means of composition. Most of his pieces are for unusual combinations or situations; most too, showing an extreme disparity between form and content, impress themselves as theatrical events in a tradition including dada, silent film and Beckett. He has taught composition and music theatre at Darmstadt, in the USA and at the Cologne Musikhochschule.
Compositions: Anagrama, 4 solo vv, speaking chorus, 11 insts, 1955-8; Sur scène, 6 performers, 1958-60; Sonant, gui, harp, db, drums, 1960; Improvisation ajoutée, org, 1961-2; Match, 2 vc, perc, 1964; Tremens, music theatre, 1963-5; Str Qt, 1965-7; Hallelujah, chorus, 1967-8; Staatstheater, opera personnel, 1967-70, ★Hamburg, 1971; Variationen ohne Fuge, orch, 1971-2; Kantrimusik, music theatre, 1973-5; MM51, pf, 1977; Aus Deutschland, song opera, ★1981; Die Erschöpfung der Welt, opera, ★1985

Films: Match, 1966; Hallelujah, 1967-9; Ludwig van, 1969-70; MM51, 1977; Un chien andalou (music for Buñuel-Dali film), 1982
[UE, Peters; DGG]

Kammermusik (Chamber Music) Title of 7 Baroque-concerto-like works by Hindemith and of a Hölderlin fantasy by Henze.

Karg-Elert, Sigfrid (1877-1933) German composer. Studied at the Leipzig Conservatory (1896-1902) and gained the support of Grieg, as well as later that of Reger, who advised him to arrange some of his large output of harmonium pieces for the organ. In 1919 he took Reger's place at the Leipzig Conservatory. His production was prodigious in all but dramatic and orchestral genres, but it is the organ works that have survived, some being of a Bachian kind while others are tone poems in late Romantic harmony.

Katya Kabanova (Káťa Kabanová) Opera by Janáček after Ostrovsky's *The Storm*, a tragedy of love outside marriage. *Brno, 23 Nov 1921.

Kay, Ulysses (1917-) American composer. A nephew of the jazz musician King Oliver, he studied at Yale with Hindemith, at Columbia, and in Europe. In 1968 he was appointed professor at Lehman College (CUNY). His works include operas, much choral music and orchestral pieces. [AMP, Duchess]

Kelemen, Milko (1924-) Yugoslav composer. Studied at the Zagreb Academy (1945-52), with Messiaen and Aubin at the Paris Conservatoire (1954-5) and with Fortner at the Freiburg Musikhochschule. He founded the Zagreb Biennale and has taught at Zagreb (1953-68), Düsseldorf (1970-72) and Stuttgart (1973-). In his music he moved in the late 1950s from folksy neoclassicism to an avant-garde style.

Kelterborn, Rudolf (1931-) Swiss composer. Studied with Geiser at the Basle Academy, with Burkhard and with Blacher, Fortner and Bialas in Germany, where he also attended the Darmstadt courses. He has taught at Basle, Detmold (1960-68) and Zurich, while cultivating a fantastical dramatic style well shown in his operas *Die Errettung Thebens* (*Zurich, 1963), *Kaiser Jovian* (*Karlsruhe, 1967) and *Ein Engel kommt nach Babylon* (*Zurich, 1977). [Bote & Bock]

Khachaturian, Aram (1903-78) Armenian composer. Studied at the Moscow Conservatory with Myaskovsky (1929-37), during which time he began to make a name for large orchestral works whose strong melodic themes have some national colouring. He shared in the official disapproval meted out to Shostakovich and Prokofiev in 1948, though his music remained untouched by modernism of any sort. From 1950 he taught in Moscow at the Gnesin Institute and the conservatory; he also appeared internationally as a conductor of his own music.
Ballets: Gayane, 1942, rev. 1957; Spartacus, 1954, rev. 1968
Orchestral: Sym no.1, 1935, no.2, 1943, no.3, 1947; Pf Conc, 1936; Vn Conc, 1940, Vc Conc, 1946; Conc-Rhapsody, vn, orch, 1961-2; Conc-Rhapsody, vc, orch, 1963; Conc-Rhapsody, pf, orch, 1965
Few early chamber pieces, piano music, choral odes, songs

Khrennikov, Tikhon (1913-) Russian composer and administrator. Studied with Shebalin at the Moscow Conservatory (1932-6). His mellifluous folksong-style opera *Into the Storm* (*1939) won official approval, and in 1948 he took a leading part in denouncing Prokofiev, Shostakovich and Khachaturian, emerging as secretary-general of the Composers' Union, which post he retains.

Kilpinen, Yrjö (1892-1959) Finnish composer. Studied in Helsinki from 1908 to 1917 apart from periods in Vienna (1910-11) and Berlin (1913-14). His output consists mostly of songs, over 800 of them, in Lied style.

Kim, Earl (1920-) American composer. Studied with Schoenberg (1940-41) and with Sessions at Berkeley (1947-52), then taught at Princeton (1952-67) and Harvard (1967-). His works are few, in a highly refined style; they include the mixed-media Beckett settings *Exercices en route* (1963-70), *Earthlight* (1973) and *Narratives* (*Cambridge, Mass., 1979).

Kirchner, Leon (1919-) American composer. Studied with Toch and Schoenberg in Los Angeles, at Berkeley, and with Sessions in New York, then returned to Berkeley after war service. He has taught at Mills College (1952-61) and Harvard, where in 1966 he succeeded to Piston's chair. His music is large in gesture, of strong melodic movement and in a harmonic realm close to

Schoenberg and Berg, though he is not a serialist. His works include 2 piano concertos (1953, 1963), 3 quartets (1949, 1958, 1966, the third with tape) and pieces written towards the opera *Lily* (★New York, 1977) on Bellow's *Henderson, the Rain King*. [AMP, Mercury]

Klangfarbenmelodie (Timbre melody) Term introduced by Schoenberg in his *Harmonielehre* (1911) for a 'melody' defined by changes of timbre-rather than pitch. There is something of this in the middle piece of his op.16, and in much of Webern: the end of the latter's op.10 no.1, for instance, has the same note sounded successively by flute, flute plus trumpet, trumpet and celesta. Here the change of colour is from note to note, as it is in some serial music of the early postwar years (e.g. the start of Stockhausen's *Kontra-Punkte* and Babbitt's Composition for 12 Instruments), but the term does not necessarily imply such rapid discontinuity. It has regularly been used, for instance, of Webern's Bach instrumentation, where the colouring picks out motifs.

Klavierstücke (Piano Pieces) Cycle of compositions by Stockhausen, originally intended to be of 21 pieces in 6 sets, though only the first 3 collections (I–IV, V–X, XI) were finished, the next 3 pieces belonging to *Licht*. I–IV, ★Mercenier, Darmstadt, 21 Aug 1954; V–VIII, ★Mercenier, Darmstadt, 1 Jun 1955; IX, ★Kontarsky, Cologne, 21 May 1962; X, ★Rzewski, Palermo, 10 Oct 1962; XI, ★Jacobs, Darmstadt, 28 Jul 1957; XII in *Michaels Jugend* from *Donnerstag*, ★M. Stockhausen, Tel Aviv, 16 Oct 1979; XIII = *Luzifers Traum* from *Samstag*, ★M. Stockhausen, Metz, 19 Nov 1981; XIV ★P.-L. Armand, Baden-Baden, 31 Mar 1985

Klebe, Giselher (1925-) German composer. Studied at the Berlin Conservatory and with Rufer and Blacher (1946-51), then was appointed in 1957 to teach at the Detmold Academy. In the early 1950s he was associated with the new avant garde, but afterwards like Henze he began to develop a more Romantic style and to cultivate opera, drawing his own librettos from literary classics.
Operas: Die Räuber, ★1957; Die tödlichen Wünsche, ★1959; Die Ermordung Cäsars, ★1959; Alkmene, ★1961; Figaro lässt sich scheiden, ★1963; Jacobowsky und der Oberst, ★1965; Das Märchen von der schönen Lilie, ★1969; Ein wahrer Held, ★1975; Das Mädchen aus Domrémy, ★1976; Das Rendez-vous, ★1977 [Bote & Bock]

Klemperer, Otto (1885-1973) German conductor. Studied at the Frankfurt Conservatory, with Pfitzner in Berlin and much later, in the 1930s, with Schoenberg in Los Angeles. Mahler's confidence won him appointments at Prague (1907-10) and Hamburg (1910-12), followed by posts in other German towns before he became director of the Kroll Opera (1927-31). He was then conductor of the Los Angeles Philharmonic (1933-9), the Budapest Opera (1947-50) and the Philharmonia of London (1955-72), suffering during these later years from ill health that had kept him from the podium during the war. In Berlin and Los Angeles he was closely associated with contemporary music, conducting Stravinsky, Schoenberg (premieres of Suite for strings and Brahms quartet) and Hindemith (premieres of *Kammermusik no.5*, *Neues vom Tage* and *Das Unaufhörliche*); later he was renowned for the rugged grandeur of his Beethoven and Mahler. His compositions date mostly from his last few years and include 6 symphonies and 9 quartets.
☐ P. Heyworth, *Otto Klemperer*, vol.1 (1983)

Knipper, Lev (1898-1974) Russian composer. Turned to music only in 1922, after army service, and studied in Moscow with Glier and Berlin with Jarnach. His satirical opera The North Wind (1929-30) fell, like Shostakovich's similar The Nose, under official displeasure, and he worked thereafter in a blander style, composing 14 symphonies (some including rousing choral songs) and other orchestral works.

Knussen, Oliver (1952-) English composer. Studied with Lambert in London (1963-9) and Schuller at Tanglewood (1970-73). His music is rich in strong, strange images presented with Ravelian accomplishment, but often also with a Carter-like energy.
Operas: Where the Wild Things Are, 1979-83; Higglety Pigglety Pop!, 1984-5
Orchestral: Sym no.1, 1966-7, no.2, S, chamber orch, 1970-71, no.3, 1973-79; Coursing, chamber orch, 1978-80
Chamber: Océan de terre, S, 7 insts, 1972-3, rev. 1976; Trumpets, S, 3 cl, 1975; Ophelia Dances, 8 insts, 1975; Autumnal, vn, pf, 1976-7; Cantata, ob, str trio, 1977; Sonya's Lullaby, pf, 1977-8 [Faber; Unicorn]

Kodály, Zoltán (1882-1967) Hungarian composer and teacher. Bartók's collaborator in the collection of Hungarian folk music, he also contributed to the founding of a strong compositional tradition in Hungary, if more as teacher than as composer. He studied with Koessler at the Budapest Academy (1900-05) and began collecting folksongs in 1905 with Bartók. In 1907 he visited Paris and came back with some of Debussy's music, which he introduced to Bartók; later that year he was appointed to the staff of the Academy. On 17 March 1910 a recital in Budapest included his and Bartók's first quartets, and is remembered as the début of modern Hungarian music.

Thereafter the pattern of his life changed little: he taught, composed (though there were few works after 1940), and collected, arranged and edited folk music. After the war he had a leading role in Hungarian music, and his tuneful folksong-based style (never so dense, harsh or analytic as Bartók's) became the model for younger composers. He also had the opportunity then to put into practice his view that musical education should be made available to all children through choral singing; he provided much music for that purpose.

Operas: Háry János, 1925-7; The Transylvanian Spinning-Room, 1924-32; Czinka Panna, 1946-8

Orchestral: Summer Evening, 1906; Dances of Marosszek, 1930; Dances of Galánta, 1933; 'Peacock' Variations, 1938-9; Conc for Orch, 1939-40; Sym, C, 1930s-61

Choral: Psalmus hungaricus, T, chorus, orch, org, 1923; Budavari Te Deum, S, A, T, B, chorus, orch, 1936; Missa brevis, chorus, org, 1944 (also orch version); very many songs and folksong arrangements, also solo songs

Chamber and instrumental: Str Qt no.1, op.2, 1908-9, no.2, op.10, 1916-18; Piano Music, op.3, 1909; Sonata, op.4, vc, pf, 1909-10; Duo, op.7, vn, vc, 1914; Sonata, op.8, vc, 1915; Capriccio, vc, 1915; Serenade, op.12, 2 vn, va, 1919-20; Sonatina, vc, pf, 1921-2

[Editio Musica, UE; Hungaroton]

□ P.M. Young, *Zoltán Kodály* (1964), L. Eösze, *Zoltán Kodály: his Life in Pictures* (1971, 2/1982)

Koechlin, Charles (1867-1950) French composer. Studied with Massenet, Gédalge and Fauré at the Paris Conservatoire (1890-97), then lived uneventfully as a critic, teacher (of Milhaud and Poulenc) and theorist. Meanwhile he produced an enormous body of music (over 200 opus numbers), including dozens of big orchestral scores, song cycles, large choral works, chamber music and instrumental pieces. In subject matter and style his range was similarly vast: there is a cycle of symphonic poems on Kipling's *Jungle Book* (*Trois poèmes*, with soloists and chorus, 1899-1910; *La course de printemps*, 1908-27; *La méditation de Purun Bhagat*, 1936; *La loi de la jungle*, 1939-40; *Les bandar-log*, 1939-40), a variety of works indicating his admiration of film stars (*7 Stars Symphony*, 1933), music expressing his communist sympathies, works with ondes martenot, and a harmonic palette which, though centred in the church modes, included the polytonal and occasionally atonal, often disposed with a delight in Bachian counterpoint. Very little of his work, however, escaped neglect.

Koenig, Gottfried Michael (1926-) German composer. Studied with Bialas at the Detmold Academy (1947-50) and at the Cologne Musikhochschule (1953-4), then worked for a decade in the Westdeutscher Rundfunk electronic music studio, where he composed his *Klangfiguren 2* (1955-6) and assisted Stockhausen, Ligeti, Pousseur and other composers. In 1964 he moved to Utrecht University to work on computer programs for composition and sound generation. [Peters, Tonos, UE]

Koffler, Jozef (1896-1943/4) Polish composer. Studied in Vienna with Schoenberg (1920-24) and taught at the Lwów Conservatory (1929-41); he was killed in hiding during the war. He adapted 12-note methods to textures of neoclassical clarity and to music borrowing the rhythmic and even the melodic character of Polish folk music. His works include 3 symphonies, the 15 Variations for string orchestra (1933) and a String Trio (1929). [PWM]

Kogoj, Marij (1895-1956) Yugoslav composer. Studied with Schreker and Schoenberg in Vienna (1914-18), then worked as coach and conductor at the Ljubljana Opera and also as a music critic, though mental illness caused his early retirement. His opera *Black Masks* (1929) is said to be an Expressionist drama comparable with *Wozzeck*.

Kolb, Barbara (1939-) American composer. Studied at the Hartt College (1957-64) and with Foss and Schuller at Tanglewood. She worked as an orchestral clarinettist and has taught at Brooklyn college (1973-5) and Wellesley College (1975-). Her works include many for instrumental ensemble. [Boosey]

Kolisch, Rudolf (1896-1978) Austrian-American violinist. Studied in Vienna, where he had composition lessons from Schreker and Schoenberg; the latter married his sister Gertrud in 1924. Two years before that he had formed a quartet, which existed until 1939 and made a point of performing new works: they gave the first performances of Schoenberg's Third and Fourth Quartets and his Quartet Concerto, Bartók's Fifth, Berg's Lyric Suite, and Webern's Trio and Quartet. Living in America from 1935, Kolisch led the Pro Arte Quartet from 1942.

Kol nidre (All vows) Schoenberg's setting of the prayer for Yom Kippur, with his own adaptations to the text. *cond Schoenberg, Los Angeles, 4 Oct 1938.

König, Hirsch (King Stag) Opera by Henze and H. von Cramer after Gozzi, an elaborate fairytale concerning a king who takes animal form. *Berlin, 23 Sep 1956. Rev. as *Il re cervo, or The Errantries of Truth*, *Kassel, 10 Mar 1963.

Kontakte (Contacts) 4-channel tape piece by Stockhausen, to be played either alone or with additions from pianist and percussionist, whose parts pick up signals from the tape and anticipate its gambits. *Tudor, Caskel, Cologne, 26 Oct 1961.

Kontarsky, Aloys (1931-) German pianist. Studied with Schmitz-Gohr and Frank at the Cologne Musikhochschule (1952-5) and with Erdman in Hamburg (1955-7). As a soloist, duo player (with his brother Alfons) and ensemble musician (with Stockhausen's group from 1964) he was closely associated with contemporary music, for which his quick, exact control of rhythm and sonority was admirably suited. The Kontarskys gave the first performance of Stockhausen's *Mantra*, which they recorded, along with the 4-hand music of Debussy, Ravel, Bartók, Boulez and Zimmermann. Aloys alone gave the first complete performance of Stockhausen's *Klavierstücke* I-XI (Darmstadt, 1966), which he also recorded.

Kontra-Punkte (Counter-Points) Work by Stockhausen for piano with 9 instruments (fl, cl, b cl, bn, tpt, trbn, harp, vn, vc) which drop out one by one as the piece moves through different harmonic regions established by the new GROUP technique. *Cologne, 26 May 1953.

Korngold, Erich Wolfgang (1897-1957) Austrian-American composer. A sensation in his boyhood: in 1907 he impressed Mahler, who recommended him to Zemlinsky for lessons; in 1910 his ballet *Der Schneeman* was produced in Vienna,

and his E major Piano Sonata of the same year won Schnabel's advocacy, while his first orchestral works, of 1911-12, were approved by Strauss. The climax came with the staging of *Die tote Stadt* (1920), after which his rate of production declined. In 1934 he went with Reinhardt to Hollywood, where he wrote film scores and instrumental works on a large Romantic scale.

Operas: Der Ring des Polykrates, *Munich, 1916; Violanta, *Munich, 1916; Die tote Stadt, *Hamburg and Cologne, 1920; Das Wunder der Heliane, *Hamburg, 1927; Die Kathrin, *Stockholm, 1939
Orchestral: Schauspiel Ouvertüre, 1911; Sinfonietta, 1912; Pf Conc for left hand, C♯, *1923; Vn Conc, D, 1946; Symphonic Serenade, B, str, *1947; Sym, F♯, 1951-2
Chamber: Str Qt no.1, A, *1924; no.2, E♭, 1935; no. 3, D, 1945

Koussevitzky *See* KUSEVITSKY.

Krenek (Křenek), **Ernst** (1900-) Austrian-American composer. Studied with Schreker in Vienna (1916-20) and Berlin (1920-23), then visited Switzerland (1923-5) and Paris, where he was influenced by Stravinsky's neoclassicism. He subsequently worked at the Kassel Opera (1925-7) before the wild success of his mildly jazzy opera *Jonny spielt auf* gave him financial security: the work was staged all over Europe, including the USSR, and also in New York. He moved to Vienna and wrote more operas, including *Karl V*, in which he began to use 12-note methods. Speculative serialism continued to be his style after he moved to the USA in 1939, settling in Los Angeles in 1947.

Operas: Zwingburg, *Berlin, 1924; Der Sprung über den Schatten, *Frankfurt, 1924; Orpheus und Eurydike, *Kassel, 1926; Jonny spielt auf, *Leipzig, 1927; Der Diktator, Das geheime Königreich, Schwergewicht (triple bill), *Wiesbaden, 1928; Leben des Orest, *Leipzig, 1930; Karl V, *Prague, 1938; Pallas Athene weint, *Hamburg, 1955; Der goldene Bock, *Hamburg, 1964; Sardakai, *Hamburg, 1970
Many works in all other genres
[UE, Bärenreiter]
☐ E. Krenek, *Horizons Circled* (1974)

Kroll Opera Branch of the Berlin State Opera set up at the Kroll Theatre (whence the name) in 1927, with Klemperer as director. The enterprise survived only 4 seasons, but its devotion to contemporary work (operas by Stravinsky, Schoenberg, Janáček, Weill and Hindemith), its high musical standards and its adventurous productions have made it a lasting ideal of what a modern opera house might be.

Kulturbolschewismus (Cultural bolshevism) Term used by Nazi officials in denigrating the music of Stravinsky, Schoenberg and others, presumably because they associated artistic radicalism with revolutionary POLITICS.

Kunstbolschewismus *See* KULTURBOLSCHEWIS-MUS.

Kurtág, György (1926-) Hungarian composer. Studied with Veress and Farkas at the Budapest Academy (1946-55), and with Deutsch, Milhaud and Messiaen in Paris (1957-8), where he was impressed by what he heard at the Domaine Musical concerts. In his String Quartet op.1 he initiated a style of Webernian precision and brevity, influenced too by similar qualities in Bartók's piano music. His works have remained few and small, though their expressive reach, particularly where a solo voice is involved, is often on a quite different scale. There is also in his music an ingenious wit, most obviously in the volumes of partly educational piano music. His son, also György Kurtág, is a composer too, one of his father's pupils at the Budapest Academy, where the elder Kurtág has taught since 1968.

Str Qt, 1959; Wind Qnt, 1959; 8 Pf Pieces, 1960; 8 Duos, vn, cimbalom, 1961; Signs, va, 1961; The Sayings of Péter Bornemisza, S, pf, 1963-8; In Memory of a Winter Sunset, S, vn, cimbalom, 1969; 4 Capriccios, S, 14 insts, 1972; Splinters, cimbalom/ pf, 1973; 4 Songs, B, 7 insts, 1973-5; S.K. Remembrance Noise, v, vn, 1974-5; Plays and Games, pf, vols. 1-4, 1973-6; 12 Microludes, str qt, 1977-8; Omaggio a Luigi Nono, chorus, 1979; Messages of the Late Miss R.V. Troussova, S, small orch, 1976-80; 15 songs, S, vn, cimbalom, db, 1981-2; 8 Tandoori Choruses, 1984 [Editio Musica; Hungaroton, Erato]

Kurzwellen (Shortwaves) Work by Stockhausen for live electronic ensemble of 4 musicians, each also equipped with a shortwave radio. ★Bremen, 5 May 1968. Also realized with tapes of Beethoven instead of shortwave signals as *Kurzwellen mit Beethoven (Stockhoven-Beethausen Opus 1970)*. ★Düsseldorf, 17 Dec 1969.

Kusevitsky, Sergey (Koussevitzky, Serge) (1874-1951) Russian-American conductor. Began

his careeer as a DOUBLE BASS player: he made his conducting début with the Berlin Philharmonic in 1908. The next year he founded a publishing house (Editions Russes de Musique) and an orchestra, with which he gave the first performance of Skryabin's *Prometheus*. After the Revolution he was based in Paris, where he continued his activities as publisher (much of Stravinsky's music from *Petrushka* to *Perséphone* appeared under his imprint) and conductor, giving the first performances of Stravinsky's Symphonies of Wind Instruments and Piano Concerto, and the Ravel-Musorgsky *Pictures at an Exhibition*. In 1924 he became conductor of the Boston Symphony, which he remained for 25 years, conducting the first performances of works by Copland (Organ Symphony), Prokofiev (Symphony no.4), Roussel (Symphony no.3) and many others. He founded the Koussevitzky Music Foundation as a memorial to his wife Natalie, with funds to commission new works.

L

La Barbara, Joan (1947-) American composer and singer. Studied at Syracuse and New York universities, then active as performer with Reich, Glass, Cage, Lucier and others. Her own works, usually vocal, profit from her experience in experimental and minimal music.

Laderman, Ezra (1924-) American composer. Studied with Wolpe (1946-9) and Luening at Columbia (1950-52); has taught at Sarah Lawrence College and from 1971 at the State University of New York at Binghamton. Most of his works are vigorously conceived on a large scale: they include operas, symphonic compositions and vocal orchestral pieces, as well as a series of quartets. [OUP]

Lady Macbeth of the Mtsensk District, The (Ledi Makbet Mtsenskovo uyezda) Opera by Shostakovich and Preys after Leskov, the story of a multiple murderess treated with wild flamboyance and parody. ★Leningrad, 22 Jan 1934. In 1936 the work was denounced in *Pravda* (*see* POLITICS) and withdrawn, to appear under a somewhat laxer régime in revised form, as *Katerina Izmaylova*. ★Moscow, 8 Jan 1963.

Lambert, Constant (1905-51) English composer. Studied with Vaughan Williams and Morris at the Royal College of Music from 1922, and soon became a member with Walton of the Sitwell set (*Façade* is dedicated to him). He was the first English composer commissioned by Dyagilev (*Romeo and Juliet*, *Monte Carlo, 1926), and spent much of his life in ballet as a conductor and composer (*Pomona*, *Buenos Aires, 1927; *Horoscope*, *London, 1938; *Tiresias*, *London, 1951). His concert works include *The Rio Grande* for piano, chorus and orchestra (1927), an exuberant mix of the Hispanic, the jazzy and the Delian. [Chester, OUP]
□ C. Lambert, *Music Ho!* (1934, 3/1966); R. Shead, *Constant Lambert* (1973)

Langlais, Jean (1907-) French composer and organist. Blind from infancy, he studied with Dupré and Dukas at the Paris Conservatoire and also had lessons with Tournemire; in 1945 he succeeded to Tournemire's and Franck's post at Ste Clotilde. He has also taught at the National Blind Institute and the Schola Cantorum. His music, in the modal Tournemire tradition, consists very largely of organ works and mass settings.

Lansky, Paul (1944-) American composer. Studied with Perle at Queens College (1961-6) and with Cone, Westergaard, Babbitt and Randall at Princeton (1966-9), later working with Perle on his 12-note modal system and teaching at Princeton (from 1969). His compositions are intimate, using electronic (*mild and leise*, tape, 1976) or instrumental (*Crossworks*, ensemble, 1975-6) resources with elegant intelligence. [Nonesuch]

La Rochelle French town, site of the Rencontres Internationals d'Art Contemporain, which assumed the functions of the Royan Festival in 1973. Stockhausen and Boulez featured prominently on early programmes there, followed by Ferneyhough.

Lazarof, Henri (1932-) Bulgarian-American composer. Studied at the Sofia Academy, in Jerusalem, with Petrassi in Rome (1955-7) and at Brandeis (1957-9), then joined the faculty at UCLA in 1962. His works, mostly instrumental, show him abreast of developments in European serial music.

League of Composers Organization founded in New York in 1923 to promote contemporary music, its concerts including works by Stravinsky,

Schoenberg, Bartók, Copland and many others. It also published the journal *Modern Music*. In 1954 it merged with the ISCM.

Leeuw, Ton de (1926-) Dutch composer. Studied with Badings (1947-9), with Messiaen and Thomas de Hartmann in Paris (1949-50), and with Jaap Kunst for musical ethnology (1950-54), then worked for Dutch radio before his appointment in 1960 to teach at the Amsterdam Conservatory. His music shows a wish for oriental stasis, often assisted by the disposition of performers in space, combined with influences from Pijper, Boulez and *musique concrète*. [Donemus]

LeFanu, Nicola (1947-) English composer. The daughter of Elizabeth Maconchy, she studied at Oxford and the Royal College of Music, and later in master classes with Petrassi and Davies; in 1977 she began teaching at King's College, London. Her works encompass all genres from music theatre (*Antiworld*, 1972; *Dawnpath*, 1977) to chamber music. [Novello]

Lehár, Franz (1870-1948) Austrian composer. Studied with Foerster at the Prague Conservatory (1882-8), also gaining advice from Fibich and Dvořák. He worked as a military bandmaster until success as a waltz composer enabled him to retire in 1902. The most popular of his many operettas came during the next few years: *Die lustige Witwe* (*1905), *Der Graf von Luxemburg* (*1909) and *Zigeunerliebe* (*1910), all first produced in Vienna, where he spent most of the rest of his life.

Lehrstück (Teaching piece) Term probably coined by Brecht for works he designed as exercises, involving amateur performers, intended to raise the political and artistic consciousness of both performers and audiences. Music played a part in all of them. They include (with composers indicated): *Lehrstück* (1929, Hindemith), *Der Lindberghflug* (1929, Weill and Hindemith), *Der Jasager* (1930, Weill), *Die Massnahme* (1930, Eisler), *Die Ausnahme und die Regel* (1930, Dessau) and *Die Horatier und die Kuriatier* (1934, Kurt Schwaen). *See* GEBRAUCHSMUSIK.

Leibowitz, René (1913-72) Polish-French composer and teacher. Studied with Schoenberg and Webern in Berlin and Vienna (1930-33), and settled in 1945 in Paris, where he gave instruction in 12-note methods to Boulez, Nigg and others. His book *Schoenberg and his School* (New York, 1949, r1975) had even wider influence, though his compositions – mostly in Schoenbergian genres while including some operatic and other reflections of his French literary interests – have been neglected. [Bomart, UE]

Leighton, Kenneth (1929-) English composer. Studied at Oxford and in Rome with Petrassi, then later returned to teach at Oxford (1968-70) before being appointed professor at Edinburgh. His output consists largely of sacred music and of concertos and instrumental pieces, in a vigorous, chromatic style owing something to Hindemith and Berg. [Lengnick, Novello, OUP]

Liadov See LYADOV.

Liapunov See LYAPUNOV.

Licht Cycle ultimately to be of 7 operas by Stockhausen for the evenings of a week. See DONNERSTAG AUS LICHT, Der JAHRESLAUF, SAMSTAG AUS LICHT.

Liebe der Danae, Die (Danaë's Love) Opera by Strauss and Josef Gregor after Hofmannsthal's draft, the last of this composer's modern interpretations of mythological persons, scored on an opulent scale. ★Salzburg, 16 Aug 1944 (dress rehearsal for cancelled production).

Liebermann, Rolf (1910-) Swiss composer and opera administrator. Studied with Scherchen in Zurich and Vogel in Ascona, then worked as a radio producer and orchestral manager in Switzerland (1945-57). Most of his compositions date from this period, including the operas *Leonore 40 /45* (★Basle, 1952), *Penelope* (★Salzburg, 1954) and *Die Schule der Frauen* (★Louisville, 1955), and the Concerto for jazz band and orchestra (1954). He gave up composing to take charge of the operas at Hamburg (1959-73) and Paris (1973-80), being responsible for the commissioning of works from Kagel, Penderecki, Messiaen and others.

Lied von der Erde, Das (The Song of the Earth) Symphony by Mahler in 6 songs alternately for tenor and contralto, setting German adaptations of Chinese poems. ★cond Walter, Munich, 20 Nov 1911.

Ligeti, György (1923-) Hungarian composer. Born near Kolozsvár (now Cluj in Romania), he studied at the conservatory there with Farkas (1941-3) and then at the Budapest Academy with Farkas, Veress and Jardányi (1945-9). In 1950 he began teaching at the Academy while also publishing music in the accepted post-Kodály style. At the same time, however, he was writing more adventurous works, using what he could discover of Schoenberg, Webern and middle-period Bartók; though these works, including the *Musica ricercata* for piano and the First Quartet, could not be performed in Hungary at the time.

In 1956, after the Russian invasion, he left for Vienna and then made for Cologne, where he worked in the electronic music studio and prepared a widely read analysis of Boulez's *Structures Ia*. His interest in the new serialism was evidently intense, but he had doubts on many points of theory and aesthetics. He retained the notion of repertories of musical objects; he focused his attention, though, on large formal shapes rather than minutiae, working towards an ideal of slow, seamless change, involving CLUSTERS, in parts of *Apparitions* and the whole of ATMOSPHÈRES (1961), both for orchestra. His way of organizing more abrupt material was to relate it to patterns of speech, often with ironic and even humorous effect (AVENTURES, 1962). These 2 works of 1961-2 thus provided him with the 'clocks and clouds' of which much of his later music has been composed.

The clouds, though, have changed. In *Atmosphères* they are differentiated only to the extent of being more or less dense, but in the finale of the *Requiem* and in *Lontano* (1967) he started to work towards and around defined harmonic events, even including open octaves. Meanwhile the speaking clocks of *Aventures* were becoming elaborate machines in the Second Quartet, and these rediscoveries of harmony and rhythm were followed by a rediscovery of melody in the tangled web of *Melodien* (1971). Such profusion, though, is exceptional. Normally the music is highly contrived and artificial, which is not too surprising in a work for 2 pianos (1976) but becomes fascinatingly odd in an opera (*Le* GRAND MACABRE) and still odder within the Brahmsian world of the Horn Trio.

Operas: Le GRAND MACABRE, 1974-7; The Tempest, in progress

Orchestral: Apparitions, 1958-9; ATMOSPHÈRES, 1961; Requiem, S, Mez, chorus, orch, 1963-5; Vc Conc, 1966; Lontano, 1967; Ramifications, str, 1968-9; Chamber Conc, 1969-70; Melodien, 1971; Double Conc, fl, ob, orch, 1972; Clocks and Clouds, female vv, orch, 1972-3; San Francisco Polyphony, 1973-4

Choral: Night, Morning, 8vv, 1955; 3 Phantasien, 16vv, 1983; Hungarian Studies, 16vv, 1983

Vocal: AVENTURES, 3 solo vv, 7 insts, 1962; Nouvelles aventures, same ensemble, 1962-5

Chamber: 6 Bagatelles, wind qnt, 1953; Str Qt no. 1, 1953-4, no. 2, 1968; 10 Pieces, wind qnt, 1968; Trio, vn, hn, pf, 1982

Keyboard: Musica ricercata, pf, 1951-3; Study no. 1 'Harmonies', org, 1967, no. 2 'Coulée', 1969; Continuum, hpd, 1968; Monument, Selbstportrait, Bewegung, 2 pf, 1976; Hungarian Rock, hpd, 1978; Passacaglia ungherese, hpd, 1978

Tape: Glissandi, 1957; Artikulation, 1958

[Schott, UE, Peters; Wergo, DG]

☐ *Ligeti in Conversation* (1983), P. Griffiths, *György Ligeti* (1983)

live electronic music Music requiring electronic means in its performance, though normally the term excludes simple tape playback and the use of manufactured electronic instruments. The possibilities therefore include using amplification to exaggerate and alter sounds (Cage's *Cartridge Music*, Stockhausen's *Mikrophonie I*), applying some form of modulation, especially ring modulation (Stockhausen's *Mixtur* and *Mantra*), employing tape recorders to record and playback during performance (Stockhausen's *Solo*), using specially constructed instruments (*see* ELECTROCHORD, ELECTRONIUM) and using digital equipment in the variation and projection of sounds (Boulez's *Répons*). Cage's *Imaginary Landscape no. 1* (1939) is usually credited as the first example of live electronic music, but the genre really got under way in the 1960s, when Cage and Tudor began to work regularly with electronics, and when in Europe various ensembles began to specialize in music of this kind (*see* AMM, GENTLE FIRE, INTERMODULATION, STOCKHAUSEN). For many composers since then – Stockhausen, Cage, Glass and Young, for example – electronics have become a quite natural part of concert giving.

Lloyd, George (1913-) English composer. Studied with Farjeon at the Royal Academy of Music and gained early success as a composer of opera (*The Serf*, ★Covent Garden, 1938), but in the 1950s ill health obliged him to retire, and his music began to be rediscovered only in the 1980s. His works include 9 symphonies and 4 piano concertos.

Loeffler, Charles Martin (1861-1935) Alsatian-American composer. Studied the violin and composition in Berlin and Paris, and in 1881 went to the USA. He was assistant leader of the Boston Symphony (1882-1903), then lived as a composer and teacher. He was influenced by contemporary French music and by Classical subject matter (*A Pagan Poem* for orchestra with obbligato piano, cor anglais and trumpets), though in later years he admired Gershwin. [G. Schirmer]

London Sinfonietta Orchestra founded in 1968 with David Atherton as conductor, specializing in 20th c. music. They have given the first performances of works by Berio, Stockhausen, Henze, Birtwistle, Davies, Goehr, Carter, Varèse and many others, and have recorded music by Stravinsky, Weill, Schoenberg, Berg, Stockhausen, Berio, Birtwistle, etc.

Loriod, Yvonne (1924-) French pianist. Studied with Messiaen at the Paris Conservatoire in the early 1940s. He composed his *Visions de l'Amen* (1943) for the 2 of them to play, and there were important piano parts for her in many of his subsequent major works; in 1962 they were married. Her resonant brilliance of colour and her command of rapid toccata movement suit her particularly to Messiaen's music, which indeed she has influenced through her playing; but she was also involved in early performances of Barraqué and Boulez. Her sister Jeanne is an exponent of the ondes martenot.

Los Angeles US city, not only the home of the film industry but also a favourite point of exile for European artists, its inhabitants including Schoenberg (1934-51), Stravinsky (1940-69), Krenek (1948-) and Klemperer (1933-9). Schoenberg and Stravinsky are said to have met there only at Werfel's funeral.

Lourié, Arthur (1892-1966) Russian-American composer. Studied at the St Petersburg Conservatory but soon left to pursue his own investigations of atonality, mostly in small piano pieces departing from late Skryabin. He was music commissar (1918-21), then left for Berlin and Paris (1924-41), where he became attached to Stravinsky's circle, and where he turned to a modal style influenced sometimes by Russian church music. In 1941 he moved to the USA.

Operas: The Feast During the Plague, 1935; The Blackamoor of Peter the Great, 1961

Orchestral: Sonata liturgica, A vv, chamber orch, 1928; Conc spirituale, pf, solo vv, chorus, orch, 1929; Sym no. 1, 1930, no. 2, 1939

Piano: Synthesis, Quatre préludes fragiles, Three Sonatinas, Formes en l'air, all 1915; several later pieces

Much other vocal music, three str qts
[Editions Russes de Musique, Fischer, G. Schirmer]

Love for Three Oranges, The (Lyubov k tryom apelsinam) Opera by Prokofiev after fantastic fairytale play by Gozzi. ★cond Prokofiev, Chicago, 30 Dec 1921

Lucier, Alvin (1931-) American composer. Studied at Yale (1950-56), Brandeis (1958-60) and Darmstadt (1961), then worked at Brandeis (1962-70) and Wesleyan University (1970-). He was a member of the Sonic Arts Union (1966-73), performing live electronic music including his own *Vespers* (1968) for people in the dark using echolocation devices to test the acoustic environment. Other works have similarly been concerned with room acoustics. [Composer-Performer Edition]

Luening, Otto (1900-) American composer. Studied in Munich (1915-17) and at the conservatory in Zurich (1919-20), where he also had private lessons with Jarnach and Busoni. In 1920 he moved to Chicago, and then held various teaching posts, notably at Columbia University (1944-68), where in 1952 he and Ussachevsky set up the studio that later became the Columbia-Princeton Electronic Music Center. His works are notably diverse in style and genre. The electronic pieces include *Fantasy in Space* (1952), composed from flute sounds, and *Gargoyles* for violin and tape (1960); with Ussachevsky he produced works for orchestra and tape: Rhapsodic Variations (1953-4), *A Poem in Cycles and Bells* (1954) and the ebullient Concerted Piece (1960). [Highgate, Peters; CRI, Columbia]

Lulu Opera by Berg after Wedekind's plays *Erdgeist* (1895) and *Die Büchse der Pandora* (1901), concerning the rise and degradation of a woman who is pure sensuality. Part of the composition of the third act, and much of its orchestration, remained unfinished at Berg's death, and his widow eventually forbade completion, so that the opera was long performed in a 2-act version. ★Zurich, 2 Jun 1937. Helene Berg's death in 1977 made possible the presentation of the full score, completed by Cerha. ★cond Boulez, Paris, 24 Feb 1979.

Lumsdaine, David (1931-) Australian composer. Studied in Sydney before moving in 1952 to London, where he studied at the Royal Academy of Music and privately with Seiber. He remained in London as a teacher and editor, then took an appointment at Durham University in 1970. His music shares with that of Banks a clear-cut strength of image and form: the movement may be purposefully directed or meditatively static, but the ideas always have character and definition.
Orchestral: Episodes, 1968; Salvation Creek with Eagle, chamber orch, 1974; Evensong, brass band, 1975; Sunflower, chamber orch, 1975; Hagoromo, 1975-7
Vocal: Missa brevis, SATB, org, 1964; Annotations of Auschwitz, S, 6 insts, 1964; Story for a Time of Disturbance, Bar, 11 insts, 1965; Easter Fresco, S, 4 insts, 1966, rev. 1971; Aria for Edward John Eyre, S, 2 narrators, ensemble, 1972; My Sister's Song, S, 1974
Instrumental: Kelly Ground, pf, 1964; Flights, 2 pf, 1967; Mandala I, wind qnt, 1968; Mandala II, 5 insts, 1969; Looking-Glass Music, brass qnt, tape, 1970; Kangaroo Hunt, pf, perc, 1971; Caliban Impromptu, pf trio, electronics, 1972; Ruhe sanfte, sanfte Ruh', pf, 1974
[UE]

Lutosławski, Witold (1913-) Polish composer. His reputation rests, like Carter's, on a rather small number of works completed after his 40th year and belonging to an individual world of instrumental gesture and form. In his case the hallmarks include a French-inspired euphony of harmony and scoring, a poetic elegance (even when dramatic or mournful), and often a discreet balance of metred movement with aleatory passages building a more static yet subtle web of figures.

His delayed arrival at this style was due at least in part to political developments in Poland. He had studied the piano with Lefeld and composition with Maliszewski at the Warsaw Conservatory (1932-7), and begun to compose in a neoclassical style. But the war restricted his activities: he worked with Panufnik as a café pianist and arranged much music for that purpose. Then, when the war was over, he was obliged to follow party precepts in the new Stalinist Poland, which resulted in works of folk-music character, though done with a Bartókian perfection of technique. The change came with his *Funeral Music* for strings in memory of Bartók (1958), even if the undisguised motivic working of that piece was unusual: it was a hearing of Cage's Concert for Piano and Orchestra that opened the door to the aleatory loosening in *Venetian Games* and subsequent works, followed in the Third Symphony and surrounding pieces by a more defined and directed style that profits from earlier delicacies of texture.

Orchestral: Symphonic Variations, 1936-8; Sym no.1, 1941-7, no.2, 1965-7, no.3, 1983; Overture, str, 1949; Little Suite, 1950-51; Conc for Orch, 1950-54; Dance Preludes, cl, chamber orch, 1955; Funeral Music, str, 1954-8; 3 Postludes, 1958-60; Venetian Games, chamber orch, 1960-61; Livre pour orchestre, 1968; Vc Conc, 1969-70; Preludes and Fugue, 13 str, 1970-72; Mi-parti, 1975-6; Paganini Variations, pf, orch, 1977-8; Novelette, 1978-9; Double Conc, ob, harp, str, 1980; Chain 1, chamber orch, 1983

Vocal orchestral: Silesian Triptych, S, orch, 1951; 5 Songs, Mez, 30 insts, 1958; 3 Poems of Henri Michaux, chorus, orch, 1961-3; Paroles tissées, T, chamber orch, 1965; Les espaces du sommeil, Bar, orch, 1975

Chamber: Recitativo e arioso, vn, pf, 1951; Dance Preludes, cl, pf, 1954; Bucolics, va, vc, 1962; Str Qt, 1964; Sacher Variation, vc, 1975; Epitaph, ob, pf, 1979

Piano: 2 Studies, 1941; Variations on a Theme of Paganini, 2 pf, 1941; Folk Melodies, 1945; Bucolics, 1952; Invention, 1968

[Chester, PWM]

□ B.A. Varga, *Lutosław ski Profile* (1976); S. Stucky, *Lutosław ski and his Music* (1981)

Lutyens, Elisabeth (1906-83) English composer. Daughter of the architect Sir Edwin Lutyens, she studied with Darke at the Royal College of Music (1926-30) and took a leading part in the Macnaghten-Lemare concerts of contemporary music in London (1933-7). In her Chamber Concerto no.1 for 9 instruments (1939) she arrived at a variety of Webernian serialism, being one of the first English composers to use 12-note methods (she would have had contact with Schoenberg and Webern through her husband Edward Clark, who was instrumental in bringing these composers to England to conduct for the BBC). In later years she was an influential teacher and friend of younger British composers; her own output was large (over 150 works with opus numbers), and covered all genres from opera and music theatre to small-scale ensemble and instrumental music. [Belwin-Mills, Schott, Olivan]

□ E. Lutyens, *A Goldfish Bowl* (1972)

Lyadov, Anatol (1855-1914) Russian composer. Studied with Rimsky-Korsakov at the St Petersburg Conservatory (1870-78), where he then taught. Famously indolent, though contriving to produce a decent output of orchestral pieces, piano music and songs, he failed to fulfil Dyagilev's commission for a *Firebird* score, so that the task passed

to Stravinsky. The works he did complete include the Rimskyan tone poems *Baba-Yaga* (?1891-1904), *The Enchanted Lake* (1909) and *Kikimora* (1909).

Lyapunov, Sergey (1859-1924) Russian composer. Studied with Tchaikovsky and Taneyev at the Moscow Conservatory (1878-83), but inclined more to the nationalist school and went to St Petersburg for lessons with Balakirev. In 1893 he went on a folksong-collecting expedition with Balakirev and Lyadov; he later made arrangements and used folksong themes in his works, which include many virtuoso miniatures for the piano. He also taught in St Petersburg and remained there after the Revolution, though he died in exile in Paris.

Lyric Suite (Lyrische Suite) String quartet by Berg in 6 movements, of mixed serial and non-serial foundation and increasing divergence of speed (Allegretto giovale, Andante amoroso, Allegro misterioso–Trio estatico, Adagio appassionato, Presto delirando–Tenebroso, Largo desolato). The work is officially dedicated to Zemlinsky and quotes from his Lyric Symphony, as well as from *Tristan*, though unofficially it was intended as a memento of Berg's attachment to Hanna Fuchs-Robettin, including a setting of Baudelaire's 'De profundis clamavi' that is 'sung' by the instruments in the finale. *Kolisch Quartet, Vienna, 8 Jan 1927. Berg arranged the second, third and fourth movements for string orchestra as Three Pieces from the Lyric Suite. *Berlin, 31 Jan 1929.

M

Machover, Tod (1953-) American composer. Studied with Carter and Sessions at the Juilliard School, then did work on computer composition at Stanford before taking charge of musical research at the Institut de Recherche et de Coordination Acoustique/Musique, where his works included *Soft Morning, City!* for soprano, double bass and tape (1980).

Maconchy, Elizabeth (1907-) English composer. Studied with Wood and Vaughan Williams at the Royal College of Music (1923-9) and in Prague with Jirák. During the 1930s she became known in

England and central Europe as a composer of chamber music in a tough-minded Bartókian style, and this she has continued to pursue, notably in her 13 string quartets. However, her output also includes operas, orchestral works, choral pieces and songs. [Boosey, Chester, OUP]

McPhee, Colin (1900-64) American composer and musical ethnologist. Studied at the Peabody Conservatory, in Toronto and with Le Flem and Philipp in Paris (1924-6), then moved to New York, where he had lessons with Varèse. He spent 2 years in Bali (1934-6), and it is his Balinese pieces that have excited most interest: *Tabuh-tabuhan* for 2 pianos and orchestra (1936) and *Balinese Ceremonial Music* for 2 pianos (1940). After the war he taught in Los Angeles and prepared his study *Music in Bali* (New Haven, 1966, r1976).

Madama Butterfly Opera by Puccini, Giacosa and Illica after Belasco's play. ★Milan, 17 Feb 1904. This 2-act version was a failure and Puccini quickly prepared a revision in 3 acts (★Brescia, 28 May 1904), though since the 1970s productions have justified including some of the earlier material, which fills out the Japanese background and lets Pinkerton off less lightly.

Maderna, Bruno (1920-73) Italian composer and conductor. Appeared before the war as a child violinist and conductor, then studied composition with Malipiero at the Venice Conservatory and, after the war, conducting with Scherchen, who guided him towards 12-note composition. In 1951 he went to Darmstadt for the first time, when the courses were also attended by Nono and Stockhausen. Berio was another of his early companions: they founded an electronic music studio at the Milan station of Italian radio in 1955. That was also the year he first taught at Darmstadt, where he made his home, while conducting regularly in Milan, London and the Netherlands. His repertory was stongest in the 20th c., and he was a generous promoter of his fellow composers' works; his own convey the same largeness of spirit.
Stage: Hyperion, ★Venice, 1964; Satyricon, ★Scheveningen, 1973
Orchestral: Ob Conc no.1, 1962, no.2, 1967, no.3, 1973; Quadrivium, 1969; Vn Conc, 1969; Grande aulodia, fl, ob, orch, 1970; Juilliard Serenade, small orch, tape, 1971; Aura, 1972; Biogramma, 1972; Giardino religioso, small orch, 1972
Instrumental and tape pieces, arrangements
[Ricordi, Suvini Zerboni]

magic square Arrangement of numbers so that each horizontal or vertical row adds up to the same sum. E.g.:

1	6	2	7	3	8	4	9	5
6	2	7	3	8	4	9	5	1
2	7	3	8	4	9	5	1	6
7	3	8	4	9	5	1	6	2
3	8	4	9	5	1	6	2	7
8	4	9	5	1	6	2	7	3
4	9	5	1	6	2	7	3	8
8	5	1	6	2	7	3	8	4
5	1	6	2	7	3	8	4	9

This is the square used in Davies's *Ave maris stella*, where the numbers are interpreted as pitch classes and durational values; other works by him use magic squares less blatantly.

Magnard, Albéric (1865-1914) French composer. Studied at the Paris Conservatoire with Dubois and Massenet (1886-8), then privately with d'Indy. His music, with its own dark seriousness and solemn candour, includes the opera *Bérénice* (Paris, 1911) and 4 symphonies (no.4 in C♯ minor, 1913).

Mahagonny 'Songspiel' by Weill and Brecht (★Baden-Baden, 1927), extended to make a full-length opera of corruption and decadence set in a mythical Wild West: *Aufstieg und Fall der Stadt Mahagonny* (Rise and Fall of the City of Mahagonny). ★Leipzig, 9 Mar 1930.

Mahler, Gustav (1860-1911). Austrian composer and conductor. Though all his works can be understood as chapters in a profoundly inward-seeking autobiography, what he produced has influenced quite decisively such otherwise heterogeneous composers as Schoenberg and Bernstein, Shostakovich and Webern, Britten and Henze. In this respect, at least, composers were in advance of their audiences, for Mahler's music was not widely performed before the 1960s. Previously his large forms were considered as Brucknerian grandiosities without Brucknerian simplicity, but latterly their complexity has been appreciated as the necessary vehicle for the expression of ironic distance, obsession, anxiety and nostalgia. Mahler needed too a language aware of earlier certainties (sonata form, diatonic harmony, homophony, the 4-movement symphonic ideal) but straining in new directions: towards continuous development, atonality (notably in the first movement of the Tenth Symphony), textures of simultaneous individualized lines (*see* HETEROPHONY) and symphonic structures including songs and extra movements.

He studied with Fuchs and Krenn at the Vienna Conservatory (1875-8) and also attended lectures by Bruckner, then worked as a teacher while composing his cantata *Das klagende Lied*. In 1880 he began his career as a conductor, at first in minor towns, but afterwards at the opera houses in Prague (1885-6), Leipzig (1886-8), Budapest (1888-91) and Hamburg (1891-7), moving on in each case because of disagreements with the management. In Leipzig he presented his own completion of Weber's *Die drei Pintos* (1888), but apart from the early abandoned *Rübezahl* (*c*. 1880), he made no attempts at opera composition: from the first his music sprang from a highly subjective, individual viewpoint, and where words were needed they naturally came from lyric poetry rather than drama.

Song and symphony emerged together. The First Symphony (?1884-1888) used themes from the cycle *Lieder eines fahrenden Gesellen* (Songs of a journeying lad, 1883-5) and developed its typically Romantic tone of alienation into something more acutely personal. Then the early Romantic compilation *Des Knaben Wunderhorn* (The Boy's Magic Horn) – believed in Mahler's time to contain genuine folk poetry – became his source for orchestral songs, some included in the Second, Third and Fourth Symphonies (1888-1900), each of which finds a way towards appeasement. In the Second this comes in a vision of resurrection in the choral finale; the Third moves from a massive half-hour allegro in D minor through instrumental and vocal movements to an adagio finale in D major; and the Fourth, more conventionally laid out in 4 movements instead of the Second Symphony's 5 and the Third's 6, ends with a simple song of heavenly bliss.

In 1897 he had converted from his native Jewish to the Christian faith in order to secure his appointment as director of the Vienna Court Opera. During his decade there he was responsible for Mozart and Wagner productions reported to have been as musically impressive as they were dramatically integrated, with the help of radically simplified designs by Alfred Roller: this was where 20th c. opera as performance art began. In 1902 he married Alma Schindler, by whom he had 2 daughters, Maria and Anna.

This was also a time of abundant creative work. The Fourth Symphony was finished, and followed within 6 years by 4 more, of which nos 5-7 are all purely orchestral, though related to musical and psychological themes from his contemporary settings of Rückert. In particular these works are centred on the threat of death: the *Kindertotenlieder*

(1901-4) had appallingly foreshadowed the death of his elder daughter in 1907, and in the Sixth Symphony (1903-4) he faced his own extinction. There is a notable change from the serene or triumphant endings of the earlier symphonies, and though the lack of songs is compensated by picturesque movements (the Adagietto for harp and strings in the Fifth Symphony; the 2 nocturnes in the Seventh), these symphonies are more unified in structure. Pessimism of spirit is thus combined with supreme artistic confidence – a confidence that enabled Mahler to symphonize hymn and drama in the 2 massive parts of his Eighth Symphony, setting the *Veni, Creator Spiritus* and the finale of Goethe's *Faust* for soloists, choirs and a characteristically large orchestra (though the nickname 'Symphony of a Thousand' exaggerates).

In Vienna he was a beacon to such younger composers as Zemlinsky, Schoenberg, Berg and Webern, but as usual he made enemies, and in 1907 he left for New York, where he was conductor of the Metropolitan (1908-10) and the Philharmonic (1909-11). He returned to Austria for the summers, though, and there composed *Das* LIED VON DER ERDE, the Ninth Symphony and what he completed of the Tenth. There are new features here: pentatonics in *Das Lied von der Erde*, more polyphonic textures in the Ninth Symphony and extreme chromaticism in the Tenth. There is, too, a return of the slow finale in the first 2 works, contributing to a tone of regretful leave-taking, though the Tenth Symphony (realized in the 1960s and 1970s by Deryck Cooke) may have been intended as more affirmative.

Symphonies: no.1, ?1884-1888, rev. 1893-6; no.2, with S, A, chorus, 1888-94, rev. 1903; no.3, with A, women's chorus, boys' chorus, 1893-6, rev. 1906; no.4, with S, 1892, 1899-1900, rev. 1901-10; no.5, 1901-2, later rev.; no.6, 1903-4, rev. 1906; no.7, 1904-5, later rev.; no.8, with 8 solo vv, chorus, boys' chorus, 1906; *Das* LIED VON DER ERDE, with T, A/Bar, 1908-9; no.9, 1908-9; no.10, 1910, unfinished

Orchestral songs from Des Knaben Wunderhorn: Der Schildwache Nachtlied, 1892; Verlor'ne Müh, 1892; Trost im Unglück, 1892; Wer hat dies Liedlein erdacht?, 1892; Das irdische Leben, 1892-3; Des Antonius von Padua Fischpredigt, 1893; Rheinlegendchen, 1893; Lob des hohen Verstandes, 1896; Lied des Verfolgten im Turm, 1898; Wo die schönen trompeten blasen, 1898; Revelge, 1899; Der Tamboursg'sell, 1901

Other vocal orchestral works: Das klagende Lied, S, A, T, chorus, orch, 1880, rev. 1892-3, 1898-9;

Lieder eines fahrenden Gesellen, ?1883-1885; Kindertotenlieder, 1901-4; 5 Rückert Lieder, 1901-2
Songs with piano: Lieder, T, pf, 1880; Lieder und Gesänge, vol. 1, 1880-83, vols 2-3 (Des Knaben Wunderhorn), 1887-90
Chamber: PfQt, a, first movement only, ?1876-8
□ D. Mitchell, *Gustav Mahler*, vol.1 (1958, 2/1980), vol. 2 (1975); M. Kennedy, *Mahler* (1974)

Makropulos Case, The (Věc Makropulos) Opera by Janáček after Čapek's play, a mixture of fantasy and cutting realism centred on a lawsuit pursued by a woman who has magically survived through 3 centuries. ★Brno, 18 Dec 1926.

Malipiero, Gian Francesco (1882-1973) Italian composer. Studied at the Vienna Conservatory (1898-9) and with Bossi in his native Venice (1899-1902) and Bologna (1904), but was most influenced by his discovery of early Italian music in the Biblioteca Marciana (he later made many arrangements and editions of works by Monteverdi, Vivaldi, etc) and by experiences in Paris in 1913: gaining the friendship of Casella and hearing *The Rite of Spring*. He suppressed his earlier music and began writing more splintered yet lyrical works, held in tension among the poles of Stravinsky, Debussy and early music. His most fascinating pieces come from this period, followed after 1930 by years of more complete synthesis and stability.
Stage: Pantea (ballet), 1917-19, ★Venice, 1932; L'orfeide (operatic trilogy: La morte delle maschere; Sette canzoni; Orfeo, ovvero L'ottava canzone), 1918-22, ★Düsseldorf, 1925; S Francesco d'Assisi (mystery), 1920-21, ★Perugia, 1949; 3 commedie goldoniane, 1920-22, ★Darmstadt, 1926; Filomela e l'infatuato (opera), 1925, ★Prague, 1928; Merlino maestro d'organi (opera), 1926-7, ★Palermo, 1972; Il mistero di Venezia (operatic trilogy), 1925-8, ★Coburg, 1932; Torneo notturno (opera), 1929, ★Munich, 1931
Many later operas, orch works, chamber music (8 str qts), etc
[Ricordi, UE, Chester, Suvini Zerboni]

Manchester School Name used to bracket together Birtwistle, Davies and Goehr, all of whom were pupils of Hall at the Royal Manchester College of Music in the mid-1950s.

mandolin Used as a serenade instrument in Mahler's Seventh Symphony and Schoenberg's Serenade, though both these composers also made it part of the normal orchestra, Mahler in his

Second and Eighth Symphonies and *Das Lied von der Erde,* Schoenberg in his Variations, *Von heute auf morgen* and *Moses.* Webern used it in his opp. 10, 26 and 29. The Viennese associations were only confirmed when Stravinsky brought it into his *Agon.* Boulez has used it in his *Pli selon pli* and *Eclat/ Multiples.*

Mantra Work by Stockhausen for 2 pianos ring modulated with sine tones, his first to be based on a melodic formula. ★Kontarskys, Donaueschingen, 28 Oct 1970.

marimba Xylophone with resonators, entering the modern orchestra from Africa by way of Latin America and light music. Grainger used it before the second world war, but it only became common after 1940, when Creston wrote a concerto for it. Milhaud wrote a concerto for marimba and xylophone (1947), and there are parts for the instrument in Messiaen's *Chronochromie*, Boulez's *Pli selon pli* (2), Stockhausen's *Gruppen* and *Zyklus*, and Davies's *Ave maris stella* and other works. *See also* XYLOPHONE.

Markevich, Igor (1912-83) Russian-Italian composer and conductor. Was brought up in Switzerland and Paris, where he studied with Boulanger and came to the notice of Dyagilev, who commissioned his Piano Concerto (1929). In the 1930s he made a reputation as a composer, notably with his ballet *Icare* (1932) and Milton cantata *Le paradis perdu* (1933-5). During the war he settled in Italy and thereafter worked mostly as a conductor.

Marteau sans maître, Le (The Hammer Unmastered) Work by Boulez interlocking settings of and commentaries on 3 poems by Char, their tightly controlled savagery equalled in the music for contralto, alto flute, viola, guitar, vibraphone, xylorimba and percussion. Perhaps the outstanding classic of the postwar avant garde, it had enormous influence as a model of wild imaginativeness given serial authority and as an instrumental ideal, combining wind, string and percussion instruments and European with Indonesian (vibraphone) and African (xylorimba) resonances. ★cond Rosbaud, Baden-Baden, 18 Jun 1955.

Martin, Frank (1890-1974) Swiss composer. The son of a Geneva Calvinist minister, he was permanently marked by a performance of the St Matthew Passion heard when he was 10, but though he had already begun to compose, it took him another 4 decades to establish what would be his mature style. In the meantime he studied privately with Joseph Lauber, worked with Jaques-Dalcroze (from 1926) and was influenced by the French music that Ansermet brought to Geneva after the first world war. In his First Piano Concerto (1933-4) he began to use 12-note methods, but his harmony remained in the luminous suspension of diatonic discords. Finally, perhaps as a result of Bartók's presence in Switzerland in the mid-1930s, he added Bartók to his personal pantheon of Bach, Debussy and Schoenberg, and created his first masterpiece in the Tristan oratorio Le vin herbé. In 1946 he moved to the Netherlands, commuting to teach at the Cologne Musikhochschule (1950-57), where his pupils included Stockhausen.

Stage: Das Märchen vom Aschenbrödel (ballet), 1941, ★Basle, 1942; Der Sturm (opera), 1952-5, ★Vienna, 1956; Le mystère de la Nativité (oratorio-spectacle), 1957-9, ★Salzburg, 1960; Monsieur de Pourceaugnac (opera), 1961-2, ★Geneva, 1963

Oratorios: Le vin herbé, 1938-41; In terra pax, 1944; Golgotha, 1945-8; Pilate, 1964; Requiem, 1971-2

Vocal orchestral: 6 Monologe aus 'Jedermann', A/Bar, pf, 1943, orch version 1949; Maria-Triptychon, S, vn, orch, 1968-9

Orchestral: Ballades with solo a sax, 1938, fl, 1939, pf, 1939, trbn/t sax, 1940, vc, 1949, va, 1972; Petite symphonie concertante, harp, hpd, pf, str, 1945; Conc, 7 wind, perc, str, 1949; Vn Conc, 1950-51; Hpd Conc, 1952; Etudes, str, 1955-6; Vc Conc, 1965-6; Pf Conc no.2, 1968-9; 3 danses, ob, harp, str, 1970; Polyptyque, vn, str, 1972-3

Chamber, choral, instrumental pieces

[UE]

Martino, Donald (1931-) American composer. Studied with Sessions and Babbitt at Princeton (1952-4) and Dallapiccola in Florence (1954-6), then taught at Princeton (1957-9), Yale (1959-69) and the New England Conservatory (1969-). A clarinettist himself, he has written much for his own and other solo instruments in music of strong, vital gesture yet also of breadth and sophistication.

Orchestral: Pf Conc, 1965; Mosaic, 1967; Vc Conc, 1972; Ritorno, 1976; Triple Conc, cl, b, cl, cb cl, 1977

Chamber: Conc, wind qnt, 1964; Notturno, 6 insts, 1973

Instrumental: Parisonatina, vc, 1964; B, a, b, b, it, t, cl, 1966; Strata, b cl, 1966; Pianissimo, pf, 1970

[Ione]

Martinů, Bohuslav (1890-1959) Czech composer. Studied the violin with Suk at the Prague Con-servatory (1906-10) but was expelled for indolence; he then lived as a teacher and violinist in the Czech Philharmonic (1918-23), returned briefly to Suk for composition lessons, and settled in Paris (1923-40). There he had lessons with Roussel and was impressed also by Stravinsky, jazz and neo-classicism, while retaining the charm of Czech folk music. On the fall of France he left by way of Lisbon for the USA, where, though homesick, he lived for most of the rest of his life except for periods in Nice (1953-5) and Rome and Switzer-land (1956-9). His output is immense, and very varied in style, though the Roussel connection was often important and the best of his works (*Julietta*, the Sixth Symphony) have a febrile inventiveness within sustained diatonic chords and progressions.

Operas: Julietta, 1936-7, ★Prague, 1938; Mirando-lina, 1954, ★Prague, 1959; The Greek Passion, 1956-9, ★Zurich, 1961

Ballets: Kitchen Revue, 1927; Špalíček, 1931-2

Orchestral: La bagarre, 1926; Le Jazz, 1928; Jazz Suite, 1928; Sym no. 1, 1942, no. 2, 1943, no.3, 1944, no.4, 1945, no. 5, 1946, no.6, 1951-3; Sinfo-nietta 'La Jolla', pf, orch, 1950; Frescoes of Piero della Francesca, 1953; many concs for pf (4), vn, 2 vn (2), vc, hpd, ob, etc

Choral: Field Mass, Bar, male vv, orch, 1939; Gil-gamesh (oratorio), 1954-5

Much other choral, vocal, chamber (7 str qts), pf music

[Boosey; Supraphon]

□ B. Large, *Martinů* (1975)

Martyre de Saint-Sébastien, Le 'Mystery' by d'Annunzio lavishly setting out the mythology of the beautiful saint holding to Christianity amid a decadent paganism that wants to see him as Ado-nis; Debussy provided modal orchestral pieces, choruses and songs for the spectacle, and engaged Caplet's help in the instrumentation. ★Paris, 22 May 1911.

Marx, Joseph (1882-1964) Austrian composer. Studied humanities at Graz University, not com-mitting himself to composition until he was 26. Then in 4 years (1908-12) he wrote the 120 songs on which his reputation rests; they are of a Wolfian character, setting poems from Heyse's *Italienisches Liederbuch* and others by contemporary poets more associated with the Second Viennese School (Rilke, Mombert, Storm, Giraud-Hartleben). In later years he worked as a teacher and critic, and turned to chamber and orchestral composition in a conservative style. [UE]

Mather, Bruce (1939-) Canadian composer. Studied with Beckwith at Toronto University (1953-9), with Milhaud and Messiaen in Paris (1959-62) and with Leland Smith at Stanford (1962-4), then in 1966 took an appointment at McGill University. Musically he aligns himself with the later Boulez, his works including a set of 5 *Madrigaux* for female soloists and small ensembles (1967-73).

Mathias, William (1934-) Welsh composer. Studied with Berkeley at the Royal Academy of Music (1956-9), since when he has taught at University College, Bangor. He is a prolific and vigorous composer, with a large output particularly of orchestral and choral music, in a decisive style forged out of Bartók, Hindemith and Britten. [OUP]
☐ M. Boyd, *William Mathias* (1974)

Mathis der Maler (Mathis the Painter) Opera by Hindemith to his own libretto on the life of Matthias Grünewald and the problematic choice facing the artist between engagement in just temporal struggles and devotion to art. The production was preceded by the appearance of a symphony drawn from the score, its movements named after masterpieces by Grünewald: Engelkonzert, Grablegung, Versuchung des heiligen Antonius. *Berlin, 12 Mar 1934 (sym); Zurich, 28 May 1938 (opera).

Matthews, Colin (1946-) English composer, brother of David. Studied with Whittall at Nottingham University and with Maw, then worked with Britten and with Cooke on his performing version of Mahler's Tenth Symphony. He has written much for orchestra, including his Fourth Sonata (1974-5) and Cello Concerto (1984), his complex, atonal style having an objectified and abstracted Mahlerian intensity, brilliantly coloured. [Faber]

Matthews, David (1943-) English composer, brother of Colin. Studied at Nottingham University and with Milner, then like his brother worked with Cooke on Mahler's Tenth; he has also been associated with Tippett, on whom he wrote a short study (London, 1979). His music is basically diatonic and includes symphonies, string quartets and songs. [Faber]

Mavra Short opera by Stravinsky and Boris Kochno after Pushkin, dedicated to the memory of Pushkin, Glinka and Tchaikovsky. It is a comedy in short numbers briskly scored for a wind-led orchestra: Mavra is a hussar hired as a maidservant by his beloved to outwit her mother. *Paris, Ballets Russes, 1 Jun 1922.

Maw, Nicholas (1935-) English composer. Studied with Berkeley at the Royal Academy of Music (1955-8) and with Boulanger and Deutsch in Paris (1958-9), since when he has worked as a copyist and university teacher (at Cambridge 1966-70, Exeter and Yale). His early works show a bewildering range of enthusiasms, from Webern to Strauss by way of Britten and Bartók, but out of these he has created a coherent, richly textured yet strongly harmonically directed music.
Opera: One Man Show, 1964; The Rising of the Moon, *Glyndebourne, 1970
Orchestral: Scenes and Arias, S, Mez, A, orch, 1962, rev. 1966; Sinfonia, small orch, 1966; Sonata, str, 2 hn, 1967; Life Studies, 15 str, 1973-6; Serenade, small orch 1973-7; La vita nuova, S, small orch, 1979
Chamber: Str Qt no. 1, 1965; no. 2, 1982; Personae, pf, 1973
[Boosey; Chandos]

Meale, Richard (1932-) Australian composer. Studied as a pianist at the NSW Conservatorium but is self-taught as a composer, influenced by the music of Messiaen and Boulez, and by courses in Asian music he attended at UCLA in 1960-61. His works include the opera *Juliet's Memoirs* (1974-5), orchestral pieces (Nocturnes, 1965-7; *Very High Kings*, 1968; *Viridian*, str, 1978) and chamber music. [Boosey, UE]

mechanical instruments Discounting those machines that require electricity, the most important have been the PIANOLA and the musical box.

Medtner *See* METNER.

Mellers, Wilfrid (1914-) English composer. Studied with Leavis at Cambridge (1933-8) while taking composition lessons with Rubbra and Wellesz in Oxford, then taught at the universities of Cambridge (1945-8), Birmingham (1948-59), Pittsburgh (1960-63) and York (1964-82). His breadth of knowledge, daring and literary panache have won him wider audiences for his books than for his compositions: the former include studies of American music (*Music in a New Found Land*, London, 1964, r1975) and 20th c. composition (*Caliban Reborn*, New York, 1967). His musical works are numerous and diverse, ranging from early chamber pieces in an English vein of neoclassicism to the exultant *Yeibichai* for combined jazz, orchestral, vocal and electronic forces (1968).

Melos Monthly journal for new music founded by Scherchen, published 1920-34 and 1946-74, then amalgamated with the *Neue Zeitschrift für Musik*.

Mennin, Peter (1923-) American composer. Studied with Lockwood at Oberlin College (1941-2) and with Hanson and Rogers at the Eastman School (1943-7), then taught at the Juilliard School (1947-58) and the Peabody Conservatory (1958-62) before becoming president of the Juilliard School. His music is in the American diatonic tradition of Harris and Schuman, and includes 8 symphonies besides other orchestral and large-scale vocal works. [Fischer]

Menotti, Gian Carlo (1911-) Italian-American composer. Studied at the Milan Conservatory (1923-7) and with Scalero at the Curtis Institute (1928-33), where he became a close companion of Barber's (later he wrote the libretto for the latter's *Vanessa*). His first opera *Amelia Goes to the Ball*, a 1-act comedy, established his ready gift for the theatre, but it was outdone in success after the war by *The Medium* and by his first full-length work, *The Consul*, conveying a rawness of emotional expression that has perhaps unfairly evoked comparison with Puccini.
Amelia Goes to the Ball, *Philadelphia, 1937; The Old Maid and the Thief, *NBC radio, 1939; The Island God, *New York, 1942; The Medium, *New York, 1946; The Telephone, *New York, 1947; The Consul, *Philadelphia, 1950; Amahl and the Night Visitors, *NBC TV, 1951; many later operas, also ballets, orch pieces, etc
[G. Schirmer, Ricordi]

Mer, La (The Sea) Set of '3 symphonic sketches' by Debussy, almost a symphony in D♭ major, with a scherzo surrounded by 2 accumulating allegros of emphatic statement swayed by mutability. The movements are 'De l'aube à midi sur la mer' (From dawn to noon on the sea), 'Jeux de vagues' (Waveplays) and 'Dialogue du vent et de la mer' (The wind's dialogue with the sea). *Paris, 15 Oct, 1905.

Messager, André (1853-1929) French composer and conductor. Studied with Fauré and Saint-Saëns at the Ecole Niedermeyer (1869-74),

and set out on double career, at first having most success as an operetta composer (*Véronique*, 1898). But increasingly he won renown as a Wagner conductor in Paris and London; he was also responsible for the first performance of *Pelléas et Mélisande*, which is dedicated to him.

Messiaen, Olivier (1908-) French composer and teacher. His understanding of Debussy and Stravinsky, coupled always with the Roman Catholic faith that has been at the heart of all his work, led him towards a conception of music as static rather than dynamic, concerned with statement and decoration rather than with development. This encouraged him to look for parallels and stimulus in a wide variety of non-developmental musical cultures – notably ancient Greek, Sanskrit and Indonesian – as well as in the songs of birds. He has also worked consistently with a group of MODES OF LIMITED TRANSPOSITIONS that neutralize long-range harmonic forces by drawing diatonic chords into configurations based on symmetrical divisions of the octave, notably the diminished-7th chord and the augmented triad. All these features make his music quite inimitable, yet his openness to new ways of making music – whether through serialism or a resort to oriental qualities of instrumentation and time-scale – has made him one of the century's most remarkable composition teachers, his pupils including Barraqué, Boulez and Stockhausen.
He himself studied at the Paris Conservatoire (1919-30) with the Gallons, Caussade, Emmanuel, Dupré and Dukas, and took the post of organist at La Sainte Trinité in Paris immediately thereafter. His early career was that of an organist-composer: his first important works were cycles for his own instrument and symphonic meditations on aspects of faith. However, he was also a member of La JEUNE FRANCE, and his marriage in 1931 to Claire Delbos brought forth song cycles on themes of familial love, as expressed in the fervent surrealist imagery of his own texts (*Poèmes pour Mi*, *Chants de terre et de ciel*; all later works also set his own words or compilations). Meanwhile his technical repertory grew: his special modes already form the basis of his earliest published works; to them he added in *La Nativité du Seigneur* a delight in rhythmic irregularity coming partly from ancient Indian musical theory.
In 1939 he was called up for military service, which lasted until he was captured the next year: then at prisoner-of-war camp he wrote the QUATUOR POUR LA FIN DU TEMPS. In 1942 he re-

turned to the Conservatoire to teach, and acquired a lively group of students including Boulez, Nigg and the pianist Yvonne Loriod, his devoted interpreter and later his wife (Claire Messiaen was confined to hospital with a wasting disease). Several of his most important works date from the next few years, including the VISIONS DE L'AMEN, the TROIS PETITES LITURGIES, the VINGT REGARDS, HARAWI and the TURANGALÎLA-SYMPHONIE. Then came a brief period when he took part in his pupils' exploration of 12-note methods, though his interest was not in serialism but in the construction of artificial musical universes, as in his influential MODE DE VALEURS ET D'INTENSITÉS (1949-50).

During the 1950s almost all his music was based on birdsongs, which had already appeared occasionally; however, the preservation of characteristic instrumental, rhythmic and even modal features make these works distinctively his own. The main effect of the birds is to make his colouring brighter in the search for equivalents to avian plumage (he has often spoken of a relationship between sound and colour), and also to intensify the tendency of his rhythm to move in quick even values. This had come in the first place from Stravinsky, with whom he shares a view of rhythm in terms of individual units rather than groups defined by metre and phrase, and a fascination with purely rhythmic construction, as in his NON-RETROGRADABLE RHYTHMS.

In the early 1960s birdsong music began to be mixed with other kinds: abstract constructions and mountainscapes in the orchestral *Chronochromie*, and plainsong and rich harmonies in *Couleurs de la Cité Céleste*, which is as kaleidoscopic in its mosaic form as in its colouring. Then he returned to the more symmetrical and liturgical forms of his earlier music, and began a process of bringing together the various components of a language developed over 4 decades. This process involved creating room for heterogeneity rather than attempting a synthesis, which would have been against the nature of his art; it has therefore given rise to works of large dimensions: the oratorio La TRANSFIGURATION, the orchestral *Des canyons aux étoiles*... and the opera SAINT FRANÇOIS D'ASSISE.

Orchestral: Les offrandes oubliées, 1930; Le tombeau resplendissant, 1931; Hymne au Saint Sacrement, 1932; L'Ascension, 1932-3; TURANGALÎLA-SYMPHONIE, pf, ondes martenot, orch, 1946-8; Réveil des oiseaux, pf, orch, 1953; Oiseaux exotiques, pf, 11 wind, 7 perc, 1955-6; Chronochromie, 1959-60; 7 haïkaï, pf, 13 wind, 6 perc, 8 vn, 1962; Couleurs de la Cité Céleste, pf, 13 wind, 6 perc,

1963; Et exspecto resurrectionem mortuorum, 34 wind, 3 perc, 1964; Des canyons aux étoiles..., pf, 43 insts, 1971-5

Choral: O sacrum convivium!, SATB/S, org, 1937; 3 petites liturgies de la Présence Divine, 36 female vv, pf, ondes martenot, perc, str, 1943-4; 5 rechants, 12 solo vv, 1949; La TRANSFIGURATION DE NOTRE SEIGNEUR JÉSUS-CHRIST, 1965-9

Solo vocal: 3 mélodies, v, pf, 1930; La mort du nombre, S, T, vn, pf, 1930; Vocalise, S, pf, 1935; Poèmes pour Mi, S, pf, 1936, orch version 1937; Chants de terre et de ciel, S, pf, 1938; HARAWI, S, pf, 1945

Chamber: Thème et variations, vn, pf, 1932; QUATUOR POUR LA FIN DU TEMPS, cl, vn, vc, pf, 1940-41; Le merle noir, fl, pf, 1952

Organ: Le banquet céleste, 1928; Diptyque, 1930; Apparition de l'église éternelle, 1932; L'Ascension, after orch work, 1933-4; La Nativité du Seigneur, 1935; Les corps glorieux, 1939; Messe de la Pentecôte, 1949-50; Livre d'orgue, 1951; Verset pour la fête de la Dédicace, 1960; Méditations sur le mystère de la Sainte Trinité, 1969

Piano: Preludes, 1928-9; Fantaisie burlesque, 1932; Pièce pour le tombeau de Paul Dukas, 1935; Rondeau, 1943; Visions de l'Amen, 2 pf, 1943; 20 regards sur l'Enfant-Jésus, 1944; Cantéyodjayâ, 1949; 4 études de rythme (Ile de feu 1, MODE DE VALEURS ET D'INTENSITÉS, Neumes rythmiques, Ile de feu 2), 1949-50; CATALOGUE D'OISEAUX, 1956-8; La fauvette des jardins, 1970

[Leduc, Durand, UE]

□ O. Messiaen, *Technique of My Musical Language* (1957); P. Griffiths, *Olivier Messiaen and the Music of Time* (1985)

Metner, Nikolay (Medtner, Nicolas) (1880-1951) Russian composer and pianist. Studied with Safonov and Arensky at the Moscow Conservatory (1892-1900), and was encouraged by Taneyev to devote himself to composition. In 1921 he left Russia and in 1925 settled in Paris, though as a representative of high Russian Romanticism he found less favour there than in England and North America, and in 1935 he moved to London. His works include 3 piano concertos (c, 1914-18; c, 1920-27; e, c.1940-43), much solo piano music and many songs to Russian and German texts. [Editions Russes de Musique, Novello]

metric modulation Term introduced by Carter for a technique of changing the pulse from one passage to the next, and usually changing the metre too, by introducing the new rhythmic character as a cross-rhythm within the old. For instance, in bars 22ff of his First Quartet the cello defines a 4/4 metre at crotchet = 120; the viola then enters in triplet crotchets and establishes a new movement in 3/2 metre at minim = 90. There is thus no connection with Blacher's technique of variable metres, where the pulse rate is not changed.

Metz French town, site of the Rencontres Internationales de Musique Contemporaine taking place annually in November since 1972, and presenting works by Stockhausen, Boulez, Kagel, Xenakis, etc.

Metzger, Heinz-Klaus (1932-) German writer on music. Studied at the Freiburg Musikhochschule (1949-52) and Tübingen University (1952-4), and also had lessons in composition with Deutsch in Paris. He was closely associated in the 1950s with the Darmstadt circle, for whom he played a role of philosophical apologist similar to that which Adorno played for the Second Viennese School. In the 1960s he began to find American experimental music more inviting to his Hegelian-Marxist analysis, but he has written on a wide range of music in the journal *Musik-Konzepte*, which he founded with Rainer Riehn in 1977.

Miaskovsky *See* MYASKOVSKY.

microtones Intervals smaller than an octave. Alternatives to the fixed 12-note scale have been considered by theorists from the time when such scales began to exert their hegemony, with the rise of keyboard instruments in the late Renaissance; and no doubt they have always been practised by choirs and keyboardless ensembles. The construction of special instruments in the 20th c., such as Fokker's 31-note organ or Partch's 43-note percussion instruments, simply extends these subtleties of tuning.

But microtones have also been used on their own account, beginning with the introduction of quarter tones by Carrillo and Foulds in the 1890s. The climax of this interest came in the 1920s, when Hába was founding a whole school of quarter-tone and sixth-tone composition in Prague, Carrillo was writing quarter-note music for Stokowski, and Vishnegradsky was composing for quarter-tone pianos in Paris, while a more decorative use of quarter tones appeared in Ives and Bartók (*The Miraculous Mandarin*). Performing quarter-tone and sixth-tone music is physically (if not aurally and intellectually) straightforward for singers and

string players, but these composers also worked with pairs of pianos tuned a quarter tone apart (Ives, Vishnegradsky) or with specially constructed instruments (Hába, Carrillo). Hearing microtonal music may present more difficulties, since the ear's long experience of semitonal music predisposes it to interpreting smaller intervals as mistunings.

Possibly for that reason, interest in quarter-tone and sixth-tone musical systems has declined since the 1950s, to be replaced by usages that may appear less contrived: the decorative use of quarter tones within monody (Boulez's *Improvisation sur Mallarmé III*) and the free employment of the whole pitch spectrum in electronic music. However, where electronic music asks to be heard in terms of pitch relations, it is very often composed within the 12-note system (Babbitt) or else within what amounts to a new tuning rather than an involvement of small intervals (Stockhausen).

Midsummer Night's Dream, A Opera by Britten and Pears after Shakespeare. *Aldeburgh, 11 Jun 1960.

Mikrokosmos 6 volumes of piano music by Bartók, progressing from beginners' pieces to concert works, and providing also a journey through the composer's creative world that includes studies in particular matters of modality, rhythm and construction as well as fully achieved works (notably the final 6 Dances in Bulgarian Rhythm, nos 148-53 of the collection). Bartók arranged 7 pieces from Mikrokosmos for 2 pianos (1940) and recorded many items from the last 3 volumes (Hungaroton).

Mikrophonie Title of 2 works by Stockhausen which use electronics in live performance: hence 'microphony'. *Mikrophonie I* is for 6 performers causing, picking up and electronically controlling small resonances from a tam-tam. *Brussels, 9 Dec 1964. *Mikrophonie II* is for 12 singers ring modulated against an electric organ, with taped 'windows' onto more positive works (*Gesang der Jünglinge, Carré, Momente*). *Cologne, 11 Jun 1965.

Milhaud, Darius (1892-1974) French composer. A byword for creative fruitfulness: he produced *c*.450 works with opus numbers, including full-length operas, a large number of orchestral works, cantatas and 18 string quartets, besides smaller pieces of every description. To offer a summary of such an output would be presumptuous, especially when only a very small part of it is in regular performance. Even his celebrated property of bitonality is difficult to judge when his musical connections with Stravinsky and Koechlin remain obscure. Certainly he learned from these composers, and also from jazz, developing a style of mild diatonicism given interest by compound metres, syncopation and bitonal tensions. It seems likely that he produced his best music during his twenties and early thirties, following studies with Gédalge, Dukas and Widor at the Paris Conservatoire, and following a crucial meeting with Claudel. It was in his music for Claudel's translation of the *Oresteia* (1913-22) that he made adventurous use of bitonality, rhythmic speech and percussion. He also travelled with Claudel to Rio de Janeiro as his secretary (1917-18) and visited New York (1922), so that the pervasive influence of South American music and jazz was acquired on the spot. He remained a frequent traveller, and after spending the years 1940-47 at Mills College in Oakland, California, he divided his time between teaching there and at the Conservatoire until in 1971 he retired to Geneva.

Full-scale operas: Christophe Colomb, 1928, ★Berlin, 1930; Maximilien, 1930, ★Paris, 1932; Bolivar, 1943, ★Paris, 1950; David, 1952, ★Jerusalem, 1954; La mère coupable (completion of trilogy with Il barbiere di Siviglia and Le nozze di Figaro), 1964, ★Geneva, 1965; Saint Louis, roi de France, 1970, ★RAI, 1972

Small operas: Les malheurs d'Orphée, 1925, ★Brussels, 1925; Le pauvre matelot, 1926, ★Paris, 1927; 3 opéras minutes (L'enlèvement d'Europe, L'abandon d'Ariane, La délivrance de Thésée), 1927, ★Wiesbaden, 1928

Ballets: L'homme et son désir, 1918; Le BOEUF SUR LE TOIT, 1919; La CRÉATION DU MONDE, 1923; Salade, 1924; Le train bleu, 1924

Incidental music: Agamemnon, 1913-14; Protée, 1913-19; Les choëphores, 1915; Les euménides, 1917-22

Orchestral: 6 chamber syms, 1917-23; 12 syms, 1939-61; concs for pf (5), vn (3), va (2), vc (2), ob, cl, harp, 2 pf, perc, mar and vib, hpd; many other works

Choral music, songs, chamber music, pf pieces, children's music

[UE, Eschig, Heugel, Salabert]

□ D. Milhaud, *Notes without Music* (1952)

Milner, Anthony (1925-) English composer. Studied with Seiber (1944-8) and with Morris at the Royal College of Music (1945-7), then taught at various institutions in London. His works are basically diatonic and often expressive of his Roman Catholic faith, though including more cantatas for concert performance than liturgical settings. [Novello, UE]

minimal music Term normally applied not to music in which the material actually is minimal (at the extreme Cage's *4' 33"*) but rather to works based on the repetition of short figures: i.e. the music of Reich, Riley, Glass, etc. There are adumbrations of this art in Cage (e.g. *Music for Marcel Duchamp*, 1947), but its more immediate sources were in the music created by Young and Riley (*In C*) in the mid-1960s, to which Reich and Glass in the late 1960s added a notion of process, or gradual change effected within ostinato textures. Early works of minimalism, such as Reich's *4 Organs* (1969) or Glass's *Music in Fifths* (also 1969) have the beauty of streamlined simplicity, but the tradition has proved capable of elaboration, as in Reich's later works and Glass's operas. It has also gained numerous adherents in the USA and in Europe, besides influencing composers who, like Ligeti, arrived at repetitive material independently.

Miraculous Mandarin, The (A csodálatos mandarin) Pantomime by Bartók to scenario by Menyhért Lengyel: the mandarin is lured by a prostitute and murderously attacked by her accomplices, but does not die until his lust has been assuaged. The score is Bartók's most wildly imaginative for orchestra. ★Cologne, 27 Nov 1926.

Miroirs (Mirrors) Book of 5 piano pieces by Ravel, of more Lisztian than Debussian picturesqueness: 'Noctuelles', 'Oiseaux tristes', 'Une barque sur l'océan', 'Alborada del gracioso', 'La vallée des cloches'. ★Viñes, Paris, 6 Jan 1906.

mixed media Term applied to works in which musical, dramatic, verbal and visual stimuli may be combined other than in such conventional genres as opera. The idea probably grew out of the happening, and often a similar degree of cheerful chaos is involved, as in Cage's *Theatre Piece* (1960), *Variations V* (1965) or *HPSCHD* (1967-9). Composers within the avant-garde tradition, however, have sometimes tried to compose for multifarious events in a very precise way: examples include Stockhausen's *Originale* (1961) and practically the whole output of Kagel.

mobile form Term used, by association with Calder's mobiles, of works in which composed sections may be arranged in time as chance or choice disposes. This has been most usually a European sort of ALEATORY composition, practised notably by Boulez (Third Piano Sonata, *Domaines*, *Eclat*), Stockhausen (*Klavierstück XI*, *Momente*), Berio (*Epifanie*) and others, though Brown too has created musical mobiles. Most works of this kind date from the late 1950s and 1960s; the greater interest in long-range harmonic process since then has brought about a decline, measured in Boulez's successive revisions of his *Pli selon pli*.

mode Term which may signify (i) one of the 'church modes' of medieval European music, (ii) any similar choice of pitches, transposable onto any level (thus Haydn's op.1 quartets are all based on the same mode, the major), or (iii) a choice of pitches implying also certain melodic patterns (this is the way with, for example, the ragas of Indian music and similar concepts in Arab, Indonesian and Japanese music).

Western art music from the 17th c. to the early 20th c. was distinguished by an extreme reduction in the number of available modes to 2: major and minor. One symptom of the growing instability of this system around 1900 was the introduction of other modes, including the church modes (Debussy, Emmanuel), the PENTATONIC mode (Puccini, Mahler), modes from folk music (Bartók, Vaughan Williams) and invented modes, including most notably the whole-tone mode (Debussy). Of these, the most important were the church modes, since they underlie most European folk music as well. The commonest are the most ancient, the 'authentic modes' (all shown here starting on C): Dorian (C–D–Eb–F–G–A–Bb–C), Phrygian (C–Db–Eb–F–G–Ab–Bb–C), Lydian (C–D–E–F♯–G–A–B–C) and Mixolydian (C–D–E–F–G–A–Bb–C). The Dorian and Phrygian modes are clearly near neighbours of the minor, and have often been used in that context (e.g. the Dorian D minor of Sibelius's String Quartet and the Phrygian G minor of Debussy's). The Lydian mode, with its distinctive tritone, is potentially more disruptive, and has been used precisely for that quality by Bartók, Davies and others; Bartók also made much use of a mode he discovered in Romanian music, consisting of a Lydian bottom half and a Mixolydian top: C–D–E–F♯–G–A–Bb–C (see his Music for Strings, etc). This is sometimes called the 'acoustic scale', since it approximates to the early members of the harmonic series.

Disruptiveness of the major-minor system is not just a feature of the Lydian mode and its relatives,

however. Where a major scale, for instance, contains the notes of major triads to be built on its tonic, 4th and 5th, a Mixolydian scale permits major triads on its tonic, 4th and 7th. This is why the church modes were so difficult to accommodate in 18th c. and 19th c. diatonic music, and why they have assisted in the 20th c. in new varieties of tonality, as displayed in the music of Bartók, Vaughan Williams and others.

The whole-tone mode, with no triads at all and an abundance of tritones, is still more opposed to conventional tonality, and was used by Debussy as a primary means of achieving harmonic stasis; Messiaen has similarly used his MODES OF LIMITED TRANSPOSITIONS. Other invented modes, however, may well come nearer the major-minor system, and it is possible to imagine modal systems which penetrate the major-minor to produce rich networks of ambiguous harmonic relations. This is so, for instance, in Davies' music: his Second Symphony is in a B minor where the normal dominant of F♯ is in conflict with a modal dominant of E♯.

Modes which imply particular melodic patterns remain unusual in western music, though there are examples in Messiaen (e.g. the '*Boris* motif' associated with much of his second-mode music in the 1930s and 1940s) and Stockhausen (*see* FORMULA); MINIMAL MUSIC could also be seen in this light.

Mode de valeurs et d'intensités (Mode of durations and volumes) Piano piece by Messiaen using an array of 36 pitches, each with its own duration, volume and manner of attack. The organization is not serial, but the piece greatly influenced the onset of total serialism. ★Messiaen, Tunis 1950.

modernism Term commonest in American writing on music in the 1930s (cf modern Music), when such composers as Varèse, Schoenberg, Bartók, Stravinsky, Cage, Antheil, Webern and Copland might all be described as modernists, or even ultramodernists. In writing about contemporary culture more generally, the term 'modern movement' implies the new sensibility that emerged around the time of the first world war, and that was expressed in the paintings of Picasso and Kandinsky, the novels of Joyce and Proust, and the music of Schoenberg and Stravinsky. The movement is widely regarded as having lost its momentum by the 1960s; hence the invention of the unlikely term 'post-modernism'. 'Modernism' suggests a conscious pushing-back of the frontiers, and so is not inappropriate in connection with composers who have seen this as their aim: Varèse and Boulez, for instance. 'Post-modernism' may equally be a useful term in writing and thinking about music which is no longer arrowed to the future but timeless in its survey of as much of human culture as its composer can encompass: the later Berio provides examples.

Modern Music Journal published in New York by the League of Composers from 1925 to 1946, including articles and reviews by Sessions, Copland, Cage, etc.

Modern Psalms Collection of works on which Schoenberg was engaged in his last year. Several were written, but only 1 was partly composed. *Cologne, 29 May 1956.

modes of limited transpositions Term coined by Messiaen for modes which contain repeating intervallic units, and which therefore can be transposed only a limited number of times before the same set of pitches is produced. For instance, the 'first mode' is the whole-tone mode (repeating unit 2 semitones), which in these terms has but 2 transpositions: C–D–E–F♯–G♯–A♯–C and C♯–D♯–F–G–A–B–C♯. The 'second mode' has a repeating unit of 2–1 semitones (C–D–D♯–E♯–F♯–G♯–A–B–C), the 'third mode' one of 2–1–1 semitones (C–D–D♯–E–F♯–G–G♯–A♯–B–C), the 'fourth mode' one of 3–1–1–1 semitones (C–D♯–E–F–F♯–A–A♯–B–C) and the 'sixth mode' one of 2–2–1–1 semitones (C–D–E–F–F♯–G♯–A♯–B–C). All divide the octave symmetrically, the symmetry being that of the diminished 7th chord (second mode), augmented triad (third mode) or tritone (fourth and sixth modes). They lend themselves therefore to static harmony.

modulation Apart from its classical sense of gradual movement from one key to another, the term has acquired wider implications from its use in electronic technology (*see* AMPLITUDE MODULATION, FREQUENCY MODULATION, RING MODULATOR). Stockhausen's coinage of 'INTERMODULATION' arises from here, while simple 'modulation' may indicate ring modulation or, more loosely, any process by which a musical parameter (pitch, loudness, timbre, placing, etc) is subjected to steady change. One could thus speak of a glissando as an instance of pitch modulation.

Moeran, E(rnest) J(ohn) (1894-1950) English composer. Studied at the Royal College of Music (1913-14) and then, after war service, with Ireland.

His small output places him with other English pastoralists of the time, including his teacher and Vaughan Williams; it includes most notably a Symphony in G minor (1934-7). [Novello]
□ S. Wild, *E.J. Moeran* (1973)

Momente (Moments) Work by Stockhausen for soprano, 4 choral groups, 8 brass, 2 electric organs and 3 percussionists, setting various texts in a flowing sequence of segments each concentrating on particular aspects of colour, pitch and duration. *cond Stockhausen, Cologne, 21 May 1962, in longer form at Donaueschingen, 16 Oct 1965. The 'Europa version' extends the work to full concert length and makes it more celebratory in tone. *cond Stockhausen, Bonn, 8 Dec 1972.

moment form Term introduced by Stockhausen, implying that the listener's concentration should be on the 'moment', or section with some defined character which may last for a moment or over a minute (it is an enlargement of the concept of group). This kind of form is exemplified by *Kontakte*, *Carré* and most particularly by the work called 'Moments' (see above), which – in keeping with the principle that relationships between moments are not so important – allows changes in the ordering of sections. However, this aspect of mobile form is hedged with limitations, and virtually abolished in the 1972 version of the work, though the idea of music as composed of moments has remained important to Stockhausen.

Mompou, Federico (1893-) Spanish composer. Studied in Paris (1911-1914) and also spent the years 1921–41 there, living otherwise in Barcelona. His works consist almost entirely of piano miniatures and songs of a shy naive melancholy, influenced by Satie. [Salabert, Eschig]

monody Music on 1 line, i.e. without counterpoints or chords. Uncommon from the 15th c. to the end of the 19th c. in western music (with notable exceptions in *Tristan*), it became possible again in the 20th c. with the dissolution of the major-minor system that had required vertical harmony. Perhaps the earliest examples are Debussy's *Syrinx* (1913) and Stravinsky's 3 Pieces for clarinet (1919), followed by other works for solo wind instrument or voice. Birtwistle's *Monody for Corpus Christi* is in fact for soprano, flute, horn and violin, though like much of his music it is monodic in essence.

Montemezzi, Italo (1875-1952) Italian composer. Studied at the Milan Conservatory, then lived
as a composer in Italy and California (1939-49).
L'amore dei tre re was much his most successful
work, in a Puccinian style with some Wagnerian
enrichment.
Operas: Giovanni Gallurese, ★Turin, 1905; Hel-
lera, ★Turin, 1909; L'amore dei tre re, ★Milan,
1913; La nave, ★Milan, 1918; La notte di Zoraima,
★Milan, 1931; L'incantesimo, ★NBC, 1943
[Ricordi]

Moog, Robert (1934-) American inventor and
manufacturer of a brand of SYNTHESIZER.

Moore, Douglas (1893-1969) American composer. Studied with Parker at Yale and with Tournemire, d'Indy and Boulanger in Paris (1919-21), and
taught at Barnard College in Columbia University
(1926-62). He was one of the first successful American composers of opera, generally choosing rural
and pioneer subjects as apt to his distinctly American lyrical gift.
Operas: White Wings, 1935; The Devil and Daniel
Webster, ★New York, 1939; The Emperor's New
Clothes, ★New York, 1949; Giants in the Earth,
1950; The Ballad of Baby Doe, ★Central City, Colorado, 1956; Gallantry, ★New York, 1958; Wings
of the Dove, ★New York, 1961; The Greenfield
Christmas Tree, ★Baltimore, 1962; Carrie Nation,
★Lawrence, Kansas, 1966 [Boosey, Fischer, Chappell, G. Schirmer, Galaxy]

Moses und Aron Opera by Schoenberg, treating
the Biblical story as a parable of the imperative of
truth. Moses (*Sprechgesang* role) speaks with God,
but it is his brother Aron (Aaron, tenor) who can
speak with the Israelite people, though his colouring of Moses' austere vision leads to the barbaric
error of the Dance around the Golden Calf.
Schoenberg wrote the text for the short third act
but did not set it. ★Hamburg, 12 Mar 1954

Mosolov, Alexander (1900-73) Russian composer. Fought in the civil war (1918-20), then studied with Glier, Myaskovsky and Prokofiev at the
Moscow Conservatory (1922-5). He was a leading
member of the Association for Contemporary
Music, writing songs of a Musorgskian intensity
and satirical edge (*3 Children's Scenes, 4 Newspaper
Announcements*, both 1926) as well as Futurist
machine music (piano sonatas; orchestral piece *The
Foundry*, 1926-8). With the fall of the ACM he
came under criticism and turned to a much more
conventional style, sometimes with folk
influences. His later works include 5 symphonies,
concertos and oratorios.

motif (motive) Used in its English but more commonly in its French form to indicate a small group
of notes deemed to be of importance in a composition (CELL is a synonym). For instance, the finale of
Bartók's Fifth Quartet may be said to be based on
the motif of a 4-note scale fragment. The difference
between motif and SET is that the former implies a
fixed shape whereas the latter is more abstractly a
collection of pitch classes not defined in transposition or order.

movement The Baroque and Classical concept
was already being undermined by Beethoven's
time, and this process has continued, so that works
may be of symphonic scope yet contained within a
single span (e.g. Schoenberg's First Quartet and
Chamber Symphony, Sibelius's Seventh Symphony). Another symptom of unease with the notion is the Second Viennese School's preference for
'piece' ('Stück') in atonal works, where there is not
the harmonically motivated continuity expected
to obtain between movements in diatonic works;
though both Schoenberg and Webern wrote readily in movements once serialism had brought a return of comprehensible directedness.
   Debussy called one of his piano IMAGES 'Mouvement', seemingly just to mean 'motion'. On the
other hand, Stravinsky's use of the word in his
Symphony in 3 Movements and his miniature
piano concerto Movements seems more pointed.
To the traditional sense of symphonic entity he
adds the literal meaning: these are 'ways of moving', and perhaps they are also movements like
those of watches. Boulez has looked to other analo-
gies in preferring the term FORMANT.

Muldowney, Dominic (1952-) English composer. Studied at Southampton University with Harvey, in London with Birtwistle and at York University with Rands and Blake. In 1976 he joined the
music staff at the National Theatre in London. His
works are distinguished by a circumspect, wry and
inquisitive attitude to the conventions and traditions of his chosen genres, including the theatrical.
They include settings of Brecht, 2 string quartets
(1973, 1980) and concertos for piano (1983) and
saxophone (1984). [UE]

multiphonics Chords produced by fingering
techniques on woodwind instruments; *see* BARTO-
LOZZI.

Mumma, Gordon (1935-) American composer. Studied at the University of Michigan (1952-3) and was co-founder with Ashley of the Cooperative Studio for Electronic Music at Ann Arbor (1958-66) and of the ONCE FESTIVALS (1961-8); the 2 then joined with Behrman and Lucier in the Sonic Arts Union (1966-73), performing live electronic music. Also in 1966 he began working with CUN-NINGHAM. Many of his compositions are in mixed media; many too, like the *Hornpipe* (1967) he wrote for himself as solo hornist, involve digital equipment in live performance, or 'cybersonics' to use his own term. [Odyssey, Mainstream].

Muradeli, Vano (1908-70) Russian composer. Studied with Shekhter and Myaskovsky at the Moscow Conservatory, and was prominent in the Composers' Union from 1939 until his opera *The Great Friendship* (*Moscow, 1947) surprisingly precipitated the purges of 1948 (*see* POLITICS). Later cantatas and party songs secured his rehabilitation.

Musgrave, Thea (1928-) Scottish composer. Studied at Edinburgh University (1947-50), privately with Gál, and in Paris with Boulanger (1950-54). During the next decade she wrote somewhat dour 12-note music, but the mid-1960s brought a more flamboyant style, particularly in a sequence of concertos casting instruments and groups as characters in vivid imaginary dramas, and in her successful operas.
Operas: The Decision, *London, 1967; The Voice of Ariadne, *Snape, 1974; Mary, Queen of Scots, *Edinburgh, 1977; A Christmas Carol, *Norfolk, Virginia, 1979; Harriet, the Woman Called Moses, *Norfolk, Virginia, 1985
Concertos: Chamber Concs nos 1-3, 1962, 1966, 1966; for Orch, 1967; Cl, 1967; Hn, 1971; Va, 1973; Orfeo II, fl, str, 1975
[Chester, Novello]

music Almost every entry in this book testifies to how much the notion of music has changed since 1900. In the first place, the range of sounds that could be considered musical has vastly increased. In 1899 it was still possible, at least in Vienna, for Schoenberg's *Verklärte Nacht* to be turned down because it contained an improper chord, and yet by 1937 it was being claimed, at least by Cage, that no sound is out of bounds. Nor are these isolated phenomena, for in the intervening 38 years had come atonality, 12-note composition, athematic music, ametrical music, music for percussion alone and music for mechanical and electronic instruments.

Either one had to accept that music had powerfully changed, or one was obliged to erect some distinction between music and non-music. Composers on both sides of the fence felt this need: Pfitzner in his adherence to 19th c. criteria, Varèse in his invention of the term 'organized sound' for his own work. Generally, though, the widened meaning of 'music' has been accepted, even if in the process the nature and purpose of the art have been further obscured (*see* AESTHETICS).

Music for Strings, Percussion and Celesta Work by Bartók for antiphonal string orchestras and a percussion group that includes, besides the celesta, piano, harp, xylophone, timpani and noise instruments. A single theme runs through the 4 movements, in a slow-fast-slow-fast pattern. *Basle, 21 Jan 1937.

music theatre 1. Term preferred to 'opera' by Felsenstein and other producers (and critics) with the intention of drawing attention to the dramatic nature of the art. 2. Combination of music and theatre on a small scale, often in an unconventional manner, though without the multiplicity of means suggested by mixed media: music theatre is avant-garde, mixed media composition is generally experimental. The genre has sometimes been given an ancestry including Monteverdi's *Combattimento*, Stravinsky's *Soldier's Tale* and *Renard*, and Schoenberg's *Pierrot lunaire*, but its continuous history hardly goes back before 1960, and those composers who have interested themselves in it have tended to create their own traditions, sometimes with their own ensembles. Examples include Davies' works for the Fires of London (though here *Pierrot* is incontestably a model) and Goehr's triptych for the Music Theatre Ensemble, which also presented Birtwistle's *Down by the Greenwood Side*. Other composers who have worked in this area include Berio, Bussotti, Henze and Kagel, and from an earlier period Weill (*Mahagonny* 'Songspiel') and Falla (*El retablo*).

Musica Elettronica Viva Live electronic ensemble of mostly American musicians (Alan Bryant, Frederic Rzewski, Alvin Curran, etc) active in Rome, 1966-71. The group developed a marked social consciousness, working with improvisation and inviting members of the audience to take part in performances. Their collective work *Spacecraft* is recorded on Mainstream MS 5002.

Musica Nova Festival of contemporary music held in Glasgow in 1971, 1973, 1976, 1979, 1981 and 1984, featuring new orchestral works by Berio, Davies, Birtwistle, Goehr, Casken and others.

Musica Viva Annual festival of contemporary music in Munich, founded by Hartmann in 1945. It played an important part in the immediate postwar years in reintroducing to Germany the music of Stravinsky, the Second Viennese School, Bartók, etc, and was the prototype for festivals at Royan, Hamburg, Bremen, Warsaw and elsewhere.

Musikblätter des Anbruch Monthly journal, house organ of Universal Edition, published 1919-37, from 1929 as *Anbruch*.

musique concrète Music created on disc (originally) or tape by simple techniques of editing, reversal and speed-changing worked on recordings of natural sounds: instrumental, vocal or other. The technique and the name were invented by Schaeffer in 1948, and at first the term *musique concrète* was used in opposition to ELECTRONIC MUSIC, which was created with purely synthetic sounds. However, since the two techniques were combined in Varèse's *Poème électronique* and Stockhausen's *Gesang der Jünglinge* there has no longer been much point in the distinction, and *musique concrète* has become more a historical term for pieces created by Schaeffer and his associates in Paris in the late 1940s and 1950s.

Myaskovsky, Nikolay (1881-1950) Russian composer. Associated with progressive composers including Prokofiev, and studied with Lyadov and Rimsky-Korsakov at the St Petersburg Conservatory (1906-11). His career was interrupted by service in the war and then in the Red Army until 1921, when he was appointed to the Moscow Conservatory. There he remained to his death, while writing long cycles of symphonies (27), quartets (13) and piano sonatas (9): his symphonies, in particular, were highly regarded in Russia and abroad during his lifetime, showing an individual mind at work within thoroughly conventional (though usually 3-movement) forms.
Symphonies: no.1, c, 1908; no.2, c♯, 1910-11; no.3, a, 1913-4; no.4, e, 1917-8; no.5, D, 1918; no.6, e♭, 1922-3; no.7, b, 1922; no.8, A, 1924-5; no.9, e, 1926-7; no.10, f, 1927; no.11, b♭, 1931-2; no.12, g, 1931-2; no.13, b♭, 1933; no.14, C, 1933; no.15, d, 1933-4; no.16, F, 1935-6; no.17, g♯, 1936-7; no.18, C, 1937; no.19, E♭, band, 1939; no.20, E, 1940; no.21, f♯, 1940; no.22, b, 1941; no.23, a, 1941; no.24, f, 1943; no. 25, D♭, 1946; no.26, C, 1948; no.27, c, 1949-50.

N

Nabokov, Nicolas (1903-78) Russian-American composer. A cousin of the novelist, he studied with Rebikov in St Petersburg and Yalta (1913-20), at the Stuttgart Conservatory (1920-22) and with Juon and Busoni at the Berlin Hochschule (1922-3). In 1926 he settled in France; Dyagilev commissioned his ballet-oratorio *Ode* (1928). Then in 1933 he moved to the USA, where he taught at various institutions, but in 1952 he was back more or less permanently in Paris: he organized the Festival of 20th c. Music there that year. His works include a collaboration with Auden and Kallman on an opera after *Love's Labour's Lost* (*Brussels, 1973).

Nancarrow, Conlon (1912-) American-Mexican composer. Studied at the Cincinnati Conservatory (1929-32) and privately in Boston with Slonimsky, Piston and Sessions (1933-6). In 1937 he fought in the Spanish Civil War, and in 1940 he settled in Mexico. His interest in complex cross-rhythms led him from 1950 to compose exclusively for the player piano, which can execute his canons in voices moving at different speeds, simultaneous accelerandos and ritardandos, etc, these being contained in a series of over 40 studies.

Nebenstimme (Ger. 'next voice') Schoenberg's term for the next to main voice in polyphony, which he marked with an 'N' in scores from op. 16 onwards. *See* HAUPTSTIMME.

neoclassicism The revival of 18th c. or earlier musical precepts. This is a matter of much analytical, aesthetic and even moral dispute, growing out of the fact that the two parts of the word imply a dual focus: a neoclassical work may well ask to be understood not just as a musical experience. Often this irony is very evident in Stravinsky's music: in, for example, his *Pulcinella* (1919-20), which is often credited as the first neoclassical composition, though it was preceded by Prokofiev's 'Classical' Symphony (1916-17). Stravinsky himself described how *Pulcinella* was motivated not by respect for the Neopolitan originals but by love, by a love that takes possession and so distorts. And he admitted to the same ironizing love in his later works, where he turned his attention to Handelian oratorio and Verdian opera (*Oedipus Rex*), to the Brandenburg Concertos ('Dumbarton Oaks' Concerto), to Mozartian comedy (*The Rake's Progress*) and so on. Sometimes the latter opera is regarded as bringing his neoclassical phase to a closing peak, though it is hard to be sure that his later admiration for Webern was not musically expressed in quite as ironic a fashion. More generally the quality of his irony becomes less brittle when he is dealing with music to which he is close in technique: his adaptation of Tchaikovsky in *The Fairy's Kiss* produced one of his smoothest works.

Stravinsky's neoclassicism struck a responsive chord in a great many of his contemporaries, especially in Paris, as may be seen in the music of Ravel, Prokofiev, Roussel, Poulenc, Martinů and many others. For most of them, though, the irony tended to soften not through nearness but through time, so that by the 1930s and 1940s the parading of Haydnish forms and Bachian counterpoint had become merely a retrieval of the established genres of symphony, sonata and grand opera. The same development can also be seen at the same time in the music of Hindemith, whose Brandenburg-like *Kammermusiken* gave way to symphonies and concertos of a more 19th c. character. Indeed, because irony has normally been regarded as a component of neoclassicism, works like Prokofiev's Fifth Symphony and Hindemith's *Mathis der Maler* are rarely counted as neoclassical. To the extent that they take from the past, they do so in a genuine attempt to restore past values, not to react against them or use them as quoted authorities.

There may yet be unconscious irony, which is the justification for counting much of Schoenberg's music of the 1920s and 1930s as neoclassical. Schoenberg himself was firmly opposed to the movement: his little cantata *Der neue Klassizismus* (1925) mocks 'der kleine Modernsky' for wanting to don papa Bach's wig. Yet his Piano Suite includes Baroque dance movements (gavotte, musette, etc) and his Wind Quintet and Third String Quartet revive 4-movement symphonic form after a gap of 30 years in his output. Probably he would have argued that the lessons of the old masters are of continuous importance, and that his practice was simply Classical, not neoclassical. However, there is such a gulf between his serial style and the diatonic harmony of Bach and Mozart that a gap between content and form is bound to become apparent, and give the music a sense of ironically pacing through old kinds of movement.

Where he turned to the adaptation of past music, in the Cello Concerto and String Quartet Concerto, the irony becomes inescapable: *Pulcinella* itself is not more deeply split between the 18th c. and the 20th c.

Schoenberg and Stravinsky both became neoclassicists at the same time, immediately after the first world war, when many artists were moving towards styles of greater orderedness: Picasso even provides clear parallels with Stravinsky in his reconceptions of Ingres and Velazquez, for instance, while in Germany the trend towards Neue Sachlichkeit was apparent in Kandinsky's new geometrical style or in Bauhaus design. But though neoclassicism is most associated with the inter-war period, something very like it had been present in music from the 1890s, when Busoni began to reintroduce what he hoped were Mozartian clarity and Bach-style counterpoint, and when Reger began to appeal very directly to Bach in his orchestral and keyboard music – not to mention the 'back to Bach' strain in the late music of Brahms. All these composers shared Stravinsky's dissatisfaction with the subjectivity that had entered music since the 18th c., but perhaps neoclassicism implies a greater negation of the 19th c. and hence a greater irony, than they were prepared to countenance.

neoromanticism Term sometimes used of the music composed in the 1930s and 1940s by Prokofiev, Hindemith, etc, suggesting a return to 19th c. values.

Neue Sachlichkeit (New Objectivity) Term used in the 1920s by German writers to denote a movement away from the subjective expression characteristic of Romanticism; in music it best fits Hindemith's and Weill's works of that period, though obviously it is part of the same phenomenon as neoclassicism.

New Music 1. Used as a term, almost a slogan, to indicate music which is not merely new but avantgarde. *Le marteau sans maître* was new music; Shostakovich's Tenth Symphony was not. The implied distinction was unhelpful and is now, after the end of the avant-garde tradition, redundant. 2. Cowell's imprint for publications of scores and records from 1927 to the 1950s, featuring works by Ives, Ruggles, Antheil, Crawford Seeger, Rudhyar, etc.

New Romanticism A term as thorny as neoclassicism. It was introduced in the 1970s in the USA to describe a return on the part of many composers to large, smooth gestures, big forms, standard genres and sometimes also diatonic harmony. However, it could be applied equally to the insistence on subjective expression made by La JEUNE FRANCE in 1936, or imposed by the Soviet Composers' Union in the same year. Romanticism is perhaps more in the ear of the listener than in the mind of the composer, and its evaluation may well be influenced by background circumstances; subjectivity almost demands as much.

New Simplicity Term coined in the 1970s to describe music influenced by MINIMAL MUSIC, and associated most often with younger German, Scandinavian and Dutch composers.

New York American city of unusually diverse and influential musical culture in the 20th c. Ives did most of his composing there in the first 2 decades of the century; it was then a major centre of jazz, the home of the American musical and an importantly stimulating environment to Copland, Varèse and others between the wars. Weill and Bartók spent their last years there as refugees, finding employment in different branches of the city's musical life. Other aspects of its Protean character are to be found in the postwar music of Bernstein, Cage and Carter, all of whom profited from contacts with New York artists working in other fields (ballet, painting, poetry).

Nielsen, Carl (1865-1931) Danish composer. Studied as a violinist at the Copenhagen Conservatory (1884-6) and played in orchestras while continuing studies with Rosenhoff and starting seriously to compose. From the first he reacted against the Romanticism represented in Scandinavian music by such composers as Grieg and Gade, but though he venerated the Classical masters (he had played quartets from boyhood) his music is rarely neoclassical: his concentration was not on past aspects of style but instead directly on the basic materials of music, and he used the widened harmonic vocabulary of his day within symphonic forms clearly, even starkly directed by tensions between pitches and chords which sometimes generate progressive tonality. He was also a conductor, especially of his own music, and teacher at the Copenhagen Conservatory (1916-19).

Operas: Saul and David, 1898-1901, ★Copenhagen, 1902; Maskarade, 1904-6, ★Copenhagen, 1906
Symphonies: no.1, g, 1890-92; no.2 'The Four Temperaments', 1901-2; no.3 'Sinfonia espansiva', 1910-11; no.4 'The Inextinguishable', 1914-16; no.5, 1921-2; no.6 'Sinfonia semplice', 1924-5
Other orchestral works: Helios, overture, 1903; Vn Conc, 1911; Pan and Syrinx, 1917-18; Fl Conc, 1926; Cl Conc, 1928
Chamber: Str Qt no.1, g, 1887-8, rev. 1897-8, no.2, f, 1890, no.3, E, 1897-8, no.4, F, 1906, rev. 1919; Str Qnt, G, 1888; Serenata in vano, 5 insts, 1914; Wind Qnt, 1922
Instrumental: Vn Sonata no.1, A, 1895, no.2, 1912; Commotio, org, 1931; pf music
Many cantatas, smaller choral pieces, songs
[Hansen; Unicorn]
□ C. Nielsen, *Living Music* (1953), *My Childhood* (1953); R. Simpson, *Carl Nielsen* (1952, 2/1979)

Nigg, Serge (1924-) French composer. Was a contemporary of Boulez in Messiaen's class at the Conservatoire (1941-6) and Leibowitz's private classes (1945-8), though he spent longer with both teachers and was strongly influenced by Messiaen (in his symphonic poem *Timour*, 1944) before joining in the enterprise of serialism. Boulez dedicated the early *Notations* to him, and he responded with his Variations for piano and decet (1947). However, his political affiliations soon made him choose a more immediate style: he visited Eastern Europe several times and wrote cantatas with a powerful social message (*Le fusillé inconnu* for singer, speaker and orchestra, 1949). Later orchestral works, such as the orchestral *Jérôme Bosch-Symphonie* (1960) and *Visages d'Axel* (1967), show another change to wild and bizarre imaginativeness. [Jobert, Billaudot; ORTF Inédits]

Nightingale, The (Solovey, Le rossignol) Short opera by Stravinsky and Mituzov after Andersen. ★Ballets Russes, Paris, 26 May 1914. Much of the music from the 2 later acts was put into the symphonic poem *Chant du rossignol* (★cond Ansermet, Geneva, 6 Dec 1919), made into a ballet by Massine with designs by Matisse (★Ballets Russes, Paris, 2 Feb 1920).

Noces, Les (Svadebka, The Wedding) Ballet ('Russian choreographic scenes') by Stravinsky, choreographed by Nijinska and designed by Goncharova. It is in 4 choral tableaux: 'At the Bride's House', 'At the Bridegroom's House', 'The Bride's Departure' and 'The Wedding Feast'. Stravinsky took some years to find the right medium for his ceremonial machine. The composition for soloists and chorus (1914-17) was first given orchestral accompaniment (1917), then the first 2 scenes were scored for an ensemble of pianola, 2 cimbaloms, harmonium and percussion (1919), and finally the voices gained the support of 4 pianos and percussion (1921-3). ★Ballets Russes, cond Ansermet, Paris, 13 Jun 1923.

noise Often used to indicate sound without definite pitch. 'White noise' notionally contains an even distribution of all frequencies; 'coloured noise' is this filtered.

Nono, Luigi (1924-) Italian composer. He was a central member with Boulez and Stockhausen of the European avant garde of the 1950s, combining musical radicalism with a passionate commitment to left-wing politics, from which his music has drawn strength, urgency and a fierce beauty. His political activism has also led him to discontent with conventional means of musical performance. For though he has like Verdi found opera a convenient medium in which to make calls for freedom, he has also made much use of electronic and other non-traditional materials, and he has given concerts of his music in factories.

Venetian born, he studied with Malipiero at the conservatory there (1943-5) and was then a pupil of Maderna and (from 1948) Scherchen, who conducted his *Variazioni canoniche* (on the set of Schoenberg's *Ode to Napoleon*) at Darmstadt in 1950. The next year at Darmstadt he met Stockhausen and Goeyvaerts, and was influenced by them in his practice of the serialism he had already learned from Scherchen. He favoured wedge-shaped all-interval series, a close numerical control of durations, and contrapuntal lines moving rapidly among different voices or instruments, though an Italian lyricism breaks through all his constraints. Works of the late 1960s and early 1970s tend to be more broadly conceived, in an equivalent to poster art, while the later works are curiously intimate and calm. In 1955 he married Schoenberg's daughter Nuria.

Operas: INTOLLERANZA 1960; Al gran sole carico d'amore, 1972-5, ★Milan, 1975, rev. ★Milan, 1978; Prometeo, opera without action, ★Venice, 1984

Choral: Epitaffio per Federico García Lorca (España en el corazon, S, Bar, vv, insts; Y su sangre ya viene cantando, fl, chamber orch; Memento, speaker, speaking vv, chorus, orch), 1951-3; Liebeslied, vv, insts, 1954; Il mantello rosso (ballet), S, Bar, vv, orch, 1954; La victoire de Guernica, vv, orch, 1954; Il canto sospeso, S, Mez, T, vv,

orch, 1955-6; La terra e la compagna, S, T, vv, insts, 1957-8; Coro di Didone, vv, perc, 1958; Un volto, del mare, vv, tape, 1968-9; Y entonces comprendió, 6 female vv, chorus, tape, electronics, 1969-70; Ein Gespenst geht um in der Welt, S, vv, orch, 1970, rev. 1971; Siamo la gioventù del Vietnam, unison, 1973

Other vocal works: Ha venido, S, 6 female vv, 1960; Sarà dolce tacere, 8 solo vv, 1960; Canti di vita e d'amore (Sul ponte di Hiroshima, S, T, orch; Djamila Boupachà, S; Tu, S, T, orch), 1962; Canciones a Guiomar, S, 6 female vv, insts, 1962-3; La fabbrica illuminata, S, tape, 1964; A floresta è jovem e cheja de vida, S, 3 speakers, cl, bronze sheets, tape, 1967; Como una ola de fuerza y luz, S, pf, orch, tape, 1971-2; Donde estas Hermano?, 2 S, Mez, A, 1982; Quando stanno morendo (Diario polacco no. 2), 4 female vv, fl, vc, electronics, 1982; Omaggio a György Kurtág, A, tuba, fl, electronics, 1983

Orchestral: Variazioni canoniche, chamber orch, 1950; Composizione no. 1, 1951; 2 espressioni, 1953; Canti per 13, 13 insts, 1954-5; Incontri, 24 insts 1955; Varianti, vn, orch, 1957; Composizione no. 2 (Diario polacco), 1958-9; Per Bastiana Tai-Yang Cheng, orch, tape, 1967

Other instrumental works: Polofonica-Monodia-Ritmica, 7 insts, 1951; . . .sofferte onde serene. . ., pf, tape, 1976; Con Luigi Dallapiccola, 6 perc., 1979; Fragmente-Stille, str qt, 1980

Tape: Omaggio a Emilio Vedova, 1960; Ricorda cosa ti hanno fatto in Auschwitz, 1966; Contrappunto dialettico alla mente, 1967-8; Non consumiamo Marx, 1969; Musiche per Manzù, 1969; Für Paul Dessau, 1975

[Ricordi, Schott; DG, Wergo]

non-retrogradable rhythm Term used by Messiaen for a group of durations in a symmetrical pattern, e.g.

Nordheim, Arne (1931-) Norwegian composer. Studied at the Oslo Conservatory (1948-52) and with Andersen, Baden, Brustad and Holmboe, then worked as a music critic (1960-68) before assuming an international career as a composer and performer of his own live electronic music. His works tend to be scored for large forces (or tape) in a radiant or dramatic cluster style, or else to be musical dialogues for small groups.

Orchestral: Canzona, 1960; Epitaffio, orch, tape, 1963; Éco, S, choruses, orch, 1967; Floating, 1970;

Greening, 1973; Doria, T, orch, 1974-5; Spur, accordion, orch, 1974-5; The Tempest (ballet), orch, tape, 1979

Instrumental: Respons I, 2 perc, tape, 1966-7; Signaler, accordion, elec gui, perc, 1967; Colorazione, elec org, perc, elec, 1968; Dinosauros, accordion, tape, 1970

Tape: Evolution, 1966; Solitaire, 1968
[Hansen; Philips]

Nørgård, Per (1932-) Danish composer. Studied with Holmboe, at the Copenhagen Conservatory (1952-5) and with Boulanger in Paris (1956-7), then taught at the conservatories of Odense (1958-61), Copenhagen (1960-65) and Århus (1965-), where he has established an open-minded compositional school. During the 1950s his music was in the Sibelius tradition, but at the end of that decade he began to write in a more fragmentary style, though still covering broad harmonic spans by means of repetitive figuration. The static nature of his music is further enhanced by a dwelling on the harmonics of a particular note, these being sprayed in variegated orchestral colours (Symphony no.2). His rhythm tends to be based on uneven motifs within a regular pulse, making his music eminently suitable for dancing.

Operas: The Labyrinth, 1963; Gilgamesh, 1971-2; Siddharta, ★Stockholm, 1983; The Divine Tivoli, ★Århus, 1983

Ballets: The Young Man Shall Marry, 1964; Gipsy Tango, 1967

Orchestral: Sym no.1 'Sinfonia austera', 1954, no.2, 1970, no.3, with chorus, 1972-5; no.4, 1981; Constellations, str, 1958; Fragment VI, 1959-61; Iris, 1967; Luna, 1968; Voyage into the Golden Screen, chamber orch, 1968; Twilight, 1977; Illuminationi, 1984; Vc Conc, 1985

Choral, chamber, piano, tape music, songs
[Hansen; Caprice, EMI]

Nose, The (Nos) Opera by Shostakovich and various librettists after Gogol, a satirical fantasy about a nose which departs from its owner to lead an independent existence, musically traced with parody and startling effect. ★Leningrad, 18 Jan 1930.

notation Changes in music in the 20th c. have naturally wrought havoc with the symbolic notation of earlier centuries, though equally the old notational system has influenced the course music has taken even at its most radical: the durational serialism of Boulez's first book of *Structures*, for in-

stance, is in essence more a notational than an aural phenomenon. But much commoner are the developments in notation necessitated by new sound material, such as:

1. *Chromatic notes.* These involve a plethora of accidentals in conventional notation, and new systems have been invented to cope with the problem more economically (e.g. Equiton, Klavarscribo), but they require performers to learn a whole new language and have been used in only a very few publications (e.g. Zimmermann's *Monologe* in his own adaptation of usual symbols).

2. *Microtones.* Various alterations of the normal accidental signs have been used.

3. *Clusters.* Cowell's invention of vertical bands between marked pitches has been followed in most piano publications. Band notation for orchestral clusters occurs in Penderecki's scores.

4. *Irregular rhythms.* These bring about a great complication of conventional notation, which is founded on division by 2. Many composers have sought ease of use before accuracy by employing TIME-SPACE NOTATION.

5. *New vocal techniques.* Schoenberg placed crosses on the note stems to indicate SPRECHGESANG in *Pierrot lunaire*, and there are similar adaptations in works by Berg, Berio, etc.

6. *New instrumental techniques.* A whole range of new symbols has been introduced, with little systematization.

7. *Aleatory music.* Again the range is vast, including GRAPHIC NOTATION.

8. *Electronic music.* There are special problems here, in that no score may intervene between composition and performance. Some works have been published, either to show how a work was composed (e.g. Stockhausen's *Studie II*) or as 'listening scores' to guide the aural experience of the work (e.g. Stockhausen's *Hymnen* and Ligeti's *Artikulation*). In works for tape and live performers some representation of the former will usually be necessary, often involving a mixture of graphics and conventional symbols (e.g. Stockhausen's *Kontakte*).

Many composers, including for example Carter and Babbitt, have found it possible to write music even in the last quarter of the 20th c. within the normal symbolic notation, if with an unusually fastidious use of it. But others, seeking new sounds and new ways of evoking a musical response from performers, have been obliged to look elsewhere: the scores of Cage, Stockhausen, Berio and Ligeti include most of the important innovations. What remains unclear for both groups, of course, is the precise relationship between notation and sound. The scores of Babbitt are perhaps no less likely than those of Bach to arouse controversy about authentic style, while certain idiosyncratic notations, such as Cage's graphics or Stockhausen's plus-minus system, seem intended not so much to define sounds as to evoke styles of performance that may be lost. For many composers, too, notation has ceased to provide a faithful representation of how music sounds. The music of Xenakis notoriously sounds a lot easier than it looks, and Cage's PREPARED PIANO music makes notation no longer an image of sound at all but only a programme of instructions, as it was in the Middle Ages.

□ J. Cage, *Notations* (1969); G. Read, *Modern Rhythmic Notation* (1978)

note row *See* SET.

Novák, Vítězslav (1870-1949) Czech composer. Studied with Dvořák at the Prague Conservatory (1889-95), and was then decisively influenced by the folk music of Bohemia and Moravia as well as by Janáček's use of the latter. His style, however, was much more luxuriant than Janáček's, and is best displayed in his works of 1900-10, including the symphonic poems *In the Tatra Mountains* (1902) and *Toman and the Wood Nymph* (1906-7), the *Sonata eroica* (1900) and tone poem *Pan* (1910) for piano, and the cantata *The Storm* (1908-10). In 1909 he was appointed professor of composition at the Prague Conservatory, and he then composed little until his last years. [UE, Czech State Publishers; Supraphon]

O

oboe The repertory has been greatly expanded since the mid-1960s by Holliger, both through his own compositions and through works written for him (e.g. Berio's *Sequenza VII* and *Chemins IV*, Castiglioni's *Aleph* and concertos with harp by Henze, Krenek, Lutosławski, etc), many of these with BARTOLOZZI sounds. The oboe d'amore, pitched a minor 3rd lower, has been used in the orchestra by Strauss (*Symphonia domestica*) and others; the cor anglais, a 5th below the normal oboe, is common in orchestras and ensembles (there is also a sonata for it by Hindemith). The lowest member of the family, an octave below the oboe, is the baritone oboe (sometimes called bass oboe), which is to be distinguished from the HECKELPHONE.

Obukhov, Nikolay (1892-1954) Russian composer. Studied with Shteynberg and Tcherepnin at the St Petersburg Conservatory, and was, like Lourié and Roslavets, influenced by late Skryabin towards 12-note composition, at which he arrived in 1914. He then wrote a number of fervently ecstatic settings of Balmont, including 'J'attendrai' (1915) and 'Le sang' (1918) for voice and piano. In 1918 he moved to France, where he designed an electronic instrument, the 'croix sonore', which he used with voices and piano duet in his major continuing work *La livre de vie*, with which most of his subsequent output was associated. [Durand, Rouart Lerolle, Salabert]

Octandre Work by Varèse in 3 short movements for wind septet and double bass, named after octandrous flowers, which have eight stamens. ★New York, 13 Jan 1924.

Ode to Napoleon Buonaparte Setting by Schoenberg of Byron's poem, implicitly turning its invective against a later dictator (Hitler) and bending 12-note composition towards the E♭ of Beethoven's Napoleon symphony. The lines are declaimed in *Sprechgesang* with accompaniment for piano and string quartet or string orchestra. ★Mark Harrell, Steuermann, NYPO/Rodzinsky, New York, 23 Nov 1944.

Oedipus Rex Opera–oratorio in 2 short acts by Stravinsky and Cocteau, the Sophoclean tragedy being monumentalized in panels of sung Latin, introduced by a narrator speaking in the audience's language. ★Ballets Russes, Paris, 30 May 1927.

Oliver, Stephen (1950-) English composer. Studied at Oxford with Leighton and Sherlaw Johnson. He has worked mostly in the theatre, writing a great variety of operas (e.g. *Tom Jones*, ★Snape, 1976), a musical (*Blondel*, ★London, 1983) and music for the Royal Shakespeare Company. [Novello]

Oliveros, Pauline (1932-) American composer. Studied at Houston University (1949-52) and with Robert Erickson (1954-60), and worked at the San Francisco Tape Music Center (1961-7), teaching thereafter at the University of California at San Diego. Her *I of IV* (1966) is remarkable in having been composed on tape in real time, rather than by studio techniques, but most of her work has been in mixed media. [Bowdoin College Press]

ONCE Festival Annual festival of experimental music directed by Ashley and Mumma at Ann Arbor, Michigan, 1961-8. There was also a ONCE Group specializing in mixed media pieces.

ondes martenot Electronic melody instrument invented by Maurice Martenot (1898-1980) as the 'ondes musicales' (musical waves): he gave the first demonstration of it at the Paris Conservatoire on 20 Apr 1928 in a *Poème symphonique* by Dimitrios Levidis. In 1929 Varèse used it to substitute for the sirens in a Paris performance of *Amériques*; he then scored for 2 ondes martenot in *Ecuatorial* (1933-4). The instrument was also used in the 1930s and 1940s by Milhaud (Suite with piano), Koechlin (*Seven Stars Symphony*), Jolivet (*Danse incantatoire*, Concerto), Messiaen (*Fête des belles eaux*, *Trois petites liturgies*, *Turangalîla*), Honegger (*Jeanne d'Arc au bûcher*) and Boulez (first version of *Le visage nuptial*, Quartet); Boulez played the ondes as music director for Barrault. The vogue for the instrument in French music came to an end with the invention of *musique concrète*, though not before it had acquired a repertory demanding its survival. It produces sound from the modulation of 2 oscillators, one at fixed frequency and the other variable, in response either to a keyboard ('clavier') or to the movement of a ring on a ribbon ('ruban'), the latter generating glissandos. Controls are available to change the timbre (by means of filters) and volume.

open form Alternative term for MOBILE FORM.

opera The form began with the arrival of long-range diatonic harmony around 1600, and has seemed indissoluble from that musical system, which in its naturally progressive movement readily supports narrative. Indeed, it is notable that the most successful opera composers of the 20th c.– Puccini, Strauss, Prokofiev, Janáček and Britten – have written diatonically, and it has been argued, by Boulez for one, that opera was dead because its language was dead. Support for that view might seem to come from the operas of Berg and Henze, for example, which reintroduce tonality.

However, one can take another lesson from *Wozzeck*. The central character there is in search of the logical explanation of his existence that diatonic harmony might have provided (and which it still provides for Marie); atonality is the appropriate medium for his confusion, and for the pathological views of those around him. Similarly in *Pelléas et Mélisande* conventional harmony is reserved for a few moments when the characters are in control of their feelings and actions; otherwise their dissociation and instability are matched by similar features in the music. And indeed the association of diatonic music with normality and chromatic music with abnormality is an operatic device as old as Monteverdi. The only new challenge in essentially non-diatonic opera is that of finding an apt dramatic framework for essentially abnormal behaviour. In the stage works of Berg, Henze, Schoenberg, Davies and others this framework is provided by a single deranged mentality (*Erwartung*, *8 Songs for a Mad King*) or by situations of emotional extremity. But Stravinsky's *Oedipus Rex* shows another possibility, that of making the action abnormal in style by presenting it as ceremony; his later *Rake's Progress* does the same thing more subtly by making the ceremony that of operatic theatre, creating a work that is 'opera' in quotes.

Most successful operas since the mid-1920s, when *Turandot*, *Wozzeck* and *Oedipus Rex* were all presented for the first time, have opted for a Bergian or a Stravinskian kind of drama, or more rarely for a mix of the two (Weill's *Mahagonny*, for instance). The movement, quickened by the fashion for ZEITOPER, was then hampered by the effective closure of the German theatres to new works after 1933, and by the concentration by younger composers on purely musical works after 1945. In the late 1960s, too, it seemed that the future of musical drama lay in the new modes of music theatre and mixed media. However, the operas written since the mid-1970s by Stockhausen, Ligeti, Birtwistle, Berio and others have proved the genre's capacity to assimilate the innovations of these modes and to generate non-narrative kinds of theatre.

The most notable 20th c. operas have separate entries in this book (see the list of contents).

orchestra The increase in the size and colour range of the orchestra reached to its extreme in the first decade of the century, with Schoenberg's scoring for an enormous ensemble in his *Gurrelieder* (8 flutes, 7 clarinets, 10 horns, etc) and with the introduction of unusual instruments by Strauss and Mahler (heckelphone, mandolin, guitar, harmonium, cowbells, hammer, etc). Schoenberg's First Chamber Symphony (1906), scored for 15 soloists, has usually been regarded as marking a reaction against that trend, a reaction that gained pace with the anti-Romantic movement which followed the first world war. Since then the term 'orchestra' has meant anything from the septet of *The Soldier's Tale* to the 100+ groupings of Varèse's *Amériques* or Messiaen's *Saint François d'Assise*.

However, most symphony orchestras have a salaried personnel appropriate for the performance of Tchaikovsky or Brahms, so that there has always been a tension between what can be imagined and what will be played. Some composers have sought to relieve that tension by forming their own orchestras (Cage's percussion ensemble, for instance); some orchestras have sought to do the same by adapting themselves flexibly to composers' requirements, though for economic reasons such ensembles (the CONTEMPORARY CHAMBER ENSEMBLE, DOMAINE MUSICAL, GROUP FOR CONTEMPORARY MUSIC, LONDON SINFONIETTA) have normally been small. Where composers have wanted to write for larger resources, they have had to use an essentially 19th c. grouping, which can be varied in any of 4 main ways:

1. *Omission*. Examples include Stravinsky's Symphonies of Wind Instruments, Symphony of Psalms (lacking violins and violas) and other works.

2. *Expansion of the percussion*. Here it is not hard for 3 or 4 players to make a great deal of difference. Tuned percussion ensembles are prominent in the orchestras of Messiaen, Boulez, Davies and others.

3. *New seating arrangements*. The usual pattern can be changed to facilitate new blendings (Boulez's *Figures-Doubles-Prismes*), to mingle the players with the audience (Xenakis's *Terretektorh*) or to divide the musicians into separate ensembles (Stockhausen's *Gruppen*, Carter's A Symphony of Three Orchestras).

4. *Electronic additions*. Combining orchestra with tape causes problems of synchronization unless the 2 are separated in time (as they are in Varèse's *Déserts*); nevertheless, there are works of this kind by Babbitt, Pousseur, Nordheim, Stockhausen and others. Stockhausen has also applied electronic transformation to orchestral sound in *Mixtur* and later works.

Orff, Carl (1895-1982) German composer. Graduated from the Munich Academy in 1914 and after the war had lessons with Kaminski. In 1924 he and Dorothee Günther founded a school influenced by Jaques-Dalcroze's ideas, which led in the 1950s to a method of encouraging children to sing and play simple percussion instruments (the *Orff-Schulwerk*). Meanwhile he had made his name as a composer with *Carmina burana* (*Frankfurt, 1937), setting rowdy medieval poems to rudimentary mechanical music derived from *Les noces*. His later works were nearly all operas and ceremonials of the same kind. [Schott; DG]

organ The ecclesiastical aura of the instrument is a conservative influence on its repertory, and much 20th c. organ music lies within the established traditions of Germany (Reger, Pepping), Austria (Schmidt, David), England (Parry, Howells) and France (Vierne, Langlais). However, Messiaen's music shows so extreme a development of the French tradition as to represent something new, in his idiosyncratic use of registers (particularly his use of unbalanced timbres), his rhythmic demands and his production of large-scale concert works. Others have followed him in finding the organ specially suited to grand virtuosity (Ligeti) or spiritual meditation (Davies).

organized sound Term preferred by Varèse as avoiding the connotations of 'music'. The score of his *Déserts* refers to 'organized sound' on tape.

Ornstein, Leo (1892-) Russian–American composer. Studied at the Petrograd Conservatory and, after his move to New York in 1907, at the Institute of Musical Art. He made European tours as a pianist in 1913 and 1914, and returned with works by Debussy, Ravel, Schoenberg and Skryabin which he introduced to New York, along with his own modernist piano pieces, including the *Dwarf Suite* (1913), *Impressions de Notre Dame* (1914), *Three Moods* (1914), *Wild Men's Dance* (c.1915), *Poems of 1917*, etc. In 1920 he virtually abandoned his career as a pianist, and at the same time his music became more orthodox. He taught at the Philadelphia Music Academy and founded the Ornstein School of Music there. [Schott, Fischer]

Orpheus Subject of operas by Milhaud, Casella, Krenek, Malipiero and Birtwistle, ballets by Stravinsky, Henry and Henze, and a film by Cocteau. Stravinsky's score was written for Balanchine (*New York, 28 Apr 1948).

Osborne, Nigel (1948-) English composer. Studied with Leighton and Wellesz at Oxford (1967-70), and with Rudziński in Warsaw (1970-71); in 1978 he was appointed lecturer at Nottingham University. His music is that of an acute, penetrating mind stimulated as much by social concerns as by a fascination with 20th c. Russian literature. His works include a Flute Concerto (1980) and two Sinfonias for orchestra (1982, 1983), besides settings of Russian poetry in *The Sickle* for soprano and orchestra (1975) and *I am Goya* for bassbaritone and mixed quartet (1977). [UE; Unicorn]

oscillator Valve or other electronic device producing a wave form, the foundation of electronic musical instruments.

Owen Wingrave Opera by Britten and Myfanwy Piper after Henry James, a ghost story that is also a tract against militarism. It was written for BBC television (*broadcast 16 May 1971), though presenting no obstacles to stage performance (*Covent Garden, 10 May 1973).

P

Paik, Nam June (1932-) Korean composer. Studied at the universities of Tokyo (1952-6) and Munich (1956-7), with Fortner at the Freiburg Musikhochschule (1957-9) and at Cologne University (1958-62). While in Cologne he was associated with Stockhausen (he took part in the original *Originale*), but the main influences on him were already those of Cage and the Fluxus movement (see his *hommage à john cage* for 2 pianos which are destroyed during the performance, 3 tape recorders, projections, and live actions involving eggs, toy cars and motorbikes, 1959). In 1964 he moved to New York, and in 1970 to Los Angeles.

palindrome The word has been taken into musical discourse to indicate pieces which repeat the same events backwards after a midpoint. This would have been exceedingly difficult to achieve in tonal music, but it has proved a convenient principle of form building in atonal music, as in the second movements of Berg's Chamber Concerto and Webern's Symphony. In neither of these cases, nor in most musical palindromes, is the repetition exact.

Palmgren, Selim (1878-1951) Finnish composer. Studied with Wegelius at the Helsinki Conservatory (1895-9) and in Italy and Germany with Busoni and others. His works include 5 piano concertos, piano pieces and songs.

pandiatonicism Term coined by Slonimsky to indicate the use of all the notes of the diatonic scale in non-resolving chords, e.g. the 6th in jazz and Messiaen, the 7th and 9th in Debussy and Ravel.

pantonality Term preferred to 'atonality' by Schoenberg.

Panufnik, Andrzej (1914-) Polish-British composer. Studied with Sikorski at the Warsaw Conservatory (1932-6) and was then a conducting pupil of Weingartner's. His pre-1944 compositions were lost during the Warsaw rising. After the war he made a career in Poland as conductor and composer until in 1954 he moved to England. His works are typically based on small note groups, developed in an atmosphere of intense solemnity. They include symphonies, concertos, large-scale choral pieces and a few compositions on a smaller scale. [Boosey]

Parables for church performance Trilogy of music theatre pieces by Britten and Plomer for soloists and ensemble (fl, hn, tpt, a trbn, harp, perc, chamber org, va, db): *Curlew River*, *Orford, 12 Jun 1964; *The Burning Fiery Furnace*, *Orford, 9 Jun 1966; *The Prodigal Son*, *Orford, 10 Jun 1968.

parameter Aspect of musical sound: pitch, duration, volume or timbre. The term gained currency with the advent of total serialism in Europe in the early 1950s, when all these aspects were subjected to separate serial control.

Paris An important centre of compositional activity throughout the 20th c. thanks to its being home or chief musical metropolis for Debussy, Stravinsky (1920-39), Honegger, Messiaen, Boulez, Barraqué and many others. Before the first world war its musical life was dominated by Debussy, Ravel and then the Ballets Russes. Between the wars it was a notable centre of neoclassicism, influenced by Stravinsky's presence, though La JEUNE FRANCE offered a different perspective. And since 1945 Messiaen and Boulez have been leading figures, the latter directing the Domaine Musical and later the Institut de Recherche et de Coordination Acoustique/Musique. Works introduced at the Opéra have included Roussel's *Padmâvatî* (1923), Milhaud's *Maximilien* (1932) and *Bolivar* (1950), and Messiaen's *Saint François d'Assise* (1983), and at the Opéra-Comique Debussy's *Pelléas et Mélisande* (1902), and Ravel's *L'heure espagnole* (1911).

Parker, Horatio (1863-1919) American composer and teacher. Studied with Chadwick in Boston and Rheinberger in Munich (1882-5), then returned to the USA, where he worked as a church musician and as professor of music theory at Yale (1894-1919). His highly conventional works include the oratorio *Hora novissima* (1893) and much other sacred music, besides 2 operas.

Partch, Harry (1901-76) Amercan composer. Californian born and largely self-taught, he developed during the 1920s and 1930s his own theory of music. Taking his authority from the Greeks, he argued for music as a 'corporeal' rather than an intellectual art, acting on spectators at theatrical performances and using the natural intervals of just intonation (he built his own percussion and wind instruments for this purpose in a 43-note scale). His own major works were therefore dramatic, their drama enhanced by the striking presence of his instruments. They included *Barstow* (1941), *US Highball* (1943), *Oedipus* (1951), *The Bewitched* (1955) and *Delusion of the Fury* (1969). [CRI]

Payne, Anthony (1936-) English composer and critic. Studied at Durham University (1958-61) and began career as a critic in 1965, publishing a concise study *Schoenberg* (London, 1968) and later one of Frank Bridge (London, 1984). His music shows an unusual deployment of avant-garde gestures within ample forms suggesting his admiration for Delius and Bax: the symphonic poem, often for small ensemble with or without solo voice, has become his characteristic mode of expression (*The World's Winter*, 1976; *The Song of the Clouds*, 1979-80). [Chester]

Peeters, Flor (1903-) Belgian composer and organist. Studied at the Lemmens Institute in Mechelen and privately with Dupré; in 1923 he joined the staff at the institute and became assistant organist at St Rombout's Cathedral in the same city. Later he taught at the conservatories of Ghent (1931-8), Tilburg (1935-48) and Antwerp (1948-68). His works consist mostly of choral and organ music for the Catholic rite, influenced by his friend Tournemire.
□ J. Hofmann, *Flor Peeters* (1978)

Pelléas et Mélisande Play by Maeterlinck, a tragedy of love and jealousy set in a shadowy unreality. Fauré and Sibelius wrote incidental music for it; Schoenberg made it the subject of a symphonic poem (*cond Schoenberg, Vienna, 26 Jan 1905); and Debussy set most of it as an opera (*Paris, 30 Apr 1902). No other literary work since Goethe's *Faust* has attracted such attention from musicians during its author's lifetime.

Penderecki, Krzysztof (1933-) Polish composer. Studied with Malawski and Wiechowicz at the Krakow Conservatory (1955-8), where he has taught since graduating. In 1959 he won 3 first prizes in a national competition, and at the beginning of the 1960s he came suddenly to international fame for the emotional drive he obtained from sonorities that had been more abstractly deployed in the scores of Xenakis, Stockhausen and others: clusters, new string effects and a variety of percussion sounds. These activate a range of orchestral works from *Anaklasis* and the *Threnody for the Victims of Hiroshima* to the First Symphony; they are important too in the Expressionist ambience of his opera *The Devils* and large-scale religious canvases. In the early 1970s his music began to become more thematic, and eventually to achieve a Brucknerian solemnity of purpose and pace on the basis of simple motivic material.

Operas: The Devils of Loudun, 1968, *Hamburg, 1969; Paradise Lost, 1975-8, *Chicago, 1978
Choral orchestral: Psalms of David, vv, perc, 1958; Dimensions of Time and Silence, 1960; St Luke Passion, 1963-5; Dies irae, 1967; Cosmogonia, 1970; Utrenja, 1969-71; Canticum canticorum, 1972; Magnificat, 1974; Te Deum, 1979; Polish Requiem, 1980-83
Orchestral: Epitafium, str, perc, 1958; Emanations, str, 1958; Anaklasis, str, perc, 1960; Threnody for the Victims of Hiroshima, str, 1960; Fluorescences, 1961; Fonogrammi, 1961; Polymorphia, str, 1961; Canon, str, tapes, 1962; Sonata, vc, orch, 1964; Capriccio, ob, str, 1965; De natura sonoris I, 1966, II, 1971; Capriccio, vn, orch, 1967; Pittsburgh Overture, wind, timp, 1967; Actions, jazz group, 1971; Partita, hpd, chamber orch, 1971; Preludium, wind, dbs, 1971; Vc Conc no.1, 1972; Sym no.1, 1972-3; The Dream of Jacob, 1974; Vn Conc, 1976; Sym no.2, 1979-80; Vc Conc no.2, 1981-2; Va conc, 1982-3
Other works: Strophes, S, reciter, 10 insts, 1959; 3 Miniatures, vn, pf, 1959; Str Qt no.1, 1960, no.2, 1968; Psalmus, tape, 1961; Capriccio, vc, 1968; Ecloga VIII, 6 male vv, 1972
[Moeck, Schott]

pentatonic Using only 5 of the 12 notes. The commonest pentatonic mode is that without minor 2nds, e.g. C–D–E–G–A–C. This is the basis of much folk music from around the world, and has been used by composers as diverse as Dvořák, Mahler, Puccini, Bartók and Messiaen.

Pepping, Ernst (1901-) German composer. Studied with Gmeindl at the Berlin Hochschule (1922-6), where he later taught (1953-68), besides working at the Spandau Church Music School from 1934 until his retirement. His works consist mostly of choral and organ music for Lutheran use in a revival of Baroque style stemming from Hindemith. They include the *Spandauer Chorbuch* originally published in 20 volumes (1934-8) and concertos, fugues, partitas and chorale preludes for the organ. [Bärenreiter, Schott]

percussion Group of instruments requiring a striking action: this would include the piano, which indeed has been treated as a percussion rather than a legato instrument by many 20th c. composers (e.g. Stravinsky in *Les noces*). The family may be divided into 'tuned' (or 'pitched') and 'untuned' (or 'unpitched', or 'noise') instruments, depending on whether or not there is a clear sensation of pitch in the sound. Apart from the piano, the former group includes various kinds of BELL, CELESTA, CENCERROS, CIMBALOM, CROTALES, glockenspiel, MARIMBA, TIMPANI, VIBRAPHONE, XYLOPHONE, xylorimba. The latter group is enormous: a survey of the scores of Varèse, Cage, Messiaen, Stockhausen and Davies would show many of the possibilities. *See also* FLEXATONE, GONGS.

The modern growth in the importance of percussion instruments began as part of the growth of the orchestra in the 1890s: Mahler is the outstanding example for both, and stands behind the passages scored for percussion alone in Berg (op. 6 no.1) and Webern (op.6 no.4). But the complex cross rhythms of Varèse's percussion scoring, right from *Amériques*, indicate a new readiness to make music just with noise instruments, as he then went on to do in most of his *Ionisation* (1931), which is generally counted the first western work for percussion alone, though *Les noces* and Milhaud's *Les choëphores* had been scored for voices and percussion. Milhaud had also written a concerto for percussion and chamber orchestra. During the 1930s and 1940s Cage organized percussion ensembles and wrote much for them; a further repertory has evolved for the 6-man team of Les Percussions de Strasbourg, who made their début in 1961 and have commissioned works from Barraqué, Stockhausen, Birtwistle and others.

The literature for solo percussionist is small, but has one classic in Stockhausen's *Zyklus*. Within the orchestra, though, the percussion ensemble has kept its importance, not least among those composers who have been influenced by the gamelan or by African drumming. Some serialists have found it difficult to accommodate unpitched instruments: there are few such in, for example, later Webern or later Boulez (except as timekeepers in *Rituel*). Boulez, however, in his *Pli selon pli*, *Eclat/Multiples* and *Répons* has made tuned percussion the very centre of his orchestra.

□ J. Blades, *Percussion Instruments and their History* (1970, 2/1974)

performance Schoenberg once said that modern music was not difficult; it was just badly played. And though standards of execution have vastly improved, as gramophone records can show, the performance of new works can rarely be undertaken under conditions which might assure a good account of the score. Some composers (e.g. Babbitt) have for that reason preferred to work in the electronic studio; others have perhaps intended to lessen the difficulties by allowing for IMPROVISATION or lesser degrees of ALEATORY freedom, though whether these make the performer's task easier or harder is a moot point. Much 20th c. music, especially that of the 1950s, does present severe problems of speed of reaction, particularly in defining dynamic nuances and complexities of rhythm and metre. It seems likely, therefore, that this music will remain associated with specialist performers (*see* ORCHESTRA, etc).

'Performance art' is a term sometimes applied to a branch of musical-dramatic activity done by solo performers such as Laurie ANDERSON.

Perle, George (1915-) American composer and musicologist. He studied with Wesley LaViolette at De Paul University (1934-8) and later with Krenek, then taught at the University of Louisville (1949-57), that of California at Davis (1957-61) and Queens College, New York (1961-). He was one of the first Americans in the 1930s to interest himself in 12-note music, and he began developing his own system of hierarchies within a 12-note context, producing music that tends to be euphonious in its sound but highly sophisticated in its harmonic relations and in its deployment of an irregular pulse. His works includes songs and orchestral pieces but mostly chamber music, including 7 quartets (no.5, 1960, rev. 1967; no.6, 1969; no.7, 1973). [Presser; Nonesuch, CRI]

□ G. Perle, *Serial Composition and Atonality* (1962, 4/1978); *Twelve-Tone Tonality* (1978)

Perséphone 'Melodrama' by Stravinsky and Gide for tenor and reciter, adult and children's choruses, and orchestra. It is a classical rite of spring, created for Ida Rubinstein and her company. ★Paris, 30 Apr 1934.

Persichetti, Vincent (1915-) American composer and teacher. Studied with Nordoff and Harris at the Philadelphia Conservatory and the Curtis Institute, then taught at the former institution (1942-62) and the Juilliard School (1947-). His works are abundant and various in style; he has also published a HARMONY textbook. [Elkan-Vogel]

Perspectives of New Music Twice-yearly journal first published in 1962 and edited by Benjamin Boretz. It has been much associated with the Princeton school of 12-note composition and computer music, though it has also included important articles on a wide range of 20th c. music from Schoenberg to Stockhausen.

Peter Grimes Opera by Britten and Eric Crozier after Crabbe, the story of an intemperate misfit within a small, narrow-minded and hypocritical community in a fishing town on the east coast of England. ★London, 7 Jun 1945.

Petrassi, Goffredo (1904-) Italian composer and teacher. Studied at the Conservatorio di S Cecilia in Rome with Bustini (1928-33), and taught composition there from 1939 to 1959, when he moved to the Accademia di S Cecilia. His early works were in a neoclassical style near to Hindemith and Casella, who recognized and encouraged him, but he has steadily developed in reaction to Bartók, the later Stravinsky and Webern. The abiding dynamism and instrumental virtuosity of his music are well shown in the sequence of concertos for orchestra (no.1, 1933-4; no.2, 1951; no.3, 1952-3; no.4, str, 1954; no.5, 1955; no.6, 1956-7; no.7, 1961-2, rev. 1964; no.8, 1970-72). His other works include choral pieces and much chamber and instrumental music. [Ricordi, Suvini Zerboni, UE]

Petrushka Ballet ('burlesque in 4 scenes') by Stravinsky and Benois, choreographed by Fokine: the agonies of the puppet Petrushka are presented within the mechanical bustle of a shrovetide fair in St Petersburg. ★Ballets Russes, Paris, 13 Jun 1911. Stravinsky arranged *3 mouvements de Pétrouchka* for piano in 1921 and reorchestrated the whole ballet more economically in 1946.

Pettersson, Allan (1919-80) Swedish composer. Studied with Olsson and Blomdahl at the Stockholm Conservatory (1930-39), then played the viola in the Stockholm Philharmonic (1939-51) before studying further in Paris with Honegger and Leibowitz. He was little known until Dorati performed his Seventh Symphony in 1968; after this he wrote 8 more symphonies, usually in one long movement (no.9 plays for 1¼ hours) and in a dour style striving for diatonic resolution. [Suecia]

Pfitzner, Hans Erich (1869-1949) Geman composer. Studied at the Hoch Conservatory in Frankfurt with Knorr and Kwast (1886-90), then worked as a teacher and conductor in Coblenz, Mainz, Berlin (1897-1908), Strasbourg (1908-20), again Berlin (1920-29) and Munich (1930-33). The end of the war found him destitute in Munich, but he spent his last years as a pensioner of the Vienna Philharmonic. He was fiercely opposed to Schoenberg, Berg and Strauss, all of whom he felt to be betraying the great German Romantic tradition. But he was no blinkered conservative: his opera *Palestrina* indicates the depth at which he was prepared to argue the moral responsibility of art, and his musical thinking was conscientious when it was not profound. The best of him is probably to be found in *Palestrina*, the cantatas and the songs.
Operas: Der arme Heinrich, 1891-3, ★Mainz, 1895; Die Rose vom Liebesgarten, 1897-1900, ★Elberfeld, 1901; Palestrina, 1912-15, ★Munich, 1917; Das Herz, 1930-31, ★Berlin, 1931
Cantatas: Vom deutscher Seele, 1921; Das dunkle Reich, 1929
Orch and chamber works, many songs

phantasy Title implying a single-movement instrumental composition, probably one more diffuse than the word 'sonata' would imply. Schoenberg used the term for his last instrumental piece, op.47 for violin and piano; ★Adolph Koldofsky, Leonard Stein, Los Angeles, 13 Sep 1949. In 1905 W.W Cobbett had established a prize for chamber-music phantasies (he liked the association with viol fancies of the 16th and 17th c.); Bridge, Vaughan Williams, Britten and others wrote works of this kind.

Philippot, Michel (1925-) French composer. Studied with Dandelot at the Paris Conservatoire (1946-8) and with Leibowitz (1948-50). In 1949 he was among the first to work in Schaeffer's *musique concrète* studio, where he created several pieces during the next decade (*Ambiance nos.1-2*, 1959). He was then an executive with French radio (1960-70) and professor at the University of São Bernardo do Campo in Brazil. [Salabert]

Philomel Work by Babbitt and Hollander for a soprano to sing with a tape of synthesized sounds and recorded soprano: the music explores the moment of transformation from woman into bird in the Ovidian story.

piano The list of those who have notably enlarged the piano literature in the 20th c. would have to include Rakhmaninov and Boulez, Debussy and Bartók, Stravinsky and Messiaen, Stockhausen and Prokofiev, Ives and Ravel, Schoenberg and Cowell, Cage and Fauré. It must be obvious that no convenient summary of 20th c. piano music is conceivable, though there is truth in the oft repeated assertion that this century has seen the paino recognized as a percussion instrument. Indeed the change in sensibility can be dated quite precisely to the few years before the first world war, when Stravinsky wrote *Petrushka*, Bartók his *Allegro barbaro* and Cowell his first pieces. Since then the piano has been recognized as a percussion instrument by association (in *Les noces* and Bartók's Sonata for pianos and percussion), and has even been converted into a percussion instrument (*see* PREPARED PIANO, STRING PIANO). The piano has also become a regular member, even a leader of the percussion ensemble of the orchestra in works by Messiaen, Boulez, Stockhausen, etc. Moreover, a realization of the percussive nature of the instrument has encouraged a wider exploration of its resonance characteristics, notably in the music of Schoenberg (who used the technique of silently depressing keys to release their strings) and Boulez.

Such new techniques have signalled the fact that the piano in the 20th c. is no longer the amateur's instrument it was in the 19th c. Very little of Schoenberg, Rakhmaninov, Ives or Boulez, for example, is plausible amateur repertory, and the piano has ceased to be the regular medium for disseminating orchestral and chamber works. Where composers did make their works available in keyboard form, as Stravinsky often did, this seems largely to have been a hang-over from 19th c. publishing practice or else a practical convenience, facilitating the rehearsal of a ballet or concerto. In the particular case of Stravinsky, though, the piano form may represent an original, since we know that he habitually composed at the piano. Messiaen too has acknowledged as separate the tasks of 'composition' and 'orchestration', without normally publishing keyboard versions of his orchestral works. For Ravel, however, orchestration was very definitely an optional extra, so that a large part of his output exists in piano and orchestral forms, both suitable for concert performance (it has been discovered too that the 4-hand scores of the *The Rite of Spring* and *Petrushka* are more than utilitarian).

The repertory of 20th c. music for 2 or 4 hands is obviously too vast for a quick survey. The important piano concertos include those of Bartók, Stravinsky, Rakhmaninov, Prokofiev, Schoenberg, Ravel, Busoni and Carter, besides Messiaen's several works for piano and orchestra; the rarer literature of double piano concertos includes works by Berio and Bartók.

pianola During its heyday, just after the first world war, the mechanical piano aroused the interest of several composers, notably Stravinsky. Automatic reproduction suited his aesthetic of non-interpretation, and also the nature of the instrument seemed well adapted to the dry, percussive sonorities he was preferring. In 1917 he wrote an Etude for pianola, and he planned to include a pianola in *Les noces*, besides arranging other pieces for the instrument. Since the 1920s the popularity of the pianola has considerably declined among public and composers alike, but Nancarrow has found it a stimulating medium.

Pierrot lunaire (Moonstruck Pierrot) Set of '3 times 7' poems by Albert Giraud in translations by Otto Erich Hartleben and musical settings by Schoenberg for reciting voice (in *Sprechgesang*) with quintet (vn + va, vc, fl + piccolo, cl + b cl, pf). This is one of the key works of 20th c. music – even its solar plexus, as Stravinsky said – opening avenues of mixed chamber music to be followed by Stravinsky, Boulez and many others, of small-scale theatre to spur Henze and Davies, and most generally of atonal harmony used to the quite clearly appropriate ends of expressing alienation, violence and nostalgia. ★Albertine Zehmer (actress who commissioned the work), quintet/ Schoenberg, Berlin, 16 Oct 1912

Pierrot Players *See* FIRES OF LONDON.

Pijper, Willem (1894-1947) Dutch composer. Studied with Johan Wagenaar in Utrecht (1911-16), then taught at the conservatories of Amsterdam (1918-30) and Rotterdam (1930-47). In 1920 he introduced his technique of composing whole works or movements out of a small cell of 3 or 4 notes, this having more in common with Bartók than with Webern. His works include the opera *Halewijn* (1933), 3 symphonies (1917, 1921, 1926), songs and chamber pieces. [Donemus]

Piston, Walter (1894-1976) American composer. Studied at Harvard (1920-24) and in Paris with Boulanger and Dukas (1924-6), then returned to Harvard, where he taught until 1960. He wrote textbooks on *Harmony* (New York, 1941, 2/1962), *Counterpoint* (New York, 1947) and *Orchestration* (New York, 1955), and had Carter, Bernstein and others among his pupils. His own works have the ease and fluency of American-Parisian neoclassicism; they include 8 symphonies, various concertos, 5 string quartets and the ballet *The Incredible Flutist* (1938). [AMP, Boosey]

pitch class Set of all pitches with the same name, irrespective of register; e.g. the pitch class C includes all Cs. The term was introduced by Babbitt for a concept that had been implicit in 12-note serialism from the first, since Schoenberg considered the set as a set of pitch classes, not pitches.

Pizzetti, Ildebrando (1880-1968) Italian composer. Studied at the Parma Conservatory (1895-1901) with Giovanni Tebaldini, who encouraged in him an interest in Renaissance music; this duly influenced the arioso style of his operas. He returned to the Parma Conservatory as a teacher (1907-8), then taught at the conservatories of Florence (1908-24) and Milan (1924-36), and the Accademia di S Cecilia in Rome (1936-58). During the 1930s he distanced himself from radical trends in Italian music, though his world had always been a conservative one, looking to Debussy, Musorgsky and Monteverdi.
Operas: Fedra, 1909-12, ★Milan, 1915; Debora e Jaele, 1915-21, ★Milan, 1922; Assassinio nella cattedrale (after Eliot), 1957, ★Milan, 1958
Other works: Requiem, chorus, 1922; other choral pieces, songs, orch works, chamber music
[Ricordi, Sonzogno]

Pli selon pli Work by Boulez for soprano and orchestra, based on sonnets by Mallarmé. The 5 movements contain small-scale aleatory freedoms and have proved mutable to a larger degree in succeeding versions:
Don, S, pf, 1960; S, orch, 1962
Improvisation sur Mallarmé I: Le vierge, le vivace et le bel aujourd'hui, S, 7 perc, 1957; S, small orch, 1962
Improvisation sur Mallarmé II: Une dentelle s'abolit, S, 9perc, 1957
Improvisation sur Mallarmé III: A la nue accablante tu, S, small orch, 1959, rev. 1983
Tombeau, S, orch, 1959-62
★Ilse Hollweg, NDR SO/Rosbaud, Hamburg, 13 Jan 1958 (*Improvisations I-II*); Eva Maria Rogner SWF SO/Boulez, Cologne, 13 June 1960 (whole work)

pluralism The use of different styles within a work, and sometimes simultaneously. It was Bernd Alois Zimmermann's term for COLLAGE.

Poème électronique Tape piece by Varèse, made from recordings of percussion instruments, a solo voice, a musical performance (of the composer's *Etude pour 'Espace'*), electronic tones and natural sounds. It was commissioned to be heard within the Philips pavilion designed by Le Corbusier for the 1958 Brussels Exposition (★2 May).

Poem of Ecstasy, The (Le poème de l'extase) Orchestral work by Skryabin, inspired by his growing faith in art's power to cause spiritual exhilaration. ★New York, 1908.

point Isolated note in a musical composition. The study of Webern encouraged many young European composers around 1950 to work with single notes in serially organized processes: the effect of TOTAL SERIALISM, particularly, was to produce a fabric of points (see Messiaen's MODE DE VALEURS ET D'INTENSITÉS, Boulez's *Structures Ia* and Stockhausens's *Kreuzspiel*). The phase was brief: Boulez in *Structures Ib* and Stockhausen in the significantly named *Kontra-Punkte* worked with larger melodic units (Stockhausen's term was 'group'). However, it did make the word 'pointillisme' a common term of description for avant-garde music of the 1950s, though perhaps the nearer parallels with Seurat are in Debussy, where clouds rather than points are at issue.

politics Music would seem the unlikeliest medium for political statement, and yet it is perhaps in the musical field, more than in that of any other form of artistic expression, that political correlatives and consequences have been most hotly claimed in the 20th c. The essential contention, yet to be supported by argument, is simple: it is that there is some community of mentality between artistic and political revolution. The Nazis evidently were sure there was: hence their immediate disparagement of anything that threatened the status quo of major–minor harmony (Stravinsky, Bartók, Schoenberg and eventually Hindemith were all branded as exponents of KULTURBOLSCHEWISMUS). From a different perspective, the ASSOCIATION FOR CONTEMPORARY MUSIC in Russia took a similar view, welcoming anything new in music as appropriate to a new society: hence the opportunities available in the 1920s to such composers as Roslavets, Mosolov, Deshevov, Popov, Protopopov and the young Shostakovich.

However, the Russian Association for Proletarian Music took the different and in many ways contrary view that music in a socialist state should be comprehensible to everyone (see SOCIETY), which for them meant adherence to the familiar: folksong, and a musical style rooted in the age of Borodin, Tchaikovsky and Musorgsky. In 1931 the ACM collapsed, and though the success of the RAPM was moderated the next year by the foundation of the Union of Soviet Composers, earlier adventurousness was suppressed in the interests of SOCIALIST REALISM. In 1936 Shostakovich was publicly criticized for FORMALISM, and the charge was repeated in 1948 when Andrey Zhdanov instituted a period of severe artistic repression that lasted until after Stalin's death in 1953.

Since then the tension between political and musical radicalism has been argued again and again, though essentially from the two viewpoints represented in the Soviet Union in the 1920s by the ACM and the RAPM. Pousseur, for instance, has tried to find parallels between musical and political organizations, suggesting that PLURALISM might be the expression of a tolerant socialism; and Cage, though eventually despairing of the artist's usefulness in changing the world, has argued similarly. On the other hand, Cardew in the mid-1970s was powerfully stating the case for a musical language already familiar to the 'broad masses' and for a critical examination of past music for its political content.

The cynic might argue that the real enemy of artistic liberty is certainty, whether it comes from the right or from the left, for it is régimes of both persuasions, Nazi and Stalinist, who have been most repressive. On the other hand, the problems of political expression in music are vividly illustrated by the variety of styles in which this has been attempted, by Shostakovich, Nono, Bush, Pousseur, Wolff, Durey, etc, making socialist music quite as diverse as any other repertory in the 20th c.

Polovinkin, Leonid (1894-1949) Russian composer. Studied with Myaskovsky, Glier and others at the Moscow Conservatory (1914-24), where he returned as teacher (1926-32). During the 1920s he was a leading member of the Association for Contemporary Music, producing piano pieces and orchestral works (*Telescope I*, 1926, *II*, 1928) influenced by Schoenberg and young French composers. After the fall of the ACM he wrote simpler music, including ballets for children.

polymetre The presence together of musical lines in different metres. This is not uncommon in 14th c. song, but it then disappeared, apart from such special cases as the Act I finale of *Don Giovanni*, until the 20th c. There are many instances in Ives, where different kinds of music are superposed (*Three Places*, Fourth Symphony, etc), and also in Stockhausen (*Gruppen*), Carter, Messiaen, etc.

polyphony Music in more than one part. The distinction from HETEROPHONY is confused: classically, the voices in heterophony are expressions of the same melody at different speeds, whereas those in polyphony may be independent, though fused together by regulated tempo relationships and by harmonic principles. Usage of these terms in relation to 20th c. music has tended to concentrate on the degree of fusion rather than the nature of the voices, so that Webern's String Quartet is described as polyphonic even though the lines are all expressions of the same 12-note set, and Messiaen's *Turangalîla-Symphonie* is described as heterophonic even when the parts have no evident melodic connection. Boulez has further extended the term by suggesting the possibility of a monody being a 'latent polyphony' (where the secondary voices may survive vestigially as grace notes), and by proposing too the ideas of 'polyphony of polyphonies', 'polyphony of heterophonies', etc. His whole manner of composing suggests a garden of forking paths, where more or less complex polyphonies are always at hand to ornament monodies: this is almost schematically presented in his *Domaines*, but it dates back at least as far as his *Polyphonie X*, whose title embodies a favourite notion that polyphonic lines might be connected not just vertically but also diagonally, through time. Babbitt, too, has developed the concept of polyphony, if in a more organized manner:

in his music polyphonic lines may not be present as distinct melodic voices, but may be separated rather by separate organizations of timbre, dynamic, time point, etc.

If the same word may be used of, say, a flute solo in *Le marteau sans maître* (VIII, bars 81-3), a guitar piece by Babbitt (his Composition, described by him as being a 6-part polyphony), an orchestral texture of numerous independent melodies by Ligeti (*San Francisco Polyphony*) and a mass by David or Pepping, then clearly the term is losing any precision of meaning it had. What may be asserted, nevertheless, is that 20th c. music has seen a widespread revival of polyphony after the tendency of music in the 19th c. to be homophonic. This is very obvious in Schoenberg's earliest works; it was remarked by Webern; and it is implicit in neoclassicism.

polyrhythm Term embracing polymetre and the more traditional conflict of 2 rhythms within the same metre (i.e. cross-rhythm).

polytonality The presence of more than one key at a time. If there are 2 simultaneous keys the term is BITONALITY; the accurate sensation of more than 2 keys at a time is dubious.

Ponce, Manuel (1882-1948) Mexican composer. Trained and worked in Mexico as pianist and organist before leaving in 1904 for Europe, where he studied further in Bologna and Berlin. He returned to Mexico to teach, compose and study folk music, apart from a period in Paris (1925-33). His works consist mostly of songs and pieces for piano and guitar, in Hispanic style. [Peer, Schott]

Popov, Gavriil (1904-72) Russian composer. Studied at the Leningrad Conservatory with Shcherbachov and made a notable contribution to the radical movement in Soviet music with his Sextet (1927); his later works are monumental choral pieces and symphonies.

Porter, Quincy (1897-1966) American composer. Studied with Parker and David Smith at Yale (1915-20), with d'Indy in Paris (1920-21) and with Bloch in New York and Cleveland, where he taught at the Institute of Music (1923-8). He then returned to Paris for three years before taking appointments at Vassar College (1932-8), the New England Conservatory (1938-46) and Yale (1946-65). His musical style was one of smooth, scalic melodies moving with rhythmic purposefulness

through chromatic polyphony: his works include 9 quartets (1923, 1925, 1930, 1931, 1935, 1937, 1943, 1950, 1958), besides other chamber music, 2 symphonies, smaller orchestral pieces and songs. [Presser, New Valley]

post-modernism *See* MODERNISM.

Poulenc, Francis (1899-1963) French composer. His great talent was to turn Stravinsky's irony into distinctly French modes of chic and charm, and it was a talent that emerged early. Having heard *The Rite* during its first season, he began lessons in 1915 with Viñes, through whom he came into contact with Satie, Auric and others (formal training in composition came only in 1921-4, when he took lessons with Koechlin). His early sonatas show him alert to Stravinsky's rapid development during the period of the Symphonies of Wind Instruments and the Octet, while at the same time he was following Cocteau's aesthetic in combining popular materials and sophisticated wit in his songs, notably *Cocardes*. He was the most natural candidate for membership of Les Six, and kept a Cocteau-like regard for style, elegance, classical mementos and suave modernity in his music of the 1920s and early 1930s.

In 1935, however, he rediscovered his Catholic faith, and there followed a sequence of sacred works whose meaning remains equivocal in the light of his previous superb detachment and exquisiteness (which these works continue in musical style). There is the question of whether gravity is being explored as a mode of expression (as seems clearly to be the case in the Organ Concerto) or whether it is genuinely intended. Such difficulties do not arise in his 2 short operas, the absurd setting of Apollinaire's *Les mamelles de Tirésias* and the smartly sentimental underscoring of Cocteau's *La voix humaine*, nor generally in the many songs, representing a genre in which he excelled. After the second world war he appeared internationally in song recitals with Pierre Bernac, and also recorded much of his song and piano output.

Operas: Les mamelles de Tirésias, 1944, ★Paris, 1947, Dialogues des carmélites, 1953-6, ★Milan, 1957; La voix humaine, 1958, ★Paris, 1959

Orchestral: Les biches (ballet with chorus), 1923; Concert champêtre, hpd, orch, 1927-8; Aubade, pf, 18 insts, 1929; Conc, d, 2 pf, orch, 1932; Conc, g, org, timp, str, 1938; Les animaux modèles (ballet), 1940-41; Sinfonietta, 1947; Pf Conc, 1949

Choral: Litanies à la vierge noire, SSA, org, 1936; Mass, G, SATB, 1937; 4 motets pour un temps de pénitence, SATB, 1938-9; Salve Regina, SATB, 1941; Figure humaine, 12vv, 1943; 4 petites prières de St François d'Assise, male, vv, 1948; Stabat mater, S, 5vv, orch, 1950, 4 motets pour le temps de noël, 1951-2; Ave verum corpus, SMezA, 1952; Laudes de St Antoine de Padoue, male vv, 1957-9; Gloria, S, vv, orch, 1959; 7 répons de ténèbres, child S, vv, orch, 1961

Chamber: Sonata, 2 cl, 1918, rev. 1945; Sonata, cl, bn, 1922; Sonata, hn, tpt, trbn, 1922, rev. 1945; Trio, ob, bn, pf, 1926; Sextet, wind qnt, pf, 1932-9; Sonata, vn, pf, 1942-3, rev. 1949; Sonata, vc, pf, 1948; Sonata, fl, pf, 1956; Sonata, cl, pf, 1962; Sonata, ob, pf, 1962

Songs: Le bestiare (Apollinaire), 1918-19; Cocardes (Cocteau), 1919; Poèmes de Ronsard, 1924-5; Chansons gaillardes, 1925-6; Airs chantés (Moréas), 1927-8; 3 poèmes de Louise Lalanne, 1931; 4 poèmes (Apollinaire), 1931; 5 poèmes (Jacob), 1931; 8 chansons polonaises, 1934; 4 chansons pour enfants, 1934; 5 poèmes (Eluard), 1935; Tel jour, telle nuit (Eluard), 1936-7; 3 poèmes (de Vilmorin), 1937; 2 poèmes (Apollinaire), 1938; Miroirs brulants (Eluard), 1938-9; Fiançailles pour rire (de Vilmorin), 1939; Banalités (Apollinaire), 1940; Chansons villageoises (Fombeure), 1942; Métamorphoses (de Vilmorin), 1943; 2 poèmes (Aragon), 1943; 2 mélodies (Apollinaire), 1946; 3 chansons (Lorca), 1947; Calligrammes (Apollinaire), 1948; La fraîcheur et le feu (Eluard), 1950; Le travail du peintre (Eluard), 1956; La courte paille (Carème), 1960; many single nos

Melodrama: L'histoire de Babar, 1940-45

Piano: Sonata, 4 hands, 1918; 3 mouvements perpétuels, 1918; Suite, C, 1920; 6 Impromptus, 1920; Promenades, 1921; Napoli, 1925; 2 novelettes, 1927-8; 3 Pieces, 1928; Nocturnes, nos 1-8, 1929-38; Improvisations nos 1-15, 1932-59; Villageoises, 1933; Les soirées de Nazelles, 1930-36; Sonata, 2 pf, 1952-3

[Chester, Heugel, Eschig, Rouart Lerolle]

□ H. Hell, *Francis Poulenc* (1959); P. Bernac, *Francis Poulenc* (1977)

Pousseur, Henri (1929-) Belgian composer. Studied at the Liège Conservatory (1947-52), with Absil at the Brussels Conservatory (1952-3) and with Froidebise, who introduced him to Webern's music. Also important were his meetings with Boulez in 1951 and Stockhausen in 1954: he became a regular teacher at Darmstadt (1957-67) and participant in the avant-garde movement. He was particularly concerned with aleatory form, in *Scambi* for segments of tape to be assembled, in *Mobile* for 2

pianos, and in the opera *Votre Faust*, where eventualities can be decided by the audience. This libertarian attitude led to a view of music as a potential model of Utopian society, whether addressed to a society of musicians in works for group improvisation or to a larger company in such pieces as *Couleurs croisées*, an orchestral transformation of the song 'We shall overcome'. Pousseur would see his concern with harmony, present throughout his work, as also of social import.

Opera: Votre Faust, 1960-67, ★Milan, 1969

Orchestral: Symphonies, 15 insts, 1954-5; Rimes, with tape, 1958-9; Trait, 15 str, 1962; Couleurs croisées, 1967; Les éphémerides d'Icare II, pf, 18 insts, 1970; L'effacement du Prince Igor, 1971; Chronique illustrée, with Bar, 1976

Chamber: 3 chants sacrés, S, str trio, 1951; Qnt, cl, b cl, vn, vc, pf, 1955; Madrigal I, cl, 1958, II, 4 insts, 1961, III, 6 insts, 1962; Répons, 7 insts, 1960; Ode, str qt, 1960-61

Piano: Exercices, 1956; Mobile, 2 pf, 1956-8; Caractères, 1961; Apostrophe et 6 reflections, 1964-6

Tape: Seismogrammes I-II, 1954; Scambi, 1957; Electre, 1960; 3 visages de Liège, 1961; Jeu de miroirs de Votre Faust, 1967; Parabol Mix I-III, 1973, Liège à Paris, 1977

[UE, Suvini Zerboni, Wergo]

Powell, Mel (1923-) American composer. Was a noted jazz pianist before studying with Toch in Los Angeles (1946-8) and Hindemith at Yale, where he joined the faculty (1958-72), then taught at the California Institute of the Arts. His music is in a 12-note style of vivid, organic imagery, and consists mostly of tape pieces and works for small ensembles. [G. Schirmer]

preludes Genre of piano music cultivated by Skryabin, Rakhmaninov and Debussy, whose first book comprises 1. 'Danseuses de Delphes' (Delphi Dancers), 2. 'Voiles' (Sails), 3. 'Le vent dans la plaine' (The Wind on the Plain), 4. 'Les sons et les parfums tournent dans l'air du soir' ('Sounds and odours turn in the evening air': a line from Baudelaire), 5. 'Les collines d'Anacapri' (The Hills of Anacapri), 6. 'Des pas sur la neige' (Steps on the Snow), 7. 'Ce qu'a vu le vent de l'ouest' (What the Westwind Saw), 8. 'La fille aux cheveux de lin' (The Flaxen-Haired Girl), 9. 'La sérénade interrompue' (The Interrupted Serenade), 10. 'La cathédrale engloutie' (The Submerged Cathedral), 11. 'La danse de Puck' (Puck's Dance), 12. 'Minstrels'.

The second book contains 1. 'Brouillards'

(Mists), 2. 'Feuilles mortes' (Dead Leaves), 3. 'La Puerta del Vino' (a gateway at the Alhambra), 4. 'Les fées sont d'exquises danseuses' (Fairies are Exquisite Dancers), 5. 'Bruyères' (Heaths), 6. 'General Lavine–eccentric' (a music-hall puppet), 7. 'La terrasse des audiences du clair de lune' (The Terrace for Moonlit Audiences), 8. 'Ondine', 9. 'Hommage à S. Pickwick Esq., P.P.M.P.C., 10. 'Canope' (Canopus: ancient Egyptian site), 11. 'Les tierces alternées' (Alternating Thirds), 12. 'Feux d'artifice' (Fireworks).

prepared piano Instrument with objects inserted between the strings: a screw and a piece of cardboard in Cage's *Second Construction* (1940), and a small bolt, a screw with nuts and 11 pieces of fibrous weather stripping in his *Bacchanale* (also 1940). The technique was introduced by Cage, who also named the instrument (on the score *Bacchanale*; in the *Second Construction* he still uses Cowell's term of string piano). Later works by Cage involve more preparations (45 in the Sonatas and Interludes) and come with precise instructions as to where the objects should be placed, though the exact effect will depend on the nature of the objects and of the piano into which they are introduced. Notionally, the prepared piano allows the composer to experiment with sound in a way unrivalled before the arrival of electronic music; however, the freedom passes in effect to the performer, since the sounds cannot be prescribed. This was to have far-reaching consequences in Cage's work, as was the subtle but radical change in the nature of notation. Prepared piano music is notated in the normal way, but the normal correspondence between symbol and sound is lost: a notated C may sound as a percussive rustle. Notation thus becomes a system of instructions to the performer and not a visual representation of the music.

Cage has not returned to the prepared piano since his Concerto (1950-51), nor have many other composers written for it.

Pribaoutki Russian rhymes. Stravinsky's work of this title is a setting of 4 rhymes for baritone and mixed octet, but he used poems of the same sort in *Berceuses du chat* for contralto and 3 clarinets, *Renard* and *Les noces*.

Prinz von Homburg, Der Opera by Henze and Bachmann after Kleist, a work with a German military setting but marking the composer's absorption in early 19th c. Italian opera. ★Hamburg, 22 May 1960.

process music *See* MINIMAL MUSIC.

progressive tonality The term is used of symphonic music which ends in a key other than of its origin, excepting the trivial case of minor-key works ending in the tonic major. Probably the first notable examples are among Mahler's symphonies, his Second moving from C minor to Eb major (though this is a step executed a semitone down by Bach's B minor Mass), his Fourth from G major to E major, etc. There is movement of tonality too in the symphonic works of Nielsen, Simpson and others.

Prokofiev, Sergey (1891-1953) Russian composer. As a musical ironist he probably has no equal in the 20th c. apart from the supreme one of Stravinsky, yet he seems always to have wanted of himself a more integrated form of expression. The result was a creative career of unusual variety and sudden change, from bitter sarcasm to the most indulgent Romanticism – from, in one short period, the artful fantasy of *The* LOVE OF THREE ORANGES to the wild hysteria of *The* FIERY ANGEL. His restlessness manifested itself also on the banal level of geography: he left Russia soon after the Revolution, then lived in the USA and in Paris, but in the 1930s gradually returned to assume an awkward place as a composer in a society that had not decided what it wanted of its artists.

He had lessons from Glier in his boyhood, then studied at the St Petersburg Conservatory (1904-14), where his courses with Lyadov, Rimsky-Korsakov, Tcherepnin and others were less important than the friendships he made with Myaskovsky and Asafyev. In 1914 he visited London and met Dyagilev, who commissioned a ballet; however, his first effort, *Ala and Lolli*, came to nothing (its music went into the *Scythian Suite*), and his second, *Chout*, was held up by the outbreak of war. He returned to Petrograd and wrote *The* GAMBLER, as well as his first exercise in neoclassicism, the *Classical* Symphony, consciously modelled on the form and manners of Haydn's time, and his lyrical First Violin Concerto.

In May 1918 he left for the USA, where he quickly wrote *Three Oranges* for the Chicago Lyric Opera and began *The Fiery Angel*. He then returned to Paris (1920-21), in the first place to revise *Chout* for Dyagilev, and while in France he continued to work on a variety of fronts: there was the outgoing, virtuoso Third Piano Concerto, written for himself to play and contrasting with the complex Second and the bumptious First; there was also a symbolist cantata on Balmont's *They are Seven*. In the winter of 1921-2 he was back in Chicago for the staging of *Three Oranges*, but after that he made Paris his centre for the next dozen years. His works remained various, ranging from the machine-age futurism of the Second Symphony and the ballet *Le pas d'acier* to the grace of another ballet, *L'enfant prodigue*, and the intense, fevered excitement of another symphony, the Third, drawn from *The Fiery Angel*.

In 1933 he made his first visit to the USSR since leaving, and increasingly he began to write for Soviet audiences: ROMEO AND JULIET was commissioned by the Kirov in Leningrad in 1934. Finally in 1936 he took up permanent residence in Moscow with his wife and 2 sons. The time was not propitious: Shostakovich had just been condemned for *Lady Macbeth*, and his own *Romeo and Juliet* was rejected. At first he wrote only utility music, including patriotic cantatas, incidental music for the theatre and cinema (though this included an important score for Eisenstein's *Alexander Nevsky*) and the instructive *Peter and the Wolf*. His first Soviet opera, *Semyon Kotko*, was dropped after its first season; his second, *The Duenna*, was not staged for several years; and his third, WAR AND PEACE, had no complete performance until after his death.

He found himself more attuned to Soviet taste in his imposing Fifth Symphony (1944) and his second full-length ballet, *Cinderella*, but he was a principal target of the criticism meted out to composers in 1948, and the works of his last years have generally been regarded as anodyne in response to this. He died on the same day as Stalin.

Operas: The GAMBLER, 1915-17, rev. 1927-8; The LOVE FOR THREE ORANGES, 1919; The FIERY ANGEL, 1919-23, rev. 1926-7; Semyon Kotko, 1939, *Moscow, 1940; The Duenna (Betrothal in a Monastery), 1940-41, *Leningrad, 1946; WAR AND PEACE, 1941-3, rev. 1946-52; The Story of a Real Man, 1947-8, *Moscow, 1960

Ballets: Chout, 1915, rev. 1920, *Paris, 1921; Le pas d'acier, 1925-6, *Paris, 1927; L'enfant prodigue, 1928-9, *Paris, 1929; Sur le Borysthène, 1930-31, *Paris, 1932; ROMEO AND JULIET, 1935-6; Cinderella, 1940-44, *Moscow, 1945; The Tale of the Stone Flower, 1948-53, *Moscow, 1954

Symphonies: no.1 'Classical', D, 1916-17; no.2, d, 1924-5; no.3, c, 1928; no.4, C, 1929-30, rev. 1947; no.5, B♭, 1944; no.6, E♭, 1945-7; no.7, c♯, 1951-2

Concertos: for pf, no.1, D♭, 1911-12, no.2, g, 1912-13, rev. 1923, no.3, C, 1917-21, no.4, B♭, left hand, 1931, no.5, G, 1931-2; for vn, no.1, D, 1916-

17, no.2, g, 1935; for vc, e, 1933-8, rev. 1950-52 as Sym-Conc; Vc Concertino, g, 1952

Suites: Scythian Suite, 1915; Lieutenant Kijé, 1934; others from operas and ballets

Cantatas: They are Seven, T, vv, orch, 1917-18, rev. 1933; Alexander Nevsky, Mez, vv, orch, 1939

Melodrama: Peter and the Wolf, narrator, orch, 1936

Chamber: Overture on Hebrew Themes, c, cl, pf qnt, 1919; Qnt, g, ob, cl, vn, va, db, 1924; Str Qt no.1, b, 1930, no.2, F, 1941; Sonata, C, 2 vn, 1932; Sonata, f, vn, pf, 1938-46; Sonata, D, fl/vn, pf, 1943-4; Sonata, C, vc, pf, 1949

Piano: Sonata no.1, f, 1909, no.2, d, 1912, no.3, a, 1917, no.4, c, 1917, no.5, C, 1923, rev. 1952-3, no.6, A, 1939-40, no.7, B♭, 1939-42, no.8, B♭, 1939-44, no.9, C, 1947; Sarcasms, 1912-14; Visions fugitives, 1915-17

Songs: 2 Poems, 1910-11; The Ugly Duckling, 1914; 5 Poems (Balmont), 1915; 5 Poems (Akhmatova), 1916; 5 Poems (Balmont), 1921; 3 Romances (Pushkin), 1936

[Boosey, Soviet State Publishers]

□ S.I. Shlifshteyn, ed. *Sergey Prokofiev* (1960, 2/ 1968); I.V. Nestyev, *Prokofiev* (1961); C. Samuel *Prokofiev* (1971)

Prometheus, the Poem of Fire (Prométhée, le poème du feu) Work by Skryabin for piano, orchestra, COLOUR organ and chorus in the last stages. *Moscow, 1911.

proportional notation *See* TIME-SPACE NOTATION.

Prozession (Procession) Work by Stockhausen for live electronic ensemble, composed in plus-minus notation defining not the material but how the players react to one another and to quotations from other Stockhausen works that they introduce. *Helsinki, 21 May 1967.

Puccini, Giacomo (1858-1924) Italian composer. The son, grandson, great-grandson and great-great-grandson of church musicians in Lucca, he was expected to follow his father (who had died when he was 5), but hearing *Aida* when he was 17 made him decide on an operatic career. He studied at the Milan Conservatory (1880-83) with Bazzini and Ponchielli, and won success with his first opera *Le villi* (1884), then international acclaim with *Manon Lescaut* (1893). Despite an incoherent plot and a story of trivial sentimentality, this has moments of harmonic and orchestral boldness comparable only with the contemporary works of Strauss and Mahler. There is a similar friction between novelettish characters and sometimes searching music in *La Bohème* (1896), *Tosca* (1900) and MADAMA BUTTERFLY (1904): in particular, Puccini was aware of Debussy, and his reduction to pentatonic principles cuts to raw levels of emotion as surely as does Schoenberg's chromaticizing. In doing so, however, the music can often seem exploitative, and all these works have moments of loving cruelty (the death of Mimì, the whole middle act of *Tosca* and the finale of *Madama Butterfly*), besides being geared to symphonic scores that may appear to manipulate the character towards emotional extremity.

Partly because of this tastelessness, the 3 operas of 1896-1904 have been as much vilified as adored, and their successors La FANCIULLA DEL WEST (1910) and *La rondine* (1917) have not been so widely admired; nor have the three 1-act operas of *Il* TRIT-TICO (1918). However, his last opera was again to become a staple of the repertory: TURANDOT (1926). Here the exotic setting allowed him to profit from Stravinsky and Schoenberg as well as Debussy, while there was opportunity also for his characteristic glorification of cruelty to be expressed not only in the stage action but also in the demands made of the singers. Demanding much of himself too, he was unable to complete the finale, which was posthumously added by Alfano.

☐ M. Carner, *Puccini* (1958, 2/1974)

Pulcinella 'Ballet with song' by Stravinsky, the music for 3 singers and chamber orchestra being dislocated from arias and instrumental pieces attributed to Pergolesi. The ballet originally had a *commedia dell'arte* setting, choreographed by Massine and designed by Picasso. ★Ballets Russes/Ansermet, Paris, 15 May 1920. The suite includes 11 of the 18 numbers and omits the soloists.

pulse 1. Audible rhythmic regularity. This is a characteristic of most music, though it has been weakened, complicated and sometimes obliterated with the arrival of 20th c. conceptions of musical time. 2. Single burst of electric power. Stockhausen's *Kontakte* was composed from the outputs of pulse generators at different rates.

Punch and Judy Opera by Birtwistle and Stephen Pruslin, a ritual of quest and murder based on traditional puppet plays, and scored for chamber forces. ★Aldeburgh, 8 June 1968.

Q

Quatuor pour la fin du temps (Quartet for the End of Time) Work by Messiaen for clarinet, violin, cello and piano, his only chamber piece and the most compact survey of his musical worlds. There are 8 movements based on imagery from the Apocalypse: 1 'Liturgie de cristal' (Crystal Liturgy; abstract rhythmic process), 2 'Vocalise, pour l'ange qui annonce la fin du temps' (Vocalise, for the Angel who Announces the End of Time: ecstatic song), 3 'Abîme des oiseaux' (Abyss of the Birds: clarinet solo), 4 'Intermède' (Interlude: sprightly dance without piano), 5 'Louange à l'éternité de Jésus' (Praise to the Eternity of Jesus: adagio for cello and piano), 6 'Danse de la fureur, pour les sept trompettes' (Dance of Fury, for the Seven Trumpets: mostly for quartet in loud unison), 7 'Fouillis d'arcs-en-ciel, pour l'ange qui annonce la fin du temps' (Bundles of Rainbows, for the Angel who Announces the End of Time: development section), 8 'Louange à l'immortalité de Jésus' (Praise to the Immortality of Jesus: adagio for violin and piano). ★Henri Akoka (cl), Jean La Boulaire (vn), Etienne Pasquier (vc), Messiaen, Stalag VIIIA, Görlitz, Silesia, 15 Jan 1941.

Quilter, Roger (1887-1953) English composer. Studied with Knorr at the Hoch Conservatory, Frankfurt, then lived on private income as a composer mostly of songs, setting English, Elizabethan and Romantic poetry with a light elegance.

☐ T. Hold, *The Walled-in Garden* (1978)

quotation Music alluding incidentally to other music is not common before the 20th c. but becomes so from Berg (Lyric Suite, Violin Concerto) and Ives onwards. There are notable examples in Zimmermann, Berio (SINFONIA), Shostakovich (Fifteenth Symphony), etc.

R

Rachmaninov *See* RAKHMANINOV.

ragtime Musical style distinguished by syncopated and often pentatonic melodies in square, symmetrical forms. Its heyday was the period from the late 1890s to around 1915, when it was succeeded by jazz, and its main practitioners were black American pianists in Missouri (Scott Joplin) and on the east coast (James P. Johnson). Stravinsky used elements of the style in his *Rag-Time, Soldier's Tale* and *Piano-Rag-Music*, all from 1918-19 and sparked off by published ragtime music that Ansermet had brought back from the USA; there are also ragtime moments in Ives's First Piano Sonata and other works. In the 1970s there was a revival of ragtime, and Bolcom and others began writing rags.

Rainier, Priaulx (1903-) South African composer. Studied at the Royal Academy of Music from 1920 and remained in London as a violinist, teacher and composer. Her earlier works (String Quartet, 1939; *Barbaric Dance Suite* for piano, 1949) have a rhythmic ingenuity that relates as much to African music as to Bartók or Stravinsky. Later pieces are more compressed and less tonal. [Schott]

Rake's Progress, The Opera by Stravinsky, Auden and Kallman after Hogarth's paintings of a young man's downfall, engineered in the opera by his devilish alter ego. The work is scored for Mozartian forces and looks to the Mozart-da Ponte operas, as well as to Monteverdi, Donizetti and Verdi: it was the final triumph of Stravinsky's neoclassicism. *cond Stravinsky, Venice 11 Sep 1951

Rakhmaninov, Sergey (1873-1943) Russian composer and pianist. Studied with Ziloti, Taneyev and Arensky at the Moscow Conservatory (1885-92), then began successful career as a composer, in a style owing much to Tchaikovsky and, in his piano music, Chopin. However, the première of his First Symphony (1895) was a failure, and he lost faith in his abilities, turning to conducting. He returned to composition with his Second Piano Concerto (1900-01), whose success restored his self-belief:

the next 15 years were the most productive of his life. But he again abandoned composition after leaving Russia at the end of 1917. The next year he settled with his family in the USA (he had been there for the first time in 1909 to give the first performance of his Third Piano Concerto), and he began a new career as a concert pianist, touring internationally and making recordings of his own and other music. In 1926 he started to compose again, his American works bringing a new lustre to his Russian Romanticism.

Operas: Aleko, 1892, *Moscow, 1893; The Miserly Knight, 1903-5, *Moscow 1906; Francesca da Rimini, 1900-05, *Moscow, 1906
Choral orchestral: The Bells, with S, T, Bar, 1913; 3 Russian Songs, 1926
Orchestral: Pf Conc no.1, f♯, 1890-91, rev. 1917, no.2, c, 1900-01, no.3, d, 1909, no.4, g, 1926, rev. 1941; Prince Rotislav, 1891; The Rock, 1893; Caprice bohémien, 1892-4; Sym no.1, d, 1895, no.2, e, 1906-7, no.3, a, 1935-6, rev. 1938; The Isle of the Dead, 1909; Rhapsody on a Theme of Paganini, pf, orch, 1934
Piano: Morceaux de fantaisie (includes Prelude, c♯), 1892; Fantaisie-tableaux (Suite no.1), 2 pf, 1893; Morceaux de salon, 1893-4; 6 Duets, 1894; Moments musicaux, 1896; Suite no.2, 2 pf, 1900-01; Variations on a Theme of Chopin, 1902-3; 10 Preludes, 1903; Sonata no.1, d, 1907, no.2, b♭, 1913, rev. 1931; 13 Preludes, 1910; Etudes tableaux, 2 sets, 1911, 1916-7; Variations on a Theme of Corelli, 1931
Choral: Liturgy of St John Chrysostom, 1910; All-Night Vigil, 1915
Songs, chamber pieces, pf arrangements
[Foley, Gutheil, Editions Russes de Musique, Boosey]
□ G. Norris, *Rakhmaninov* (1976)

Randall, James Kirtland (1929-) American composer. Studied at Columbia, at Harvard, and with Sessions and Babbitt at Princeton, where in 1957 he began teaching. His works, generally using computer sound generation, include *Quartets in Pairs* (1964) and *Mudgett: Monologues by a Mass Murderer* (1965). [CRI, Nonesuch]

Rands, Bernard (1935-) English composer. Studied at Bangor with Reginald Smith Brindle (1953-8) and in Italy with Vlad (1958), Dallapiccola (1959-60) and Berio (1960-62), also attending the Darmstadt summer courses of 1961-4. In 1967-9 he was at the universities of Princeton and Illinois, after which he taught at York University and then the University of California at San Diego. His music has been most conspicuously influenced by Berio's, both in his enjoyment of solo virtuosity and in his approach to verbal language. Among his works are cycles of *Memos* for soloist (I, db, 1971; II, trbn, 1973; III, vc, 1974; IV, org, 1975; V, pf, 1975) and *Ballads* for vocal forces (I, Mez, 5 insts, 1970; II, v, pf, 1970; III, S, tape, 1973; IV, 8 solo vv, 21 insts, 1980). [UE]

Rape of Lucretia, The Opera by Britten and Ronald Duncan after André Obey, the first of Britten's works for soloists and a small orchestra. The legend is enacted with post-Christian commentary from Male and Female Chorus. ★cond Ansermet, Glyndebourne, 12 Jul 1946.

Ravel, Maurice (1875-1937) French composer. He may represent at its most extreme the tendency in 20th c. music for individual ideas to be perfectly self-contained, leaving no room for development. In attaining this ideal he made himself a master of orchestration as well as of his own instrument, the piano, to the extent that many of his works exist in forms for both media, both forms being so well fashioned that they have the status of originals. His creation of musical objects (rather than thematic subjects) was also a mark of his expressive objectivity: much of his music emerged under the cover of some picturesque illustrative purpose, whether as ballet music or tone poetry, the motifs often chosen from legends, faraway places and fairy-tales, or else, in various dance pieces, from the mechanisms of musical movement.

He studied at the Paris Conservatoire (1889-95), while being impressed too by hearing Javanese gamelan and Russian orchestral music at the 1889 Exposition. Among his acquaintances were Ricardo Viñes, who championed his and Debussy's piano music, as well as Chabrier and Satie, who influenced his first pieces. He then went back to the Conservatoire (1897-1900) for further studies with Gédalge and Fauré, and retained an association with the place even longer, competing for the Prix de Rome until 1905 without success, though by then he was already the acclaimed composer of the orchestral song cycle *Shéhérazade*, the F major String Quartet and various piano pieces. A scandal ensued, but nothing checked his creative output, and when Dyagilev arrived in 1909 he was a natural choice for a commission: the result was his longest work, DAPHNIS ET CHLOÉ.

The arrival of the Ballets Russes also brought Stravinsky to Paris, and Ravel quickly became one of the Frenchmen closest to him, personally and musically. One of Stravinsky's Japanese Lyrics was dedicated to him, and he replied with his *3 poèmes de Stéphane Mallarmé* (1913), 1 of which is dedicated to Stravinsky (though not the harmonically abstruse third song, which perversely he inscribed to Satie). During the war his life was disrupted by service as a driver and by the death of his mother (1917), for whom he probably cared more than for any other human being (he remained unmarried and, it would seem, chaste). As with Debussy, the war also excited his musical patriotism, expressed, as well as his delight in dance forms, in the suite Le TOMBEAU DE COUPERIN (1914-17).

This is hardly more than accidentally neoclassical, though he certainly combined with such contemporaries as Stravinsky and Roussel in making his harmony more spare and non-triadic around this time, especially in the sonatas for violin with cello (1920-22) and with piano (1923-27). His opera L'ENFANT ET LES SORTILÈGES, however, needs a wide variety of harmonic characters to create its picture-book images, and his 2 piano concertos show a return to denser textures, whether dark and bass-heavy in that for left hand alone (1929-30) or brash and bright in the partly Gershwinesque G major work (1929-31). His last years were a period of gradual decline as he fell victim to Pick's disease: he wrote nothing after the Don Quixote songs, one of many works showing the Spanish zest he felt he inherited from his Basque mother.

Operas: L'HEURE ESPAGNOLE 1907-9; L'ENFANT ET LES SORTILÈGES, 1920-25

Ballets: Ma mère l'oye (Mother Goose), 1911, ★Paris, 1912; DAPHNIS ET CHLOÉ, 1909-12; Adélaïde (= Valses nobles et sentimentales), 1912, ★Paris, 1912; La valse, 1919-20, ★Paris, 1928; Boléro, 1928, ★Paris, 1928

Orchestral: Shéhérazade, overture, 1898; Une barque sur l'océan, 1906, rev. 1926; Rapsodie espagnole, 1907-8; Pavane pour une infante défunte, 1910; Alborada del gracioso, 1918; Le tombeau de Couperin, 1919; Tzigane, vn, orch, 1924; Fanfare pour 'L'éventail de Jeanne', 1927; Menuet antique, 1929; Pf Conc, left hand, 1929-30; Pf Conc, G, 1929-31

Vocal orchestral: Myrrha, 3 solo vv, orch, 1901; Alcyone, 3 solo vv, orch, 1902; Alyssa, 3 solo vv, orch, 1903; Shéhérazade, Mez, orch, 1903; Don Quichotte à Dulcinée, Bar, orch, 1932-3; orchestrations of songs

Chamber: Sonata, vn, pf, 1897; Str Qt, F, 1902-3; Introduction and Allegro, harp, fl, cl, str qt, 1905; Pf Trio, 1914; Sonata, vn, vc, 1920-22; Berceuse, vn, pf, 1922; Tzigane, vn, pf, 1924; Sonata, vn, pf, 1923-7

Vocal chamber: 3 poèmes de Stéphane Mallarmé, S, 9 insts, 1913; Chansons madécasses, S, fl, vc, pf, 1925-6

Songs: Un grand sommeil noir (Verlaine), 1895; Sainte (Mallarmé), 1896; Chanson du rouet (de Lisle), 1898; Si morne! (Verhaeren), 1898; 2 épigrammes de Clément Marot, 1896-9; Manteau de fleurs (Gravollet), 1903; Noël des jouets (Ravel), 1905; 5 mélodies populaires grecques, 1904-6; Histoires naturelles (Renard), 1906; Les grands vents venus d'outremer (de Régnier), 1907; Sur l'herbe (Verlaine), 1907; Vocalise-étude, 1907; Tripatos, 1909; Chants populaires, 1910; 2 mélodies hébraïques, 1914; Ronsard à son âme, 1923-4; Rêves (Fargue), 1927

Choral: 3 chansons (Ravel), SATB, 1914-15

Piano: Sérénade grotesque, *c*.1893; Menuet antique, 1895; Sites auriculaires, 2 pf, 1895-7; Pavane pour une infante défunte, 1899; Jeux d'eau, 1901; Sonatina, 1903-5; MIROIRS, 1904-5; GASPARD DE LA NUIT, 1908; Menuet sur le nom d'Haydn, 1909; Ma mère l'oye, 4 hands, 1908-10; Valses nobles et sentimentales, 1911; A la manière de Borodine, 1913; A la manière de Chabrier, 1913; Prelude, 1913; Le TOMBEAU DE COUPERIN, 1914-17; Frontispice, 2 pf 5 hands, 1918; La valse, 2 pf; Bolero, 2 pf

Orchestration of Musorgsky's *Pictures at an Exhibition*, 1922

[Durand, Eschig]

□ A. Orenstein, *Ravel* (1975); R. Nichols, *Ravel* (1977)

Rawsthorne, Alan (1905-71) English composer. Studied at the Royal Manchester College of Music (1926-30) with Merrick for the piano and Keighley for composition, then took further piano lessons with Petri (1930-31). After returning to England he taught at Dartington (1932-5), then moved to London to concentrate on composition. Influenced by Hindemith, he wrote mostly in standard abstract genres a music of fastidiousness, smooth accomplishment and occasional open wit.

Orchestral: Pf Conc no.1, 1939, rev. 1942, no.2, 1951; Street Corner, overture, 1944; Ob Conc, 1947; Vn Conc no.1, 1948, no.2, 1956; Sym no.1, 1950, no.2, with S, 1959, no.3, 1964; Vc Conc, 1965; Double Pf Conc, 1968

Chamber: Str Qt no.1, 1939, no.2, 1954, no.3, 1964; Cl Qt, 1948; Pf Trio, 1962; Qnt, pf, woodwind, 1962-3; Pf Qnt, 1968; Ob Qt, 1970; Qnt, cl, hn, vn, vc, pf, 1970

[OUP]

recording The claim is sometimes made that 20th c. music has been influenced by the new possibility for listeners to acquaint themselves with a work through repeated experience: music could thus be more complex and quicker in its thought processes. However, it seems unlikely that Schoenberg and Webern in 1908 were envisaging the possibility of their works being recorded when they wrote the first atonal pieces. Indeed, few serious works, other than operatic arias, were recorded before the 1920s, and even since then the representation of new music in recorded form has been patchy. Among the composers to play, conduct or supervise more than the occasional performance for recording have been Elgar, Strauss, Rakhmaninov, Stravinsky, Britten, Copland, Bernstein, Boulez and Stockhausen. On the other hand, Bartók recorded no concerto, Schoenberg recorded only his *Pierrot lunaire*, and of Webern's conducting there survives only a performance of his orchestration of some of Schubert's German dances.

These discrepancies obviously limit the value of recordings in conveying information about performance practice, but there are other problems too. Tempos may be constrained by the need to contain a movement or section on one side of a record, and cuts may be entertained for the same reason. The style of recording may not be adequate to reproduce the composer's intended balance, particularly in orchestral works recorded with many microphones. And the performers may not have had sufficient experience of the work. Difficulties of all these kinds are evident when one examines recordings of the same work made by a composer at different times: Stravinsky's recordings of *Petrushka* and *The Rite of Spring*, for instance, or Boulez's of *Le marteau sans maître* and *Pli selon pli*.

If recordings are dubious tools in the search for 'authentic' style, they have obviously been essential to electronic music and their usefulness in propagating new music is also less equivocal. Given the costs of mounting performances of unknown works and the uncertainties of box-office response, it is inevitable that new music should be most widely disseminated through recordings and radio broadcasts. It may therefore be some advantage that Babbitt and Boulez are not as commercially successful as their contemporaries among rock musicians, since there has been little temptation for record companies to manipulate serious composers. On the contrary, recordings have often had to be funded by institutions or foundations in order for them to be possible at all, though it is perhaps unfortunate that serious composers have not been encouraged to use the recording medium creatively in the way that has been available to rock musicians since the mid-1960s. Records of serious music tend to be precisely records: documents of works intended for the concert hall or broadcasting service. Kagel's *1898*, commissioned by Deutsche Grammophon for their 75th anniversary, is a rare example of a work made to be recorded.

Refrain Work by Stockhausen for piano, celesta and vibraphone, the 3 players also using additional percussion and consonantal sounds. The striking score prints the 'refrain' on a transparent strip, so that it may interfere with the music at different points in different performances. ★Tudor, Cardew, Rockstroh, Berlin, 2 Oct 1959.

Reger, Max (1873-1916) German composer. With Schoenberg he was one of the most richly gifted Germanic composers of his generation, and like Schoenberg he was at once zealously conservative of his tradition and strongly compelled to follow the consequences of Wagner's harmony. Possibly the essential difference was that his cast of mind was more academic than analytic, so that he tended to favour solutions vouchsafed by history: the solutions of variation form and fugue above all. There are also signs, for instance in the first movement of his D minor String Quartet, that the dictates of correct form are being applied without much reference to the highly undisciplined material placed therein. This sort of gap between form and content is an abiding characteristic of Reger's art, though his style is scarcely less distinctive in works of freer form.

A prolific composer and organist from boyhood, he was impressed by a visit to the Bayreuth festival when he was 15 and from 1890 was a pupil of Riemann. From 1901 to 1907 he lived in Munich, moving from there to Leipzig, where he taught until 1911. He was then conductor of the court orchestra at Meiningen (1911-14), from whence he moved to Jena. Composing abundantly all the while, he still found time for visits abroad, notably to London (1909) and St Petersburg (1906), where he earned the admiration of Prokofiev though not of Stravinsky.

Orchestral: 2 Romances, with vn, 1900; Sinfonietta, 1904-5; Serenade, G, 1905-6; Variations and Fugue on a Theme of Hiller, 1907; Vn Conc, A, 1907-8; Symphonischer Prolog zu einer Tragödie, 1908; Pf Conc, f, 1910; Eine Lustspielouvertüre, 1911;

Konzert im alten Stil, 1912; Eine romantische Suite, 1912; 4 Tondichtungen nach Böcklin, 1913; Eine Ballettsuite, 1914; Variations and Fugue on a Theme of Mozart, 1914; Eine vaterländische Ouvertüre, 1914; Variations and Fugue on a Theme of Beethoven, 1915; Suite im alten Stil, 1916

Choral orchestral: Gesang der Verklärten, 1903; Psalm 100, 1908-9; Die Nonnen, 1909; Die Weihe der Nacht, 1911; 2 Gesänge, 1915

Chamber: 2 Str Qts, op.54, g, A, 1900; Pf Qnt, c, 1901-2; Str Qt, op.74, d, 1903-4; Serenade, D, fl, vn, va, 1904; Str Trio, a, 1904; Pf Trio, e, 1907-8; Str Qt, op. 109, Eb, 1909; Pf Qt, d, 1910; Str Sextet, F, 1910; Str Qt, op. 121, f♯, 1911; Pf Qt, a, 1914; Serenade, G, fl/vn, vn, va, 1915; Str Trio, d, 1915; Cl Qnt, A, 1915

Sonatas with piano: Vc, op.28, g, 1898; Vn, op.41, A, 1899; Cl, op.49, no.1 A, no.2 f♯, 1900; Vn, op.72, C, 1903; Vc, op.78, F, 1904; Vn, op.84, f♯, 1905; Cl/Va, op.107, Bb, 1908-9; Vc, op.116, a, 1910; Vn, op.122, e, 1911; Vn, op.139, c, 1915

Works for solo violin: 4 Sonatas, op.42, d, A, b, g, 1900; 7 Sonatas, op.91, a, D, Bb, b, e, G, a, 1905; 8 Preludes and Fugues, op.117, 1909-12; 6 Preludes and Fugues, op.131a, 1914

Piano: Variations and Fugue on a Theme of J.S. Bach, 1904; Variations and Fugue on a Theme of Beethoven, 2 pf, 1904; Variations and Fugue on a Theme of Mozart, 2 pf, 1914; Variations and Fugue on a Theme of Telemann, 1914; much else

Organ: Chorale Fantasia 'Ein' feste Burg', 1898; Fantasia and Fugue, c, 1898; Chorale Fantasia 'Freu' dich sehr', 1898; Sonata no.1, f♯, 1899, no.2, d, 1901; Chorale Fantasia 'Wie schön leucht't uns', 1900; Chorale Fantasia 'Wachet auf', 1900; Chorale Fantasia 'Halleluja! Gott zu loben', 1900; Sym Fantasia and Fugue, 1901; Variations and Fugue on an Original Theme, f♯, 1903; Suite, g, 1905; Introduction, Passacaglia and Fugue, e, 1913; Fantasia and Fugue, d, 1915; much else

Songs, choral pieces, etc

Reich, Steve (1936-) American composer. Studied philosophy at Cornell University (1953-7) and composition at the Juilliard School (1958-61) and Mills College (1962-3), where his teachers included Milhaud and Berio. He worked at the San Francisco Tape Music Center in 1964-5 and then at his own studio in New York, where in the late 1960s he began giving performances with his own ensemble. His starting point for such performances was that of ostinatos in exceedingly slow canon: this sprang from an electronic phenomenon, that of 2 or more tape recorders gradually getting out of phase with one another (hence his use of the word 'phasing' for processes of this kind). He thus became one of the principal figures of MINIMAL MUSIC, creating works for his group of largely percussion instruments, with whom he appeared internationally from the beginning of the 1970s, following a study visit to investigate Ghanaian drum music in 1970. His work since then has shown increasing subtlety of design, though still with textures of modal repetition, as well as an ability to use larger resources with the same polished finesse he had brought to composing for small formations. Around 1980 he released his scores for performance by any musicians, having previously reserved them for his own ensemble.

It's gonna rain, tape, 1965; Come out, tape, 1966; Piano Phase, 2 pf, 1967; Violin Phase, vn, tape/4 vn, 1967; Pendulum Music, electronics, 1968; 4 Organs, 4 electronic org, maracas, 1970; Phase Patterns, 4 electronic org, 1970; Drumming, perc, vv, piccolo, 1971; Clapping Music, 2 musicians, 1972; 6 Pianos, 6 pf, 1973; Music for Mallet Instruments, Voices and Organ, 1973; Music for Pieces of Wood, 1973; Music for 18 Instruments, 1976; Variations for Winds, Strings and Keyboards, 1978; Octet, 1979; Telihim, vv, insts, 1981; The Desert Music, chorus, orch, ★Cologne, 1984; Music for Percussion and Keyboards, 1984 [UE; DG, ECM]

□ S. Reich, *Writings about Music* (1974)

Reihe, Die (Ger. 'the row') 1. Periodical edited by Eimert and Stockhausen, with 8 numbers published between 1955 and 1962 by Universal Edition of Vienna (in 1958-68 these appeared in English translation). The journal was an important means of communication (or obfuscation) for the avant garde, publishing classic articles by Stockhausen, Boulez, Pousseur, Ligeti and Cage, and concentrating in each issue on a particular topic: electronic music (1), Webern (2), 'musical craftsmanship' (3), young composers (4), 'reports, analyses' (5), speech and music (6), 'form-space' (7), the last number being designated 'retrospective'.

2. Ensemble founded by Cerha in Vienna in 1958 to specialize in 20th c. music. They have recorded works by Varèse, Ligeti, etc.

Reimann, Aribert (1936-) German composer. Studied with Blacher and Pepping at the Hochschule für Musik in West Berlin (1955-9), and since then has worked as composer and pianist, notably in recitals of 20th c. Lieder with Fischer-Dieskau, with whom he has recorded Schoenberg, Webern, Berg, Schreker, etc. His own works include several for Fischer-Dieskau in an expansive Expressionist style, as well as the operas *Ein Traumspiel* (★Kiel, 1965), *Melusine* (★Schwetzingen, 1971), *Lear* (★Munich, 1978) and *Die Gespenstersonate* (★Berlin, 1984). [Schott; DG]

Renaissance instruments 20th c. revivals of early music have brought old instruments once more into the performing domain, though apart from the HARPSICHORD none has gained a large modern repertory. Most 20th c. recorder music is educational, though Frans Brueggen commissioned Berio's *Gesti* and Michael Vetter has composed for the recorder, besides playing the instrument in Stockhausen performances. Consorts of Renaissance instruments are used on stage in Davies' *Taverner* and on the concert platform in works by Gilbert, Kagel, Lutyens and others.

Renard (Reynard, Bayka) 'A burlesque in song and dance' by Stravinsky, setting Russian popular rhymes in a farmyard fable of 4 animal characters 'to be played by clowns, dancers or acrobats'. The scoring is for 2 tenors, 2 basses and a 14-piece band including a cimbalom. ★Ballets Russes/Ansermet, Paris, 18 May 1922.

resonance The resounding of upper partials was a problem for music of closely organized harmony: hence the cultivation in the 19th c. of a legato style for the piano, for instance. In the 20th c., however, resonance phenomena have become important to western music, whether through the use of metal and string PERCUSSION, through the introduction of new PIANO techniques, through the use of bell and other resonating sounds in electronic works (e.g. Harvey's *Mortuos plango*), through the exploration of resonance by live electronic means (as by Lucier) or through the instrumental imitation of resonance (as in Stravinsky's Symphonies of Wind Instruments and other works). Resonances, particularly bell resonances, are among the central images of Stravinsky; Boulez's *Eclat/Multiples* and *Répons* are consciously based on the contrast between resonating and non-resonating sounds, which is implicit also in much of Bartók and Messiaen.

Respighi, Ottorino (1879-1936) Italian composer. Studied with Torchi and Martucci at the Liceo Musicale in Bologna (1891-1901) and with Rimsky-Korsakov in Russia (1900-01, 1902-3), then lived in Bologna and Rome (from 1913) as a conductor, teacher, pianist and composer. The lessons with Rimsky were crucial to his development of a brilliant orchestral technique, sometimes combined with the modes and materials of early music.

Operas: La bella dormente nel bosco, ★Rome, 1922; Belfagor, ★Milan, 1923; La campana sommersa, ★Hamburg, 1927; Belkis, ★Milan, 1932; Maria Egiziaca, ★Venice, 1932; La fiamma, ★Rome 1934; Lucrezia, ★Milan, 1937

Ballets: La boutique fantasque (after Rossini), ★London, 1919; Scherzo veneziano, ★Rome, 1920

Orchestral: Fontane di Roma (Fountains of Rome), 1914-16; Conc gregoriano, with vn, 1921; Pini di Roma (Pines of Rome), 1923-4; Conc in modo misolidio, with pf, 1925; Vetrate di chiesa (Church Windows), 1925; Gli uccelli (The Birds, after hpd pieces), 1927; Trittico botticelliano, 1927; Impressioni brasiliane, 1928; Feste romane (Roman Festivals), 1928; Antiche arie e danze (Ancient Airs and Dances), 3 sets, 1917, 1923, 1931; Conc a 5, ob, tpt, pf, vn, db, str, 1933

Vocal: Lauda per la Natività del Signore, S, Mez, T, chorus, 8 insts, 1928-30; other works

[Bongiovanni, Bote, Ricordi, UE]

Réti, Rudolph (1885-1957) Serbian-American writer on music. Studied in Vienna at the academy and university, and worked there as a pianist and critic before moving to the USA in 1938. He developed a theory of composition as the working-out of small cells, his books including *The Thematic Process in Music* (New York, 1951) and *Tonality-Atonality-Pantonality* (London, 1958). *See* ANALYSIS.

retrograde Playing lines backwards is a stock feature of the canonic art, whence its occurrence in, for example, no. 18 of *Pierrot lunaire*. Schoenberg then made it an integral feature of serialism, retrograding being one of the basic operations to be applied to 12-note sets. The harmonically directed nature of music in the 18th and 19th c. had made retrograding almost impossible (the finale of the *Hammerklavier* Sonata provides the only notable instance), but in the 20th c. it has been quite permissible for music to be turned backwards, whether on the small and abstract scale in 12-note composition or on the larger scale of whole sections in the palindromes of Berg (Chamber Concerto, *Lulu*), Webern (Symphony) and Stravinsky (*Canticum sacrum*).

Revueltas, Silvestre (1899-1940) Mexican composer. Studied in Mexico City (1913-16), at St Ed-

ward College, Austin (1916-18), and with Borowsky and Kochansky at the Chicago Musical College (1918-20, 1922-6). Chávez made him assistant conductor of the Mexico SO (1929-35); he also taught at the national conservatory. His works include vigorous and colourful orchestral scores like *Sensemayá* (1938), influenced by Mexican street music and *The Rite of Spring*. [Southern]

Reynolds, Roger (1934-) American composer. Studied engineering at the University of Michigan, then composition with Finney and Gerhard (1957-60). He took part in the ONCE Festivals and has written for mixed media, often including electronics. In 1969 he was appointed professor at the University of California at San Diego, but he has also worked frequently in Europe, notably at IRCAM. [Peters]

rhythm Nothing is changeless, and so rhythm is an inevitable consequence of all music, since rhythm is the composed and/or perceived alteration of musical elements in TIME. It may therefore be misleading to suggest that 20th c. music has been distinguished by a revival of rhythm: the truth is rather that metre and phrasing have often been lost, so that individual beats become more prominent. *The Rite of Spring* is classically the score that first shows this, through several techniques: the rapid exchange of time signatures so that there is no stable metre, the accenting of events against a prevailing metre, the piling-up of cross rhythms, and the insistence on every beat as of equal importance, producing regular pulsation rather than metre. However, all these techniques can be observed in earlier music by Debussy, Bartók and the Second Viennese School (their atonal works): *The Rite* is therefore not the origin but rather the first emphatic triumph of a new view of rhythm at the extremes of instability and pulsing.

Rhythmic instability has suggested to many composers the possibility of inventing rhythms independently of other parameters. Varèse would seem to be doing this in his percussion polyphonies of unrelated, irregular lines. Messiaen certainly regards rhythm as an independent element when he writes canons that work in terms of durations but not pitches, creates non-retrogradable rhythm, introduces rhythmic formulae taken from a Sanskrit treatise, or interprets number patterns as durations. His dissociation of rhythm from harmonic construction has parallels in such medieval techniques as rhythmic modality and isorhythm, and has influenced Boulez and Stockhausen in moving towards TOTAL SERIALISM (Babbitt, by contrast, has sought an integration of rhythmic and pitch domains in his TIME-POINT system).

Rhythmic pulsation has arisen often through contacts with oriental cultures (Cage, Reich) or rock (Riley, Souster), or else through the imitation of Baroque toccata movement (Stravinsky, Hindemith, Boulez), this sometimes influenced, notably in the 1920s, by a futurist machine aesthetic.

Riegger, Wallingford (1885-1961) American composer. Studied with Goetschius at the New York Institute of Musical Art (1905-7) and with Bruch in Germany (1908-10), where he returned as a conductor in 1914-17. Back in the USA he began seriously to compose (his op.1 was the Piano Trio in B minor, 1919-20), though he soon grew dissatisfied with his thoroughly traditional style. Living in New York, and acquainted with Varèse, Ruggles, Cowell and Ives, he developed through 3 years of silence (1923-6) his own style of atonal counterpoint in driving rhythm.

Orchestral: Study in Sonority, 10 vn or multiple thereof, 1926-7; Dichotomy, chamber orch, 1931-2; Canon and Fugue, 1941; Sym no.3, 1946-7, no.4, 1957; Music for Brass Choir, 1948-9; Variations, with pf, 1953; Dance Rhythms, 1955; Variations, with vn, 1959; Duo, with pf, 1960

Chamber: Str Qt no.1, 1938-9, no.2, 1948, no.3, 1945-7; Pf Qnt, 1951; Nonet, brass, 1951; Wind Qnt, 1952; Conc, pf, wind qnt, 1952; Movement, 2 tpt, trbn, pf, 1957

Ballets, choral pieces, songs, pf music
[AMP, New Music, G. Schirmer]

Rieti, Vittorio (1898-) Italian-American composer. Studied in Milan and, after the first world war, with Respighi in Rome, where he was helped too by Casella. He fell under the influence of Les Six and divided his time between Paris and Rome, composing for Dyagilev (*Barabau*, 1925, choreographed by Balanchine). In 1940 he moved to the USA, teaching in Baltimore (1948-9), Chicago (1950-53) and New York (1955-64), and composing fluently in all genres, especially ballet, orchestral and chamber music. [AMP, UE]

Rihm, Wolfgang (1952-) German composer. Studied at the Karlsruhe Musikhochschule, where he began teaching in 1973. He composes prolifically in an Expressionist style, his works including 5 string quartets and various settings of Nietzsche, Artaud, Hölderlin, Wölfli, etc. [UE]

Riley, Terry (1935-) American composer. Studied with Erickson at the San Francisco State College (1955-7) and at the University of California at Berkeley (1960-61). In 1962-64 he worked in the studios of French radio, where he became interested in the overlapping repetitions of small tonal motifs: his *Keyboard Studies* (1963) and *In C* (1964) were among the early classics of MINIMAL MUSIC. In 1972 he began teaching at Mills College. [Columbia]

Rimsky-Korsakov, Nikolay (1844-1908) Russian composer. Studied at naval cadet school in St Petersburg (1856-62), where he came under the influence of Balakirev. He was then away at sea (1862-5), but resumed his musical activities on his return: he heard Berlioz conduct in Russia in the winter of 1867-8 and became known in the Balakirev circle as a gifted orchestrator (he was later to complete and adapt works by Musorgsky and Borodin). Orchestral works and operas duly loomed large in his output, showing his brilliant instrumentation and his love of the exotic. He also taught, at the St Petersburg Conservatory (1871-1908) and privately, his pupils including Glazunov, Lyadov and Stravinsky. Only his 20th c. works are noted below.

Operas: Servilia, 1900-01, ★St Petersburg, 1902; Kashchey the Immortal, 1901-2, ★Moscow, 1902; Pan Voyevoda, 1902-3, ★St Petersburg, 1904; The Legend of the Invisible City of Kitezh, 1903-5, ★St Petersburg, 1907; The Golden Cockerel, 1906-7

Vocal orchestral: From Homer, S, Mez, A, female vv, orch, 1901

ring modulator Electronic device which produces from 2 inputs of frequencies x and y outputs of $x+y$ and $x-y$. Thus if the inputs are in a simple ratio, e.g. 440 Hz and 220 Hz, the outputs will also be in a simple ratio (in this case 660 Hz and 220 Hz). In other words, the more consonant the inputs, the more consonant the outputs will be: Stockhausen's *Mantra* makes use of this property of ring modulators as monitors of harmony, while other works by him, such as *Mixtur*, use them more to achieve new sonorities from conventional instruments.

Rite of Spring, The (Vesna svyashchennaya, Le sacre du printemps) Ballet by Stravinsky, 'scenes of pagan Russia', to a scenario worked out with Nicolas Roerich, choreographed originally by Nijinsky. There are 2 parts, each moving from a slow and hesitant introduction to a loudly pulsating finale, 'Dance of the Earth' in the first part and 'Sacrificial Dance' in the second. The scoring is for a large orchestra of quintuple woodwind, 8 horns, 5 trumpets, 3 trombones, 2 tubas, percussion and strings. ★Ballets Russes/Monteux, Paris, 29 May 1913.

Rochberg, George (1918-) American composer. Studied with Szell and Mannes at the Mannes School (1939-42), and with Scalero and Menotti at the Curtis Institute (1945-7), where he taught from 1948 to 1954. In 1950 he met Dallapiccola in Rome, and was impressed by the expressive power of 12-note music. He was then an editor for Presser (1951-60) before his appointment as professor at the University of Pennsylvania. His early works lean towards Stravinsky, Hindemith and Bartók, after which came his engagement with Schoenbergian and then, from around 1957, Webernian serialism. In the early 1960s he began to work with collage, quoting from Boulez, Berio, Varèse and Ives in his quartet *Contra mortem et tempus*. His Third Quartet (1972) and later works go beyond quotation to a revival of past styles, notably those of Mahler and the later Beethoven.
Orchestral: Night Music, chamber orch, 1949; Sym no.1, 1949-57, no.2, 1955-6, no. 3, with solo vv and chorus, 1966-9, no. 4, 1976; Cheltenham Conc, small orch, 1958; Time Span, 1962; Apocalyptica, band, 1964; Zodiac, 1965; 3 Black Pieces, 1965; Music for the Magic Theater, 15 insts, 1965; Black Sounds, wind, perc, 1965; Imago mundi, 1973; Vn Conc, 1975
Vocal: David the Psalmist, T, orch, 1954; Blake Songs, S, 8 insts, 1961; Tableaux, S, 11 insts, 1968; Songs in Praise of Krishna, S, pf, 1970; Phaedra, Mez, orch, 1973-4
Chamber: Str Qt no.1, 1952, no.2, with S, 1959-61, no.3, 1972, no.4, 1977, no.5, 1978, no.6, 1978, no.7, 1980; PfTrio, 1963; Contra mortem et tempus, fl, cl, vn, pf, 1965; Electrikaleidoscope, 5 insts, 1972; Pf Qnt, 1975
Piano: 12 Bagatelles, 1952; Bartokiana, 1959; Nach Bach, or hpd, 1966; Carnival Music, 1971
[Presser; Nonesuch, CRI]

Rodrigo, Joaquín (1902-) Spanish composer. Blind from the age of 3, he studied with Antich in Valencia (1920-23) and with Dukas in Paris (1927-32), where he also gained much from an acquaintance with Falla. He remained for the most part in Paris and Gemany until 1939, when he returned to Madrid; he was appointed professor at the university there in 1947. His music is Hispanic

in a lyrical, charming and colourful manner familiar from his ubiquitous *Concierto de Aranjuez* for guitar and orchestra (1939). There are also concertos for piano, violin, cello, harp, flute, guitar duo and guitar quartet. [Chester, Eschig, Schott, Salabert]

Roger-Ducasse, Jean (1873-1954) French composer. Studied with Fauré at the Paris Conservatoire, where he later taught (1935-40); he was also a school music inspector. His works are those of a conscientious, independent mind influenced by Fauré and Debussy: they include the large-scale Faustian cantata *Au jardin de Marguérite* (1901-5), the ballet *Orphée* (★Paris, 1926) and the opera *Cantegril* (★Paris, 1931). [Durand]

Roland-Manuel (Lévy, Roland Manuel) (1891-1966) French composer. Studied with Roussel and Ravel, whose musical follower and biographer he became. He was also closely associated with Stravinsky, contributing much to the latter's *Poetics of Music*: the statement there of an aesthetic of Classical restraint and perfection has more to do with his own music than Stravinsky's. His small output includes operas and ballets, oratorios, orchestral pieces, chamber music and songs. [Durand]

Roldán, Amadeo (1900-1939) Cuban composer. Studied in Madrid with del Campo, then in 1921 settled in Havana, where he revived musical life through his activities as composer, quartet leader, conductor and teacher. A mulatto, he used Afro-Cuban music in his works, together with a *Rite*-like dynamism. His output includes the ballets *La rebambaramba* (1927-8) and *El milagro de Anaquillé* (1928-9, rev. 1931), as well as *Ritmicas I-IV* for wind quintet and piano (1930) and *V-VI* for percussion ensemble (1930), of which the latter were with Varèse's *Ionisation* the first western works for percussion alone. [New Music, Southern]

Romeo and Juliet (Romeo i Dzhuletta) Ballet by Prokofiev after Shakespeare, one of the few full-length ballet scores of high quality. ★Brno, 30 Dec 1938. There are two orchestral suites (1936) and a book of 10 pieces arranged for piano (1937).

Ropartz, Guy (1864-1955) French composer. Studied with Dubois and Massenet at the Paris Conservatoire (1885-6) and privately with Franck, whose circle of devoted admirers he joined. He directed the conservatoires at Nancy (1894-1919) and Strasbourg (1919-29), then retired to his native Brittany, where he continued to compose abundantly. His works include the symphonic poems *La cloche des morts* (1887) and *La chasse du Prince Arthur* (1912), 5 symphonies (1894, 1900, 1905: choral, 1910, 1944) and 6 string quartets (1893, 1911, 1924, 1933, 1940, *c*.1950). [Baudoux, Durand, Lerolle, Schola Cantorum]

Rorem, Ned (1923-) American composer. Studied with Sowerby in Chicago (1938-9), at the Curtis Institute (1943), at the Juilliard School (1945-8) and privately with Thomson, Diamond and Copland. he then lived in Morocco (1949-51) and in Paris (1951-7), where he studied further with Honegger and gained the friendship of Poulenc, Milhaud and Auric. In 1958 he returned to New York. His works include a great many songs and choral pieces, operas, symphonies, chamber music and several diaries of a colourful life in Paris and New York. [Boosey]

Rosenberg, Hilding (1892-1985) Swedish composer. Studied with Eldberg at the Royal Academy in Stockholm (1915-16), and later with Stenhammer. He also visited Germany and Paris in 1920-21, which brought him into creative contact with the music of Schoenberg, Hindemith and Stravinsky, though these influences were to be moulded into a Nordic symphonic style. In the 1930s and 1940s he was active as a conductor in Sweden and abroad; in the 1950s he was important as a teacher.

Operas: Journey to America, ★Stockholm, 1932; Marionettes, ★Stockholm, 1939; The Isle of Felicity, ★Stockholm, 1945; The House with 2 Doors, ★Stockholm, 1970

Radio opera: Joseph and his Brethren, ★Swedish radio, 1946-8

Symphonies: no.1, 1917, rev. 1919, rev. 1971; no.2 (Sinfonia grave), 1928-35; no.3 (The 4 Ages of Man), 1939, rev. 1952; no.4 (The Revelation of St John), Bar, chorus, orch, 1940; no.5 (Hortulanus), A, chorus, orch, 1944; no.6 (Sinfonia semplice), 1951; no.7, 1968; no.8 (In candidum), chorus, orch, 1974

Much other music of all kinds

[Nordiska Musikförlaget]

□ M. Pergament *Hilding Rosenberg* (1956); P.H. Lyne, *Hilding Rosenberg: Catalogue of his Works* (1970)

Rosenkavalier, Der (The Chevalier of the Rose) Opera by Strauss and Hofmannsthal, set in 18th c. Vienna though suffused with sublime anachronism by the waltz. The Marschallin, a grande dame

in early middle age, distances herself from her adolescent lover Oktavian and points him towards the young Sophie: all 3 are soprano roles. A comic subplot centres on the buffo bass Baron Ochs. ★Dresden, 26 Jan 1911. Strauss drew from the score 2 waltz sequences (1911, 1944) and a suite (1945).

Roslavets, Nikolay (1881-1944) Russian Composer. Studied with Vasilenko at the Moscow Conservatory (1902-12), and during the next few years developed a 12-note style out of late Skryabin. After the Revolution he was active in the Association for Contemporary Music, but in 1930 he disappeared from Soviet musical life until his music was revived half a century later, following performances and analytical interest in the west.

Orchestral: Sym 1922; Vn Conc, 1925

Chamber: Nocturne, ob, harp, 2 vn, vc, 1913; Méditation, vc, pf, 1921; Sonata, vc, pf, 1921; 3 danses, vn, pf, 1921; 5 str qts, 1913, ?, 1920, ?, 1941; 3 pf trios, ?,?, 1921; 5 vn sonatas, *c*.1913-14,?,?, *c*.1924, ?

Piano: 3 compositions, 1914; 3 études, 1914; Quasi prélude, Quasi poème, 1915; Prelude, 1915; 5 Preludes, 1919-22; 2 poèmes, 1920; Sonata no.5, 1923

Songs: 3 compositions, 1913; Paysages tristes, 1913; 4 compositions, 1913-14

Choral works, agit-prop songs

Roussel, Albert (1869-1937) French composer. Served in the navy before resigning his commission in 1894 to study in Paris with Gigout, then with d'Indy at the Schola Cantorum (1898-1909). While there he began teaching counterpoint within the school, his pupils including Varèse and Satie; he also wrote several important works. In 1909 he took his new wife on a tour of India and south-east Asia: the exotic in his music, therefore, was learned at first hand. He saw active service in the first world war while writing his Indian opera *Padmâvatî*; then in 1922 he settled on the Normandy coast. His later music became harmonically more acerbic, structurally more clear-cut and rhythmically more forceful, paralleling developments in Ravel and Stravinsky, and contrasting with the Impressionist filigree of his works before the war.

Operas: Padmâvatî, 1914-18, ★Paris, 1923; Le testament de la tante Caroline, 1932-3, ★Olomouc, 14 Nov 1936

Ballets: Le festin de l'araignée, 1912, ★Paris, 1913; Bacchus et Ariane, 1930, ★Paris, 1931; Aenéas, 1935, ★Brussels, 1935

Orchestral: Sym no.1 (Le poème de la forêt), 1904-6, no.2, B♭, 1919-21, no.3, g, 1929-30, no.4, A,

1934; Pour une fête de printemps, 1920; Suite, F, 1926; Conc, small orch, 1926-7; Pf Conc, G, 1927; Little Suite, 1929; Sinfonietta, str, 1934; Rapsodie flamande, 1936; Vc Concertino, 1936

Choral orchestral: Evocations, A, T, Bar, vv, orch, 1910-11; Psalm 80, T, vv, orch, 1928

Chamber: Pf Trio, 1902; Divertissement, wind qnt, pf, 1906; Vn Sonata no.1, d, 1907-8, no.2, A, 1924; Impromptu, harp, 1919; Joueurs de flûte, fl, pf, 1924; Ségovia, gui, 1925; Serenade, fl, harp, str trio, 1925; Trio, fl, va, vc, 1929; Str Qt, D, 1931-2; Andante and Scherzo, fl, pf, 1934; Str Trio, 1937

Songs: 4 poèmes (de Regnier), 2 sets, 1903, 1907; Flammes (Jean-Aubry), 1908, 2 poèmes chinois, 3 sets, 1907-8, 1927, 1932; 2 mélodies (Jean-Aubry, Oliphant), 1918; 2 mélodies (Chalupt), 2 sets, 1919, 1933-4; 2 poèmes (Ronsard), v, fl, 1924; Odes anacréontiques, 2 sets, 1926; Jazz dans la nuit, 1928; 2 idylles, 1931; A Flower Given to my Daughter (Joyce), 1931; 2 mélodies (Ville), 1935

Piano: Rustiques, 1904-6; Suite, f♯, 1909-10; Sonatina, 1912; Prelude and Fugue, 1932-4; 3 Pieces, 1933

[Durand]

□ B. Deane, *Albert Roussel* (1961)

row Alternative name for SERIES

Royan Festival Annual showcase held at the casino of the French Atlantic-coast town from 1964 to 1973, including first performances of works by Barraqué, Xenakis, Amy and others. Along with Donaueschingen, Warsaw and Zagreb it was one of the star venues in the great age of new music festivals.

Rubbra, Edmund (1901-) English composer. Studied with Scott, and with Holst at Reading University (1920-21) and the Royal College of Music (1921-5). He then made a career as a pianist, composer, critic and teacher, notably as lecturer at Oxford (1947-68). In 1948 he converted to Roman Catholicism. His individual style has links with Holst, Ireland, Bax and Vaughan Williams, but with its own contrapuntal energy and diatonic conscientiousness.

Symphonies: no.1, 1935-7; no.2, 1937; no.3, 1939; no.4, 1941; no.5, 1947-8; no.6, 1954; no.7, 1957; no.6, 1966-8; no.9 (Sinfonia sacra), with S, A, Bar, SATB, 1971-2; no.10 (Sinfonia da camera), 1974; no.11, 1978-9

Other works: much choral music, other orch pieces, 4 str qts (1933, 1952, 1962-3, 1976-7), inst music, songs

[Lengnick; Lyrita]

Rudhyar, Dane (Chennevière, Daniel) (1895-) French-American composer. Studied at the Paris Conservatoire (1912-13) but was mostly self-taught. In 1916 he moved to the USA, and in 1926 took citizenship under a Hindu name. During the next few years some of his works appeared under Cowell's New Music imprint, showing a strong Skryabin influence, but after 1930 he devoted himself less to composition than to astrology. [New Music, Presser]

Ruggles, Carl (1876-1971) American composer. Studied with Paine at Harvard (1903-7), then worked as a conductor in Winona, Minnesota. After 1917 he divided his time between New York and Vermont, supported by patronage in his activities as composer and painter. Apart from a hymn tune composed as a memorial to his wife, all his works date from 3 decades after the first world war, when he was in touch with Varèse, Cowell and Ives: Varèse had his music performed by the International Composers' Guild, Cowell published it in his New Music edition, and Ives respected another American prepared not to be cosy. Ruggles' music is, however, much more integrated than Ives's, being marked by long, thrusting lines in atonal counterpoint of compact form.

Orchestral: Men and Mountains, 1924; Portals, str, 1925; Sun-Treader, 1926-31; Organum, 1944-7

Vocal: Toys, v, pf, 1919; Vox clamans in deserto, S, small orch, 1923; Exaltation, unison vv, 1958

Chamber: Mood, vn, pf, *c*.1918; Angels, 6/7 brass, 1938; Evocations, pf, 1935-43

[New Music, American Music Edition; Columbia]

Russolo, Luigi (1885-1947) Italian composer. Associated first with Futurism as a painter, he published a manifesto in 1913 calling for an art of noises, and later the same year demonstrated the first of his intonarumori, constructed to make such a thing possible. In his last years he returned to painting.

Rzewski, Frederic (1938-) American composer and pianist. Studied with Thompson and Spies at Harvard (1954-8) and with Strunk at Princeton (1958-60). During the next decade he was mostly in Europe: he gave the first performance of Stockhausen's *Klavierstück X* (1962) and was a founder member of Musica Elettronica Viva. His work with this ensemble took on political overtones, and the pieces he has composed since returning to the USA in 1971, mostly evoking comparisons with virtuoso piano works of the 19th c., have been vehemently committed to left-wing protest. In 1977 he took a teaching post at the Liège Conservatory.

Les moutons de Panurge, any insts, 1969; Coming Together, speaker, insts, 1972; The People United will never be Defeated, pf, 1975; A Long Time Man, pf, orch, ★1980

S

Sacher, Paul (1906-) Swiss patron and conductor. Studied in Basle and in 1926 founded his Basle Chamber Orchestra, for whom he commissioned works from Stravinsky, Bartók, Honegger, Martin, Britten and many others. He also supported contemporary composers through his work at the Basle Music Academy, of which he was founder principal (1954-69), and through his assembling of one of the most important collections of 20th c. manuscripts. Boulez, Lutosławski, Holliger and others wrote works for his seventieth birthday.

Saint François d'Assise Opera by Messiaen in 8 tableaux portraying moments in the spiritual life of the saint. The work is scored for soloists with a chorus of 150 and an orchestra of 120, including 3 ondes martenot. ★Paris, 28 Nov 1983.

Saint-Saëns, Camille (1835-1921) French composer. A contemporary of Brahms, he is the earliest composer considered here, and merits inclusion simply because he remained active as a composer to the end of his long life, after the deaths of Mahler and Debussy. His best music, however, had been composed long before the 20th c. began, and he was intolerant of new developments: he disparaged Debussy and was horrified by The Rite. Nevertheless, his late music often shows qualities of leanness and elegance comparable with the contemporary output of his friend Fauré or even of Ravel. Only his 20th c. works are noted below.

Orchestral: Vc Conc no.2, d, 1902; Caprice andalous, vn, orch, 1904; Ouverture de fête, 1910; Morceau de concert, harp, orch, 1918; Cyprès et lauriers, org, orch, 1919; Odelette, fl, orch, 1920

Chamber: Vc Sonata no.2, F, 1905; Str Qt no.2, G, 1918; Ob Sonata, D, 1921; Cl Sonata, E♭, 1921; Bn Sonata, G, 1921

Operas, choral music, songs, pf and org pieces

Sallinen, Aulis (1935-) Finnish composer. Studied with Merikanto and Kokkonen at the Sibelius Academy in Helsinki (1955-60), where he joined the staff in 1965. After using 12-note methods in his music of the 1960s, he began around 1970 to work on a Sibelian time scale, and to integrate diatonic concords with clusters of a Ligetian kind. His first 3 symphonies seemed to mark him out as Sibelius's most likely successor, but since the mid-1970s he has made a name also as a composer of opera, in a boldly eclectic style.

Operas: The Horseman, 1973-4, ★Savonlinna, 1976; The Red Line, 1977-8, ★Helsinki, 1978; The King Goes Forth to France, 1982-3, ★Savonlinna, 1984

Orchestral: Mauermusik, 1962; Vn Conc, 1968; Chorali, 1970; Sym no.1, 1971, no.2, with perc solo, 1972, no.3, 1975, no.4, 1979; Chamber Music I, str, 1975, II, a fl, str, 1976; Vc Conc, 1976

Chamber: Str Qt no.1, 1958, no.2, 1960, no.3, 1969, no.4, 1971, no.5, 1983; Sonata, vc, 1971; Canto and Ritornello, vn, 1975

Choral works, songs

[Fazer, Novello]

Salome Opera by Strauss to Hedwig Lachmann's German translation of the Wilde play, concerning the Herodian princess's destructive sexual fascination with John the Baptist. ★Dresden, 9 Dec 1905.

Salzburg Site of the first ISCM Festival in 1923 and regularly of the Salzburg Festival, which has given the first performances of Strauss's *Die Liebe der Danae*, Henze's *The Bassarids* and Berio's *Un re in ascolto*.

Salzedo, Carlos (1885-1961) French-American composer and harpist. Studied at the Paris Conservatoire (1896-1901) and moved to New York to take a post as harpist with the Metropolitan Opera (1909-13). He then worked as a chamber musician, teacher and co-founder with Varèse of the International Composers' Guild, though his own works have more in common with Ravel and Hindemith than with the modernist world of that organization. All of them involve the harp, whether as soloist (*Scintillation*, 1936; Suite, 1943; *Prélude fatidique*, 1954), or with other instruments (Sonata with pf, 1922; Concerto with 7 wind, 1925-6), or in ensembles (*Bolmimerie*, 7 harps, 1919; *Pentacle*, 2 harps, 1928).

[G. Schirmer]

Samstag aus Licht (Saturday from Light) Opera by Stockhausen to his own libretto, the second completed of his 7-evening cycle *Licht*. It is in 4 separately performable scenes: *Luzifers Traum, oder Klavierstück XIII* (Lucifer's Dream, or Piano Piece XIII), a fantastic sequence of pianism dreamed by the solo bass as Lucifer; *Kathinkas Gesang als Luzifers Requiem* (Kathinka's Song as Lucifer's Requiem), a long mimed and played solo for the flautist Kathinka Pasveer with 6 percussionists; *Luzifers Tanz* (Lucifer's Dance), a ballet scored for wind band disrupted by Michael's entrance as trumpeter; and *Luzifers Abschied* (Lucifer's Farewell), a slow ceremonial for chanting male chorus, organ and trombones. There is also an overture *Samstags-Gruss* (Saturday's Greeting) for brass and percussion. *Milan, 25 May 1984.

Satie, Erik (1866-1925) French composer. His independence, simplicity and irony opened him to a variety of canonizations: as the discoverer of new harmonic possibilities for Debussy, as the furnisher of blankness for Cocteau, and as the pioneer of non-intention for Cage. He was all of these, though whether by accident or design it is hard to know, just as it is difficult to be sure whether the baldness of much of his music is chosen or merely the result of weakness of technique. Certainly he himself felt insecure about his competence, to the extent of taking lessons in counterpoint, fugue and orchestration with Roussel and d'Indy at the Schola Cantorum in 1905-8, long after his undistinguished attendance at the Paris Conservatoire (1879-86).

His first important works were the sets of three *Sarabandes* (1887), *Gymnopédies* (1888) and *Gnossiennes* (1890), where his harmonic venturings run to unresolved 7ths and 9ths and a revival of church modes. This came about as part of an absorption in medieval Christianity, which led him to an association with the Rosicrucian movement: most of his works of 1891-5 were written for imaginary esoteric ceremonies. It was also during this period that he met Debussy, while his other activities included playing the piano at the Chat Noir café in Montmartre, where he lived.

In 1898 he moved to the industrial suburb of Arcueil-Cachan, but he continued to work as a café pianist (and composer) in Montmartre, walking to and fro each day. Some of his café music went into the *3 morceaux en forme de poire* (3 Pear-Shaped Pieces: in fact there are 7) for piano duet, allegedly named so because Debussy had criticized his form. Otherwise he wrote little until 1913, when the championship of Viñes, Ravel and, from 1915, Cocteau made him fashionable. Dyàgilev com-

missioned a ballet, *Parade*, which is a suite of small pieces laid out for an orchestra including typewriter and siren, but most of his miniatures were for the piano, often having absurd titles and always in a flat, repetitive style. He continued, though, to work with novel harmonies, such as chords in 2nds, 4ths, 5ths and 7ths in the second of the 5 Nocturnes (1919), and in the music for a film sequence in his ballet *Relâche* he anticipated Antheil and Cage in planning music by the duration of sections. Meanwhile his cultivation of bareness extended to such relatively ambitious projects as the 'symphonic drama' *Socrate*, a half hour chant in plainsong modality with totally unassuming instrumental support, as well as to FURNITURE MUSIC, written to be ignored. With Cocteau's imprimatur he became the model for Les SIX, replaced in 1923 by the Ecole d'Arcueil of Cliquet-Pleyel, Désormière, Sauget and Jacob. Despite all his admirers, however, he has remained inimitable.

Orchestral: En habit de cheval, 1911; 5 grimaces, 1914; Parade (ballet), 1917; La belle excentrique, 1920; Mercure (ballet), 1924; Relâche (ballet), 1924
Larger vocal works: Messe des pauvres, chorus, org/pf, 1895; Geneviève de Brabant (marionette opera), vv, pf, 1899; Socrate, v/vv, orch, 1918
Songs: Elégie, 3 mélodies, Chanson, 1887; Salut drapeau!, 1891; Bonjour Biqui!, 1893; Tendrement, Je te veux, Le diva de l'Empire, *c*.1900; 3 poèmes d'amour, 1914; 3 méodies, 1916; 4 petites mélodies, 1920; Ludions, 1923
Piano duet: 3 morceaux en forme de poire, 1890-1903; En habit de cheval, 1911; Aperçus désagréables, 1908-12; Parade, 1917; La belle excentrique, 1920; 3 petites pièces montées, *c*.1920
Piano solo: Allegro, 1884; Valse-ballet, Fantaisie-valse, 1885; 4 ogives, 1886; 3 sarabandes, 1887; 3 gymnopédies, 1888; 3 gnossiennes, 1890; Première pensée Rose+Croix, 1891; Le fils des étoiles, 3 preludes, 1891; Fête donnée par des Chevaliers Normands, 2 préludes du Nazaréen, Uspud, 1892; Vexations, *c*.1893; Prélude d'Eginhard, Danses gothiques, Modéré, 1893; Prélude de la porte héroïque du ciel, 1894; Pièces froides, 1897; Jack-in-the-Box, 1899; Poudre d'or, *c*.1901; Le Piccadilly, *c*.1904; Prélude en tapisserie, Passacaille, 1906; Nouvelles pièces froides, 1906-10; 4 préludes flasques, 3 véritables préludes flasques, 1912; Le piège de méduse, Descriptions automatiques, Embryons desséchés, Croquis et agaceries d'un gros bonhomme en bois, Chapitres tournés en tous sens, Vieux sequins et vieilles cuirasses, Menus propos enfantins, Engantillages pittoresques, Pecadilles importunes, Les pantins

dansent, 1913; Sports et divertissements, Heures séculaires et instantanées, Les 3 valses du précieux dégoûté, 1914; Avant-dernières pensées, 1915; Sonatine bureaucratique, 1917; 5 Nocturnes, 1919; Rêverie de l'enfance de Pantagruel, *c*.1920; Premier menuet, 1920

Chamber: Le piège de méduse, 8 insts, 1913; Choses vues à droite et à gauche (sans lunettes), vn, pf, 1914; Musique d'ameublement (with Milhaud), pf, 3 cl, trbn, 1920; Sonnerie pour reveiller le bon gros Roi des Singes, 2 tpt, 1921

[Rouart Lerolle, Salabert, UE]

□ R. Myers, *Erik Satie* (1948); *The Writings of Erik Satie*, ed. N. Wilkins (1976)

Sauguet, Henri (1901-) French composer. Born and brought up in Bordeaux, he studied there with Canteloube, then went to Paris in 1923 on Milhaud's encouragement and joined the Ecole d'Arcueil around Satie. His large output ranges from operas to *musique concrète*, but includes most notably a number of ballets (*La chatte*, choreographed by Balanchine for Dyagilev, 1925). [Heugel, Salabert, Eschig, Ricordi]

saxophone The alto in Eb and tenor in Bb are common in the 20th c. orchestra (e.g. in Bartók's *Wooden Prince*); much rarer are the soprano in Bb (Birtwistle's *The Triumph of Time*), the baritone in Eb (Stockhausen's *Gruppen*) and the bass in C (Schoenberg's *Von heute auf morgen*). The solo repertory includes Debussy's *Rapsodie* with piano, Hindemith's Sonata with piano, and concertos by Glazunov and Muldowney, all for alto saxophone; there is also a repertory of quartets for soprano, alto, tenor and baritone.

Saxton, Robert (1953-) English composer. Studied with Lutyens (1970-74), with Holloway at Cambridge, and with Berio, then taught in London, Oxford and Bristol. His early works, e.g. *Echos of the Glass Bead Game* for wind quintet (1975), are fastidiously worked in a Boulezian style of ornamentation, which has gradually gained a stronger harmonic motive power in such pieces as his Concerto for Orchestra (1983-4). [Chester]

Schaeffer, Pierre (1910-) French composer. Studied at the Ecole Polytechnique and joined French radio as a technician in 1936. In 1948 he created the first pieces of *musique concréte*: Etude violette, Etude au piano, Etude aux tourniquets, Etude aux chemins de fer and Etude pathétique. He then welcomed professional composers into his studio, which in 1951

was established as the Groupe de Musique Concrète, and he worked with Henry on the *Symphonie pour un homme seul* (1950-51) and electronic opera *Orphée 53* (1953). But that year he left the group, to return only briefly in 1958-60, when his works included *Etude aux allures* (1958), *Etude aux sons animés* (1958) and *Etude aux objets* (1959). Afterwards he abandoned composition for teaching and theoretical divagations.

Schafer, Raymond Murray (1933-) Canadian composer. Studied at the Toronto Conservatory (1945-55) and with Weinzweig at Toronto University (1954-5), then moved to Europe (1956-61). He went back to Canada to teach at Memorial University, Newfoundland (1963-5) and Simon Fraser University, BC (1965-). His view of music is global, embracing concerns with education and noise pollution; his compositions, too, tend to use a wide variety of means and reference points. His books include *British Composers in Interview* (London, 1963), *The New Soundscape* (Toronto, 1969, 3/ 1972), *The Book of Noise* (Vancouver, 1970, 2/ 1973), *The Music of Ezra Pound* (New York, 1974), *E.T.A. Hoffmann and Music* (Toronto, 1975) and *The Tuning of the World* (New York, 1977), as well as pamphlets on working with children.

Schat, Peter (1935-) Dutch composer. Studied with van Baaren at the Utrecht Consevatory (1952-8), with Seiber in London and with Boulez in Basle (1960-62). Boulez was a strong influence on his early works, though he already showed an independent mind: his *Improvisations and Symphonies* for wind quintet (1960) was perhaps the first work requiring players to move about. In 1967 he visited Cuba, and most of his subsequent works have been politically motivated, often with a Pousseur-like search for a versatile harmonic organization. His works include the operas *Labyrinth* (1961-2) and *Houdini* (1974-6), 2 symphonies, etc. [Donemus; Composers' Voice]

Schenker, Heinrich (1868-1935) Austrian theorist. Studied with Bruckner at the Vienna Conservatory, and remained in the city as a pianist, composer, teacher and writer on music. His compositions were admired by Brahms, but his main contribution was in the field of ANALYSIS.

Scherchen, Hermann (1891-1966) German conductor. Mainly self-taught, he assisted Schoenberg in preparing *Pierrot lunaire*, and made his début conducting that work in 1912. In 1919 he founded *Melos*, and from the 1920s onwards he was widely active as a conductor, particularly of new music. He settled in Switzerland in 1933. Among the works he performed for the first time were Berg's *Wozzeck* fragments, Webern's orchestral Variations, the 'Dance around the Golden Calf' from Schoenberg's *Moses und Aron*, Dallapiccola's *Il prigioniero*, Henze's *König Hirsch* and Nono's *Intolleranza*.

Schillinger, Joseph (1895-1943) Russian-American teacher and composer. Studied at the Petrograd Conservatory (1914-18), then worked in Russia as a teacher, conductor and composer (*October* for piano and orchestra, 1927). In 1928 he moved to the USA, where he taught his own system of composition, notionally based on mathematical principles, in New York. Gershwin and Brown were among his pupils.
□ J. Schillinger, *The Mathematical Basis of the Arts* (1948, r1976)

Schmidt, Franz (1874-1939) Austrian composer. Studied the piano with Leschetizky and composition with Bruckner at the Vienna Conservatory. He was then cellist in the Vienna Court Opera orchestra (1896-1911), playing for much of that time under Mahler; afterwards he taught at the Vienna Academy (1914-37). He admired, and was admired by, Schoenberg, but his own fidelity to the great Austro-German tradition took a different form, that of diatonic and polyphonic symphonism having close connections with Brahms, Bruckner and Reger.
Operas: Notre Dame, 1902-4; Fredigundis, 1916-21
Oratorio: Das Buch mit 7 Siegeln, 1935-7
Orchestral: Sym no.1, E, 1896-9, no.2, E♭, 1911-13, no.3, A, 1927-8, no.4, C, 1932-3; Concertante Variations on a Theme of Beethoven, with pf left hand, 1923; Variationen über ein Husarenlied, 1930-31; Pf Conc, E♭, left hand, 1934; Fuga solemnis, wind, org, timp, 1937
Chamber: Str Qt, A, 1925; Pf Qnt, G, 1926; Str Qt, G, 1929; Qnt, B♭, cl, pf qt, 1932; Qnt, A, cl, pf qt, 1938
Organ: Fantasia and Fugue, D, 1923-4; Toccata, C, 1924; Prelude and Fugue, E♭, 1924; Chaconne, c♯, 1925; 4 Little Chorale Preludes, 1926; Fugue, F, 1927; Prelude and Fugue, E♭ 1927; 4 Little Preludes and Fugues, 1928; Chorale Prelude 'Gott erhalte', 1933; Chorale Prelude 'Der Heiland ist erstanden', 1934; Toccata and Fugue, A♭, 1935
Piano: Toccata, d, left hand, 1938
[Doblinger, UE]

□ H. Truscott, *The Music of Franz Schmidt*, vol.1: *The Orchestral Music* (1984)

Schmitt, Florent (1870-1958) French composer. Studied with Massenet and Fauré at the Paris Conservatoire, then travelled in Europe as winner of the Prix de Rome (1900). During the next few years he produced the 3 works by which he is remembered: the setting of Psalm 47 for soprano, chorus and orchestra (1904), the ballet *La tragédie de Salomé* (1907) and the Piano Quintet (1902-8), all showing a melding of influences from Debussy and Strauss. The strongly accented rhythms of *Salomé* look forward to *The Rite of Spring*, though since Schmitt revised his work in 1910 the origins of both may be in *The Firebird*. In any event, he was an early associate of Stravinsky's in Paris, and dedicatee of one of the Japanese Lyrics. He continued to write orchestral, large-scale choral and chamber music until his death. [Durand]

Schnabel, Artur (1882-1951) Austrian-American pianist and composer. Studied with Leschetizky in Vienna, then lived in Berlin (1900-33), Switzerland and the USA. During the 1930s and 1940s he made classic recordings of Beethoven and Schubert; 20th c. music featured little in his intimately known world as a performer, though as a composer he used 12-note principles, his works including 3 symphonies, 5 quartets and the late *Duodecimet*.
□ C. Saerchinger, *Artur Schnabel* (1957)

Schnebel, Dieter (1930-) German composer. Studied theology and music in Freiburg (1949-55) and was ordained as a Lutheran pastor, then taught in Kaiserslautern (1955-63), Frankfurt (1963-70) and Munich (1970-). Influenced by Kagel, he has worked with widened vocal resources (*Maulwerke*, 1968, etc), silence (*Nostalgie* for solo conductor, 1962), music for reading (*mo-no*, 1969) and arrangements of BACH, Beethoven, Webern and Wagner. [Schott; Wergo]

Schoeck, Othmar (1886-1957) Swiss composer. Studied at the Zurich Conservatory (1905-7) and with Reger at the Leipzig Conservatory (1907-8), then returned to Switzerland as composer, conductor and piano accompanist. His main works are the operas and almost 400 songs of German late Romantic character.
Operas: Don Ranudo de Colibrados, 1917-18, *Zurich, 1919; Venus, 1919-20, *Zurich, 1922; Penthesilea, 1924-5, *Dresden, 1927; Vom Fischer

159

und syner Fru, 1928-30, *Dresden, 1930; Massi-
milla Doni, 1934-5, *Dresden, 1937; Das Schloss
Dürande, 1938-9, *Berlin, 1943
[Bärenreiter, Breitkopf, Hug, UE]

Schoenberg (Schönberg), **Arnold** (1874-1951)
Austrian-American composer. With Stravinsky
one of the essential creators of 20th c. music. For
Adorno and many other writers of his generation
these 2 were polar opposites, Schoenberg advanc-
ing from within the central tradition and Stravinsky retreating into that tradition from a position
outside. This view has since been widely modified,
and Schoenberg seen as quite as much a manipula-
tor of history as Stravinsky. Nevertheless,
Schoenberg was Stravinsky's antitype in his insistence on symphonic development and on originality of idea and form. Originality was necessary because only the original could be the authentic expression of an inner vision; symphonic development was essential because this was how ideas
must be exposed and explored for the comprehen-
sion of the music's listeners. Originality obliged
him in 1908 to go beyond the norms of tonality and
form; symphonic development urged him during
the next 15 years to work out the new framework
of 12-NOTE COMPOSITION. Meanwhile his defence
of the double discipline of being new and being
logical made him one of the greatest teachers in the
history of music, his pupils including not only
Berg and Webern but also Eisler and Cage.

He was born in Vienna, the eldest of 3 children in
an orthodox Jewish family of modest means. After
his father's death he had to work in a bank to support the family (1891-5), but he pursued his musical interests, playing chamber music with friends,
taking some lessons with Zemlinsky, and composing. His D major String Quartet (1897), unpublished until after his death, is closer to Dvořák than
to Brahms (his parents were of Hungarian-Czech
origin), but the string sextet *Verklärte Nacht* (1899)
is already more earnest, combining a Brahmsian
imperative for development (and a Brahmsian
medium) with *Tristan* harmony and a Straussian
richness of colour. In songs of the same period, not
least the later orchestrated GURRELIEDER, the rich
polyphony, energetic line and sometimes contras-
tingly static, unresolved harmonies of his early
style are used to suggest deep emotional states.

In 1901 he married Zemlinsky's sister Mathilde
and moved to Berlin where he worked in a cabaret.
He also wrote *Pelleas und Melisande* (1902-3), a
symphonic poem with an extraordinary long,
polyphonic development section, bringing

together Strauss and Reger: Strauss was impressed, and recommended him to the Stern Conservatory in Berlin, where he started his career as a
teacher. But in 1903 he returned to Vienna and
there taught privately, Berg and Webern becoming his pupils in the next year. Also in 1903 *Verklärte Nacht* was first performed (it had been turned
down in 1899 as containing an inadmissible chord)
and his music began to be published.

His style now developed rapidly. In his First
Quartet (1905) and first CHAMBER SYMPHONY
(1906) he drew all 4 movements into a single span
of development, ranging into barely tonal regions.
Then in the last movement of his Second Quartet
and in *Das* BUCH DER HÄNGENDEN GÄRTEN he abandoned tonality altogether, as very soon did
Webern and, with more misgivings, Berg. During
the next few years he lived creatively outside the
known musical world: his pieces tended to be short
(in op.19 very short) or else sustained by a dramatic
argument (ERWARTUNG, *Die* GLÜCKLICHE HAND).
He also turned to painting, and began a correspondence with Kandinsky: both artists felt themselves at this stage pressed to forsake technique and
tradition (*see* EXPRESSIONISM), though Schoenberg
was also completing his harmony treatise.

Between 1911 and 1915 he again spent much of
his time in Berlin, where he made his conducting
début at the premiere of PIERROT LUNAIRE. He then
served in the Austrian army (1915-16) before starting his oratorio *Die* JAKOBSLEITER, the unfinished
testimony to the religious direction his thoughts
were taking. Meanwhile he was working towards
the principles of serialism, once more teaching in
Vienna, and running the SOCIETY FOR PRIVATE
MUSICAL PERFORMANCES. In 1923 he completed his
first serial works, opp.23-4 and the wholly 12-note
op.25. That year too his wife died, and 10 months
later he married Gertrud Kolisch, the sister of
Rudolf KOLISCH.

In 1925 he returned once more to Berlin to take
over Busoni's master classes in composition at the
Prussian Academy of Arts. There he worked with
confidence, producing chamber works, orchestral
pieces, choruses and even a comic opera all in the
12-note system but within a more normal musical
world where his reference points were Brahms,
Mozart, Reger and Mahler. He also wrote the first
2 acts of his opera *Moses und Aron*. But then in 1933
his Jewishness became a political issue. He immediately left the academy for Paris, where he formally returned to the Jewish faith (he had converted to Lutheranism in 1898 but only briefly been
a Christian believer). Later the same year he moved

to the USA, and in 1934 settled in Los Angeles for health reasons.

He remained there for the rest of his life, composing and teaching at UCLA (1936-44). In 1932-4 he had returned to tonal composition in his updating of concertos by G. M. Monn (Cello Concerto), and Handel (String Quartet Concerto), as well as in the original Suite for strings. From this point tonal and 12-note works alternated in his output, the former including the long-delayed completion of his Chamber Symphony no.2 and the Theme and Variations for wind band. The serial instrumental works, including the concertos for violin and piano and the Fourth Quartet, all show a new richness that came from a deepened understanding of how the 12-note system might be used to create large forms as whole and subtle as those of major-minor tonality. There is also in KOL NIDRE, the ODE TO NAPOLEON and SURVIVOR FROM WARSAW a revival of Expressionist intensity, though now contained within ample rhetorical gestures. The first and last express too his Jewishness, whose theological and Zionist aspects underlie his last works.

Operas: ERWARTUNG, op.17, 1909; Die GLÜCKLICHE HAND, op.18, 1910-13; VON HEUTE AUF MORGEN, op.32, 1928-9; MOSES UND ARON, 1930-32

Orchestral: Verklärte Nacht, op.4, str, arr. 1917, rev. 1943; Pelleas und Melisande, op.5, 1902-3; Chamber Sym no.1, op.9, arr. 1922, rev. 1935; Str Qt no.2, op.10, S, str, arr. ?1919; 5 Pieces, op. 16, 1909; Variations op.31, 1926-8; Begleitmusik zu einer Lichtspielscene (Accompaniment to a Film Scene), op.34, 1929-30; Vc Conc (after Monn), 1932-3; Str Qt Conc (after Handel), 1933; Suite, G, str 1934; Vn Conc, op.36, 1935-6; Chamber Sym no.2, op.38, 1906-16, 1939; Pf Conc, op.42, 1942; Theme and Variations, op.43a, concert band, 1943, arr. orch as op. 43b, 1943

Choral orchestral: GURRELIEDER, with solo vv, 1900-11; Die JAKOBSLEITER, with solo vv, 1917-22, unfinished; KOL NIDRE, op.39, with speaker, 1938; Prelude 'Genesis', op.44, 1945; A SURVIVOR FROM WARSAW, op.46, with speaker, 1947; MODERN PSALM, op.50c, with speaker, 1950, unfinished

Other choral works: Friede auf Erden (C.F. Meyer), op.13, 8vv, 1907; Der deutsche Michel (Kernstock), male vv, 1914 or 1915; 4 Pieces, op.27, SATB with 4 insts in no.4, 1925; 3 Satires (Schoenberg), SATB with 3 insts in no.3, 1925: 3 Folksongs, SATB, 1929; 6 Pieces (Schoenberg), op.35, male vv, 1929-30; 3 Folksongs, op.49, SATB, 1948; Dreimal tausend Jahre (D.D. Runes), op.50a, SATB, 1949; De profundis, op.50b, SSATBB, 1950

Chamber: Str Qt, D, 1897; Verklärte Nacht, op.4, 2 vn, 2 va, 2 vc, 1899; Ein Stelldichein, 5 insts, 1905, unfinished; Str Qt no.1, op.7, d, 1904-5, no.2, op.10, f♯, 1907-8, no.3, op.30, 1927, no.4, op.37, 1936; Chamber Sym no.1, op.9, E, 15 insts, 1906; 3 Pieces, 12 insts, 1910; Die eiserne Brigade, pf qnt, 1916; Serenade, op.24, 7 insts with B in 1 movement, 1920-23; Weihnachtsmusik, 5 insts, 1921; Wind Qnt, op.26, 1923-4; Suite, op.29, 7 insts, 1925-6; Str Trio, op.45, 1946; Phantasy, op.47, vn, pf, 1949

Songs: 2 Songs, op.1, Bar, pf, ?1898; 4 Songs, op.2, v, pf, 1899; Lied der Waldtaube (from Gurrelieder), Mez, 17 insts, arr. 1922; 8 cabaret songs, 1901; 6 Songs, op.3, Mez/Bar, pf, 1899-1903; 8 Songs, op.6, v, pf, 1903-5; 6 Songs, op.8, v, orch, 1903-5; 2 Ballads, op.12, v, pf, 1907; 2 Songs, op.14, v, pf, 1907; Das BUCH DER HÄNGENDEN GÄRTEN, op.15, v, pf, 1908-9; Am Strande, v, pf, 1909 or 1908; Herzgewächse (Maeterlinck), op.20, S, cel, harp, harmonium, 1911; 4 Songs, op.22, v, orch, 1913-16; 4 Folksong Arrangements, v, pf, 1929; 3 Songs, op.48, A/B, pf, 1933

Melodramas: PIERROT LUNAIRE, op.21, 1912; ODE TO NAPOLEON BUONAPARTE, op.41, 1942

Piano: 3 Pieces, op.11, 1909; 6 Little Pieces, op.19, 1911; 5 Pieces, op.23, 1920-23; Suite, op.25, 1921-3; Piece, op.33a, 1928-9; Piece, op.33b, 1931

Organ: Variations on a Recitative, op.40, 1941

Orchestrations: Bach: 2 chorale preludes, 1922; Bach: Prelude and Fugue, E♭, 1928; Brahms: Pf Qt, g, 1937

Many other arrangements, canons

[UE, Hansen, G. Schirmer, Schott]

□ A. Schoenberg, *Letters* (1964), *Style and Idea* (1975), *Harmonielehre* (1978); C. Rosen, *Schoenberg* (1975); H.H. Stuckenschmidt, *Arnold Schoenberg* (1977)

Schreker, Franz (1878-1934) Austrian composer. Studied with Fuchs at the Vienna Conservatory (1892-1900), and taught from 1912 at the Academy of Music there. He was also a conductor, giving the first performance of Schoenberg's *Gurrelieder*. His own creative powers were established by *Der ferne Klang*, which draws on Strauss, Mahler and Debussy to create a rich milieu for the dramatization of sensuality (Berg made the piano score, and remembered the experience when he came to write *Lulu*). The more Wagnerian *Die Gezeichneten* and *Der Schatzgräber* confirmed his reputation, and in 1920 he was invited to Berlin as director of the Hochschule für Musik. His later operas took on something of Hindemithian neoclassicism, but his reputation was already waning and his music was then little performed until the 1970s.

Operas: Der ferne Klang, *c.*1901-10, ★Frankfurt, 1912; Das Spielwerk und die Prinzessin, 1909-12, ★Frankfurt and Vienna, 1913; Die Gezeichneten, 1913-15, ★Frankfurt, 1918; Der Schatzgräber, 1915-18, ★Frankfurt, 1920; Irrelohe, 1919-23, ★Cologne, 1924; Christophorus, 1924-7; Der singende Teufel, 1924-8, ★Berlin, 1928; Der Schmied von Gent, 1929-32, ★Berlin, 1932

Other works: Chamber Sym, 23 insts, 1916; songs, mostly early
[UE]

Schuller, ˙Gunther (1925-) American composer and conductor. Studied at the St Thomas Choir School in New York (1938-42), then worked as a horn player with the Cincinnati Symphony (1943-5) and Metropolitan Opera (1945-59). He has also taught at the Manhattan School of Music (1950-63), Yale (1964-7), the New England Conservatory (1967-77) and Tanglewood. His interest in jazz has produced scholarly studies and THIRD STREAM music (e.g. *Conversations* for jazz quartet and string quartet, 1959). Most of his works are for orchestra or chamber ensemble, drawing on influences from Stravinsky, Varèse, Schoenberg and Babbitt as well as jazz. [AMP, UE]

Schuman, William (1910-) American composer. Studied at Columbia (1933-7) and at the Juilliard School with Harris (1936-8), who was the main influence on his driving, brilliant style of grand symphonism. He taught at Sarah Lawrence College (1935-45) and was president of the Juilliard School (1945-62) and of the Lincoln Center (1962-9). His works include 10 symphonies. [G. Schirmer, Presser]

Schwantner, Joseph (1943-) American composer. Studied at Chicago Conservatory College and Northwestern University (1964-8), and was appointed to the Eastman School in 1970. His works consist mostly of orchestral and chamber music, often for unusual ensembles.

Schweigsame Frau, Die (The Silent Woman) Opera by Strauss and Zweig after Ben Jonson's comedy *Epicoene*, updated to 1780 and bending towards Italian style. ★Dresden, 24 Jun 1935.

Scott, Cyril (1879-1970) English composer. Studied with Humperdinck and Knorr at the Hoch Conservatory in Frankfurt (1891-3, 1895-8), then lived in Liverpool as a composer and teacher. He became a devotee of Indian philosophy and other occultisms, reflected in the Skryabinesque character of his works, which include 3 symphonies, 2 piano concertos, many chamber works in standard genres, 3 piano sonatas and much other piano music. [Boosey, Novello, Schott, UE]

Scriabin *See* SKRYABIN

Sculthorpe, Peter (1929-) Australian composer. Studied at Melbourne University (1946-51) and with Rubbra and Wellesz at Oxford (1958-61); in 1963 he joined the staff at Sydney University. As a composer he has sought to be specifically Australian, using aborigine folklore and the music of neighbouring territories, especially Bali, often in bold, simple designs. His works include the opera *Rites of Passage* (★Sydney, 1974), a *Sun Music* cycle for orchestra and a sequence of quartets. [Faber]

Searle, Humphrey (1915-82) English composer. Studied at Oxford (1933-7), with Jacob, Morris and Vaughan Williams at the Royal College of Music (1937) and with Webern in Vienna (1937-8). Webern influenced his textures even before he began using the 12-note system, in 1946. His works include 3 powerful early cantatas (*Gold Coast Customs*, 1949; *The Riverrun*, 1951; *Shadow of Cain*, 1951), a Lisztian 12-note Piano Sonata (1951); and the opera *Hamlet* (★Hamburg, 1968). [Faber, Schott]

secondary set 12-note set formed from the second hexachord of a set and the first of a different form of the same set.

Second Viennese School Umbrella term for Schoenberg, Berg and Webern, sometimes understood to include other Schoenberg pupils, even those who, like Skalkottas, studied with him in Berlin. The idea is about as misleading as the notion that there was a 'first Viennese school' including Haydn, Mozart, Beethoven and Schubert.

Seiber, Mátyás (1905-60) Hungarian-British composer. Studied with Kodály at the Budapest Academy of Music (1919-24), then taught at the Hoch Conservatory in Frankfurt (1928-33), where he pioneered the teaching of jazz. In 1935 he settled in England, where he worked at Morley College (1942-57), conducted and wrote film music. He died in a car crash while on a lecture tour of South Africa: Ligeti dedicated *Atmosphères* to his memory. His works are diverse, showing an alert musicianly response to Bartók, to Schoenberg and to jazz.

Cantatas: Ulysses (Joyce), 1946-7; 3 Fragments (Joyce), 1957

Chamber: Str Qt no.1, 1924, no.2, 1934-5, no.3, 1948-51; 2 Jazzolettes, jazz sextet, 1929, 1933; Permutazione a 5, wind qnt, 1958; Vn Sonata, 1960 [Schott]

sequencer Electronic device able to supply a sequence of determined voltages in sound synthesis or processing. Sequencers were occasionally used in live performance and tape composition around 1970, before more powerful computers became widely available.

serialism A technique of composing with reference to series of pitch classes or other musical elements. The implication is that the series is read off in the music, from first note to last, and then repeated in some transformation, but in fact only Webern's music is ever so strictly serial. The term 12-NOTE COMPOSITION is therefore preferable in most cases, since the important criterion is not serial reading from the ideal series into the real music but rather the presence at whatever background and foreground levels of a 12-note SET. Some writers have attempted to use 'serialism' for a narrower body of music: often that produced by the Darmstadt circle in the 1950s, though composers of that milieu generated their own term in TOTAL SERIALISM. Distinctions between 'dodecaphony', 'serialism' and '12-note composition' are, moreover, impossible to sustain, and so the last has been preferred here as being of clearest meaning and widest currency.

But it cannot be applied to works in which the set consists of other than 12 notes. This may be a small repertory, but it does include works of some consequence: Schoenberg's op.23 no.2 (9 notes) and op.24 no.3 (14 notes), Stravinsky's *In Memoriam Dylan Thomas* (5 notes) and Boulez's *Le visage nuptial* (24 quarter tones).

series Ordering of pitch classes or other musical elements; the term SET is now preferred.

Sessions, Roger (1896-1985) American composer. Studied at Harvard (1910-15) and with Parker at Yale (1915-17), then taught at Smith College (1917-21) and as Bloch's assistant at the Cleveland Institute of Music (1921-5). There followed a period in Italy and Berlin, after which he resumed his teaching career at Boston University (1933-5),

Princeton (1935-45), Berkeley (1945-51) and again Princeton (1953-65). His works of the 1920s were influenced by Stravinsky and Bloch, but Schoenberg became increasingly important to him, and in the Violin Sonata of 1953 he turned to 12-note composition. There is to his music a seriousness that avoids Americanism but is distinctively American.

Operas: The Trial of Lucullus, 1947; Montezuma, 1941-63

Orchestral: 8 syms, 1927, 1944-46, 1957, 1958, 1964, 1966, 1967, 1968; Vn Conc, 1935; Pf Conc, 1956; Divertimento, 1959; Rhapsody, 1970, Double Conc, vn, vc, 1971; Concertino, 1972

Vocal orchestral: Idyll of Theocritus, S, orch, 1954; When Lilacs Last in the Dooryard Bloom'd, S, A, Bar, chorus, orch, 1970

Chamber and instrumental: 3 pf sonatas, 1928-30, 1946, 1965; 2 str qts, 1936, 1951; Sonata, vn, 1953; Str Qnt, 1958

[Marks]

□ R. Sessions, *The Musical Experience* (1950), *Questions about Music* (1970)

set Grouping of pitch classes or other musical elements; normally the reference is to a 12-note set containing all the pitch classes within the equal-tempered semitone system, though sets may also be of durations, time points, dynamic levels, etc. The term was borrowed from mathematical set theory by Babbitt.

Shaporin, Yury (1887-1966) Russian composer. Studied with Shteynberg and Tcherepnin at the St Petersburg Conservatory (1913-18), then worked in the theatre with Gorky, Blok, Mayakovsky and others. He was also a member of the Association for Contemporary Music, though after its disbandment he concentrated on major works fully within the Russian tradition, including most notably his opera *The Decembrists* (1920-53).

Shchedrin, Rodion (1932-) Russian composer. Studied with Shaporin at the Moscow Conservatory (1951-5) and quickly established himself as a brilliant orchestrator and fluent composer within a quite orthodox style. His works include the ballets *Carmen* (after Bizet, 1968) and *Anna Karenina* (1972) besides an opera, symphonies, concertos, etc.

Shebalin, Vissarion (1902-63) Russian composer. Studied with Myaskovsky at the Moscow Conservatory (1923-8) and immediately joined the teaching staff; he remained there, except for an interlude when he was removed under the Zhdanov persecution (1948-51). His works include the opera *The Taming of the Shrew* (1946-56), 5 symphonies and 9 quartets.

Shnitke (Schnittke), **Alfred** (1934-) Russian composer. Studied privately in Vienna (1946-8), where his father worked, and with Rakov and Golubev at the Moscow Conservatory (1953-61), where he remained as a teacher until 1972. He was, with Denisov and Volkonsky, one of the first Soviet composers to be touched by post-Webernian music in the 1960s, but later works display a deliberate heterogeneity of style, a sharp conflict of powerfully expressive gestures recalling his admiration for Mahler.

Orchestral: Vn Conc no.1, 1957, rev. 1962, no.2, 1966, no.3, 1978, no.4, 1981-2; Pf Conc, 1960; Double Conc, ob, harp, str, 1970; Sym no.1, 1969-72, no.2, with chorus, 1979; Conc grosso, 2 vn, hpd, str, 1977; Passacaglia, 1979-80

Chamber: Str Qt no.1, 1966, no.2, 1981; Quasi una sonata, vn, pf, 1968; Pf Qnt

[Boosey, UE; Philips]

Shostakovich, Dmitry (1906-75) Russian composer. The outstanding symphonist of the 20th c., in terms of quantity (one has to look to minor figures like Myaskovsky and Brian to cap his 15 works), certainly in terms of diversity (his symphonies find room for massive choral posters, sprawling symphonic poems and even, in no.14, a song cycle), and probably in terms of quality, if that may be judged by the richness of musical experience contained beneath the often bleak or banal surfaces of his works. And his music asks thus to be probed, since the peculiar circumstances of his being a composer in the Soviet Union – being, indeed, almost the nation's musical voice for much of his life – made it inevitable that he should operate on two fronts, the personal and the political. To take one obvious instance, his Fifth Symphony was designated 'a Soviet artist's creative reply to justified criticism', and yet many writers have agreed in finding its meekness ironic and its heroics decidedly hollow. His own awareness of such bifurcation in his creative personality remains unclear, since the authenticity of his posthumously published memoirs has been questioned. Nevertheless, his music is the most convincing evidence since Mahler's of a 20th c. distrust of the diatonic order it purports to sustain.

He studied with Shteynberg and Glazunov at the Petrograd Conservatory (1919-25): his graduation

piece was his First Symphony, which was already entirely individual and gained him a reputation in Russia and abroad. His next symphonies had loud Revolutionary finales, but they included too an assimilation of advanced western elements from music introduced by the Association for Contemporary Music. The opera *The* NOSE goes still further in that direction, while its successor *The* LADY MACBETH OF THE MTSENSK DISTRICT uses all the means at his disposal in an excess of parody and heightened emotion. This was the work that elicited the condemnation of *Pravda* in 1936 and the 'creative reply' of the Fifth Symphony in 1937 (the complex Fourth was held in reserve until 1961).

During the first months of the Soviet Union's involvement in the second world war he was in besieged Leningrad, where he began his Seventh Symphony, a massive patriotic statement dedicated to the city. However, the surrounding symphonies were more perplexing and questioning, and in the mid-1940s he began to write more chamber music, perhaps because that domain was less exposed to official reaction. Nevertheless, he was condemned along with Prokofiev and Khachaturian in 1948, after which he concentrated on innocuous oratorios until Stalin's death 5 years later. Then came his Tenth Symphony, which might have been designed as a personal vindication (it quotes his musical CIPHER). The next 2 symphonies were historical pageants in instrumental terms, but by the early 1960s it seemed possible to be more daring: the Fourth Symphony was at last performed, *The Lady Macbeth* was revived, and the Thirteenth Symphony (1962), while setting Yevtushenko's words about the Nazi massacre of Jews, was widely interpreted as a metaphorical condemnation of Stalin's atrocities.

The music of his last decade stands somewhat apart. He was suffering from ill health, and much of his work was concerned with death: the Fourteenth Symphony is a song cycle on that subject, and the Fifteenth Quartet is a memorial in 6 adagios. The harmony also became more spare and strained. In the Violin Sonata and Twelfth Quartet he made use of 12-note themes, though major-minor tonality remained to the end essential to a musical style of irony, quirkiness and extremity that could only be measured against the expectations of a system.

Operas: The NOSE, 1927-8; The LADY MACBETH OF THE MTSENSK DISTRICT, 1930-32

Ballets: The Golden Age, 1927-30; The Bolt, 1930-31; The Bright Stream, 1934-5

Symphonies: no.1, f, 1924-5; no.2 'To October', B,

with chorus in finale, 1927; no.3 'May Day', E♭, with chorus in finale, 1929; no.4, c, 1935-6; no.5, d, 1937; no.6, b, 1939; no.7 'Leningrad', C, 1941; no.8, c, 1943; no.9, E♭, 1945; no.10, e, 1953; no.11 'The Year 1905', g, 1957; no.12 'The Year 1917', d, 1961; no.13 'Babiy Yar', b♭, with B and chorus, 1962; no.14, S, B, str, perc, 1969; no.15, A, 1971

Concertos: Pf no.1, c, with tpt and str, 1933, no.2, F, 1957; Vn no.1, a, 1947-8, rev. 1955, no.2, c♯, 1967; Vc no.1, E♭, 1959, no.2, G, 1966

Suites from film scores: New Babylon, 1928; Golden Hills, 1931; Maxim, 1936-8; The Young Guard, 1947-8; Pirogov, 1947; Michurin, 1948; Encounter at the Elbe, 1948; The Fall of Berlin, 1949; Belinsky, 1950; The Unforgettable Year 1919, 1951; The Gadfly, 1955; The First Echelon, 1956; Five Days-Five Nights, 1960; Hamlet, 1963-4

Other suites: Hamlet (incidental music), 1931-2; 2 suites, jazz orch, 1934, 1938; also from ballets and operas

Other orchestral works: Scherzo, f♯, 1919; Theme and Variations, B♭, 1921-2; Scherzo, E♭, 1924; 5 Fragments, 1935; Festival Overture, 1954; Novorossisk Chimes, 1960; Overture on Russian and Kirghiz Folk Themes, 1963; Funeral-Triumphal Prelude, 1967; October, sym poem, 1967; March of the Soviet Militia, wind, 1970

Choral orchestral: Poem on the Motherland, 1947; Song of the Forests, 1949; The Sun Shines on our Motherland, 1952; The Execution of Stepan Razin, 1964

Vocal orchestral: 2 Fables (Krylov), Mez, 1922; 6 Songs, (Jap.) T, 1928-32; 6 Songs, B, 1942, orch 1971; From Jewish Folk Poetry, S, A, T, 1948, orch 1964; 6 Poems (Tsvetayeva), A, 1973; Suite (Michelangelo), B, 1974

Orchestrations: Tahiti Trot, 1928; 2 Pieces by D. Scarlatti, wind, 1928; Musorgsky: Boris Godunov, 1940, Khovanshchina, 1959, Songs and Dances of Death, 1962; 8 English and American Folksongs, 1944; Davidenko: 2 Choruses, 1962; Schumann: Vc Conc, 1966

String quartets: no.1, C, 1935; no.2, A, 1944; no.3, F, 1946; no.4, D, 1949; no.5, B♭, 1952; no.6, G, 1956; no.7, f♯, 1960; no.8, c, 1960; no.9, E♭, 1964; no.10, A♭, 1964; no.11, f, 1966; no.12, D♭, 1968; no.13, b♭, 1970; no.14, F♯, 1973; no.15, e♭, 1974

Other chamber works: Pf Trio no.1, 1923, no.2, e, 1944; 3 Pieces, vc, pf, 1923-4; 2 Pieces, str octet, 1924-5; Sonata, d, vc, pf, 1934; Pf Qnt, g, 1940; Sonata, vn, pf, 1968; Sonata, va, pf, 1975

Songs: 4 Songs (Pushkin), B, pf, 1936; 2 Songs (Svetlov), v, pf, 1945; 2 Songs (Lermontov), male v, p, 1950; 4 Songs (Dolmatovsky), v, pf, 1951; 4

Monologues (Pushkin), B, pf, 1952; 5 Songs (Dolmatovsky), B, pf, 1954; Spanish Songs, S, pf, 1956; Satires (Chorny), S, pf, 1960; 5 Songs (Krokodil'), B, pf, 1965; 7 Songs (Blok), S, pf trio, 1967; 4 Verses by Captain Lebyadkin (Dostoyevsky), B, pf, 1975

Piano: 8 Preludes, 1919-20; 5 Preludes, 1920-21; 3 Fantastic Dances, 1922; Suite, f♯, 2 pf, 1922; Sonata no.1, 1926, no.2 1942; Aphorisms, 1927; 24 Preludes, 1932-3; 6 Children's Pieces, 1944-5, 24 Preludes and Fugues, 1950-51; Concertino, 2 pf, 1953; 7 Dolls' Dances, 1952-62

[Boosey; Melodiya, Decca]

□ I. Martïnov, *Dmitry Shostakovich* (1947, r1969); N. Kay, *Shostakovich* (1971); S. Volkov, ed. *Testimony* (1979)

Shteynberg, Maximilian (1883-1946) Russian composer. Studied with Rimsky-Korsakov, Lyadov and Glazunov at the St Petersburg Conservatory, where he remained as a teacher of composition after his graduation in 1908. His works, within the Rimsky tradition, include the ballet *Métamorphoses* (*Ballet Russes, 1914) and 5 symphonies.

Sibelius, Jean (1865-1957) Finnish composer. In many other ways he was the obverse of his close contemporary Mahler, his only peer among symphonists of the early 20th c. Where Mahler's works were all autobiographical, Sibelius's generally relate to the landscapes and most especially the mythology of his country. Where Mahler's ideas tend to be long and strongly characterized, Sibelius's are often short and rudimentary, cells rather than themes. Mahler tends always towards the constant turmoil of a development, Sibelius towards steady growth in the manner of a slow introduction. Mahler's symphonies are centrifugal, with a multiplicity of distinctly various movements; Sibelius's are centripetal, with harmonious connections and even amalgamations of movements.

He showed gifts as violinist and composer from childhood, and studied with Wegelius in Helsinki (1885-9), Becker in Berlin (1889-90) and Fuchs and Goldmark in Vienna (1890-91). He then returned to Helsinki, where he completed his choral symphony *Kullervo* in 1892 and the same year married Aino Järnefelt. During the next few years he earned his living as a teacher and wrote tone poems, developing his style and establishing himself as Finland's leading composer: that position was confirmed by his *Finlandia*, while his First Symphony

(1899) gained him international interest. The work is still somewhat Tchaikovskian (Finland was at the time a Russian province), but its newness was recognized at performances in France, Germany and England, which brought him new opportunities to travel. Meanwhile in Helsinki he was often leading a disorderly existence with drinking companions, particularly around the time of his Violin Concerto (1903): this period came to an end in 1904, when he built a house outside the capital, where he lived with his wife and 4 daughters for the rest of his life.

In the Third Symphony (1904-7), of Classical lucidity, he left Russian Romanticism behind; in the Fourth (1911), insisting on the tonally disruptive tritone, he produced his bleakest work and yet one of his most typical, with its long pedal points and slow motivic expansions. The Fifth Symphony (1915), like other works, caused him trouble and needed 2 substantial revisions before it attained its unusual 3-movement form of allegro becoming scherzo (these were originally separate movements), andante, and finale of struggling heroism. After this his output slackened. Little was achieved before the pure, elusive Sixth Symphony (1923), followed swiftly by the single-movement Seventh, the incidental music for the The Tempest and the final unpeopled nature poetry of Tapiola. There were then 3 decades of SILENCE. He may have completed an Eighth Symphony but if so he burned it.

Symphonies: Kullervo, with S, Bar, male chorus, 1892; no.1, e, 1899; no.2, D, 1901-2; no.3, C, 1904-7; no.4, a, 1911; no.5, E♭, 1915, rev. 1916, 1919; no.6, d, 1923; no.7, C, 1924
Other orchestral works: En saga, 1892, rev. 1902; Karelia Overture, 1893; Karelia Suite, 1893; Spring Song, 1894; The Wood Nymph, 1895; Lemminkäinen Suite (no.3 = The Swan of Tuonela), 1893-5, rev. 1897 and later; Tiera, brass, perc, 1898; King Christian II, suite, 1898; Scènes historiques I, 1899; Finlandia, 1899; Romance, C, str, 1903; Vn Conc, d, 1903, rev. 1905; Valse triste, 1904; Pelléas et Mélisande, suite, 1905; Scene with Cranes, 1906; Pohjola's Daughter, 1906; Pan and Echo, 1906; Belshazzar's Feast, suite, 1906; Nightride and Sunrise, 1907; Swanwhite, suite, 1908; In memoriam, 1909; The Dryad, 1910; Canzonetta, str, 1911; Valse romantique, 1911; Scènes historiques II, 1912; 2 Serenades, D, g, vn, orch, 1912-13; The Bard, 1913, rev. 1914; The Oceanides, 1914; 2 Pieces vn/vc, orch 1914; 6 Humoresques, d, D, g, g, E♭, g, vn, orch, 1917; Valse lyrique, 1920; Valse chevaleresque, 1920; Suite mignonne, fl, str, 1921;

Suite champêtre, str, 1921; Andante festivo, str, 1922; Suite caractéristique, harp, str, 1922; The Tempest, prelude and 2 suites, 1925; Tapiola, 1926
Vocal orchestral: The Maiden in the Tower (opera), 1896; The Origin of Fire, Bar, male chorus, orch, 1902, rev. 1910; Luonnotar, S, orch, ?1910; Scaramouche (pantomime), 1913; many cantatas, etc
Chamber: Str Qt 'Voces intimae', d, 1909; many pieces for vn, pf; many pf pieces
Songs: 7 Runeberg Songs, op.13, 1891-2; 7 Songs, op.17, 1891-8; 6 Songs, op.36, 1899; 5 Songs, op.38, 1902-4; 6 Songs, op.50, 1906; 8 Songs, op.57, 1909; 8 Songs, op.61, 1910; 6 Songs, op.72, 1907-15; 6 Songs, op.86, 1916; 6 Songs, op.88, 1917; 6 Runeberg Songs, op.90, 1917 (all in Swed., except op.50 in Ger.)
[Breitkopf, Hansen, Hirsch, Lienau, Westerlund]
□ R. Layton, *Sibelius* (1965, 2/1978); E. Tawaststjerna, *Jean Sibelius* (1976-)

Siegmeister, Elie (1909-) American composer. Studied at Columbia (1924-7) and privately with Riegger, then in Paris with Boulanger (1927-31). On his return to the USA he wrote orchestral and choral works and a musical in a distinctively American style, influenced by jazz, blues and folksong. In 1949 he was appointed to the faculty of Hofstra University, NY. [Fischer, Marks, Mercury, Peters]

silence The absence of sound has become recognized in the 20th c. as an element of music. Busoni pointed out that silences between movements are not blank periods but moments filled with recollection and expectation: Mahler's Second Symphony was perhaps the first work in which such silences were measured, an example followed in, for instance, Boulez's *Le marteau sans maître*. But silences at the ends of works can be just as significant, and are often measured in Ligeti's works. Silence in these cases is not so much the absence of sound as its temporary disappearance – or it may threaten to be a permanent disappearance in works which, like Barraqué's Piano Sonata, are composed as dialectics between sound and silence. Alternatively there may be no dialectic: silence may be rather the ideal condition of music, allowing the listener to attend to life rather than art, as in Cage's *4' 33"*.

The complication of silence, making it controllable (Boulez), a neutral medium for music (Ligeti), an enemy of thought (Barraqué) or a friend of thoughtlessness (Cage), may not be unconnected with the many notable silences in the careers of composers in the 20th c., including those of Duparc, Dukas, Elgar, Sibelius, Varèse, Ives, Barraqué and Boulez. In all of these cases personal and even physiological explanations have been adduced, but they cannot remain entirely convincing when there are so few parallels in earlier periods. Silence in the 20th c. may speak more loudly than music.

Simpson, Robert (1921-) English composer. Studied with Howells (1942-6) and worked for the BBC (1951-80). His music has been most galvanized by the composers on whom he has written monographs: *Carl Nielsen* (London, 1952, 2/ 1979), *The Essence of Bruckner* (London, 1966) and *Beethoven Symphonies* (London, 1970). Most of his works are in traditional genres, though not at all in traditional forms: the form is, rather, very actively created by a strongly willed process of tonal conflict. The main pillars of his output are the 9 symphonies and 11 string quartets. [Lengnick]

simultaneity Term preferred to 'chord' by some composers of 12-note music on the grounds that it avoids an implication of diatonic function.

sine tone Sound of one pure frequency.

Sinfonia Work by Berio for the Swingle Singers and orchestra, originally in 4 movements (1968), with a fifth added in 1969; the third movement is a weave of quotations and vocal commentary around the scherzo from Mahler's Second Symphony.

Sirius Semi-theatrical work by Stockhausen for 4 soloists (soprano, bass, basset horn and trumpet) and tape: it is a ritual of the 4 seasons, compass points, ages of man, etc, based on a grand cycle of the TIERKREIS melodies. *Aix-en-Provence, 8 Aug 1977

Six, Les (The Six) Group named after Henri Collet's article 'Les cinq russes, les six français et M. Satie' (*Comoedia*, 16 Jan 1920): the 6 were Auric, Durey, Honegger, Milhaud, Poulenc and Tailleferre. They had been active together since 1917, largely under Cocteau's artistic leadership, but they did not long accept his demands for elegance, modernity and crisp simplicity. There was an *Album des Six* with piano pieces by all of them (1920) and a playlet-ballet by Cocteau with musical numbers by all but Durey (*Les mariés de la Tour-Eiffel*, *Ballets Suédois, Paris, 18 Jun 1921). After that they disbanded.

Skalkottas, Nikos (1904-49) Greek composer. Studied as a violinist at the Athens Conservatory

(1914-20) and from 1921 in Berlin, where he had composition lessons from Jarnach (1925-7), Schoenberg (1927-31) and Weill (1928-9). In 1933 he returned to Athens, where he worked as a back-desk violinist while composing large-scale orchestral and chamber works, most of which lay unperformed until after his death. Some of his compositions, e.g. the *Greek Dances*, are in a lively national style not so different from Dvořák's in similar works, but the majority are 12-note, and the large output of 1935-45 is mostly serial in the Schoenbergian manner. The formal models are conventional, as in Schoenberg's works of the 1920s, but the dimensions may be larger, and often the textures are dense, multithematic and multiserial.

Orchestral: Pf Conc no.1, 1931, no.2, 1937-8, no.3, 1938-9; Double Pf Concertino, 1935; Sym Suite no.1, 1935, no.2, 1944-9; 36 Greek Dances, 1931-6, rev. 1948-9; Vn Conc, 1937-8; Conc, vn, va, orch, 1939-40; 10 Musical Sketches, str, 1940; Little Suite, str, 1942; The Return of Ulysses, overture, 1942-3; Db Conc, 1942-3

Chamber: Str Qt no.1, 1928, no.2, 1929, no.3, 1935, no.4, 1940; 4 sonatinas, vn, pf; 4 suites, pf; many other works

[UE, Skalkottas Society]

Skryabin, Alexander (1872-1915) Russian composer. Showed gifts as pianist and composer from early childhood, and studied with Taneyev and Arensky at the Moscow Conservatory (1888-92), then started career as a concert pianist. Between 1894 and 1903 he was published and promoted by Belyayev, during which time he developed from a Chopinesque early style to works of more luxuriant texture and stronger rhetoric, seemingly spurred by his identification with Nietzsche's philosophy. In 1905 he turned from this to theosophy, and his music became still more individual: the harmony tends to remain static for long periods, held so by symmetrical octave divisions as in late Liszt (notably the tritone, whole-tone scale and diminished 7th chord), while melody is freed to grow in profuse ornamentation. Increasingly his expression focussed on 2 types also characteristic of late Liszt, the demonic and the voluptuous, and this concentration on a single musical state led to an output consisting mostly of short pieces with the occasional longer movement of continuous elaboration (POEM OF ECSTASY, PROMETHEUS and the sonatas of this period). He became convinced of the spiritual purpose of art, and felt himself to be working towards a *Mysterium* that would appeal to all the senses and trigger some kind of cataclysm:

hence his use of colour in *Prometheus* and his constant harmonic venturing that led him into virtual atonality in his last pieces. He died of septicaemia, leaving sketches for a *Preparatory Action* (1914-15) including 12-note chords.

Orchestral: Pf Conc, op.20, f♯, 1896; Sym Poem, d, 1896-7; Rêverie, op.24, 1898; Sym no.1, op.26, E, with chorus in finale, 1899-1900, no.2, op.29, c, 1901, no.3 'The Divine Poem', op.43, 1902-4; The POEM OF ECSTASY op.54, 1905-8; PROMETHEUS, op.60, 1908-10

Piano sonatas: no.1, op.6, 1892; no.2, op.19, 1892-7; no.3, op.23, 1897-8; no.4, op.30, 1903; no.5, op.53, 1907; no.6, op.62, 1911; no.7 'White Mass', op.64, 1911; no.8 op.66, 1912-13; no.9 'Black Mass', op.68, 1912-13; no.10, op.70, 1913

Piano preludes: 24 op. 11, 1888-96; 6 op. 13, 1895; 5 op.15, 1895-6; 5 op. 16, 1894-5; 7 op.17, 1895-6; 4 op.22, 1897; 2 op.27, 1900; 4 op.31, 1903; 4 op.33, 1903; 3 op.35, 1903; 4 op.37, 1903; 4 op.39, 1903; 4 op.48, 1905; 2 op.67, 1912-13; 5 op.74, 1914

Other piano works: Waltz, op.1, f, 1885; 3 Pieces, op.2, 1887-9; 10 Mazurkas, op.3, 1889; Allegro appassionato, op.4, 1892; 2 Nocturnes, op.5, 1890; 2 Impromptus à la mazur, op.7, 1892; 2 Etudes, op.8, 1894; 2 Pieces, op.9, left hand, 1894; 2 Impromptus, op.10, 1894; 2 Impromptus, op.12, 1895; 2 Impromptus, op.14, 1895; Allegro de concert, op.18, 1896; Polonaise, op.21, 1897; 9 Mazurkas, op.25, 1899; Fantaisie, op.28, 1900; 2 Poems, op.32, 1903; Tragic Poem, op.34, 1903; Satanic Poem, op.36, 1903; Waltz, op.38, 1903; 2 Mazurkas, op.40, 1902-3; Poem, op.41, 1903; 8 Etudes, op.42, 1903; 2 Poems, op.44, 1905; 3 Pieces, op.45, 1904-5; Scherzo, op.46, 1905; Quasi-Waltz, op.47, 1905; 3 Pieces, op.49, 1905; 4 Pieces, op.51, 1906; 3 Pieces, op.52, 1906; 4 Pieces, op.56, 1907; 2 Pieces, op.57, 1907; Albumleaf, op.58, 1910; 2 Pieces, op.59, 1910; Poem-Nocturne, op.61, 1911; 2 Poems, op.63, 1911; 3 Etudes, op.65, 1912; 2 Poems, op.69, 1913; 2 Poems, op.71, 1914; Towards the Flame, op.72, 1914; 2 Dances, op.73, 1914

[Belaieff, Jurgenson]

□ H. Macdonald, *Skryabin* (1978)

Smalley, Roger (1943-) English composer. Studied with Fricker and John White at the Royal College of Music (1961-5), with Goehr at Morley College (1962) and with Stockhausen in Cologne (1965-6). The works of this period show a Davies-like meeting of Darmstadt and the English Renaissance, but after 1967 he drew closer to Stock-

hausen: having returned to England, he was also closely associated with Stockhausen's music as a writer and broadcaster, pianist and electronic-music player (with INTERMODULATION). However, though such works as *Zeitebenen* and *Accord* clearly have their models in Stockhausen (*Hymnen* and *Mantra*), they also have a breadth that relates to his long-standing fascination with late Romantic music, to which he grew still closer in the music that followed his move to the University of Western Australia in 1976.

Orchestral: Variations, str, 1964; Gloria Tibi Trinitas I, 1965; Pulses, brass, perc, ring modulators, 1969; Strata, str, 1970-71; Konzertstück, vn, orch, 1980; Sym, 1982; Pf Conc 1982-5

Vocal: Missa brevis, 16 solo vv, 1966-7; The Song of the Highest Tower, S, Bar, chorus, orch, 1968; William Derrincourt, Bar, male vv, 13 insts, 1977

Ensemble: Str Sextet, 1964; Missa parodia II, pf, 8 insts, 1967; Zeitebenen, insts, tape, 1973; Str Qt, 1979

Piano: Pieces, I-V, 1962-5; Missa parodia I, 1967; Piece VI, 1969; Transformation I, with ring modulator, 1968-9, rev. 1971; Monody, with ring modulator, 1971-2; Accord, 2 pf, 1974-5

[Faber]

Smyth, Ethel (1858-1944) English composer. Studied with Jadassohn and Reinecke at the Leipzig Conservatory from 1877, and with Herzogenberg in Berlin. While in Germany she met Brahms, Tchaikovsky, Clara Schumann and others, gaining encouragement of her intention to compose. Her best works, including the large-scale Mass in D (1891) and the operas *The Wreckers* (1903-4, ★Leipzig, 1906) and *The Boatswain's Mate* (1913-14, ★London, 1916), have a forceful determination that also went into her work on behalf of women's suffrage. [UE, Novello, Faber]

socialist realism Official Soviet aesthetic promulgated in 1932, the underlying idea being that artists should portray the real world but bend their portraits towards the socialist future. Quite what this meant for music was never very clear: hence the problems of 1936 and 1948 (*see* POLITICS). In the west it has been sometimes used as a derogatory term in discussion of such bland party-line works as Shostakovich's oratorios.

society Since the 20th c. has had many problems in the definition of the term 'society', it is not surprising that the relationship between music and this Protean phenomenon should have been contentious. There are essentially 2 areas of dispute, concerned with the production and consumption of music. On the production side, the questions concern the degree to which composers are, should be or must be directed by the wishes of other people. On the consumption side, the principal questions are those of the relationships between particular audiences and particular kinds of music.

Curiously, most discussions of music in society, even when they have not been Marxist, have proceeded from the assumption that new music ought to have some meaning for the great majority of people. The Soviet authorities who protested at the directions taken by their composers in 1936 and 1948 (*see* POLITICS) were at least logical in seeking to change the nature of music in order to enhance its appeal. Those responsible for the dissemination of music in more liberal régimes have either left composers to the care of universities (notably in North America), tacitly admitting that new composition is simply not a social phenomenon, or else they have tried through radio programmes, advertising, educational activities, etc to encourage an audience for new music.

All these solutions present new problems. Social constraints on artists only prove effective if they are accepted: if they are imposed, then artists always have the escape of irony (*see* SHOSTAKOVICH). The approach through education and promotion, which has been chiefly characteristic of western Europe since 1945, proceeds from the unreliably founded assumption that the educators and promoters have some special knowledge equipping them to determine what music is right for what society. And the 'ivory tower' solution, though welcomed by Babbitt, risks ignoring the purpose of music as communication. Babbitt has argued that music today is no more communicable to most people than is nuclear physics or microbiology, but the analogy is not exact, since music has a long history of being widely accepted and in many different ways.

Babbitt's view is in implicit accord with Adorno's, that there is a historical inevitability about the development from Haydn to Beethoven to Brahms to Schoenberg (to Babbitt). Adorno, however, would never have concluded that music might cease to be a social phenomenon, even if he criticized Stravinsky, Sibelius and others for satisfying the expectations of bourgeois society. Indeed, for him the advance towards a Marxist society was inextricably linked to the unavoidable march towards atonality and the 12-note set. However, the increasing diversity of music, and the lack of any obvious 'progress' since the collapse of the avant-garde tradition around 1960, make it difficult to believe that music still has an impulse of its own, if it ever did have.

If it does not, then change in music must be directed either by some society or by an individual, the composer. In determining the relative weights of these alternatives, the case of isolated composers must be pertinent, and it would suggest that composers cut off for one reason or another from any consuming society (Skalkottas, Brian) may be disadvantaged, in practical terms by the lack of opportunities of performance (and in this respect music must remain a social art), in less tangible terms by uncertainty about the abilities of audiences to comprehend. Of course, it may be that isolated composers have chosen isolation as a solution to the problems of composing in the 20th c., just as silent composers may deliberately have chosen silence. But this does not alter the argument. The ultimate ideal for the individualist composer is that he/she should compose works on tape or on paper which only he/she can comprehend, and indeed it has yet to be demonstrated that this is not the most realistic view of music in the late 20th c.

However, most composers have sought a compromise between individualism and the social obedience represented in totalitarian societies by state control and in capitalist societies by commercial dictates. As far as the latter are concerned, in 1970 in the USA 'classical' music accounted for only 15% of record sales, and it would be hard to believe that music by living composers made up a large proportion even of that 15%. Inevitably the tendency has been for serious music to decline in popularity over the period – from Johann Strauss II to Cole Porter to reggae – when it has grown further apart from entertainment music. The big question is why this should have occurred, and it surely has to do with phenomena quite beyond the art itself. Meanwhile most composers have been bound to seek their audiences in small sections of society: hence the unprecedented plethora of specialist societies, festivals, etc. Even so, some have remained haunted by the Beethovenian myth that music can speak to everyman.

□ C. Ballantine, *Music and its Social Meanings* (1984)

Society for Private Musical Performances

Organization set up by Schoenberg in Vienna in 1919 to present thoroughly rehearsed concerts of new works to audiences who would come from a pure desire to increase their experience: programmes were not divulged in advance, the press were not invited, subscriptions were according to means, and applause was not required. This was a logical, if extreme reaction to the problems that Schoenberg had encountered with audiences and critics who had come ready to scoff, and indeed to the deeper issues of music's place in society: all the art's pretensions to serve as entertainment or social phenomenon were simply abandoned. The society's repertory included works by Schoenberg, Berg and Webern, and also Mahler, Reger, Ravel, Stravinsky, Bartók, etc, orchestral scores being reduced for keyboard or small ensemble. Inflation brought activities to an end in 1921.

Soldier's Tale (Histoire du soldat) Theatre piece by Stravinsky and C.F. Ramuz 'to be read, played and danced'. It is a Faustian story based on Russian folk material and requiring a narrator, 2 actors, a dancer and septet (cl, bn, cornet, trbn, perc, vn, db), the music consisting of incidental numbers and dances that gradually engulf the action. ★cond Ansermet, Lausanne, 28 Sep 1918. There is a suite, and a selection of 5 movements arranged for violin, clarinet and piano (1919).

Somers, Harry (1925-) Canadian composer. Studied with Weinzweig at the Toronto Conservatory (1942-9) and with Milhaud in Paris (1949-50), then returned to Canada and took various jobs. His works include the opera *Louis Riel* (★Toronto, 1967), orchestral, choral and chamber music. [Berandol]

sonata As a title, the word has normally been applied in the 20th c. as it was in the 19th c. to substantial works for 1 or 2 instruments, though there are exceptions, such as Debussy's Sonata for flute, viola and harp (suggesting an echo of trio sonata scoring), Bartók's Sonata for 2 pianos and percussion (apparently not called 'quartet' only because Bartók was unsure that 2 players could manage the percussion parts) and Davies' *St Michael*, a 'sonata' for 17 wind (here the reference is to Gabrieli as much as Beethoven).

Normally too, again as in the 19th c., the word implies sonata form, at least in the first movement, though the problems of defining sonata form in the 20th c. are immense. The basic pattern of statement-development-resolved statement is not uncommon among the century's tonal composers, from Mahler to Stravinsky, but the meaning of development and recapitulation may have to be altered in the absence of the diatonic functions that gave rise to these concepts. For instance, develop-

ment may be replaced by an extension of harmonic space (Webern: Symphony), by some logical process of transformation (Davies) or, very commonly, by denser textures and faster change. It is a moot point whether such techniques produce a re-vivification of sonata form or merely a reference to it. Nevertheless, sonata form was one of Schoenberg's guiding ideals once he had established the principles of 12-note composition, even though he called no work 'sonata'.

Sorabji, Kaikhosru (1892-) English composer. Largely self-taught, he played his own works in England and abroad in the 1920s and early 1930s, but then withdrew from the concert platform to live in retirement writing immense piano and orchestral works influenced by Skryabin, Busoni, Alkan, etc.

sound Music may be regarded as, at one extreme, an art of sounds placed on the neutral medium of TIME, or at the other as an art of time needing sounds in order to be perceived. But changes in 20th c. music have affected both sound and time. For instance, the range of sounds available to music has obviously increased beyond measure with the introduction of electronic music and microtones, and the expansion of harmony and the use of percussion. As a result, some composers have felt themselves to be working with sound: Varèse's preference of the term ORGANIZED SOUND to 'music' suggests this, as does the care and inventiveness that composers as various as Cage and Bartók have brought to percussion scoring. And indeed, experimenting with the prepared piano and later with electronic music synthesis made it possible for musicians to compose sounds without having to assemble an orchestra. The electronic works of Stockhausen, such as *Kontakte* or *Mikrophonie I*, present themselves very much as studies in sound, where single events or complex textures are the only musical foreground, the interest being not in specifics like pitch and rhythmic motif but rather in the whole nature of the sound. With such works of 'organized sound' at one extreme, the other might be represented by much of Schoenberg's music, since his readiness to arrange his own and other works for different media suggests the view that music is something other than the sounds in which it is embodied. This idealist position is the conventional one; it is a distinguishing feature of the 20th c. that many musicians have become more realist in their equation of music with sound, giving rise not only to Stockhausen but also to the attempted revivals of historical performance styles in order to retrieve 'what the composer heard'.

Souster, Tim (1943-) English composer. Studied with Wellesz at Oxford (1961-5), with Stockhausen at Darmstadt (1964) and privately with Bennett (1965), then worked as a BBC producer (1965-7), composer in residence at King's College, Cambridge (1969-71), assistant to Stockhausen in Cologne (1971-3) and research fellow in electronic music at Keele University (1975-7). He was also a member of INTERMODULATION and afterwards of his own group OdB: for both ensembles he has written works bringing together his interests in Stockhausen and in rock music. [OdB; Nimbus]

Sowerby, Leo (1895-1968) American composer. Studied at the American Conservatory in Chicago, and in Italy as first recipient of the American Prix de Rome (1921-4). He returned to Chicago to teach at the American Conservatory (1925-62) and serve as organist and choirmaster at St James's Episcopal Cathedral (1927-62). His works include much church music, but also 5 symphonies, 2 organ concertos, etc.

spatial music The disposition of musicians in different places had normally been reserved in the 19th c. for special effects (e.g. in *Fidelio*, the Berlioz Te Deum, *Parsifal* and Mahler's Second Symphony). It was then one of many techniques furthered by Ives, notably in his UNANSWERED QUESTION and in his dream of a 'universe symphony' for manifold groups of performers on mountain tops and plains. An electronic version of this dream occurred to Varèse as his *Espace* for ensembles communicating by radio, while Messiaen has suggested that his *Et exspecto* might suitably be performed on a mountain peak, affording lengthy reverberations for its massive chords. Ives's nearest heir, though, is Brant, whose output includes many works for separated ensembles. Carter contributed to this repertory with his *Symphony of 3 Orchestras*, and Stockhausen's *Gruppen*, also for 3 orchestras, drew attention to a concern with space apparent in many of his works: e.g. in *Gesang der Jünglinge*, which was the first electronic work for separated groups of loudspeakers (this obviously provides the easiest means of achieving spatial effects, and most subsequent electronic music has taken advantage). Works for distinct loudspeaker-groups or ensembles clearly constitute the most spectacular instances of spatial music, but space is important too in compositions that demand particular seating patterns for the orchestra, such as Bartók's Music for Strings, Percussion and Celesta, Boulez's *Figures-Doubles-Prismes* or Stockhausen's *Trans*.

speech True speech, as distinct from SPRECHGESANG, is combined with music trivially when plays or poems are given with accompaniment, though the combination may be more integrated if rhythms for the speaking voice are notated, as in Stravinsky's *Soldier's Tale* or Walton's *Façade*. Speech is still more made music when it comes from a chorus, since this takes the effect significantly further away from everyday experience: examples include Milhaud's *Les choëphores* (1915), in which this technique was pioneered, Stravinsky's *Requiem Canticles* and works by Vogel. Alternatively, most usually in opera, speech may specifically remove characters from the musical world, whether intermittently as in Berg's operas or throughout as in *Ariadne auf Naxos* and *Perséphone*.

sphaerophon Electronic melody instrument constructed by Jörg Mager in 1923, superseded by his partiturophon: both were varieties of electronic organ. In 1931 Mager was commissioned by Winifred Wagner to create synthetic bell sounds for *Parsifal*.

Sprechgesang (Ger. 'speech-song') Kind of vocal delivery between speech and song, first required by Humperdinck in his opera *Königskinder* (1897), though replaced by normal singing in the edition of 1910. It was most thoroughly exploited by Schoenberg in his *Gurrelieder, Die glückliche Hand, Pierrot lunaire, Die Jakobsleiter, Moses und Aron* (part of Moses), *Ode to Napoleon* and *A Survivor from Warsaw*. The first 4 of these, like the Humperdinck, use ordinary staff notation with some special indication: an 'x' on the note stem, as in *Die glückliche Hand* and *Pierrot*, has become standard. However, the performance of *Sprechgesang* is far from standardized. Schoenberg is most explicit in the preface to *Pierrot*, where he asks that the voice should 'give the pitch exactly, but then immediately leave it in a fall or rise': this has been taken as meaning anything from virtual singing to nightclub crooning or Expressionist dramatization. It may be significant that Schoenberg did not use the term *Sprechgesang* but rather *Sprechstimme* (speaking voice), *Sprechmelodie* (speech melody) or *Rezitation*; he also simplified his notation in the 2 last works mentioned above, using a 1-line staff so that the performer could choose his own pitch level. Berg in *Wozzeck* followed Schoenberg's recent practice and introduced a new shade, 'half sung', between *Sprechgesang* and song. Boulez's *Le visage nuptial* adds to these 'spoken intonation at the indicated pitch', between *Sprechgesang* and speech.

Starer, Robert (1924-) Austrian-American composer. Studied at the Vienna Academy (1937-8), the Jerusalem Conservatory and the Juilliard School (1947-9), where he remained as a teacher, serving also from 1963 as professor at Brooklyn College. His style is within the region of Prokofiev and Hindemith; his works include operas, ballets, symphonies, concertos, etc. [Mercury, Presser]

Stenhammar, Wilhelm (1871-1927) Swedish composer. Born into an artistic family, he studied privately and attended no conservatory. He led an active triple career as composer, pianist (especially in chamber music) and conductor, notably of the orchestra in Gothenburg (1906-22). He was also a friend of Sibelius and Nielsen, and like theirs his music developed in an individual way out of Scandinavian late Romanticism, though his inclinations were more Germanic: his late works, in particular, have a *Jugendstil* floridity crispened by Classicism.
Orchestral: Pf Conc no. 1, b♭, 1893, no. 2, d, 1904-7; Sym no. 1, F, 1902-3, no. 2, g, 1911-15; Serenade, F, 1911-13, rev. 1919
String quartets: no. 1, C, 1894; no. 2, c, 1896; no. 3, F, 1897-1900; no. 4, a, 1904-9; no. 5, C, 1910; no. 6, d, 1916
2 operas, songs, cantatas, sonatas
[Erik, Gehrman, Nordiska Musikförlaget]

Sternklang (Starsound) Work by Stockhausen for 5 electronic ensembles in a park at dusk, communicating with each other by means of musical messages sent through the air and by runner. ★Berlin, 5 June 1971.

Steuermann, Eduard (Edward) (1892-1964) Polish-American pianist. Studied in Berlin with Busoni and Schoenberg, and became the pianist of the latter's circle: he played in the first performances of *Pierrot lunaire* and many other works by Schoenberg and his pupils, was a regular performer at the Society for Private Musical Performances, and made piano scores of Schoenberg's First Chamber Symphony, *Erwartung* and *Die glückliche Hand*. In 1938 he moved to New York, where he gave the first performance of Schoenberg's Piano Concerto. He also composed atonal and 12-note pieces.

Still, William Grant (1895-1978) American composer. Studied at the Oberlin Conservatory (1917-22) and in New York with Varèse (1922-5), earning his living as an instrumentalist in theatre orchestras and arranger; from 1935 he worked for CBS. The connection with Varèse led to some early modernist essays, but from the mid-1920s he began to write large-scale, smooth diatonic works, including 5 symphonies.

Stimmung (Tuning, Mood) Work by Stockhausen for 6 singers using Asian vocal techniques and electronic amplification to project the natural harmonics of a low B♭. The 'moments' of the pieces are distinguished by different choices from the harmonic series and different 'magic words' (names of American and eastern divinities) chanted by the performers. ★Collegium Vocale Köln, Paris, 9 Dec 1968.

stochastic (Gr. *stochos* = goal) Term borrowed by Xenakis from probability theory, where it denotes a process in which the steps are governed by rules of probability. It may be, for instance that each new occurrence is ruled in some way by all those that have happened so far; this is the case in a 'Markov chain'. Early in such a process, when there is little history of events, the degree of randomness will be high, but it will then progressively decrease, and so the process tends towards a goal. Xenakis has used Markov chains and other stochastic processes as models for determining the unfolding of musical events through time, though the term 'stochastic music' has come to be used more loosely of music in which large processes are defined but small detail appears insignificant (*see* TEXTURE MUSIC).

Stockhausen, Karlheinz (1928-) German composer. The commanding figure in European music in the second half of the 20th c. – a status he acquired remarkably early in his career. He studied at the Cologne Musikhochschule (1947-51), where in 1950 he had composition lessons with Martin, though his works of this period are nothing exceptional. The change came in the summer of 1951 when he attended the Darmstadt courses: with Nono and Goeyvaerts he discussed the possibilities opened up by Messiaen's MODE DE VALEURS ET D'INTENSITÉS, possibilities for the organization of music as a process operating on individual notes according to rational laws. He went back to Cologne and wrote *Kreuzspiel* (Crossplay), a piano piece requiring also oboe, bass clarinet and 3 percussionists to articulate its crossover processes involving 12-note sets of pitch classes and durations:

performed at Darmstadt the next summer, the work immediately established his authority among composers in the vanguard of total serialism. Meanwhile he had gone to Paris in January 1952 to study with Messiaen; during 14 months there he also met Boulez and worked in Schaeffer's studio, besides composing KONTRA-PUNKTE and the first of the KLAVIERSTÜCKE. He returned to Cologne at Eimert's invitation in the spring of 1953 to co-direct the new Westdeutscher Rundfunk studio for electronic music, where he composed his 2 *Studien* in synthesized sound (among the first purely electronic works) while continuing the *Klavierstücke*. Also in 1953 he began teaching at Darmstadt.

Within 2 years he had become the acknowledged leader of the avant garde; he had also mapped out the main lines of his composing work. One of those lines is his conception of a work as the fulfilment of a design: hence the importance he has continued to attach to pre-compositional planning. Surprises may be sprung (he enjoys going beyond the system at special moments), but still the music is contained by its structure rather than achieving its form. The choice of what to put within that structure may almost be a quite independent matter. In the early 1950s almost all Stockhausen's works were based on proportioning of the various parameters with the numbers from 1 to 6, and the structure was, as in *Kreuzspiel*, the end result of a process. Since GRUPPEN, GESANG DER JÜNGLINGE and KLAVIERSTUCK XI, however, the processes have often been potentially infinite. He invented the doctrine of MOMENT FORM to cope with music which presents fragments of eternity; he also began to occupy himself more with the structure than with detailed realization. In CARRÉ, for instance, he had his scheme worked out by a pupil, Cardew, and in many works of the 1960s (*Plus-Minus*, PROZESSION, *Spiral*) there are no prescribed sound events but only new notations for patterns of change; in AUS DEN SIEBEN TAGEN even these are suppressed and only words provided as a stimulus to INTUITIVE MUSIC.

This development was partly stimulated by Stockhausen's activity as a performer of LIVE ELECTRONIC MUSIC with his own ensemble, initiated by MIKROPHONIE I. Other works of the same period show, quite differently, that concern with the invention of new sounds which had also been a characteristic of his music from the first. *Spiel*, *Punkte* and *Gruppen* are all essays in the synthesis of new timbres from the orchestra just as the *Studien*, GESANG DER JÜNGLINGE and KONTAKTE do the same

with the resources of the electronic studio. Then in the 1960s live electronic techniques brought the revelations of new worlds of sound within the tam tam (*Mikrophonie I*), orchestra (*Mixtur*) or human voice (MIKROPHONIE II, STIMMUNG). Electronics also enabled Stockhausen to bring dissimilar phenomena together, whether by the electronic imitation of natural sounds (*Gesang der Jünglinge*, *Kontakte*) or by his technique of INTERMODULATION (HYMNEN, TELEMUSIK), giving rise to his conception of his own work as unifying the musical cultures of the entire world.

Such a grandiose vision was no doubt fostered by the international acclaim his music had so long received, and it gave rise in the mid-1970s to the plan for a cycle of 7 musical ceremonies, LICHT. Works written towards this cycle have combined all the features of his art: pre-planned form schemes, musical processes (and yet also the excursions of grand gestures), new sounds (including those produced by electronic techniques), borrowings from exotic cultures (*Licht* has much more in common with the religious theatre of India, Japan or Indonesia than it has with Wagner in the manner of its musical drama, despite other obvious resemblances to *The Ring*). The processes are now based not on separate notes but on a FORMULA or formulae, as in his works of the earlier 1970s, which had included similar hieratic rituals (INORI, SIRIUS). The ability of any artist to achieve such all-embracing mythologies in the late 20th c. has been widely doubted, but the uncertain gap between aim and content, design and material, is a curious constant of his work.

If it might be tendentious to suggest that here is a real connection with Wagner, certainly the two composers are comparable in their wholesale personal identification with their art. As lecturer and performer, visiting many countries, he has been concerned exclusively with his own music. Since *Momente* most of his works have been conceived as whole-evening events or as items for Stockhausen anthologies performed by his own touring ensembles. He has also pressed for the erection of special buildings for his music (this he achieved at the Exposition at Osaka in 1970). Since 1969 he has been his own publisher; he also keeps a comprehensive archive of recordings, interviews, etc. And 3 of the 6 children of his 2 marriages (to Doris Andreae in 1951 and Mary Bauermeister in 1967) have become performers of his music.

Operas: DONNERSTAG AUS LICHT, 1977-80; SAMSTAG AUS LICHT, 1981-3; Montag aus Licht, 1984-

Orchestral: Formel, 29 insts, 1951; Spiel, 1952;

Punkte, 1952, rev. 1962-6; GRUPPEN, 1955-7; CAR-
RÉ, 1959-60; Mixtur, with ring modulators, 1964;
Stop, 1965; Dritte Region der HYMNEN, with tape,
1969; Fresco, 1969; TRANS, 1971; Ylem, 1972; IN-
ORI, 1973-4; Jubiläum, 1977

Vocal: Chöre für Doris, 1950; 3 Lieder, A, chamber
orch, 1950; Choral, 1950; MOMENTE, 1961-4, rev.
1972; MIKROPHONIE II, 1965; STIMMUNG, 1968; AT-
MEN GIBT DAS LEBEN, 1974; SIRIUS, 1975-7

Ensemble: Sonatina, vn, pf, 1951; Kreuzspiel, pf,
ob, b cl, 3 perc, 1951; Schlagquartett, pf, timp,
1952, rev. as Schlagtrio, 1974; KONTRA-PUNKTE,
1952, rev. 1953; ZEITMASZE, 1955-6; REFRAIN, 1959;
KONTAKTE, 1959-60; Plus-Minus, 1963; MIK-
ROPHONIE I, 1964; Adieu, wind qnt, 1966; HYMNEN,
1966-7; PROZESSION, 1967; KURZWELLEN, 1968; AUS
DEN SIEBEN TAGEN, 1968; Für Dr K., 6 insts, 1969;
Pole für zwei, 1969-70; Expo für drei, 1969-70;
MANTRA, 1969-70; Für kommende Zeiten, 17 text
pieces, 1968-70; STERNKLANG, 1971; ALPHABET FÜR
LIÈGE, 1972; Herbstmusik, 4 players, 1974; Musik
im Bauch, 6 perc, 1975; DER JAHRESLAUF, 1977

Solo: KLAVIERSTÜCKE I-IV, 1952-3, V-X, 1954-5
(IX-X rev. 1961), XI, 1956, XII, 1979, XIII, 1981,
XIV, 1985; Zyklus, perc, 1959; Solo, any melody
inst with tape recorders, 1965-6; Spiral, any soloist
with shortwave receiver, 1969; TIERKREIS (also in
various arrangements), 1975; Harlekin, cl, 1975;
Der kleine Harlekin, cl, 1975; Amour, cl, 1976; In
Freundschaft, melody inst, 1977

Tape: Elektronische Studien I, 1953, II, 1954;
GESANG DER JÜNGLINGE, 1955-6; KONTAKTE, 1959-
60; Telemusik, 1966; Hymnen, 1966-7

[UE, Stockhausen; DG]

□ J. Cott, ed., *Stockhausen: Conversations* (1973);
K.H. Wörner, *Karlheinz Stockhausen* (1973); J.
Harvey, *The Music of Stockhausen* (1975); R. Maco-
nie, *The Works of Karlheinz Stockhausen* (1976)

Strauss, Richard (1864-1949) German composer.
With Puccini, Berg and Britten, one of the few
composers to have written more than one successful opera in the 20th c. Like Puccini's, his career was
divided across the centuries; like Britten's, his output was divided between operas and other works.
But the two divisions coincided: all the great symphonic poems and a large proportion of the Lieder
date from the 1880s and 1890s, while from *Feuersnot* (1900-01) onwards he was nearly always at
work on an opera, except in his last years. The
abrupt change may be attributed to uncertainties
about what sort of a composer he wanted to be: it
was not the only time he suddenly switched his en-

thusiasms, for in the mid-1880s he had gone from
being the expected heir of Brahms to being the follower of Wagner and Liszt, and then in ROSEN-
KAVALIER he was to execute one of the most supreme volte-faces in the history of art, turning quite
aside from the frenzied Expressionism of his ELEK-
TRA. Probably it would be wrong to seek any deep
psychological motivation in any of these turn-
abouts: indeed, one of the characteristics of his
creativity is its lack of a grounding in his own
psyche, its refusal of self-expression (the 'self' of
Ein Heldenleben or *Intermezzo* is evidently a dramatization). While normally taken as one of the most
Romantic of 20th c. composers, his Romanticism
was a means to give pleasure rather than make
autobiographical statements: in this respect he was
an antipole to his contemporary Mahler.

Born in Munich, the son of the principal horn-
player in the court orchestra, he composed from
boyhood: he never went to a conservatory, for his
career was already well under way when he left
school in 1882. He conducted in Meiningen (1885-
6), Munich (1886-9, 1894-8), Weimar (1889-94)
and Berlin (1898-1908), after which the success of
his operas allowed him to retire to his villa at Gar-
misch with his wife and family, though he made
frequent appearances as a guest conductor of his
works, some of which he recorded. During the
Nazi years he remained in Germany, his easygoing
nature bringing him disapprobation from both
sides: from the authorities because he worked with
a Jewish librettist (Stefan Zweig), and from anti-
Nazis because he accepted official honours and
made no criticism of the government. CAPRICCIO
was intended as his operatic swansong; after it he
returned to orchestral music and Lieder.

Operas: Guntram, 1892-3, ★Weimar, 1894; Feuers-
not, 1900-01, ★Dresden, 1901; SALOME, 1903-5;
ELEKTRA, 1906-8; Der ROSENKAVALIER, 1909-10;
ARIADNE AUF NAXOS, 1911-12; Die FRAU OHNE
SCHATTEN, 1914-18; INTERMEZZO, 1918-23; Die
ÄGYPTISCHE HELENA, 1923-7; ARABELLA, 1929-32;
Die SCHWEIGSAME FRAU, 1933-4; FRIEDENSTAG,
1935-6; DAPHNE, 1936-7; Die LIEBE DER DANAE, 1938-
40; CAPRICCIO, 1940-1

Orchestral: Burleske, d, pf, orch, 1885-6; Aus Ita-
lien, 1886; Don Juan, 1888-9; Macbeth, 1886-8,
rev. 1889-91; Tod und Verklärung, 1888-9; Till
Eulenspiegels lustige Streiche, 1894-5; Also sprach
Zarathustra, 1895-6; Don Quixote, 1896-7; Ein
Heldenleben, 1897-8; Symphonia domestica,
1902-3; Le bourgeois gentilhomme, incidental
music, 1912, suite, 1918; Josephs-Legende, ballet,
1912-14; Eine Alpensinfonie, 1911-15; Schlag-

obers, ballet, 1921-2, suite, 1932; Parergon zur Symphonia domestica, pf left hand, orch, 1924; Panathenäenzug, pf left hand, orch, 1927; Hn Conc no.2, 1942; 2 sonatinas, wind, 1943, 1944-5; Metamorphosen, 23 str, 1945; Ob Conc, 1945; Duet–Concertino, cl, bn, str, harp, 1947

Choral orchestral: Taillefer, 1903; Bardengesang, 1905; Die Tageszeiten, 1928; Austria, 1929; Olympic Hymn, 1934

Choral: 2 Songs, 16vv, 1897; 2 Male Choruses, 1899; 3 Male Choruses, 1899; Deutsche Motette, 4 solo vv, 16vv, 1913; An den Baum Daphne, 9vv, 1943

Orchestral songs (dating indicates composition/ orchestration): Zueignung, 1885/1940; Cäcilie, Morgen, 1894/1897; Ruhe, meine Seele, 1894/ 1948; Liebeshymnus, 1896/1897; Das Rosenband, Meinem Kinde, 1897/1897; Mein Auge, Befreit, 1898/1933; Ich liebe dich, 1898/1943; Wiegenlied, 1899 /?1916; Notturno, Nächtlicher Gang, 1899/ 1899; Muttertändelei, 1899/1900; Des Dichters Abendgang, Freundliche Vision, Winterweihe, Winterliebe, 1900/1918; Waldseligkeit, 1901/ 1918; Das Thal, 1902/1902; Die heiligen drei Königen, 1903-6/1906; Frühlingsfeier, 1903-6/ 1933; Der Einsame, 1906/1906; Lied der Frauen, 1918/1933; An die Nacht, Ich wollt' ein Sträusslein, Säusle, Als mir dein Lied, Amor, 1918/1940; 3 Hymns (Hölderlin), 1921/1921; Das Bächlein, 1933/1935; 4 Last Songs, 1948/1948

Songs (20th c. only): 8 op.49, 1900-01; 6 op.56, 1903-6; Krämerspiegel (Kerr), cycle, 1918; 6 op.67, 1918; 6 op.68, 1918; 5 op.69, 1918; Sinnspruch, 1919; Durch allen Schall, 1925; Gesänge des Orients, 1928; 4 op.87, 1922-35; Wie etwas sei leicht, 1930; Zugemessne Rythmen, 1935; 3 op.88, 1933-42; Xenion, 1942

[Boosey]

□ Correspondence with Hofmannsthal (1961), Rolland (1968), Zweig (1977); N. Del Mar, *Richard Strauss*, 3 vols (1962-72, r1978)

Stravinsky, Igor (1882-1971) Russian composer. His huge impact on western music was sensed notoriously by the audience at the first performance of his RITE OF SPRING and has become steadily more apparent as the 20th c. has advanced. Quite simply, his works question the assumptions on which western music had been grounded since the Renaissance, those of harmonic consistency, even metrical flow, thematic development, goal direction and, at the deepest level, the major–minor system. By introducing into music new modes – some from Russian folk and church music, but most importantly the mode of alternating major and minor 2nds derived from Rimsky-Korsakov (Messiaen's second mode in different circumstances) – he was able to disrupt diatonic harmony in ways that sound perfectly controlled but have proved difficult to analyse: *The Rite* remains, with its near contemporary *Erwartung*, one of the great cruces of 20th c. musical analysis. Its harmonic revolution is accompanied, still more forcibly, by a change in rhythm. Stravinsky's TIME is not the regularly ruled canvas of most western music; the unit is not the phrase of similar bars but rather the pulse, from which irregular bars and irregular phrases may be built. And then these changes in harmony and rhythm are naturally accompanied by changes in form. His music does not move purposefully towards a resolution; the non-diatonic harmony and the irregular rhythm forfeit the subtle precision with which music has traditionally made it possible for the future to be predicted. There is no stability through time, and so Stravinsky's forms tend to consist of separate fragments, even if they are often arranged to give the illusion of a progressive form.

Stravinsky was born at Oranienbaum (now Lomonosov), the third of 4 sons of a principal bass at the Mariinsky Theatre in St Petersburg: until he was 28 his life was divided between that city and the family's summer estate at Ustilug, where he continued to spend the holidays after his marriage in 1906 to his cousin Katerina Nossenko (there were 2 sons and 2 daughters of the union). He read law at St Petersburg University (1901-5), and had private lessons in composition with Rimsky from 1902 until the latter's death in 1908. The next year he came to the notice of Dyagilev when his *Scherzo fantastique* and *Feu d'artifice* were performed in St Petersburg. Dyagilev immediately commissioned him to orchestrate 2 numbers for his Chopin ballet *Les sylphides*, and then asked him for an original score, FIREBIRD.

Preparations for that took him to Paris, and out of Russia, for the first time in 1910. During the short remaining time before the first world war he travelled widely in western Europe, meeting Schoenberg in Berlin and hearing *Pierrot lunaire*. Meanwhile his music developed with extraordinary speed, and the still largely Rimskyesque *Firebird* was succeeded by the wholly original PETRUSHKA and *Rite* besides such curiosities as the mystic cantata *Star-Visaged* and the exquisite Balmont songs and Japanese lyrics. By 1914, though his reputation rested on no more than these few works, he was widely regarded as one of the leading modernist composers.

The war he spent in Switzerland, which he had already found to be congenial (much of *The Rite* had been written there). Creatively, though, he found his sources in Russia, whose folk poetry provided him with texts for ballets in song (LES NOCES, RENARD) and for cycles of ditties (PRIBAOUTKI). His style became much more economical, requiring small ensembles, featuring lean counterpoints of small melodic ideas, tending to the barest minimum in some of the contemporary piano duets. It was a time of distillation, but as ever he was open to new musical tastes, including RAGTIME in the SOLDIER'S TALE (1918).

After the war Dyagilev's company was back on tour, and for them he wrote PULCINELLA (1919-20), opening a long period of interrogation of the past, or NEOCLASSICISM. He chose, like most of his Russian associates, to remain in exile, but he continued at first to write exceedingly Russian works, notably the opera MAVRA and even the distinctly Orthodox, though Latin-chanting, SYMPHONY OF PSALMS. Another feature of his music at this time was his preference for wind and percussion sonorities: his percussive use of the piano in *Petrushka* was continued in *Les noces* and the solo works he wrote for himself in 1923-5, while the clear articulation of woodwinds in particular suited his purposes in the SYMPHONIES OF WIND INSTRUMENTS and the Octet. However, strings appear again in the 2 works that mark the early highpoint of his neoclassicism, OEDIPUS REX (1926-27) and APOLLO (1927-8), the latter very deliberately exploiting their euphony.

During the next decade he turned more to large-scale instrumental forms than theatre works: there was the Capriccio for piano and orchestra, the Violin Concerto, the Concerto for 2 pianos, the DUMBARTON OAKS Concerto and eventually the Symphony in C (1938-40). Partly the reasons were material: after Dyagilev's death in 1928 he had no home company, and he was now writing largely on commission. But he put these circumstances to creative use, increasing the subtlety and accuracy of his irony so that it could be pointed not just at broad aspects of style (as in the Handel-Verdi of *Oedipus rex*) but at the atmospheres of particular works (the Brandenburg concertos in *Dumbarton Oaks*) or at structural procedures as removed from his own as sonata form (Symphony in C).

In 1939, while he was at work on that symphony, his wife and his mother died, and he left France, his home since 1920, for the United States. His mistress Vera Sudeikina followed him, and they were married in 1940, settling that summer in Hollywood. There the Symphony in C was finished, and followed by another, 'in Three Movements'. Other works of this period suggest an unsettled composer, willing to write for an elephant ballet (*Circus Polka*), a film of *Jane Eyre* (material used in the *Ode*) or a popular jazzman (*Ebony Concerto*). The later 1940s brought a returned integration, with the ballet ORPHEUS, the Mozartian opera RAKE'S PROGRESS, and the glowing but austere Mass for chorus and wind.

Completed before the opera, the Mass looks forward to the work that followed it, the CANTATA (1951-2), in its medievalism. The root of that medievalism, though, lay in the music of Schoenberg and Webern, which he creatively rediscovered in the Cantata and succeeding works: the Septet (for an ensemble close to that of Schoenberg's Suite op.29), IN MEMORIAM DYLAN THOMAS, the CANTICUM SACRUM, AGON and THRENI (1957-8), of which the last was his first wholesale essay in 12-note composition, the earlier works using smaller sets. This 'conversion' caused some perturbation after 3 decades during which he and Schoenberg had been seen as the rival popes of music, and yet, without touching deeper reasons in his creative personality, one can adduce several contributory factors: the facilitation provided by Schoenberg's death in 1951; the interests in Schoenberg and Webern prompted in him by CRAFT; and his observation of what young composers in Europe were about.

After *Threni* his works were all 12-note, all of short duration, and many of them memorial in character, including the *Requiem Canticles* (1965-6) with which his creative career effectively ended. In 1967 his health began to fail, and his other career as a conductor of his own music also came to an end, though not before he had recorded a large part of his output. In 1969 he and his wife moved to New York, where he died. His funeral took place in Venice.

Operas: The NIGHTINGALE, 1908-9, 1913-14; MAVRA, 1921-2; OEDIPUS REX, 1926-7; The RAKE'S PROGRESS, 1948-51

Ballets: The FIREBIRD, 1909-10; PETRUSHKA, 1910-11; The RITE OF SPRING, 1911-13; RENARD, 1915-16; Les NOCES, 1914-23; PULCINELLA, 1919-20; APOLLO, 1927-8; Le BAISER DE LA FÉE, 1928; PERSÉPHONE, 1933-4; JEU DE CARTES, 1936; Circus Polka, 1942; Scènes de ballet, 1944; ORPHEUS, 1947; AGON, 1953-4

Other dramatic works: SOLDIER'S TALE, 1918; The FLOOD, 1961-2

Works for full orchestra: Sym no.1, E♭, 1905-7;

Scherzo fantastique, 1907-8; Feu d'artifice, 1908; Chant du rossignol, 1917; 4 Studies, 1914-28; Capriccio, pf, orch, 1928-9; Vn Conc, 1931; Sym, C, 1939-40, 4 Norwegian Moods, 1942; Ode, 1943; Scherzo à la russe, 1943-4; Sym in 3 Movements, 1942-5; Greeting Prelude, 1955; Movements, with pf, 1958-9; Variations, 1963-4; Canon on a Russian Popular Tune, 1965

Works for reduced orchestras: Rag-Time, 11 insts, 1918; SYMPHONIES OF WIND INSTS, 1920; 2 suites, 1917-25; Pf Conc, 1923-4; Preludium, 1936-7; Conc, 'Dumbarton Oaks', 1938; Danses concertantes, 1941-2; Ebony Conc, cl, jazzband, 1945; Conc, D, str, 1946; Concertino, arr. 1952; Tango, arr. 1953; 8 Instrumental Miniatures, 15 insts, arr. 1962

Choral: Star-Visaged (Zvezdolikiy, Le roi des étoiles), male vv, orch, 1911-12; 4 Russian Peasant Songs, female vv, 1914-17; Pater noster, SATB, 1926, rev. 1949; SYMPHONY OF PSALMS, 1930; Credo, SATB, 1932, rev. 1949; Ave Maria, 1934, rev. 1949; Babel (cantata), 1944; Mass, TrATB, 10 wind, 1944-8; Cantata, 1951-2; Canticum sacrum, 1955; Threni, 1957-8; A Sermon, a Narrative and a Prayer (cantata), 1960-61; Anthem 'The Dove Descending', SATB, 1962; Introitus, 1965; Requiem Canticles, A, B, vv, orch, 1965-6

Songs with orchestra/ensemble: Faun and Shepherdess, Mez, orch, 1906; 3 Japanese Lyrics, S, 9 insts, 1912-13; Pribaoutki, Bar, 8 insts, 1914; Berceuses du chat, A, 3 cl, 1915-16; Pastorale, S, 4 wind, arr. 1923; Tilimbom, v, orch, arr. 1923; 3 Little Songs, v, orch, arr. 1929-30; 2 poèmes (Verlaine), Bar, chamber orch, arr. 1951; 3 Shakespeare Songs, Mez, fl, cl, va, 1953; 4 Songs, v, fl, harp, gui, 1953-4; 2 Poems (Balmont), S, 9 insts, arr. 1954; In memoriam Dylan Thomas, 1954; Abraham and Isaac, 1962-3; Elegy for J.F.K., Bar/Mez, 3 cl, 1964

Songs with piano: Pastorale, 1907; 2 mélodies (Gorodetsky), 1908; 2 poèmes (Verlaine), 1910; 2 Poems (Balmont), 1911; 3 Little Songs, 1913; 3 histoires pour enfants, 1915-17; Berceuse, 1917; 4 Russian Songs, 1918-19; The Owl and the Pussy-Cat, 1966

Chamber: 3 Pieces, str qt, 1914; 3 Pieces, cl, 1919; Concertino, str qt, 1920; Octet, wind, 1922-3; Duo concertant, vn, pf, 1931-2; Suite italienne, vn/vc, pf, 1932; Elégie, va, 1944; Septet, 1952-3; Epitaphium, fl, cl, harp, 1959; Double Canon, str qt, 1959; Fanfare for a New Theatre, 2 tpt, 1964

Piano: Scherzo, 1902; Sonata, f, 1903-4; 4 Studies, 1908; Souvenir d'une marche boche, 1915; Valse, c.1917; Piano-Rag-Music, 1919; Les 5 doigts, 1921; 3 Movements from Petrushka, 1921; Sonata, 1924; Serenade, 1925; Tango, 1940

Two pianos: Concerto, 1931-5; Sonata, 1943-4
Piano duet: 3 Easy Pieces, 1914-15; 5 Easy Pieces, 1916-17
Pianola: Etude, 1917
Arrangements: 2 Songs of the Flea (Beethoven, Musorgsky), B, orch, 1910; Song of the Volga Boatmen, orch, 1917; La Marseillaise, vn, 1919; Bluebird Pas-de-deux (Tchaikovsky), small orch, 1941; The Star-Spangled Banner, orch, 1941; Chorale Variations 'Vom Himmel hoch' (Bach), chorus, orch, 1955-6; 3 sacrae cantiones (Gesualdo), addition of missing parts, 1957-9; Monumentum pro Gesualdo, arr. of 3 madrigals for orch, 1960; Canzonetta (Sibelius), 2 cl, 4 hn, harp, db, 1963; Wolf: 2 Sacred Songs, Mez, 9 insts, 1968

[Boosey, Schott, Chester; Columbia]

□ I. Stravinsky, *An Autobiography* (1936, r1975), *Poetics of Music* (1947), *Selected Correspondence*, 3 vols. (1982-)

□ I. Stravinsky and R. Craft, *Conversations* (1959), *Memories and Commentaries* (1960), *Expositions and Developments* (1962), *Dialogues and a Diary* (1963), *Themes and Episodes* (1966), *Retrospectives and Conclusions* (1969)

□ E. W. White, *Stravinsky* (1966, 2/1979); V. Stravinsky and R. Craft, *Stravinsky in Pictures and Documents* (1968); B. Asafyev, *A Book about Stravinsky* (1982)

string piano Term introduced by Cowell for a piano in which the player operates directly on the strings, plucking or hammering.

structure 'One of the key words of our epoch', according to one of Boulez's early essays; and certainly the 20th c. has seen an unusual concern with musical structure, with the mechanisms by which moments are connected and forms built. One expression of this is in the shift from criticism to analysis in the study of music, while among composers there has been a tendency to distrust any imaginative enterprise not backed by structural meaning demonstrable in terms of some system: hence the neoclassicism of Busoni, Reger, Stravinsky, Prokofiev and Hindemith, the motivic working of Bartók, the 12-note system of Schoenberg, Berg, Webern and Babbitt, the total serialism of Boulez and Stockhausen. Babbitt has even stated that there is no note in his compositions that he cannot account for, which must represent an extreme statement of rational control over the creative process. It is easy to understand such a wish for watertight structure in an age when the old language of music (the diatonic system) has been in disarray: if the words no longer make sense, then at least one can ensure the letters are put together in patterns. More problematic is the link between composed and perceived structures, which so far has kept structuralist methods of analysis from probing far into the nature of music.

Subotnick, Morton (1933-) American composer. Studied with Milhaud and Kirchner at Mills College (1957-9), then joined the faculty (1959-66), teaching later at New York University (1966-9) and the California Institute of the Arts (1969-). He is noted as a composer of colourful and dramatic electronic music: his *Silver Apples of the Moon* (1966) was the first tape piece made for an LP record. [MCA; Nonesuch]

Suk, Josef (1874-1935) Czech composer and violinist. Studied at the Prague Conservatory (1885-92) with Dvořák, whose daughter he married. He was second violin in the Czech Quartet (1892-1933), and the composer of serious-minded music in a late Romantic style yearning into much more chromatic territory than Dvořák's. His works include the symphony *Asrael* (1905-6) and 2 quartets (1896, 1911).
□ J. Berkovec: *Josef Suk* (1968)

Surinach, Carlos (1915-) Spanish-American composer. Studied in Barcelona and Germany, then embarked on dual career as composer and conductor in Barcelona (1944-7), Paris (1947-51) and the USA (1951-). Showing high polish and not always Spanish flavour, his works include many ballets and other orchestral pieces. [AMP]

Survivor from Warsaw, A Work by Schoenberg, his last completed orchestral score. The narrator, in *Sprechgesang*, speaks Schoenberg's own words adapted from the testimonies of Jewish survivors of the Nazi terror, dramatically preparing the male chorus's expression of continuing faith. ★Albuquerque, 4 Nov 1948.

Swanson, Howard (1907-78) American composer. Studied at the Cleveland Institute of Music and in Paris with Boulanger (1938), then settled in New York in 1941. His small output, in a graceful neoclassical style, includes 3 symphonies, chamber pieces and songs. [Leeds]

Swayne, Giles (1946-) English composer. Studied at Cambridge, at the Royal Academy of Music, with Maw and with Messiaen. His earlier works are conservatively modernist within the mainstream of English music of the 1970s, but *Cry* for unaccompanied chorus (1978) is suddenly both simpler and more ambitious: a creation myth told in terms of wide consonant harmony and quasi-primitive chant. Before and after this he made a study of indigenous music in west Africa, though little of that influence can be detected in his Mozartian pastiche *Le nozze di Cherubino* (★1985). [Novello]

Swingle Singers Octet led by Ward Lemar Swingle and active 1962-73, famous for scat performances of Bach and given a place by Berio in his *Sinfonia*. Swingle founded a new group, Swingle II, in 1973, and for them Berio has written other works (*Cries, A-Ronne*).

Symbolism Artistic movement of the turn of the century, so-called because of the intensity with which inanimate objects and phenomena were scrutinized as symbols of emotional state. The term is most often associated with writers (e.g. Maeterlinck) and painters (e.g. Moreau), but Wagner's leitmotif-filled music dramas provided Symbolists with abundant precedents, and critics have pointed out that Debussy was at least as much a Symbolist as he was an Impressionist. Some of Schoenberg's works, such as the *Gurrelieder* and *Die glückliche Hand*, belong with the Nordic-Germanic Symbolism of Jacobsen, Strindberg and others, similarly Wagner-influenced, while the Russian Symbolist poets (e.g. Balmont) were an influence on Stravinsky and many other composers in the years leading up to the Revolution. The most obvious case of musical symbolism, however, is Bartók's *Bluebeard's Castle*.

Symphonies of Wind Instruments Work by Stravinsky for orchestral wind, quite non-symphonic in its abutting of short 'litanies' (his word) for different groupings: the title, he explained, was to be understood in its etymological sense of 'soundings together'. ★London, 10 Jun 1921. The revised score (1945-7) alters the scoring and detail.

symphony The form is so much a child of the diatonic system that the great symphonies of the 20th c. have inevitably come from composers using that system in some manner: Mahler, Elgar, Sibelius, Nielsen, Ives, Vaughan Williams, Stravinsky, Bax, Honegger, Shostakovich, Prokofiev.

Schoenberg's symphonies are both from among his diatonic output; Webern's singleton is 12-note; Berg's is atonal and buried as Act 2 of *Wozzeck*. Around the middle of the century the symphony came to be seen, because of its diatonic proclivities, as a conservative genre, but in the 1970s composers began to see it again as a field of adventure, perhaps because of a renewed interest in long-range harmonic, if not necessarily diatonic, processes (cf the symphonies of Davies). In view of the highly irregular character of some 20th c. symphonies – e.g. Mahler's Eighth, Berg's, Webern's, Stravinsky's 'of Psalms', Messiaen's 10-movement *Turangalîla* – useless argument has sometimes raged about whether a work is or is not a symphony. It must be obvious that the word has no defining powers, except in guiding audiences to listen against the background of the Classical 4-movement model.
☐ R. Simpson, ed. , *The Symphony*, vol. 2 (1967)

Symphony of Psalms (Symphonie des psaumes) Work by Stravinsky for chorus (with boy sopranos) and an orchestra lacking violins and violas: 'it is', he said, 'the singing of the Psalms that I am symphonizing'. The movements are introduction ('Exaudi orationem meam'), fugue ('Expectans expectavi') and apotheosis-finale ('Laudate Dominum'). *cond Ansermet, Brussels, 13 Dec 1930.

synthesizer Electronic device of which various kinds have been manufactured by Robert Moog, Donald Buchla, etc, with the idea of making available any sound by electronic synthesis. In the late 1960s and early 1970s synthesizers became popular with live electronic ensembles and rock bands; alternatively they may be used in the electronic studio, as they have been by Stockhausen, Subotnick, Carlos, etc, as well as by composers of computer music. The unique RCA Synthesizer, at the Columbia-Princeton Electronic Music Center, is the instrument favoured by Babbitt.

Szymanowski, Karol (1882-1937) Polish composer. Studied with Noskowski in Warsaw (1901-4), then lived in Berlin (1905-8), where with others he formed the Young Poland in Music group. His first works had been mostly for the piano, in a Chopinesque manner, but he now wrote his First Symphony (1906-7) under the influence of Strauss. In 1908 he returned to his native Tymoshovka in the Ukraine, but he made journeys to Italy, Sicily, Vienna, north Africa and the great Russian cities, all the while developing his tastes for the marvel-

lous and ornamental: Byzantine and Islamic art, Skryabin, Debussy and Stravinsky. All these influences came to bear on the florescence of music he produced in the years 1914-17, and then on his opera *King Roger*, a transposition of the *Bacchae* of Euripides into 12th c. Sicily. In 1919, with Poland now independent, he settled in Warsaw, and began drawing on Polish folk music rather in the manner of Stravinsky's recent work; his last works are more blandly neoclassical.
Operas: Hagith, 1913, *Warsaw, 1922; King Roger, 1918-24, Warsaw, *1926
Ballets: Mandragora, 1920; Harnasie, 1923-31
Orchestral: Sym no. 1, f, 1906-7, no. 2, B♭, 1909-10, no. 3 'The Song of the Night', with T/S and chorus, 1914-16, no. 4 (Symphonie concertante), with pf, 1932; Vn Conc no. 1, 1916, no. 2, 1933
Vocal orchestral: Love Songs of Hafiz, v, orch, 1914; Demeter, A, female vv, orch, 1917; Agave, A, female vv, orch, 1917; Stabat mater, solo vv, vv, orch, 1925-6
Songs: Songs of a Fairy-Tale Princess, 1915; 4 Songs (Tagore), 1918; Songs of the Infatuated Muezzin, 1918; 4 Songs (Joyce), 1926
Chamber: Nocturne and Tarantella, vn, pf, 1915; Myths, vn, pf, 1915; Str Qt no. 1, C, 1917, no. 2, 1927
Piano: Sonata no. 1, c, 1904, no. 2, A, 1911, no. 3, 1917; Metopes, 1915; Masques, 1916; 20 Mazurkas, 1924-5
[UE]
☐ J. Samson, *The Music of Szymanowski* (1980)

T

Tailleferre, Germaine (1892-1983) French composer. Studied at the Paris Conservatoire, where she met Auric, Honegger and Milhaud, and so became a member of Satie's circle and in due course of Les six. In later years she wrote in all genres, in a style beholden to Fauré and Ravel. [Durand, Heugel]

Takahashi, Yuji (1938-) Japanese composer and pianist. Studied at the Toho School (1954-8) and in Berlin with Xenakis (1963-5), of whose *Herma* he gave the first performance. In 1966 he went to New York to study computer composition while continuing his activities as a pianist specializing in demanding new works. [Peters]

Takemitsu, Tōru (1930-) Japanese composer. From 1948 had occasional lessons with Kiyose, but otherwise self-taught. He has been influenced by western music that itself leans towards Japan in economy of line, sophistication of colouring or non-progressive time sense: Debussy, Webern, Messiaen, Boulez. Some of his works use Japanese instruments (e.g. *November Steps* for biwa, shaku-hachi and orchestra, 1967), but most are for orchestras or ensembles of western formation. He has also composed tape pieces and much film music. [Peters, UE, Schott; DG]

Tal, Josef (1910-) Polish-Israeli composer. Studied with Hindemith at the Berlin Hochschule (1928-30), then in 1934 left for Palestine, where he taught at the Jerusalem Conservatory (1937-52) and the Hebrew University (1950-). His new surroundings and language affected his music, but the central European strain remained, and he became the most noted Israeli practitioner of 12-note and electronic music. His works include operas (*Ashmedai*, ★Hamburg, 1971), 3 symphonies, 6 piano concertos (3 with tape). [Israel Music Institute, Israeli Music Publications]

Taneyev, Sergey (1857-1915) Russian composer. Studied with Tchaikovsky at the Moscow Conservatory (1866-75), where he returned as a teacher in 1880, his pupils including Rakhmaninov and Skryabin. His music is like distilled Tchaikovsky, suave and ingratiating, but also finely worked and emotionally aloof.
Chamber (20th c. only): Str Qnt no.1, G, 1901-3, no.2, C, 1904; Str Qt no.5, A, 1903, no.6, B♭, 1905; PfQt, E, 1906; Str Trio, D, 1907; PfTrio, D, 1907; Str Trio, E♭, 1910; PfQnt, g, 1911
Choral music, songs, 4 earlier syms

Tanglewood Estate in Massachusetts, site of the Berkshire Festival, which each summer since 1964 has included a festival of contemporary music. Schuller, Copland, Messiaen and others have taught composition there.

Tansman, Alexandre (1897-) Polish-French composer. Studied at the Łódź Conservatory (1902-14) and with Rytel in Warsaw, then in 1919 moved to Paris, where he became acquainted with Stravinsky, Ravel, Milhaud and others. These friendships influenced his music, which includes operas, 7 symphonies, 8 quartets, etc.

Tavener, John (1944-) English composer. Studied with Berkeley and Lumsdaine at the Royal Academy of Music (1961-5), and enjoyed early success when his cantata *The Whale*, a graphic telling of the Jonah story, had its first performance in 1968. His subsequent development has been at once musical and spiritual, leading him to membership of the Russian Orthodox Church and the composition of music of iconic simplicity and luminosity. [Chester]

Taverner Opera by Davies to his own libretto, concerning the religious and artistic crisis presumed to have occurred in the life of the Henrician composer John Taverner when he gave up composing masses to became a persecutor of the old church. ★Covent Garden, 12 Jul 1972.

Taylor, Deems (1885-1966) American composer. Studied at New York University and privately with Oscar Coon (1908-11), and worked as a writer and broadcaster on music. He had 2 operas produced at the Metropolitan, *The King's Henchman* (★1927) and *Peter Ibbetson* (★1931), and also wrote orchestral and choral music in a fluent, European-oriented style. [Fischer]

Tcherepnin, Alexander (1899-1977) Russian-French-American composer. His father Nikolay was the composer of one of Dyagilev's early successes, *Le pavillon d'Armide* (★1908), and other ballets. In 1921 the family left Russia for Paris, where Alexander was influenced by Prokofiev. He also worked with new modes: the 'Tcherepnin scale' is identical with Messiaen's mode 3. In 1948 he moved to the USA with his family, including 2 sons who became composers, Serge (1941-) and Ivan (1943-).

Telemusik Tape piece by Stockhausen using recordings of Japanese percussion instruments (it was composed in Tokyo) and snatches of music from around the world brought together by editing and intermodulation. ★Tokyo, 25 April 1966.

Temps restitué, Le (Time Restored) The last element of his *La mort de Virgile* that Barraqué completed. ★Helge Pilarczyk, ORTF Chorus, Domaine Musical, Percussions de Strasbourg/Amy, Royan, 4 Apr 1968.

tetrachord Set of 4 pitch classes, most usually such a fragment of a 12-note set.

texture Loose but useful term for the quality of a short passage of music: the texture may be homophonic, heterophonic or contrapuntal , or it may be thin (few parts) or thick (many parts), etc.

texture music Term, sometimes mildly derogatory, for music in which texture would seem to be the main concern: i.e. qualities of melody, rhythmic interest, etc are suppressed, and instead one is presented with sound masses defined more by density, loudness and scoring. A lot of electronic music from the 1950s and 1960s fits this description, but the term is most usually applied to orchestral works of the kind represented by Ligeti's *Atmosphères* and much of Penderecki and Xenakis.

theremin Electronic melody instrument invented by the Franco-Russian physicist Léon Thérémin, and first demonstrated by him in 1920. Its pitch was determined by the distance of the player's hand from a vertical aerial. Martinů and others wrote for it, but it never attained the currency of the ondes martenot.

third stream Term introduced by Schuller in the 1950s for music drawing on both jazz and 'classical' backgrounds. Other exponents of such music have included Milhaud, Stravinsky, Banks and Babbitt.

Thompson, Randall (1899-) American composer and teacher. Studied at Harvard and with Bloch in New York (1920-21), then worked as a teacher, notably at Harvard (1948-65). He wrote much choral music, including an unaccompanied mass and a passion. [E.C. Schirmer]

Thomson, Virgil (1896-) American composer. Played the organ during his schooldays, then studied at Harvard with Hill and Davison (1919-23), interrupting his time there for a year with Boulanger in Paris (1921-2). He returned to Paris for a longer period (1925-40), during which he met Gertrude Stein and wrote with her the opera *4 Saints in 3 Acts* (1927-33), a mystifying text set with music in the simple, objective, unassuming style that soon earned him comparison with Satie. In 1940 he went back to New York as a music critic of the *Herald Tribune*, which he remained for 14 years, showing no lack of the self expression he abjured in his music. His large output after *4 Saints* includes another Stein opera, *The Mother of us All* (1947), film scores in which he explored a vein of Americana (*The Plow that Broke the Plains*, 1936; *Louisiana Story*, 1948), and a sequence of 'portraits' of friends. [Mercury, G. Schirmer; Nonesuch]

□ K. Hoover and J. Cage, *Virgil Thomson* (1959); V. Thomson, *Virgil Thomson* (1966)

Three Places in New England Work by Ives for full orchestra, published in arrangement for smaller forces. The places are 'The Saint-Gaudens in Boston Common', a slow meditation on a monument to a Revolutionary colonel and his coloured regiment; 'Putnam's Camp, Redding, Connecticut', an anecdote in music, depicting a young boy leaving a holiday outing to have a vision of another incident from the Revolutionary War; and 'The Housatonic at Stockbridge', a potentially endless slow winding of string music in dense harmony, remembering a time when Ives and his wife walked beside the Housatonic river. ★New York, 10 Jan 1931.

Threni: id est Lamentationes Jeremiae Prophetae (Threnodies: i.e. the Lamentations of Jeremiah) Work by Stravinsky, his first fully 12-note composition, set in abutting short sections for different selections from the ensemble of 6 soloists (SATTBB), chorus and orchestra. ★cond Stravinsky, Venice, 23 Sep 1958.

Tierkreis (Zodiac) Set of 12 melodies by Stockhausen , 1 for each sign, written for musical boxes used in his *Musik im Bauch* and then taken as the basic formulae for his *Sirius*. They have also been published in various instrumental and vocal arrangements, the latter setting the composer's own texts describing each sign's attributes.

timbre Quality of sound distinguishable from pitch, duration and loudness; 'colour' is the appropriate visual metaphor. The phenomenon depends on the onset characteristics and harmonic spectrum of the sound. In the 20th c. timbre has often been given more consideration than in earlier music: *see* ELECTRONIC MUSIC, KLANGFARBENMELODIE, RESONANCE, SOUND.

time Music has frequently been described as 'the art of time', but quite what this means is not clear (*see* SOUND). Stravinsky, in his dictum about music being 'powerless to *express* anything at all', goes on to say that: 'The phenomenon of music is given to us with the sole purpose of establishing an order in things, including, and particularly, the coordination between *man* and *time*.' The wording may be obscure, but his own practice enables one to suggest a certain line of interpretation, since the distinguishing aspect of his music is so much the disruption of regular, even temporal unfolding. Music from the 17th c. to the 19th had concurred with the clock: it had moved in a smooth, measured fashion, and in one direction. Stravinsky's music proclaims that there are other ways of perceiving time, other ways in which '*man*' may be coordinated with the element. The unfolding may be distinctly rough and irregular, and there may be no real progress at all, but rather a perpetual circling among the same moments (3 Pieces for quartet, Symphonies of Wind Instruments). This static conception of time is in accord with much else in 20th c. music: the decline of long-range progressive harmony, the preference for ritual rather than narrative forms and modes of theatre, the kinship with exotic cultures. However, it is easier to understand how, say, Indian music is constructed than it is to fathom how it is perceived. The audience may therefore have a more difficult task than the composer in coming to terms with other ways of experiencing time.

Among composers since *The Rite* who have gone furthest fom traditional progressiveness must be counted Cage (repetitions of the same moment in his music of the 1940s; the timelessness of total unpredictability in later works) and Messiaen (again repetitions; time reversed in his wholesale retrogradations; time vastly slowed in his adagios). *See also* DURATION, RHYTHM.

time point Concept introduced by Babbitt as a rhythmic equivalent to pitch class: its concern is not with duration but with the metrical point at which a sound starts. In a 3/4 bar one may distinguish 12 time points at intervals of a semiquaver. The time-point set (0, 10, 7, 3, 6, 11) may thus be expressed:

Duration in this system, it will be seen, is now an equivalent to interval: the gap between the last 2 time points, for instance, is 5 semiquavers (or it could be 5 semiquavers plus 1 or more bars, the bar now being an equivalent to the octave). Corresponding so closely to the pitch-class system, the time-point system lends itself to similar 12-note operations, and has been used by Babbitt in most of his works since 1957, as well as by many other composers (e.g. Wuorinen, Harvey).

time-space notation Simplified rhythmic notation introduced by Brown in 1953, and much used by other composers, e.g. Berio. Durations are indicated not by the usual symbols but simply by horizontal lines according to a fixed scale, accuracy being compensated by ease of use for the performer. Notation of this sort is obviously most practical for the representing of tape parts in scores for recorded and live sources.

timpani The introduction of pedal timpani, around the beginning of the century, made possible more rapid changes of pitch: Strauss was one of the first to take advantage of this in his *Salome*. Pedal timpani also allowed the execution of glissandos, notably used in Nielsen's Fourth Symphony and several works by Bartók (the Nielsen symphony, like *The Rite of Spring* and other works of this period, requires 2 timpanists). Other innovations have included the use of small drums for high notes (Ravel, Janáček), of particular sticks or other means of striking, and of resonating objects placed on the skins. The inevitably small solo repertory includes Carter's 8 Pieces and concertos by Robert Parris and Harold Farberman.

Tippett, Michael (1905-) English composer. Studied with Wood and Kitson at the Royal College of Music (1923-8), and with R. O. Morris (1930-32). During the 1930s he worked as a conductor, especially at Morley College in London, while gradually establishing his creative personality: his earliest unrevised works date from the end of the decade, and show a fusion of contemporary European music (Stravinsky, Bartók, Hindemith) with the sprung rhythm and polyphonic exuberance he admired in English madrigals. At the same time he was developing a consciousness of himself as an artist in society. Much of his conducting work was done for socialist organizations; he went to prison as a conscientious objector in 1943; and he produced in *A Child of our Time* a public statement on the question of good and evil, using his own words as is his custom. Sparked off by a real incident in which a Jewish boy killed a Nazi diplomat, the work is modelled on Handel's *Messiah*, but with Bach's passions also in mind, negro spirituals taking the function of chorales (blues and jazz occur in other works as representative of music in a state of natural expression).

His next project of similar scope was the opera *The Midsummer Marriage* (1946-52), where again the issue is the reconciliation of opposing traits in the human psyche: male and female, manual and intellectual, spontaneity and reflection. The theme is treated in the form of a parable on the preparation of 2 young people for union, and the treatment draws on Jung, *The Magic Flute*, Celtic myth, the metaphysical plays of Shaw, and Eliot. Typically the sources are diverse, but they are contained within a flood of rapturous lyricism and exultant dance that spilled over into the orchestral works of the next 5 years.

Change came with work on his next opera *King Priam* (1958-61), a sculptured myth set in Messiaen-style blocks. Again the style was continued in ensuing works (the Concerto for Orchestra and the Second Piano Sonata), but in the heady cantata *The Vision of St Augustine* and the modern psychological drama *The Knot Garden* he began to weld small fragments into larger, swinging continuities, somewhat in the manner of film editing. Later works, notably the Triple Concerto and *The Mask of Time*, have restored the dancing grace and ebullience of *The Midsummer Marriage*, within what he himself conceives as a late manner in the Beethoven tradition.

Operas: The Midsummer Marriage, 1946-52, ★Covent Garden, 1955; King Priam, 1958-61; ★Coventry, 1962; The Knot Garden, 1966-9, ★Covent Garden, 1970; The Ice Break, 1973-6, ★Covent Garden, 1977

Choral orchestral: A Child of our Time, 1939-41; Crown of the Year, 1958; The Vision of St Augustine, 1963-5; The Shires Suite, 1965-70; The Mask of Time, 1977-82

Orchestral: Conc, double str, 1938-9; Fantasia on a Theme of Handel, pf, orch, 1939-41; Sym no.1 1944-5, no.2, 1956-7, no.3, with S, 1970-72, no.4, 1976-7; Little Music, str, 1946; Suite, D, 1948; Fantasia concertante on a Theme of Corelli, str, 1953; Divertimento on Sellinger's Round, chamber orch, 1953-4; Pf Conc, 1953-5; Praeludium, brass, perc, 1962; Conc for Orch, 1962-3; Triple Conc, str trio, orch, 1978-9; Festal Brass with Blues, brass band, 1983

Chamber: Str Qt no.1, 1934-5, rev.1943, no.2, 1941-2, no.3, 1945-6, no.4, 1977-8; Pf Sonata no.1, 1938, rev. 1942, no.2, 1962, no.3, 1972-3, no.4, 1984; Preludio al Vespro di Monteverdi, org, 1945; Sonata, 4 hn, 1955; Music for Words Perhaps, 6 insts, 1960; The Blue Gui, gui, 1982-3

Choral: 2 Madrigals, 1942; Plebs angelica, 1943; The Weeping Babe, 1944; Dance, Clarion Air, 1952; Lullaby, 1960; Magnificat and Nunc dimittis, with org, 1961

Songs: Boyhood's End, cantata, T, pf, 1943; The Heart's Assurance, cycle, S/T, pf, 1950-51; Songs for Achilles, T, gui, 1961; Songs for Ariel, v, pf/

hpd, 1962; Songs for Dov, T, chamber orch, 1969-70

[Schott; Philips]

☐ M. Tippett, *Moving into Aquarius* (1958, 2/1974), *Music of the Angels* (1980); I. Kemp, *Tippett* (1984)

Toch, Ernst (1887-1964) Austrian-American composer. Self-taught, he began composing in a traditional diatonic style, his main works being quartets and other chamber pieces written before and after his move to Germany in 1909. In the 1920s he turned to neoclassicism along Hindemithian lines, and this manner continued after his emigration to the USA in 1934; from 1936 he lived in Los Angeles, teaching at USC and writing film music. His works include 7 symphonies (all from the 1950s and 1960s), 13 quartets, etc.

Tombeau de Couperin, Le (Homage to Couperin) Suite by Ravel, one of the earliest examples of neoclassicism in its approach to a Baroque ideal with modern means. The piano version has 6 movements: Prélude, Fugue, Forlane, Rigaudon, Menuet, Toccata. ★Marguerite Long, Paris, 11 Apr 1919. 4 of these, in the order 1-3-5-4, were later orchestrated. ★cond Rhené-Baton, Paris, 28 Feb 1920.

total serialism The organization of all possible musical parameters according to the rules of 12-note composition. Webern, though not Schoenberg, would seem to have been troubled by the inconsistency between a serial treatment of pitch and non-serial means of composition in the fields of rhythm, dynamics and instrumentation. His later works show some attempt to resolve this, particularly in the rhythmic field: e.g. his use of the duration sets 2-2-1-2 and 3-1-2-6 in the Variations op.30. This may have provided a cue for Babbitt in his use of the duration set 5-1-4-2 in his 3 Compositions for Piano (1947). Babbitt uses the retrograde form as Webern had done, but he adds the notion of 'inversion' by complementing the durations to 6, thus: 1-5-2-4. This makes possible the first real example of rhythmic serialism.

Meanwhile Messiaen's *Turangalîla-Symphonie* (1946-8) was introducing 'chromatic' durations, i.e. a scale of durations moving in steps of a demisemiquaver: ♪. ♪. ♪. ♪, ♪♪, ♪, etc. Boulez in his Second Piano Sonata (1948) began to use this scale in a serial context, but 12-note sets of chromatic durations were employed for the first time by Babbitt in his Composition for 12 Instruments (1948, independent of Messiaen). In Europe the initiative was taken by Stockhausen in his *Kreuzspiel* and Boulez in his *Structures Ia*, both written in 1951 in response to Messiaen's *Mode de valeurs et d'intensités*, and both also applying rational principles to choices from a set of dynamic levels (Boulez's piece also 'serializes' modes of attack). Since pitches, durations and dynamics were now being separately assigned to each note, the goal of total serialism might be said to have been achieved. However, the resultant scattering of musical points proved limited as a musical texture, and both composers immediately began to work with larger entities.

The ideals of total organization, though, were not lost. Stockhausen sought in his *Elektronische Studien* (1953-4) to create entirely consistent and synthetic musical worlds in which similar rules applied to the organization of pitch, rhythm and timbre, and in his *Gruppen* (1955-7) he worked with sets of tempi. And indeed all those composers touched by the avant-garde endeavours of the 1950s – even those who, like Ligeti, wrote no serial music – have continued to be fascinated by the concept of music as a construction in several different domains of sound and time.

Tournemire, Charles (1870-1939) French composer and organist. Studied with Widor at the Paris Conservatoire, and with Franck and d'Indy. In 1898 he became organist at Franck's church of Ste Clotilde. He produced a large output, including 4 operas and 8 symphonies, but is remembered almost exclusively for his organ music, consisting mostly of plainsong elaborations in a style of mystic piety: his *L'orgue mystique* (published 1927-32) is a set of 51 organ masses for the liturgical year.

Trans Work by Stockhausen, the transcription of a dream. A string orchestra is seen on stage bathed in magenta light, slowly bowing sustained chords which change with the shocks every several seconds of a weaving shuttle (on tape). Wind and percussion sound from behind, and there are occasional bizarre interjections from soloists. ★Donaueschingen, 16 Oct 1971.

Transfiguration de Notre Seigneur Jésus-Christ, La (The Transfiguration of Our Lord Jesus Christ) Work by Messiaen for 7 instrumental soloists (pf, fl, cl, vc, vib, mar, xylorimba), chorus of 100 voices and orchestra of 109. It is a full-length concert liturgy of the Transfiguration in two 'septenaries', or sequences of 7 movements: each has 2 Gospel narratives, each followed by 2 meditations, and then the finale is a huge chorale. ★Lisbon, 7 Jun 1969.

trautonium Electronic melody instrument built by Friedrich Trautwein and first exhibited by him in Berlin in 1930. It produced changes of pitch in response to the movements of the player's finger along a wire (the analogy is with the ribbon attachment of the ondes martenot). Hindemith wrote an (unpublished) *Konzertstück* for trautonium and strings, but the instrument did not acquire a repertory sufficient to ensure its survival.

Tremblay, Gilles (1932-) Canadian composer. Studied at the Montreal Conservatory and at the Paris Conservatoire (1954-61) with Messiaen, Loriod and Martenot, then returned to the Montreal Conservatory as professor (1962). His works are mostly for orchestra or mixed ensemble, used with oriental finesse. [Berandol]

trichord Set of 3 pitch classes, most usually such a fragment of a 12-note set.

Trittico, Il (The Triptych) Triple bill by Puccini comprising the tragedy *Il tabarro* (The Cloak), the melodrama *Suor Angelica* (Sister Angelica) and the comedy *Gianni Schicchi*. ★Metropolitan, 14 Dec 1918.

Trois petites liturgies de la Présence Divine (Three Little Liturgies of the Divine Presence) Work by Messiaen for mostly unison female chorus of 36 voices, string orchestra, ondes martenot, piano, celesta, vibraphone and percussion. The words are his own, hymning the presence of God in the individual ('Antienne de la conversation intérieure': Antiphon of interior dialogue), in himself ('Séquence du Verbe': Sequence of the Word) and in all things ('Psalmodie de l'ubiquité par amour': Psalmody of love's omnipresence).

trombone Apart from the inevitable Hindemith sonata, little was composed for solo trombone before Globokar. Trombone quartets appear in Stravinsky's *In memoriam Dylan Thomas* and Boulez's *Domaines*; Stravinsky also used alto and bass trombones in his *Threni* and *The Flood*.

trope Term used by Hauer for a 12-note set of unordered hexachords; there are 44 such tropes.

trumpet The trumpet in C or B♭ is the normal orchestral instrument; some 20th c. scores also include the trumpet in D made for Bach performances (e.g. *The Rite of Spring*, *Peter Grimes*), the cornet (*Petrushka*) or some sort of bass trumpet (in E♭

in *The Rite of Spring*). The solo repertory includes concertos by Hindemith (with bassoon and strings), Zimmermann and Jolivet (2), prominent parts in Shostakovich's First Piano Concerto and Honegger's Second Symphony, sonatas by Hindemith and Davies, and pieces by Wolpe.

Tudor, David (1926-) American pianist and composer. Studied with the Wolpes while working professionally as an organist (1938-48). He then became associated with Cage, whose *Music of Changes* and many later works he played for the first time; he also introduced Boulez's Second Sonata to the USA in 1950. In 1954 and again in 1958 he visited Europe with Cage, and European composers began to write for him (he is the dedicatee of Stockhausen's *Klavierstück VI*). In 1960 he began to work mostly in the field of electronic music, as both pianist (e.g. in his version of Cage's *Variations II*) and composer. He has recorded for Mainstream, Columbia, etc.

Turandot Opera by Puccini, Adami and Simoni after Gozzi's play of the Chinese princess who has her suitors slaughtered if they cannot answer 3 riddles. *Milan, 25 April 1926. The same subject had been treated by Busoni, with his own libretto. *Zurich, 11 May 1917.

Turangalîla-Symphonie Work by Messiaen for large orchestra with solo piano and ondes martenot. 'Turangalîla' is a Sanskrit word, the name of one of the rhythmic formulae of ancient Indian music; according to Messiaen 'turanga' means 'time which runs' and 'lîla' is 'divine action in the cosmos, the play of creation, of destruction, of reconstruction, the play of life and death. Lîla is also love.' There are 10 movements: the 'love' movements (2,4,6,8) are all concerned with variants of a love theme; the 'Turangalîla' movements (3,7,9) are more abstract and speculative, weighing out rhythmic patterns. The long 6th movement, resting warmly in the work's central F♯ major tonality, recalls that this is the centrepiece of the composer's Tristan trilogy. *Boston, 2 Dec 1949.

Turina, Joaquín (1882-1949) Spanish composer. Studied in his home town of Seville, in Madrid with Trago, and in Paris with d'Indy at the Schola Cantorum (1905-13), also gaining help from Falla. In 1914 he returned with Falla to Spain, where he taught at the Madrid Conservatory from 1930. His

music consists mostly of orchestral, chamber and piano pieces, in a vibrant nationalist style.

Turn of the Screw, The Chamber opera by Britten and Myfanwy Piper after the Henry James story of children in an English country house attended by ghosts. *cond Britten, Venice, 14 Sep 1954.

12-note composition Musical organization with all the chromatic notes in ordered groupings where each appears once, i.e. with 12-note sets. There are 12-note themes in the last of Berg's Altenberg songs (1912) and in Schoenberg's *Die Jakobsleiter*, but the systematic use of 12-note sets began in music created by Schoenberg and Hauer around 1920, the former's serialism and the latter's TROPES providing means for erecting order within the unbounded world of ATONALITY.

In Schoenberg's practice, right from the first, the set was used in 4 forms: prime (e.g. B♭–E–F♯–E♭–F–A–D–C♯–G–A♭–B–C, the set of his Variations op.31), retrograde (C–B–A♭ etc), inversion (B♭–E–D–F–E♭–B–F♯–G–C♯–C–A–A♭) and retrograde inversion (A♭–A–C etc). Each of these may be transposed to any level, so that there are 48 different forms available. Effectively, the 'rules' of 12-note composition end there. Still to be decided are such matters as how many set forms are to be present at the same time, how successive and simultaneous set forms are to be linked, whether set forms should be presented melodically or in chords or in some combination, not to mention larger questions of style and form. According to Schoenberg himself, 'one uses the series and then one composes as before', but quite what is meant by 'as before' has remained unclear, not least in Schoenberg's own music. Often in his music of the 1920s 1 or more set forms are presented as a theme, but the more general principle is his use of COMBINATORIALITY, which has proved a fruitful area of study for Babbitt.

Of Schoenberg's pupils, Berg never kept to a single 12-note set for a whole movement. He did not generally use retrogrades or inversions, except where the former occur in whole passages turned backwards, but he freely altered the ordering within hexachords (his sets were therefore tropes rather than series) and rotated elements within sets, besides introducing non-12-note material (most conspicuously the Bach chorale in his Violin Concerto) and emphasizing diatonic features in his harmonization. Webern, by contrast, wrote consistently in counterpoints of set forms after 1924; he never relaxed the rule of serial ordering or used more than 1 set in a work. It almost follows that his style should have been most affected by 12-note composition, with less question of composing 'as before', unless one understands the 'as before' as referring to an earlier era. For Webern recognized that 12-note composition was an invitation to closely ordered polyphony of a kind unknown since the High Renaissance: this intuition has also been important to later composers, such as Babbitt and Stravinsky.

Apart from Berg and Webern, composers to practise 12-note composition in the 1920s, 1930s and 1940s included Eisler, Wellesz, Gerhard, Skalkottas, Martin, Dallapiccola and Krenek. At the end of the 1940s and in the 1950s, however, the system (or some version of it) began to be used by a great many composers in Europe and the USA, many of them seeking ways to extend serial organization to parameters other than pitch (*see* TOTAL SERIALISM) and to develop logical methods for proceeding from one set form to another. In general, American composers, led by Babbitt and Perle, have been most concerned with combinatoriality and with ways of making 12-note music as dense with systematic order as diatonic music is, while the urge in European music in the 1950s was towards a splintering of material, the 12-note set simply ensuring a rapid circulation of all the pitch classes which might then be grouped and ordered in other ways (Nono's music shows this at an extreme, most of his works being based on the same all-interval set). '12-note music', therefore, is hardly a unified repertory, except possibly among composers in the USA. And 12-note perception, as distinct from 12-note composition, remains a matter of uncertainty.

U

Ullman, Viktor (1898-?1944) Austrian composer. Studied with Schoenberg in Vienna and Hába in Prague, where he lived until in 1942 he was interned as a Jew at Terezín. There he composed a 1-act opera, *Der Kaiser von Atlantis* (1943). In 1944 he was transferred to Auschwitz, where he is presumed to have been killed.

ultrachromaticism Making music with MICRO-TONES.

Unanswered Question, The Work by Ives. Offstage strings sound soft sustained chords, representing the silence of the seers; a trumpet asks the question of the meaning of life, to which 4 flutes reply with vain scurryings.

Universal Edition Viennese music publishing house, having a record unrivalled in the 20th c. for fostering new music. Emil Hertzka (managing director 1907–32) signed contracts with Delius and Bartók (1908), Mahler, Schoenberg and Schreker (1909), Webern and Zemlinsky (1910), Janáček (1917) and others. After the second world war UE became the publishers of Stockhausen, Boulez, Berio, Birtwistle, Osborne, etc.

Ussachevsky, Vladimir (1911-) Russian-American composer. Moved to the USA in 1931 and studied with Rogers and Hanson at the Eastman School (1935-9). In 1947 he joined the faculty at Columbia University, where he worked in electronic music with Luening. His tape pieces (e.g. *Of Wood and Brass*, 1964-5) boldly manipulate recorded sounds; he has also written choral music influenced by Orthodox traditions. [Peters, CRI]

V

Valen, Fartein (1887-1952) Norwegian composer. Studied with Elling in Copenhagen (1906-9) and Bruch in Berlin (1909-11). He then completed little before his appointment in 1927 as director of the Norwegian music collection at Oslo University library: during the interim he was working towards the style of pure 12-note polyphony he then used in a succession of large works, including 4 symphonies, piano and violin concertos, 2 quartets, etc. [Lyche]

Varèse, Edgard (Edgar) (1883-1965) French-American composer. He felt to an extreme degree the dissatisfaction of his age with the music of the past. His own works of the 1920s and 1930s are more aggressively 'modern' – in respect of the importance of percussion sounds, complexity of rhythm, strident dissonance and freedom from developmental form – than anything else of the period, and even at this time he was looking towards still further liberations that he expected from electronic music. When tape recorders became available, in the 1950s, he created 2 of the first masterpieces of music on tape, his DÉSERTS (with orchestra) and POÈME ÉLECTRONIQUE.

He studied with Roussel at the Schola Cantorum (1904-5) and Widor at the Paris Conservatoire (1905-7), then went to Berlin, where he associated with Busoni (whose *Sketch for a New Aesthetic of Music* struck a chord), Hofmannsthal (whose *Oedipus and the Sphinx* he set as an opera) and Strauss (who made possible a performance of his symphonic poem *Bourgogne*). In 1913 he returned to Paris, leaving most of his music in Berlin, where it was destroyed by fire. At the end of 1915 he took ship for the USA, and settled in New York as a composer and conductor. He was centrally active in the International Composers' Guild, and during the decade 1918-27 wrote 6 major works for orchestra or chamber orchestra. In these he used memories of the music that had impressed him in Europe – Debussy, the atonal Schoenberg and the Stravinsky of *Petrushka* and *The Rite* – but exceeded his models in his vigorous quest after the new. Melodic ideas tend to eschew harmonic implications in favour of an insistence on a single pitch (HYPERPRISM, INTÉGRALES), while the constitution of chords is determined by chromatic saturation and, most particularly, by the need for strident dissonance. Summoned by incantatory melody, the 'sound masses', as he called them, are brought together in constantly changing combinations.

In 1928-33 he was back in Paris, where he continued his exploration of new resources: he wrote IONISATION for an orchestra of percussion, and used 2 of Martenot's new instruments in *Ecuatorial*, an expression of the ancient myth that was as important to him as modern science. The work was finished in the USA, where in the later 1930s and throughout the 1940s he completed nothing, trying to get help from film companies in the production of 'organized sound', and dreaming of a work involving simultaneous broadcasts by performers around the globe (*Espace*). At the start of the 1950s he returned to composition with *Déserts*, in which the gift of a tape recorder in 1953 made it possible for him to use music on tape. However, after this work and the *Poème* he completed no more: his *Nocturnal*, one of several non-electronic projects from his last years, was completed posthumously by his pupil Chou Wen-chung.

Works for large orchestra: amériques, ?1918-21; ARCANA, 1925-7

Works for small orchestra: Offrandes, with S, 1921; HYPERPRISM, 9 wind, 7 perc, 1922-3; Octandre, 7 wind, db, 1923; INTÉGRALES, 11 wind, 4 perc, 1924-5; IONISATION, 13 perc, 1929-31; ECUATORIAL, B, 8 brass, pf, org, 2 ondes martenots, 6 perc, 1932-4; Etude pour Espace, chorus, 2 pf, perc, 1947, DÉSERTS, 14 wind, pf, 5 perc, tape, ?1950-54; Nocturnal, S, B chorus, orch, 1961

Solo: DENSITY 21.5, fl, 1936

Tape: La procession de Vergès, 1955; POÈME ÉLECTRONIQUE, 1957-8

[Colfranc; Columbia]

□ F. Ouellette, *Edgard Varèse* (1968); L. Varèse, *Varèse* (1972)

variable metres Systematic change of metre (e.g. 3/8, 4/8, 5/8 in consecutive bars) introduced by Blacher in 1950 and used also by Hartmann. There is no connection with Carter's technique of metric modulation.

Vaughan Williams, Ralph (1872-1958) English composer. Studied at the Royal College of Music (1889-91, 1895-6) and Cambridge (1891-5), his teachers including Parry, Wood and Stanford; he then had further lessons with Bruch in Berlin (1897). His first works were mostly songs and chamber pieces, influenced by English music of the period and also by folksong, which he began collecting in 1903. Lacking confidence in his technique, however, he went to Paris for lessons with Ravel (1908), and his earliest major works date from soon afterwards: they include his Housman songs *On Wenlock Edge* and his Tallis Fantasia for strings, the latter showing that glowing euphony could still be managed in an individual way with the help of 16th c. modality. These works embodied 2 of his principal expressive modes, the pastoral and the transcendent, and their frequent connection with English folksong and Tudor church music, both of which suggested modal understandings of the diatonic system.

After the first world war he joined the staff at the RCM and began regular choral and orchestral conducting, while producing a large output of music. Some relates to an English tradition of biblical mysticism: notably the Blake ballet *Job* and the long-considered opera *The Pilgrim's Progress*, of which *The Shepherds of the Delectable Mountains* is a part, and to which the Fifth Symphony is related. But other symphonies are quite different in character, the 7th coming from a score for the film *Scott of the Antarctic* and the 8th including a tuned percussion ensemble.

Operas: The Shepherds of the Delectable Mountains, 1921, *London, 1922; Hugh the Drover, 1910-14, *London, 1924; Sir John in Love, 1924-8,

*London, 1929; The Poisoned Kiss, 1927-9, *Cambridge, 1936; Riders to the Sea, 1925-32, *London, 1937; The Pilgrim's Progress, finished 1949, *Covent Garden, 1951

*Ballet:*Job, 1927-30, *London, 1931

Symphonies: A Sea Sym, with S, Bar and chorus, 1903-9; A London Sym, 1912-13; Pastoral Sym, 1921; no.4, f, 1931-4; no.5, D, 1938-43; no.6, e, 1944-7; Sinfonia antartica, with S and female chorus, 1949-52; no.8, d, 1953-5; no.9, e, 1956-7

Other orchestral works: The Wasps, overture, 1909; Fantasia on a Theme by Thomas Tallis, str, 1910; The Lark Ascending, with vn, 1914; Flos campi, with va and small chorus, 1925

Other vocal orchestral works: Sancta civitas, oratorio, 1923-5; 5 Tudor Portraits, 1935; Dona nobis pacem, cantata, 1936; Serenade to Music, 1938; An Oxford Elegy, 1947-9

Smaller choral works: Mass, g, 1920-21; church music, folksong arrs

Songs: On Wenlock Edge, T, pf qnt, 1908-9; many songs and folksong arrs with pf

Few chamber and instrumental pieces [OUP, Curwen, Stainer]

□ M. Kennedy, *The Works of Ralph Vaughan Williams* (1964); U. Vaughan Williams *R.V.W.* (1964)

Veress, Sándor (1907-) Hungarian-Swiss composer. Studied with Bartók and Kodály at the Budapest Academy (1923-32), then worked as composer and musical folklorist. In 1949 he settled in Berne, where he has taught at the conservatory and university. His music has grown out of the Hungarian tradition, employing 12-note methods since 1952; he has written copiously in all genres. [Suvini Zerboni]

Vesalii icones (Vesalius's Pictures) Work by Davies for male dancer, solo cello and quintet, in 14 movements based on anatomical drawings by the 16th c. Vesalius and on the Stations of the Cross, culminating in the resurrection of Antichrist. *London, 9 Dec 1969.

vibraphone Metallophone with resonating tubes having lids that open and close, driven by an electric motor: hence the vibration in the sound, which may be removed by having the motor turned off. The instrument was invented by Hermann Winterhoff in 1916, but at first was restricted to jazz: *Lulu* was one of the first serious scores to include it, followed by Milhaud's Concerto for marimba and vibraphone (1947) and much of Messiaen, Boulez, Henze, Stockhausen, etc.

Villa-Lobos, Heitor (1887-1959) Brazilian composer. Studied the cello as a boy, and played the guitar with popular musicians. His late teens and early 20s he spent wandering through Brazil; he then had formal lessons at the National Music Institute in Rio de Janeiro, though only briefly. In 1915 there was a recital of his music, and during the next few years he made a local reputation, enough to gain him financial support for a trip to Paris in 1923. There he caused a sensation with the brilliant, exotic colouring in his orchestral *Chôros*, drawing on Rimsky-Korsakov and Stravinsky but with a tropical exuberance (the *chôro* was a variety of Brazilian popular instrumental music). Varèse became a friend, Messiaen an admirer. In 1930 he returned to Brazil and involved himself in musical education, establishing his own conservatory in 1942. His later works include the series of *Bachianas brasileiras*, translating Bachian models of form and style into the language of Brazilian popular music.

Chôros: no.1, gui, 1920; no.2, fl, cl, 1924; no.3, male chorus, 6 wind, 1925; no.4, 3 hn, trbn, 1926; no.5, pf, 1925; no.6, orch, 1926; no.7, 7 insts, 1924; no.8, 2 pf, orch, 1925; no.9, orch, 1929; no.10, chorus, orch, 1926; no.11, pf, orch, 1928; no.12, orch, 1929; no.13, 2 orchs, band, 1929; no.14, chorus, band, orch, 1928

Bachianas brasileiras: no.1, 8 vc, 1930; no.2, orch, 1930; no.3, pf, orch, 1938; no.4, pf, 1930-36, orch 1941; no.5, S, 8 vc, 1938-45; no.6, fl, bn, 1938; no.7, orch, 1942; no.8, orch, 1944; no.9, chorus/ str, 1945

Other works: 12 syms, concs, 17 str qts, pf and gui pieces, songs

[Eschig, AMP, Ricordi)

Vingt regards sur l'Enfant-Jésus (20 Watches over the Child Jesus) Volume of piano music by Messiaen comprising: 1. 'Regard du Père' (Watch of the Father), 2. 'Regard de l'étoile' (Watch of the Star), 3. L'échange' (Exchange), 4. 'Regard de la Vierge' (Watch of the Virgin), 5. 'Regard du Fils sur le Fils' (Watch of the Son over the Son), 6. 'Par lui tout à été fait' (By him everything was made), 7. 'Regard de la Croix' (Watch of the Cross), 8. 'Regard des hauteurs' (Watch of the Heights), 9. 'Regard du temps' (Watch of Time), 10. 'Regard de l'esprit de joie' (Watch of the Spirit of Joy), 11. 'Première communion de la Vierge' (The Virgin's First Communion), 12. 'La Parole toute-puissante' (The Omnipotent Word), 13. 'Noël' (Christmas), 14. 'Regard des anges' (Watch of the Angels), 15. 'Le baiser de l'Enfant-Jésus' (The Child Jesus's Kiss), 16. 'Regard des prophètes, des bergers et des mages' (Watch of the Prophets, Shepherds and Magi), 17. 'Regard du silence' (Watch of Silence), 18. 'Regard de l'onction terrible' (Watch of the Dread Unction), 19. 'Je dors, mais mon coeur veille' (I sleep, but my heart is awake), 20. 'Regard de l'église de l'amour' (Watch of the Church of Love). *Loriod, Paris, 26 Mar 1945.

viola Instrument played by Schoenberg, Hindemith and Britten. There are concertos by Walton, Hindemith, Bartók (posthumously completed from sketches), Milhaud, Bennett and Bainbridge, and recital pieces by Hindemith, Britten, Berio, Shostakovich, etc. The viola d'amore (of similar size but normally with 7 playing and 7 sympathetic strings) was favoured by Janáček (*Katya, Makropulos*) and is featured as soloist in Hindemith's *Kammermusik no. 6* and *Kleine Sonate* op. 25 no. 2.

violin The great 20th c. concertos include those of Sibelius, Reger, Elgar, Prokofiev (2), Stravinsky, Szymanowski (2), Berg, Schoenberg, Bartók (2), Britten, Shostakovich (2) and Shnitke (4); there are important works with piano by Debussy, Ravel, Schoenberg, Stravinsky, Shostakovich, Carter etc, and the unaccompanied repertory includes sonatas by Bartók, Reger, Honegger, etc.

Vishnegradsky (Wyschnegradsky), **Ivan** (1893-1979) Russian composer. Turned from law to composition under the guidance of Sokolov (1911-14), who pointed him towards Skryabin. After the Revolution he settled in Paris and began working with artificial modes including intervals raised or lowered by a quarter tone: the 24-note scale is obtained by having 2 or 4 pianos differently tuned, and generally the music is slow and static in its strange harmony. He left projects for his music to be accompanied, Skryabin fashion, by coloured lighting over a hemispherical dome. [Belaieff; Block]

Visions de l'Amen Book of music for 2 pianos by Messiaen, being 7 images of concurrence: 1. 'Amen de la Création' (Amen of Creation), 2. 'Amen des étoiles, de la planète à l'anneau' (Amen of the Stars, the Ringed Planet), 3. 'Amen de l'agonie de Jésus' (Amen of Jesus's Agony), 4. 'Amen du désir' (Amen of Desire), 5. 'Amen des anges, des saints, du chant des oiseaux' (Amen of the Angels, the Saints, the Song of Birds), 6. 'Amen du jugement' (Amen of Judgement), 7. 'Amen de la consommation' (Amen of Consummation). *Messiaen, Loriod, Paris, 10 May 1943.

Vogel, Wladimir (1896-1984) Russian-Swiss composer. Personally influenced by Skryabin as a boy, he left Russia in 1918 and studied in Berlin with Tiessen (1919-21) and Busoni, being affected also by Schoenberg. His *3 Sprechlieder* (1922, literally 'spoken songs') initiated his use of speech, extended to polyphonic choral treatment in *Thyl Claes* (1938-45) and other works. In 1935 he settled in Switzerland, and in 1937 he began using 12-note methods.

voice The kinds of vocal production expected in 20th c. music have hugely increased to include not only speech and *Sprechgesang* but also whispering, laughing, humming and a host of effects made publicly audible by amplification. Among the key works in the postwar extension of vocal possibilities are Kagel's *Anagrama*, Berio's *Circles*, *Visage*, *Epifanie* and *Sequenza III*, Stockhausen's *Refrain*, *Carré*, *Momente*, *Mikrophonie II*, and *Stimmung*, and Davies's *8 Songs for a Mad King*.

Von heute auf morgen (From one day to the next) Opera by Schoenberg to his wife's libretto, a comedy of manners aimed at selfconsciously modern people. *Frankfurt, 1 Feb 1930.

W

Wagner-Régeny, Rudolf (1903-69) Romanian-German composer. Studied at Leipzig (1919-20) and with Schreker in Berlin (1920-23), where he remained, falling under the influence of Les Six. His opera *Der Günstling* (*Dresden, 1935) was promoted abroad by Nazi authorities, but its successors *Die Bürger von Calais* (*Berlin, 1939) and *Johanna Balk* (Vienna, 1941) proved less acceptable with their anti-totalitarianism and borrowings from Weill. He was drafted into the army, returning to composition after the war in his own 12-note system. [UE]

Walton, William (1902-83) English composer. Studied at Christ Church, Oxford (1919-20), first as a choirboy and then as an undergraduate, gaining the friendship of the Sitwells. For the next decade he lived with them in London and Italy, and used the freedom to compose. He had been impressed by Schoenberg, and wrote a quartet that Berg admired when it was played at the first ISCM Festival (Salzburg, 1923), though he later withdrew it. There was also a more cavalier response to Schoenberg's influence in *Façade* (1921-2), a set of recitations to music eschewing the anguish of *Pierrot* for a bright, smart world closer to Poulenc. He looked again towards contemporary French music in the breezy overture *Portsmouth Point*, but the Viola Concerto (1928-9) established him as a modern Romantic in the Prokofiev mould.

After that the short oratorio *Belshazzar's Feast* (1930-31) found ways of placing big Handelian-Elgarian choruses within an exotic orchestral score indebted to Stravinsky, and the First Symphony (1932-5) was again a demonstration of a deep affinity with Elgar, discovered this time by way of Sibelius. He had now set the limits of his style: most later works are for large orchestra, showing the same relish for big tunes and bold designs. Like Prokofiev, he proved an adept writer of atmospheric film music, notably for Olivier's Shakespeare productions. He also wrote a large Romantic opera *Troilus and Cressida* (1950-54), seemingly profiting from the luxuriance of his new home on Ischia, where he spent most of his last 3 decades.

Operas: Troilus and Cressida, 1950-54, ★Covent Garden, 1954; The Bear, 1965-7, ★Aldeburgh, 1967
Ballets: The Wise Virgins, 1940; The Quest, 1943
Orchestral: Portsmouth Point, 1925; Siesta, 1926; Sinfonia concertante, pf, orch, 1926-7; Va Conc, 1928-9; Sym no.1, b♭, 1932-5, no.2, 1959-60; Crown Imperial, march, 1937; Vn Conc, 1938-9; Scapino, 1940; Orb and Sceptre, march, 1953; Johannesburg Festival Overture, 1956; Vc Conc, 1956; Partita, 1957; Variations on a Theme by Hindemith, 1962-3; Capriccio burlesco, 1968; Improvisations on an Impromptu of Benjamin Britten, 1969; Varii capricci, 1976; Prologo e fantasia, 1981
Choral orchestral: Belshazzar's Feast, 1930-31; In Honour of the City of London, 1937; Coronation Te Deum, 1952-3; Gloria, 1961
Other choral works: The Twelve, SATB, org 1965; Missa brevis, 8 vv, org/orch, 1966; Jubilate, 8 vv, org, 1972; Cantico del sole, SATB, 1974
Melodramas: Façade (Edith Sitwell), reciter, 6 insts, 1921-2
Songs: 3 songs, 1932; Anon. in Love, T, gui/orch, 1959; A Song for the Lord Mayor's Table, S, pf/orch, 1962
Chamber: Pf Qt, 1918-19, rev. 1921; Str Qt, a, 1945-7; Sonata, vn, pf, 1949; 5 Bagatelles, gui, 1972

Film scores: Henry V, 1943-4; Hamlet, 1947; Richard III, 1955
[OUP]
▢ F. Howes, *The Music of William Walton* (1965, 2/1974); S. R. Craggs, *William Walton: a Thematic Catalogue* (1977)

War and Peace (*Voyna i mir*) Opera by Prokofiev to his own and Mira Mendelson's adaptation of Tolstoy, contrasting lyrical scenes wth choral tableaux for Napoleon, Kutuzov and their generals. ★Leningrad, 12 Jun 1946 (scenes 1-8), 31 Mar 1955 (11 scenes).

War Requiem Work by Britten, an oratorio-style setting of the Latin mass for the dead, interleaved with songs for tenor and baritone on war poetry of Wilfred Owen. ★Coventry, 30 May 1962.

Warlock, Peter (Heseltine, Philip) (1894-1930) English composer (as Warlock) and musical scholar (as Heseltine). Had no formal musical training, but came into contact with Delius during his teens and started composing in Delian style, later modified by his friendship with Van Dieren and his knowledge of Elizabethan music. He wrote mostly songs and choral pieces.
▢ I. A. Copley, *The Music of Peter Warlock* (1979)

Warsaw Autumn Annual festival of contemporary music instituted in 1956, and providing the main showcase for new eastern European music as well as familiarizing Polish composers with Stockhausen, Boulez, Xenakis, etc. It played a crucial part in encouraging and promoting the 'Polish school' of Lutosławski, Penderecki, Górecki, etc.

Weber, Ben (1916-) American composer. Largely self-taught, he was encouraged by Schnabel and Schoenberg, and began using 12-note methods in 1938, one of the first Americans to do so. In 1945 he settled in New York as a composer and teacher. His works, mostly in traditional abstract forms, include 2 quartets and concertos for violin and piano. [American Composers' Alliance]

Webern, Anton (von) (1883-1945) Austrian composer. Coming at the end of the Viennese tradition that reached from Haydn to his teacher Schoenberg, he moved towards oriental qualities of brevity, objectivity and fine decoration, though the motive force was not so much eastern art as nature: the wish to mirror the perfection of mountain flowers and crystal specimens. This led him to place a high value on structure. A large proportion of his music is canonic, and he welcomed the invitations of the 12-note system towards a close, tight organization of pitch relations, often around a motif of only 3 or 4 notes.

He began lessons with Schoenberg in 1904, along with Berg, who became his closest musical friend. At the same time he studied with Adler at the university, where in 1906 he took a doctorate for an Isaac edition. In 1908 he began a career as a conductor, which took him to various Austrian and German towns before he returned to Vienna in 1918. Meanwhile in his music he was moving from the Mahler-Brahms fusion of his Passacaglia (1908) into atonality in the immediate wake of Schoenberg. His first atonal pieces were, like Schoenberg's, George songs (opp. 3-4), followed by chamber and orchestral movements that became, during the years 1909-14, ever smaller: the last of the 3 Little Pieces for cello and piano consists of just 20 notes, the ultimate distillation of a Mahlerian adagio.

The problem as he saw it was that, once all 12 notes had been sounded, there was no system to suggest what ought to happen next. He found it possible, nevertheless, to seek grounds for extension in words, and all his published works of 1915-26 were songs. During this time he was active in the Society for Private Musical Performances, besides conducting the Vienna Workers' Symphony Concerts (1922-34): his conducting was widely admired for thoroughness of preparation and fidelity to the music, especially in Mahler. The texts he was setting show a gradual movement away from Mahlerian chinoiserie and Trakl's Expressionist nightmares towards liturgical texts and poems of homely piety, though paradoxically the musical style becomes increasingly astringent, the voice swinging in opp. 16-18 through 7ths, 9ths and wider intervals.

The adoption of 12-note composition, in 1924, brought no immediate change, but in his Symphony (1928) he discovered the aptness of serial methods to strict canon (1st movement) and symmetrically patterned variation (2nd movement). Thereafter his style changed little. Unlike Schoenberg, he used the 12-note system in everything he wrote, which included intricately constructed instrumental pieces like the Symphony, songs and cantatas. The words for the latter now came exclusively from the works of his friend and neighbour Hildegard Jone, who shared his sweetly expressed nature mysticism. Meanwhile, deprived of his positions and performances with the rise of the

Nazis, he had to do routine work for his publishers in order to keep his wife and family. He was shot in error by an American soldier at the liberation.

Orchestral: Im Sommerwind, 1904; Passacaglia, op.1, 1908; 5 Movements, op.5, str, arr 1928; 6 Pieces, op.6, 1909; 5 Pieces, op.10, small orch, 1911-13; Symphony, op.21, 1928; Variations, op.30, 1940

Choral: Entflieht auf leichten Kähnen, op.2, SATB, 1908; 2 Songs, op.19, SATB, 5 insts, 1926; Das Augenlicht, op.26, SATB, orch, 1935; Cantata no.1, op.29, S, SATB, orch, 1938-9; Cantata no.2, op.31, S, B, SATB, orch, 1941-3

Songs: 5 Dehmel Songs, v, pf, 1906-8; 5 Songs, op.3, v, pf, 1908-9; 5 Songs, op.4, v, pf, 1908-9; 2 Songs (Rilke), op.8, Mez, 8 insts, 1910; 4 Songs, op.12, v, pf, 1915-17; 4 Songs, op.13, S, small orch, 1914-18; 6 Songs (Trakl), op.14, S, 4 insts, 1917-21; 5 Sacred Songs, op.15, S, 5 insts, 1917-22; 5 Canons on Latin Texts, op.16, S, cl, b cl, 1923-4; 3 Traditional Rhymes, op.17, S, 3 insts, 1924-5; 3 Songs, op.18, S, Eb cl, gui, 1925; 3 Songs, op.23, v, pf, 1933-4; 3 Songs, op.25, v, pf, 1934

Chamber: Slow Movement, str qt, 1905; Str Qt, 1905; Rondo, str qt, 1906; Pf Qnt, 1907; Str Qt, a, 1907; 5 Movements, op.5, str qt, 1909; 4 Pieces, op.7, vn, pf, 1910; 6 Bagatelles, op.9, str qt, 1911-13; 3 Little Pieces, op.11, vc, pf, 1914; Sonata, vc, pf, 1914; Str Trio, op.20, 1926-7; Qt, op.22, vn, cl, t sax, pf, 1930; Conc, op.24, 9 insts, 1931-4; Str Qt, op.28, 1936-8

Piano: Kinderstück, 1924; Piece, 1925; Variations, op.27, 1935-6

Arrangements: Schubert: Deutsche Tänze, orch 1931; Bach: Fuga (Ricercata) a 6 voci, orch 1934-5 [UE, Fischer; Columbia]

□ A. Webern, *The Path to the New Music* (1963), *Letters to Hildegard Jone and Josef Humplik* (1967); W. Kolneder, *Anton Webern* (1968); H. Moldenhauer, *Anton von Webern* (1978)

We Come to the River (Wir erreichen den Fluss) 'Actions for music' by Henze and Edward Bond, an anti-militarist and anti-bourgeois extravaganza set during an imaginary civil war. ★Covent Garden, 12 Jul 1976.

Weill, Kurt (1900-50) German-American composer. Studied with Humperdinck at the Berlin Hochschule (1918-19) and with Busoni and Jarnach at the Prussian Academy of Arts (1920-23). Influenced by Busoni, but also by Schreker, Schoenberg and Stravinsky, his works of the early 1920s are stylistically disparate, but they brought him quick renown: particularly the 1-act Expressionist opera *Der Protagonist* (1924-5). In his next stage work, *Royal Palace* (1925-6), he moved towards the style of free, strained tonality founded on jazz and cabaret music that served him well in underlining Brecht's incisive social criticism in their first collaborations: *Die Dreigroschenoper* (The Threepenny Opera) and *Aufstieg und Fall der Stadt* MAHAGONNY (1927-9). The success of these works enabled him to give up the teaching and journalism he had undertaken, and to concentrate on composing, both with and without Brecht. But this brief phase of prolific activity came to an end when the Nazis took power in 1933, and he fled to Paris, where with Brecht he produced *Die 7 Todesünden* (The 7 Deadly Sins).

In 1935 he moved to New York, where he wrote music for the anti-war play *Johnny Johnson* (1936), the Jewish epic *The Eternal Road* (1935-6) and the political satire *Knickerbocker Holiday* (1938, includes 'September Song'). After 1939, however, he had no opportunity to work on anything but standard Broadway musicals.

Theatre works: Der Protagonist, 1924-5, *Dresden, 1926; Royal Palace, 1925-6, *Berlin, 1927; Der Zar lässt sich photographieren (The Tsar has his Photograph Taken), 1927, *Leipzig, 1928; MAHAGONNY, Songspiel, 1927; Die Dreigroschenoper, 1928, *Berlin, 1928; Aufstieg und Fall der Stadt Mahagonny, 1927-9; Happy End, 1929, *Berlin, 1929; Der Jasager, 1930, Berlin radio, 1930; Die Bürgschaft (Bail), 1930-31, *Berlin, 1932; Der Silbersee (Silverlake), 1932-3, *Leipzig, 1933; Die 7 Todesünden, 1933, *Paris, 1933; The Eternal Road, 1935-6, *New York, 1937; Johnny Johnson, 1936, *New York, 1936; Knickerbocker Holiday, 1938, *New York, 1938; Lady in the Dark, 1940, *New York, 1941; One Touch of Venus, 1943, *New York, 1943; The Firebrand of Florence, 1944, *New York, 1945; Street Scene, 1946, *New York, 1947; Love Life, 1947, *New York, 1948; Lost in the Stars, 1949, *New York, 1949

Orchestral: Sym no.1, 1921, no.2, 1933; Divertimento, 1922; Sinfonia sacra, 1922; Conc, vn, wind, 1924; Kleine Dreigroschenmusik, 1929

Vocal: Recordare, chorus, 1923; Der neue Orpheus, S, vn, orch, 1925; Vom Tod in Wald, B, 10 wind, 1927; Das Berliner Requiem, T, Bar, B, chorus, 15 insts, 1928; Der Lindberghflug, T, Bar, chorus, orch, 1929

[UE, AMP, Chappell; Columbia, Nonesuch, DG]
□ K.H. Kowalke, *Kurt Weill in Europe* (1979); D. Jarman, *Kurt Weill: an illustrated biography* (1982)

Weisgall, Hugo (1912-) American composer, born into a central European Jewish family who moved to the USA in 1920. He studied at the Peabody Conservatory (1927-32), with Scalero at the Curtis Institute (1934-9) and occasionally with Sessions (1932-41). He was then a military diplomat in Europe (1941-7), returning to the USA to work as a composer, conductor and teacher (Juilliard School 1957-70, Queens College 1961-). His main works are his operas, diverse in subject, but all given powerful atmosphere and dynamism by a musical style indebted to Berg.

Operas: The Tenor (after Wedekind), *Baltimore, 1952; The Stronger (after Strindberg), *Westport, 1952; 6 Characters in Search of an Author, *New York, 1959; Purgatory (Yeats), *Washington, 1961; Athaliah (after Racine), *New York, 1964; 9 Rivers from Jordan, *New York, 1968

Ballets, songs, choral music
[Presser]

Wellesz, Egon (1885-1974) Austrian-British composer. Like his friend Webern, he deeply admired Mahler, studied musicology with Adler at Vienna University, and was a pupil of Schoenberg (1905-6). But unlike Webern he continued his musicological work: he became a leading scholar in the field of Byzantine chant, and his studies of Baroque opera gave an outer skeleton to his own works in this genre, notably his Hofmannsthal setting *Alkestis* (*Mannheim, 1924). In 1938 he settled in Oxford, teaching and composing. In some works he returned to tonality, as in the Mahlerian First Symphony (1945) or Straussian opera *Incognita* (*Oxford, 1951), and generally his 12-note practice became more intuitive. His large output includes 9 symphonies, much choral and vocal music, and 9 quartets. [Doblinger, Lengnick, UE]

Westdeutscher Rundfunk (West German Radio) One of the first electronic music studios was established at their Cologne station in 1953 under the direction of Eimert and Stockhausen. Other composers to have worked there include Koenig, Pousseur, Goeyvaerts, Kagel and Krenek.

Westergaard, Peter (1931-) American composer. Studied with Piston at Harvard (1951-3), Milhaud at the Paris Conservatoire (1953-4), Sessions at Princeton (1954-6) and Fortner in Germany (1956-8), then taught at Columbia (1958-66), Amherst College (1967-8) and Princeton (1968-). His music is cool, clear and closely structured, influenced by Babbitt and Webern (some of whose music he has completed). Among his few works are the chamber opera *Mr and Mrs Discobbolos* (1966), cantatas and chamber pieces. [A. Broude, Schott; CRI]

Whittenberg, Charles (1927-) American composer. Studied with Rogers at the Eastman School (1944-8), then independently made a study of Stravinsky, Schoenberg and Webern. His earliest published works date from the early 1960s, when he was working at the Columbia-Princeton Electronic Music Center (though most of his music is for chamber forces). In 1966 he began teaching at the University of Connecticut, while continuing to practise a sophisticated, quick-thinking style of 12-note composition influenced by Babbitt and Boretz.

Williamson, Malcolm (1931-) Australian composer. Studied with Goossens at the Sydney Conservatorium (1944-50) and with Seiber and Lutyens in London, where he also encountered the music of Messiaen and Boulez. He settled in London in 1953, and made a reputation as a composer of operas and orchestral music in a style alluding variously to Stravinsky, Messiaen and Britten. In 1975 he was made Master of the Queen's Music.
Operas: Our Man in Havana, ★London, 1963; English Eccentrics, ★Aldeburgh, 1964; The Violins of Saint-Jacques, ★London, 1966
Orchestral: 5 syms, 1957, 1968-9, 1972, 1977, 1980; 3 pf concs, 1957-8, 1960, 1962; Org Conc, 1961
Choral music, songs, instrumental pieces
[Weinberger]

Wolff, Christian (1934-) American composer. Studied classics at Harvard (1951-63), where he remained on the faculty until in 1971 he was appointed associate professor of classics and music at Dartmouth College. At the beginning of the 1950s he was a member of Cage's circle, and began writing pieces of few notes and much silence. In the late 1950s and early 1960s he introduced freedoms for the performer in pursuit of a democratic idealism, which in the 1970s became political engagement. [Peters]

Wolf-Ferrari, Ermanno (1876-1948) Italian composer. Studied with Rheinberger in Munich (1892-5), where he spent much of the rest of his life. His comic operas of 1902-9 won success for their charm, wit and pastiche of 18th c. music: it was a style he tried to recapture in later works based on Goldoni.

Operas: Le donne curiose, ★Munich, 1903; I quattro rusteghi, ★Munich, 1906; Il segreto di Susanna, ★Munich, 1909; I gioielli della Madonna, ★Berlin, 1911; Gli amanti sposi, ★Venice, 1925; La vedova scaltra, ★Rome, 1931; Il campiello, ★Milan, 1936

Wolpe, Stefan (1902-72) German-American composer. Studied with Juon and Schreker at the Berlin Hochschule (1919-24), while also receiving help from Busoni and involving himself with dadaists and socialists. He continued to write propaganda music in the later 1920s and early 1930s, and like other composers of his age and milieu (Weill, Hindemith) began using jazz elements. On Hitler's assumption of power he fled to Vienna, where he had lessons with Webern (1933-4), and thence to Jerusalem (1934-8). In 1938 he settled in the USA, where he held a variety of teaching posts. His later works, mostly for instrumental ensembles, are atonal abstract dramas generated from strong gestures.
Orchestral: The Man from Midian, ballet suite, 1942; Sym, 1955-6, rev. 1964; For Pf and 16 players, 1960-61; Chamber Piece no. 1, 14 insts, 1964, no. 2, 14 insts, 1965-6
Cantatas: Street Music, Bar, speaker, 5 insts, 1963-8; Cantata for Voice, Voices and Instruments, 1963-8
Chamber: Duo im Hexachord, ob, cl, 1936; Sonata, ob, pf, 1938-41; Sonata, vn, pf, 1949; Qt, t sax, tpt, pf, perc, 1950; Piece, ob, vc, pf, perc, 1955; Qnt with Voice, Bar, cl, hn, vc, pf, harp, 1956-7; Piece in 2 Parts, fl, pf, 1960; In 2 Parts, 6 insts, 1962; Piece for 2 Inst Units, 7 insts, 1962-3; Piece in 2 Parts, vn, 1964; Trio in 2 Parts, fl, vc, pf, 1964; Solo Piece, tpt, 1966; Second Piece, vn, 1966; Str Qt, 1968-9; From Here on Farther, cl, b cl, vn, pf, 1969; Piece for Tpt and 7 Insts, 1971
Piano: Encouragements, 1943-7; 2 Studies, 1948; Dance Piece, 1950; 7 Pieces, 3 pf, 1950-51; Enactments, 3 pf, 1950-53; Form, 1959; Form IV: Broken Sequences, 1969
[Hargail, Marx]

Wood, Hugh (1932-) English composer. Studied at Oxford and privately with Lloyd Webber, Hamilton and Seiber while teaching evening classes in London; he then took appointments at the universities of Glasgow (1966-70), Liverpool (1971-3) and Cambridge (1976-). His music is 12-note, generally with a symphonic breadth that relates to Schoenberg and Berg.
Orchestral: Vc Conc, 1969; Chamber Conc, 1971; Vn Conc, 1972; Sym, 1982

Vocal: Scenes from Comus, S, T, orch, 1965; Songs to Poems by Neruda, S, chamber orch, 1973; Songs with pf, choruses
Chamber: 3 str qts, 1962, 1970, 1978; Qnt, cl, hn, pf trio, 1967
[Chester, UE; Argo]

Wooden Prince, The (A fából faragott királyfi) Ballet by Bartók to scenario by Béla Balázs. The wooden prince is a puppet made by a prince to attract a princess; she is more taken with the image than the real thing until he forsakes the magic of his guardian fairy. ★Budapest, 12 May 1917.

Wozzeck Opera by Berg to his own adaptation of Büchner's play, the story of a victimized soldier driven to murder. It is one of the key works of 20th c. opera, influential as Expressionist drama, as atonal symphonic structure, and as 'literary' opera, setting an outstanding text in largely arioso fashion. Berg prepared a concert suite of 3 fragments to stimulate interest in the work. ★Berlin, 14 Dec 1925.

Wuorinen, Charles (1938-) American composer. Studied with Luening, Beeson and Ussachevsky at Columbia, where he taught (1964-71) before moving to the Manhattan School of Music. He uses Babbitt's extensions of the 12-note system, but his music is marked by a baroque richness of imagery.
Operas: The Politics of Harmony, 1968; The W. of Babylon, 1975
Works for full orchestra: Pf Conc, 1966; Conc for amplified vn, 1972
Works for chamber orchestra: Chamber Concs for vc, 1963, fl, 1964, ob, 1965, tuba, 1971
Works for percussion orchestra: Ringing Changes, 1977; Perc Sym, 1976
Chamber: Str Qt, 1971; many other works
Tape: Time's Encomium, 1969
[Peters; Nonesuch]

X

Xenakis, Iannis (1922-) Greek-French composer. Born to Greek parents in Romania, he arrived in Greece in 1932 and studied at the Athens Polytechnic as an engineer. He worked in the resistance at the polytechnic from 1941, was wounded in 1945, and escaped to Paris in 1947. Largely self-taught in music, he came to the attention of Messiaen, with whom he studied in 1950-51; Scherchen also gave him help. But at the same time he made the acquaintance of Le Corbusier, with whom he worked on various projects, including the Philips pavilion at the 1958 Brussels Exposition, the vessel for Varèse's *Poème électronique*. By this time, though, he was beginning to make a reputation as a composer, and he came to concentrate on music.

His first published work, *Metastasis* for orchestra (1953-4), already embodies a connection between music and mathematics that has been characteristic of his art: the work is a projection of geometrical notions, achieved by glissandos (as analogous to straight lines) placed among a large body of strings, producing an extraordinary new orchestral world (again, the bold handling of newly invented sonorities was to remain typical). His interest in handling large numbers of events led him to the mathematics of probability, and so to stochastic music, which he practised in subsequent works for orchestra, ensemble or tape, some using calculations by computer. And the density of events produced music of extreme virtuosity, especially in solo pieces (*Herma* for piano, *Nomos alpha* for cello). However, in much of his music of the later 1970s and 1980s this bewildering activity has been countered by strong and simple melodies or rhythmic patterns suggestive of folk music.
Orchestral: Metastasis, 1953-4; Pithoprakta, 1955-6; Acchoripsis, 1956-7; Duel, 1959; Syrmos, str, 1959; Stratégie, 1962; ST/48, 1962; Hiketides, suite, 1964; Akrata, 16 wind, 1964-5; Terretektorh, 1965-6; Polytope de Montreal, 1967; Nomos gamma, 1967-8; Kraanerg, with tape, 1968-9; Synaphaï, pf, orch, 1969; Antikhthon, 1971; Eridanos, 1973; Erikhthon, pf, orch, 1974; Noomena, 1974; Empreintes, 1975; Jonchaies, 1977; Pour les baleines, str, 1982; Shaar, str, 1983; Lichens I, 1984
Vocal orchestral: Polla ta dhina, children's vv, orch, 1962; Cendrées, chorus, orch, 1973; Anemoessa, chorus, orch, 1979; Aïs, Bar, perc, orch, 1980; Nekuia, chourus, orch, 1981
Other choral works: Oresteia, vv, children's vv, 12 insts, 1965-6; Medea, male vv, 5 insts, 1967; Nuits, 12vv, 1967; A Colone, male vv, 18 insts, 1977; A Helene, female vv, 1977; Serment-Orkos, vv, 1981; Pour la paix, vv, tape, 1982; Chant des soleils, vv, children's vv, 12 brass, perc, 1983
Ensemble: Analogique A, 9 str, 1959; Atrées, 10 insts, 1960; ST/4, str qt, 1962; ST/10, 10 insts,

1962; Morsima-Amorsima, pf, vn, vc, db, 1962; Amorsima-Morsima, 10 insts, 1962; Eonta, pf, 5 brass, 1963; Anaktoria, 8 insts, 1969; Persephassa, 6 perc, 1969; Aroura, 12 str, 1971; Linaia-Agon, 3 brass, 1972; N'shima, 4 brass, 2 Mez, vc, 1975; Phlegra, 11 insts, 1975; Epei, 6 insts, 1976; Retours-Windungen, 12 vc, 1976; Akanthos, 8 insts, S, 1977; Ikhoor, str trio, 1978; Pleiades, 6 perc, 1978; Palimpsest, 11 insts, 1979; Khal perr, 5 brass, perc, 1983; Tetras, str qt, 1983

Duos: Charisma, cl, vc, 1971; Dmaathen, ob, perc, 1976; Dikhthas, vn, pf, 1979; Komboi, hpd, perc, 1981

Solos: Herma, pf, 1960-61; Nomos alpha, vc, 1966; Mikka, vn, 1971; Evryali, pf, 1973; Gmeeoorh, org, 1974; Psappha, perc, 1975; Theraps, db, 1975-6; Khoai, hpd, 1976; Mikka 'S', vn, 1976; Kottos, vc, 1977; Embellie, va, 1981; Mists, pf, 1981; Naama, hpd, 1984

Tape: Diamorphoses, 1957; Concret PH, 1958; Analogique B, 1959; Orient–occident, 1960; Bohor, 1962; Hibiki hana ma, 1969-70; Persepolis, 1971; Polytope de Cluny, 1972; La légende d'Eer, 1977; Mycènes A, 1978

[Salabert, Boosey; Erato, Nonesuch, RCA]

□ I. Xenakis, *Formalized Music* (1971)

xylophone Prominent in orchestral scores by Bartók, Puccini, Messiaen, Boulez and, more unusually, Schoenberg. The xylorimba, with an extended bass to give a range of 5 octaves, appears in *Le marteau sans maître* and works by Messiaen, Stravinsky, etc.

Y

Young, La Monte (1935-) American composer. Studied with Leonard Stein (1955-6), at UCLA (1957-8) and Berkeley (1958-60), and with Richard Maxfield at the New School for Social Research in New York (1960-61). In 1956-8 he wrote 12-note music, though with unusually few and long notes; then in 1959 at Darmstadt he encountered the work of Stockhausen and, still more decisively, Cage. Back in New York he was associated with the Fluxus movement, but since 1964 he has worked with repetitive figures within static harmonies in just intonation, giving performances with small groups of musicians, involving amplification and pat-

terned light shows by his wife Marian Zazeela. [Shandar]

□ L. Young and M. Zazeela, *Selected Writings* (1970)

Yun, Isang (1917-) Korean-German composer. Studied in Japan, then worked in Korea as a teacher and composer before travelling to Europe for further studies at the Paris Conservatoire with Revel (1956-7), at the Berlin Hochschule with Blacher and Rufer (1958-9) and at Darmstadt. He remained in Germany, except for a period of imprisonment in Korea (1967-9), and in 1970 began teaching at the Berlin Hochschule. His works include operas (*Sim Tjong*, 1972), orchestral pieces and chamber music, often drawing on eastern Asian culture. [Bote]

Z

Zagreb Yugoslav city, site of a biennial festival of contemporary music since 1961.

Zandonai, Riccardo (1883-1944) Italian composer. Studied with Mascagni, and was taken up by Giulio Ricordi as an opera composer. He followed in the wake of Puccini, winning most success with his d'Annunzio setting *Francesca da Rimini* (★Turin, 1914). Later works include 6 more operas and orchestral pieces.

Zeitmasze (Tempi) Work by Stockhausen for 5 woodwind (flute, oboe, cor anglais, clarinet, bassoon) working as 5 tracks in independent or conjoined tempi. ★Domaine Musical/Boulez, Paris, 15 Dec 1956.

Zeitoper (opera of the age) Term used of German operas of the late 1920s and early 1930s which dealt with contemporary society: e.g. works of this period by Hindemith, Weill, Krenek, Brand, etc. The genre was an expression of the same desire for social relevance that motivated Gebrauchsmusik and Neue Sachlichkeit (Schoenberg's *Von heute auf morgen* is a mockery of the type as well as an example).

Zemlinsky, Alexander (1871-1942) Austrian composer. Studied with Fuchs at the Vienna Conservatory (1887-92), and won Brahms's attention with his chamber music. In 1895 he met Schoenberg and gave him some advice, and in 1900 his opera *Es war einmal* was conducted by Mahler at the Court Opera. Around the same time he began his career as an opera conductor in Vienna (1899-1911) and Prague (1911-27), where he presented the first performance of Schoenberg's *Erwartung*. In his own music, however, he did not follow his friend's example: he took a keen interest in Schoenberg's development, but his rich, lyrical and sometimes oddly eccentric style kept its roots in tonality, leaning also towards Strauss and Mahler. His finest works would seem to be those he wrote in Prague, including the opera *Der Zwerg*, the Second and Third Quartets, and the Lyric Symphony. He moved from Prague to work at the Kroll under Klemperer (1927-30) and teach at the Hochschule, then fled the Nazis successively to Vienna (1933-8) and the USA. In his works of the 1930s he responded to the influences of Hindemith and Weill. After his death his music was almost forgotten until a revival began at the time of his centenary.

Operas: Sarema, 1894, ★Munich, 1897; Es war einmal, 1897-9; ★Vienna, 1900; Der Traumgörge, 1904-6, ★Nuremberg, 1980; Kleider machen Leute, 1907-9, ★Vienna, 1910, rev. 1922; Eine florentinische Tragödie, 1914-15, ★Stuttgart, 1917; Der Zwerg, 1921, ★Cologne, 1922; Der Kreidekeis, 1930-33, ★Zurich, 1933

Other stage works: Der Triumph der Zeit, ballet, 1902; Cymbeline, incidental music, 1914

Orchestral: Sym no.1, d, 1892, no.2, B♭, 1897; Die Seejungfrau, 1903; Sinfonietta, 1934

Vocal orchestral: Psalm 83, chorus, orch, 1900; Psalm 23, chorus, orch, c.1910; 6 Maeterlinck Songs, Mez/Bar, orch, 1910; Lyric Symphony, S, Bar, orch, 1922; Symphonic Songs, v, orch, 1929; Psalm 13, chorus, orch, 1935

Chamber: Trio, d, cl/va, vc, pf, 1896; Str Qt no.1, A, 1896, no.2, 1913-14, no.3, 1924, no.4, 1936

Songs, piano pieces
[UE; DG, Schwann]

Zimmermann, Bernd Alois (1918-70) German composer. Was called up into the army from his studies in Cologne and Bonn, and served in France, where he first came across the music of Stravinsky and Milhaud. In 1942 he was able to continue studies with Lemacher and Jarnach, and in 1948-50 he attended courses given by Fortner and Leibowitz at Darmstadt. He then taught at the university (1950-52) and Musikhochschule (1957-70) in Cologne. His first published works, dating from the late 1940s and early 1950s, amalgamate Schoenberg, Bartók, Stravinsky and sometimes jazz rather in the manner of the contemporary Henze, but *Perspektiven* for 2 pianos (1955-6) is much closer to Webern's symmetrical patterning. It was also one of several works he described as 'imaginary ballets', where the needs of character sometimes involved him in quoting music of the past: Bach and Messiaen, for instance, in another 2-piano work, *Monologe* (1964). He developed an aesthetic of 'pluralism', feeling that quotation impressed itself on his music by the need to cope with the past, and in his post-*Wozzeck* opera Die Soldaten (The Soldiers, 1958-64) he used quotation along with deliberate diversity of style and simultaneous actions on different stages. His last works are by contrast monochrome and bleak. He committed suicide.

Opera: Die Soldaten, 1958-64, ★Cologne, 1965

Orchestral: Conc, str, 1948; Vn Conc, 1950; Alagoana, 1940-51; Sym in 1 Movement, 1947-51, rev. 1953; Ob Conc, 1952; Canto di speranza, vc, orch, 1953, rev. 1957; Kontraste, 1953; Tpt Conc, 1954; Impromptu, 1958; Dialoge, 2 pf, orch, 1960, rev. 1965; Antiphonen, va, orch, 1961-2; Vc Conc, 1965-6; Musique pour les soupers du roi Ubu, 1966; Photoptosis, 1968; Stille und Umkehr, 1970

Vocal: Tantum ergo, 4vv, 1947; Lob der Torheit, cantata, 1948; Omnia tempus habent, cantata, 1957-8; Requiem für einen jungen Dichter, solo vv, choruses, orch, jazz group, org, tape, 1967-9; Ich wandte mich, 2 speakers, B, orch, 1970

Instrumental: Extemporale, pf, 1938-46; Vn Sonata, 1950; Enchiridion, pf, 1949-52; Sonata, va, 1955; Perspektiven, 2 pf, 1955-6; Konfigurationen, pf, 1956; Sonata, vc, 1959-60; Présence, pf trio, 1961; Tempus loquendi, fl, 1963; Monologe, 2 pf, 1964; Intercommunicazione, vc, pf, 1967; 4 Short Studies, vc, 1970

Tape: Tratto, 1966; Tratto II, 1969
[Schott; DG]

Zwilich, Ellen Taaffe (1939-) Studied with Floyd at Florida State University and with Carter and Sessions at the Juilliard School, where she took a doctorate in 1975. Her works include the orchestral *Symposium* (1975) and a Violin Concerto (1979).

Zyklus (Cycle) Work by Stockhausen for solo percussionist: the player stands in the middle of his instruments and makes a circuit of them, beginning at any of several points. ★Caskel, Darmstadt, 25 Aug 1959.

General Bibliography
and
Chronology

General Bibliography

A. Hodeir: *Since Debussy* (1961)

P.H. Lang and N. Broder, ed: *Contemporary Music in Europe* (1965)

E. Salzman: *Twentieth-Century Music* (1967)

B. Boretz and E. Cone, ed: *Perspectives on Schoenberg and Stravinsky* (1968)

R.S. Hines, ed.: *The Orchestral Composer's Point of View* (1970)

B. Boretz and E. Cone, ed: *Perspectives on American Composers* (1971)

B. Schwarz: *Music and Musical Life in Soviet Russia* (1972)

M. Cooper, ed: *The Modern Age 1890-1960*, The New Oxford History of Music vol. 10 (1974)

J. Vinton, ed: *Dictionary of Twentieth-Century Music* (1974)

J. Samson: *Music in Transition* (1977)

A. Whittall: *Music Since the First World War* (1977)

P. Griffiths: *Modern Music: A Concise History* (1978, r1984)

P. Griffiths: *Modern Music* (1980)

Chronology

There are two significant moments in the history of any work of art: when it was created, and when it first became publicly available. In the case of musical works, performance can be dated much more exactly than composition, which is one reason why works are listed here by date of the first performance. It can be objected that this misrepresents the zeitgeist, but the gap between completion and premiere is rarely significant – and where it is (for Schoenberg's stage works and much of Ives), then the pieces may be felt to belong to the time when they were unveiled to a wider world as much to the time when they were imagined.

The chronology thins out somewhat towards the present, as is natural: in music, history can normally be identified only some years after it has happened.

1901
Dvořák: *Rusalka*
Elgar: *Cockaigne*
Mahler: Symphony no.4
Rakhmaninov: Piano Concerto no.2
Strauss: *Feuersnot*

1902
Cilea: *Adriana Lecouvreur*
Debussy: *Pelléas et Mélisande*
Ives: *The Celestial Country*
Mahler: Symphony no.3
Nielsen: Symphony no.2
Ravel: *Jeux d'eau*
Schoenberg: *Verklärte Nacht*
Sibelius: Symphony no.2
Skryabin: Symphony no.2

1903
Bruckner: Symphony no.9
Elgar: *The Apostles*
d'Albert: *Tiefland*

1904
Bartók: *Kossuth*
Busoni: Piano Concerto
Debussy: *Estampes*
Delius: *Koanga*
Janáček: *Jenůfa*
Mahler: Symphony no.5
Puccini: *Madama Butterfly*

Ravel: *Shéhérazade*
Sibelius: Violin Concerto
Strauss: *Symphonia domestica*

1905
Debussy: *La mer*
Elgar: Introduction and Allegro
Lehár: *Die lustige Witwe*
Schoenberg: *Pelleas und Melisande*
Sibelius: *Pelléas et Mélisande*
Skryabin: Symphony no.3
Strauss: *Salome*

1906
Debussy: *Images* (book 1)
Elgar: *The Kingdom*
Mahler: Symphony no.6
Nielsen: *Maskarade*
Sibelius: *Pohjola's Daughter*

1907
Delius: *A Village Romeo and Juliet*
Dukas: *Ariane et Barbe-Bleue*
Massenet: *Thérèse*
Ravel: *Histoires naturelles*
Rimsky-Korsakov: *The Legend of the Invisible City of Kitezh*
Schoenberg: Chamber Symphony no.1
Sibelius: Symphony no.3
Stravinsky: Symphony in E flat
Suk: *Asrael*

1908
Delius: *Brigg Fair*
Elgar: Symphony no.1
Mahler: Symphony no.7
Rakhmaninov: Symphony no.2
Roussel: Symphony no.1
Schoenberg: String Quartet no.2
Skryabin: *Le poème de l'extase*
Webern: Passacaglia

1909
Bartók: *Two Portraits*
Rakhmaninov: Piano Concerto no.3
Reger: Prologue tò a Tragedy
Rimsky-Korsakov: *The Golden Cockerel*
Strauss: *Elektra*
Stravinsky: *Fireworks*
Vaughan Williams: *On Wenlock Edge*
Wolf-Ferrari: *Il segreto di Susanna*

1910
Bartók: String Quartet no.1
Debussy: *Ibéria, Rondes de printemps*
Elgar: Violin Concerto
Mahler: Symphony no.8
Massenet: *Don Quichotte*
Puccini: *La fanciulla del West*
Schoenberg: *Das Buch der hängenden Gärten*,
    piano pieces opp.11 and 19
Stravinsky: *The Firebird*
Varèse: *Bourgogne*
Vaughan Williams: Tallis Fantasia
Webern: Five Movements op.5

1911
Berg: String Quartet op.3
Debussy: *Le martyre de Saint Sébastien*
Elgar: Symphony no.2
Granados: *Goyescas*
Mahler: *Das Lied von der Erde*
Ravel: *L'heure espagnole*
Sibelius: Symphony no.4
Skryabin: *Prometheus*
Strauss: *Der Rosenkavalier*
Stravinsky: *Petrushka*

1912
Dukas: *La Péri*
Mahler: Symphony no.9
Nielsen: Symphony no.3, Violin Concerto
Prokofiev: Piano Concerto no.1
Ravel: *Daphnis et Chloé, Ma mère l'oye*
Roussel: *Évocations*

Schoenberg: Five Pieces op. 16, *Pierrot
    lunaire*
Strauss: *Ariadne auf Naxos* (first version)

1913
Bartók: *Deux images*
Debussy: *Jeux, Gigues, Syrinx*
Elgar: *Falstaff*
Falla: *La vida breve*
Fauré: *Pénélope*
Prokofiev: Piano Concerto no.2
Rakhmaninov: *The Bells*
Reger: *Vier Tondichtungen nach
    Arnold Böcklin*
Schoenberg: *Gurrelieder*
Stravinsky: *The Rite of Spring*
Webern: Six Pieces op.6

1914
Boughton: *The Immortal Hour*
Debussy: *Trois poèmes de Stéphane Mallarmé*
Ravel: *Trois poèmes de Stéphane Mallarmé*
Sibelius: *The Oceanides*
Strauss: *Josephs-Legende*
Stravinsky: *The Nightingale*, Three Japanese
    Lyrics

1915
Debussy: *Douze études*
Falla: *El amor brujo*
Ravel: Piano Trio
Reger: Variations and Finale on a Theme of
    Mozart
Sibelius: Symphony no.5
Strauss: *Eine Alpensinfonie*

1916
Bridge: *Summer*
Busoni: *Indianische Fantasie*
Debussy: *En blanc et noir*, Sonata for flute,
    viola and harp
Holst: *Sāvitri*
Nielsen: Symphony no.4
Strauss: *Ariadne auf Naxos* (second version)

1917
Bartók: *The Wooden Prince*
Bloch: *Schelomo*
Busoni: *Turandot, Arlecchino*
Debussy: Violin Sonata
Pfitzner: *Palestrina*
Puccini: *La rondine*
Satie: *Parade*
Szymanowski: Symphony no.3

Zemlinsky: *Eine florentinische Tragödie*

1918
Bartók: *Bluebeard's Castle*, String Quartet no.2
Holst: *The Planets*
Prokofiev: Symphony no.1
Puccini: *Il trittico*
Schreker: *Die Gezeichneten*
Stravinsky: *Histoire du soldat*

1919
Bartók: Suite op.14
Elgar: Cello Concerto
Falla: *El sombrero de tres picos*
Ravel: *Le tombeau de Couperin* (piano)
Strauss: *Die Frau ohne Schatten*

1920
Giordano: *Andrea Chénier*
Milhaud: *Le boeuf sur le toit*
Ravel: *La valse*
Satie: *Socrate*
Stravinsky: *Pulcinella, Ragtime*

1921
Fauré: Piano Quintet no.2
Hindemith: *Mörder, Das Nusch-Nuschi*
Honegger: *Le roi David*
Janáček: *Katya Kabanova, Taras Bulba*
Milhaud: *L'homme et son désir*
Prokofiev: *Le chout, The Love for Three Oranges*, Piano Concerto no.3
Stravinsky: Symphonies of Wind Instruments

1922
Bartók: Four Pieces op.12, Violin Sonata no.1
Bax: Symphony no.1
Fauré: *L'horizon chimérique*
Hindemith: *Kammermusik* no.1
Nielsen: Symphony no.5
Ravel: Sonata for violin and cello
Roussel: Symphony no.2
Stravinsky: *Mavra, Renard*
Varèse: *Offrandes*
Walton: *Façade*

1923
Bartók: Violin Sonata no.2, Dance Suite
Busoni: *Fantasia contrappuntistica*
Falla: *El retablo de Maese Pedro*
Fauré: Piano Trio

Hindemith: *Das Marienleben*
Milhaud: *La création du monde*
Roussel: *Padmâvatî*
Sibelius: Symphony no.6
Stravinsky: *Les noces*, Octet
Varèse: *Hyperprism*

1924
Gershwin: *Rhapsody in Blue*
Honegger: *Pacific 231*
Janáček: *The Cunning Little Vixen*
Poulenc: *Les biches*
Respighi: *Pini di Roma*
Ruggles: *Men and Mountains*
Schoenberg: *Erwartung, Die glückliche Hand, Serenade*, Wind Quintet
Sibelius: Symphony no.7
Strauss: *Intermezzo*
Stravinsky: Piano Concerto
Varèse: *Octandre*

1925
Berg: *Wozzeck*
Busoni: *Doktor Faust*
Copland: Music for the Theater
Nielsen: Symphony no.6
Prokofiev: Symphony no.2
Ravel: *L'enfant et les sortilèges*
Stravinsky: Piano Sonata
Varèse: *Intégrales*

1926
Antheil: *Ballet mécanique*
Bartók: Piano Sonata, *The Miraculous Mandarin*
Falla: Harpsichord Concerto
Hindemith: *Cardillac*
Janáček: *The Makropulos Affair*, Sinfonietta
Krenek: *Orpheus und Eurydike*
Milhaud: *Les malheurs d'Orphée*
Nielsen: *Flute Concerto*
Puccini: *Turandot*
Shostakovich: Symphony no.1
Sibelius: *Tapiola*
Szymanowski: *King Roger*
Webern: Five Pieces op.10

1927
Bartók: Piano Concerto no.1
Berg: Chamber Concerto, Lyric Suite
Honegger: *Antigone*
Janáček: *Glagolitic Mass*
Krenek: *Jonny spielt auf*
Prokofiev: *Le pas d'acier*

Schoenberg: String Quartet no.3
Shostakovich: Symphony no.2
Stravinsky: *Oedipus Rex*
Varèse: *Arcana*
Weill: *Royal Palace*

1928
Nielsen: Clarinet Concerto
Ravel: *Boléro*
Schoenberg: Orchestral Variations
Strauss: *Die ägyptische Helena*
Stravinsky: *Apollo, Le baiser de la fée*
Webern: String Trio
Weill: *Die Dreigroschenoper*

1929
Bartók: String Quartets nos 3 and 4
Hindemith: *Neues vom Tage*
Prokofiev: Symphony no.3, *The Gambler,*
  L'enfant prodigue
Stravinsky: Capriccio
Walton: Viola Concerto

1930
Berg: *Der Wein*
Janáček: From the House of the Dead
Prokofiev: Symphony no.4
Roussel: Symphony no.3
Schoenberg: *Von heute auf morgen*
Shostakovich: *The Nose*, Symphony no.3
Stravinsky: Symphony of Psalms
Weill: *Mahagonny*

1931
Copland: Piano Variations
Hába: *Die Mutter*
Honegger: Symphony no.1
Ives: *Three Places in New England*
Messiaen: *Les offrandes oubliées*
Ravel: Piano Concerto for the left hand
Stravinsky: Violin Concerto
Webern: Quartet op.22

1932
Prokofiev: Piano Concerto no.5
Ravel: Piano Concerto in G
Ruggles: *Suntreader*
Stravinsky: *Duo concertant*
Weill: *Die Burgschaft*

1933
Bartók: Piano Concerto no.2
Britten: Sinfonietta
Honegger: *Mouvement symphonique* no.3

Shostakovich: Piano Concerto no.1
Strauss: *Arabella*
Varèse: *Ionisation*
Weill: *The Seven Deadly Sins*
Zemlinsky: *Der Kreidekreis*

1934
Bartók: *Cantata profana*
Bax: Symphony no.5
Berg: *Lulu* suite
Hindemith: *Mathis der Maler* symphony
Messiaen: *L'Ascension*
Rakhmaninov: Paganini Rhapsody
Schmidt: Symphony no.4
Shostakovich: *The Lady Macbeth of the*
  Mtsensk District
Stravinsky: *Perséphone*
Thomson: *Four Saints in Three Acts*

1935
Bartók: String Quartet no.5
Gershwin: *Porgy and Bess*
Messiaen: *La Nativité du Seigneur*
Roussel: Symphony no.4
Strauss: *Die schweigsame Frau*
Stravinsky: Concerto for two pianos
Vaughan Williams: Symphony no.4
Webern: Concerto

1936
Berg: Violin Concerto
Britten: *Our Hunting Fathers*
Enescu: *Oedipe*
Rakhmaninov: Symphony no.3
Varèse: *Density 21.5*
Weill: *Johnny Johnson*

1937
Bartók: Music for Strings, Percussion and
  Celesta
Blitzstein: *The Cradle will Rock*
Britten: Bridge Variations, *On this Island*
Copland: *El salon Mexico*
Messiaen: *Poèmes pour Mi*
Orff: Carmina burana
Schoenberg: String Quartet no.4
Shostakovich: Symphony no.5
Stravinsky: *Jeu de cartes*
Webern: Piano Variations

1938
Bartók: Sonata for two pianos and
  percussion
Copland: *Billy the Kid*

Hindemith: *Mathis der Maler*
Honegger: *Jeanne d'Arc au bûcher*
Krenek: *Karl V*
Martinů: *Julietta*
Prokofiev: *Romeo and Juliet*
Schoenberg: *Kol nidre*
Stravinsky: 'Dumbarton Oaks' Concerto
Webern: *Das Augenlicht*, String Quartet

1939
Bartók: Violin Concerto no.2, *Contrasts*
Cage: *Imaginary Landscape* no.1
Carter: *Pocahontas*
Harris: Symphony no.3
Ives: Piano Sonata no.2
Messiaen: *Chants de terre et de ciel*
Poulenc: Organ Concerto
Prokofiev: *Alexander Nevsky*
Shostakovich: Symphony no.6

1940
Britten: *Les illuminations*, Violin Concerto
Dallapiccola: *Volo di notte*
·Schoenberg: Violin Concerto, Chamber
    Symphony no.2
Stravinsky: Symphony in C

1941
Bartók: String Quartet no.6
Britten: String Quartet no.1
Copland: Piano Sonata
Dallapiccola: *Canti di prigionia*
Messiaen: *Quatuor pour la fin du temps*

1942
Britten: Michelangelo Sonnets
Honegger: Symphony no.2
Martin: *Le vin herbé*
Shostakovich: Symphony no.7
Strauss: *Capriccio*
Stravinsky: *Danses concertantes*

1943
Britten: Serenade
Messiaen: *Visions de l'Amen*
Shostakovich: Symphony no.8
Stravinsky: Ode
Webern: Orchestral Variations

1944
Bartók: Concerto for Orchestra
Carter: Symphony no.1
Copland: *Appalachian Spring*

Hindemith: Symphonic Metamorphosis,
    Ludus tonalis
Schoenberg: *Ode to Napoleon*, Piano
    Concerto
Stravinsky: *Scènes de ballet*, Sonata for two
    pianos
Tippett: *A Child of Our Time*

1945
Britten: *Peter Grimes*, String Quartet no.2
Messiaen: *Trois petites liturgies*, *Vingt regards*
Prokofiev: *Cinderella*, Symphony no.5
Schoenberg: 'Genesis' Prelude
Shostakovich: Symphony no.9
Stravinsky: *Babel*

1946
Bartók: Piano Concerto no.3
Boulez: Piano Sonata no.1
Britten: *The Rape of Lucretia*
Copland: Symphony no.3
Honegger: Symphony no.3
Ives: Symphony no.3
Martin: *Petite symphonie concertante*
Messiaen: *Harawi*
Prokofiev: *War and Peace*
Strauss: *Metamorphosen*
Stravinsky: Symphony in Three
    Movements

1947
Cage: *The Seasons*
Carter: *The Minotaur*, Piano Sonata
Honegger: Symphony no.4
Poulenc: *Les mamelles de Tirésias*
Schoenberg: String Trio
Sessions: Symphony no.2
Stravinsky: Concerto in D

1948
Lutosławski: Symphony no.1
Schoenberg: *A Survivor from Warsaw*
Stravinsky: *Orpheus*, Mass
Vaughan Williams: Symphony no.6

1949
Britten: *Spring Symphony*
Dallapiccola: *Il prigioniero*
Messiaen: *Turangalîla-symphonie*, *Cinq
    rechants*
Schoenberg: Phantasy

1950
Boulez: Piano Sonata no.2
Carter: Cello Sonata

Copland: Piano Quartet, Clarinet Concerto
Messiaen: *Quatre études de rythme*
Strauss: *Vier letzte Lieder*

1951
Boulez: *Polyphonie X*
Britten: *Billy Budd*
Cage: *Imaginary Landscape* no.4
Honegger: *Symphony no.5*
Messiaen: *Messe de la Pentecôte*
Stockhausen: *Kreuzspiel*
Stravinsky: *The Rake's Progress*
Vaughan Williams: *The Pilgrim's Progress*

1952
Babbitt: *Du*
Boulez: *Structures Ia*
Cage: *Water Music, 4' 33"*
Henze: *Boulevard Solitude*
Messiaen: *Livre d'orgue*
Shostakovich: Twenty-Four Preludes and
  Fugues
Stockhausen: *Spiel*
Stravinsky: Cantata

1953
Britten: *Winter Words*
Carter: String Quartet no.1
Messiaen: *Le réveil des oiseaux*
Shostakovich: Symphony no.10
Stockhausen: *Kontra-Punkte*
Vaughan Williams: *Sinfonia antartica*

1954
Britten: *The Turn of the Screw*
Nono: *La victoire de Guernica*
Schoenberg: *Moses und Aron*
Stockhausen: *Studien I-II, Klavierstücke I-IV*
Stravinsky: Septet, *In memoriam Dylan
  Thomas*
Varèse: *Déserts*

1955
Boulez: *Le marteau sans maître*
Davies: Trumpet Sonata
Nono: *Incontri*
Shostakovich: Violin Concerto no.1
Stockhausen: *Klavierstücke V-VIII*
Tippett: *The Midsummer Marriage*
Xenakis: *Metastasis*

1956
Barraqué: *Séquence*
Carter: Orchestral Variations

Henze: *König Hirsch*
Messiaen: *Oiseaux exotiques*
Nono: *Il canto sospeso*
Stockhausen: *Zeitmasze, Gesang der
  Jünglinge*
Stravinsky: *Canticum sacrum*
Vaughan Williams: Symphony no.8

1957
Boulez: Piano Sonata no.3
Britten: *The Prince of the Pagodas*
Poulenc: *Dialogues des Carmélites*
Shostakovich: Symphony no.11, Piano
  Concerto no.2
Stockhausen: *Klavierstück XI*
Stravinsky: *Agon*
Xenakis: *Pithoprakta*

1958
Boulez: *Doubles, Poésie pour pouvoir*
Britten: *Nocturne*
Cage: Concert for Piano and Orchestra
Henze: *Ondine*
Stockhausen: *Gruppen*
Stravinsky: *Threni*
Varèse: *Poème électronique*
Vaughan Williams: Symphony no.9

1959
Blomdahl: *Aniara*
Davies: *Prolation*
Dutilleux: Symphony no.2
Messiaen: *Catalogue d'oiseaux*
Poulenc: *La voix humaine*
Stockhausen: *Zyklus, Refrain*

1960
Barraqué: *. . . au delà du hasard*
Berio: *Circles*
Boulez: *Pli selon pli*
Britten: *A Midsummer Night's Dream*
Carter: String Quartet no.2
Kagel: *Anagrama*
Messiaen: *Chronochromie*
Penderecki: *Anaklasis*
Shostakovich: String Quartet no.8
Stockhausen: *Carre, Kontakte*
Stravinsky: Movements

1961
Berio: *Epifanie*
Boulez: *Structures II*
Cage: *Atlas eclipticalis*
Carter: Double Concerto

Gerhard: Symphony no.3
Henze: *Elegy for Young Lovers*
Ligeti: *Atmosphères*
Nono: *Intolleranza*
Shostakovich: Symphony no.4
Varèse: *Nocturnal*

1962
Britten: *War Requiem*
Copland: *Connotations*
Shostakovich: Symphony no.13
Stockhausen: *Momente*
Stravinsky: *The Flood*

1963
Bernstein: *Kaddish Symphony*
Henze: Symphony no.5
Ligeti: *Aventures*
Messiaen: *Sept haïkaï*
Tippett: Concerto for Orchestra

1964
Britten: *Curlew River*, Cello Symphony
Messiaen: *Couleurs de la Cité Céleste*
Sessions: *Montezuma*
Stockhausen: *Mikrophonie I*
Stravinsky: *Abraham and Isaac, Elegy for J.F.K.*

1965
Berio: *Laborintus II*
Birtwistle: *Tragoedia*
Boulez: *Eclat*
Carter: Piano Concerto
Davies: Second Taverner Fantasia
Ligeti: Requiem
Messiaen: *Et exspecto resurrectionem mortuorum*
Stockhausen: *Mikrophonie II*
Stravinsky: Orchestral Variations

1966
Babbitt: *Relata I*
Barraqué: *Chant après chant*
Henze: *The Bassarids*
Stockhausen: *Solo, Telemusik*
Stravinsky: *Requiem Canticles*
Xenakis: *Terretektorh*

1967
Davies: *Antechrist*
Goehr: *Arden must die*
Ligeti: Cello Concerto, *Lontano*
Shostakovich: Violin Concerto no.2
Stockhausen: *Hymnen, Prozession*

1968
Barraqué: *Le temps restitué*, Concerto
Berio: *Sinfonia*
Birtwistle: *Punch and Judy*
Dallapiccola: *Ulisse*
Davies: *Revelation and Fall*
Pousseur: *Votre Faust*
Shostakovich: String Quartet no.12
Stockhausen: *Stimmung, Kurzwellen*

1969
Babbitt: *Relata II*
Birtwistle: *Verses for Ensembles*
Cage: *HPSCHD*
Davies: *Eight Songs for a Mad King, Vesalii icones, Worldes Blis*
Ligeti: String Quartet no.2
Messiaen: *La Transfiguration*
Shostakovich: Symphony no.14
Stockhausen: *Spiral*

1970
Babbitt: String Quartet no.3
Berio: *Opera*
Carter: Concerto for Orchestra
Ligeti: Chamber Concerto
Stockhausen: *Mantra*

1971
Bernstein: *Mass*
Britten: *Owen Wingrave*
Kagel: *Staatstheater*
Ligeti: *Melodien*
Reich: *Drumming*
Stockhausen: *Trans*

1972
Birtwistle: *The Triumph of Time*
Bussotti: *Lorenzaccio*
Davies: *Taverner*
Ligeti: Double Concerto
Messiaen: *Méditations sur le mystère de la Sainte Trinité*
Shostakovich: Symphony no.15

1973
Boulez: '*. . . explosante-fixe . . .*'
Britten: *Death in Venice*
Carter: String Quartet no.3
Davies: *Stone Litany*
Reich: Music for Mallet Instruments, Voices and Organ
Shostakovich: String Quartet no.14

1974
Henze: *Tristan*
Messiaen: *Des canyons aux étoiles . . .*
Shostakovich: String Quartet no.15
Stockhausen: *Inori*

1975
Boulez: *Rituel*
Davies: *Ave maris stella*
Ferneyhough: *Transit*
Ligeti: *San Francisco Polyphony*
Shostakovich: Viola Sonata
Stockhausen: *Tierkreis*

1976
Berio: *Coro*
Britten: String Quartet no.3
Carter: *A Mirror on which to Dwell*
Glass: Einstein on the Beach
Henze: *We Come to the River*
Ligeti: *Monument — Selbstporträt — Bewegung*
Shnitke: Piano Quintet
Stockhausen: *Sirius*

1977
Birtwistle: *Silbury Air*
Carter: A Symphony of Three Orchestras
Davies: *A Mirror of Whitening Light*
Stockhausen: *Der Jahreslauf*
Xenakis: *Jonchaies*

1978
Boulez: *Notations*
Carter: *Syringa*
Davies: Symphony no.1
Ligeti: *Le grand Macabre*

1979
Birtwistle: *. . . agm . . .*
Rochberg: 'Concord' quartets
Tavener: *Thérèse*
Tippett: String Quartet no.4

1980
Carter: *Night Fantasies*
Glass: *Satyagraha*
Reich: Variations for Winds, Strings and Keyboards

1981
Adams: *Harmonium*
Boulez: *Répons*
Davies: Symphony no.2
Stockhausen: *Donnerstag*

1982
Berio: *La vera storia*
Ligeti: Horn Trio

1983
Boesmans: *La passion de Gilles*
Messiaen: *Saint François d'Assise*
Reich: *The Desert Music*

1984
Berio: *Un re in ascolto*
Birtwistle: *Secret Theatre*
Glass: *Akhnaten*
Stockhausen: *Samstag*
Tippett: *The Mask of Time*

1985
Carter: *Penthode*
Davies: Symphony no.3
Goehr: *Behold the Sun*
Kagel: *Sankt-Bach-Passion*